Fodor's UpCLOSE

SAN FRANCISCO

the complete guide, thoroughly up-to-date

SAVVY TRAVELING: WHERE TO SPEND, HOW TO SAVE

packed with details that will make your trip

CULTURAL TIPS: ESSENTIAL LOCAL DO'S AND TABOOS

must-see sights, on and off the beaten path

INSIDER SECRETS: WHAT'S HIP AND WHAT TO SKIP

the buzz on restaurants, the lowdown on lodgings

FIND YOUR WAY WITH CLEAR AND EASY-TO-USE MAPS

Previously published as *The Berkeley Guide to San Francisco*

FODOR'S TRAVEL PUBLICATIONS, INC.

NEW YORK • TORONTO • LONDON • SYDNEY • AUCKLAND

www.fodors.com/

FODOR'S UPCLOSE™ SAN FRANCISCO

Editor: Amy McConnell

Editorial Contributors: Jennifer Brewer, Deke Castleman, Kathleen Dodge, Sharon Silva, Suzanne Stein, Sharron Wood

Editorial Production: Tracy Patruno

Maps: David Lindroth *cartographer*; Steven Amsterdam *map editor*

Design: Fabrizio La Rocca, *creative director*; Allison Saltzman, *cover and text design*; Jolie Novak, *photo editor*

Production/Manufacturing: Rebecca Zeiler

Cover Art: Mark E. Gibson/The Stock Market

CONTENTS

3. SHOPPING *84*

4. FOOD *95*

5. CAFÉ CULTURE *121*

6. AFTER DARK *127*

7. WHERE TO SLEEP *150*

8. THE GREAT OUTDOORS *169*

9. DAY AND WEEKEND TRIPS *186*

INDEX *229*

TRAVELING UPCLOSE

H ave a picnic on a hilltop park bench. Go to a festival. Commune with nature. Memorize the symphony of the streets. And if you want to experience the heart and soul of San Francisco, whatever you do, don't spend too much money.

The experience of San Francisco that every true traveler yearns for is one thing that money can't buy. In fact, if you have it, don't use it. Traveling lavishly is the surest way to turn yourself into a sideline traveler. Restaurants with white-glove service are great—sometimes—but they're usually not the best place to find the perfect clam chowder with sourdough bread. Doormen at plush hotels have their place, but not when your look-alike room could be anywhere from Dusseldorf to Detroit. Better to stay in a more intimate place that truly gives you the atmosphere you traveled so far to experience. Don't just stand and watch—jump into the spirit of what's around you.

If you want to see San Francisco up close, this book is for you. We'll show you the local culture, the offbeat sights, the bars and cafés where tourists rarely tread, and the B&Bs and other hostelries where you'll meet fellow travelers—places where the locals would send their friends. And because you'll probably want to see the famous places if you haven't already been there, we give you tips on losing the crowds, plus the quirky and obscure facts you want as well as the basics everyone needs.

OUR GANG

Who are we? We're artists and poets, slackers and straight arrows, and travel writers and journalists, who in our less hedonistic moments report on local news and spin out an occasional opinion piece. What we share is a certain footloose spirit and a passion for the City by the Bay, which we celebrate in this guidebook. Shamelessly, we've revealed all of our favorite places and our deepest, darkest travel secrets, all so that you can learn from our past mistakes and experience the best part of San Francisco to the fullest. If you can't take your best friend on the road, or if your best friend is hopeless with directions, stick with us.

JENNIFER BREWER is a San Francisco–based travel writer whose work has recently taken her to Eastern Europe, the Middle East, and Asia. A native Californian, she still thinks the Golden State is one of the most breathtaking places on earth.

DEKE CASTLEMAN learned his budget-traveler skills in the mid-1970s in Alaska, the most expensive state in the country, waiting for a job on the Trans-Alaska Pipeline. Now he divides his time between Las Vegas, where he edits the *Las Vegas Advisor;* and the Sierras, where he indulges in the free pleasures of nature.

KATHLEEN DODGE grew up in the San Francisco Bay Area and still calls it her favorite corner of the world—and home. She can be spotted on fair-weather weekends chatting with proprietors of small wineries in Napa and Sonoma Valleys, two of her favorite getaways.

JONATHAN LEFF has traded in the challenge of exploring Yosemite National Park for another kind of adventure: He currently lives in Lithuania, where he writes for a weekly newspaper.

SHARON SILVA, our dining updater, has been a regular contributor to *San Francisco Magazine* for more than a decade. She currently covers restaurants for San Francisco Sidewalk, an on-line city guide.

JENNIFER WEDEL is a freelance writer whose favorite splurge is the Big Dipper at the Santa Cruz Boardwalk—for the fleeting glimpse of an expanse of blue ocean before the first plunge to certain death.

SHARRON WOOD got some last budget-travel yearnings out of her system by visiting San Francisco's most happening nightspots and bargain hotels, before starting her new job as managing editor of On the Road, Inc., a new business travel on-line venture.

A SEND-OFF

Always call ahead. We knock ourselves out to check all the facts, but everything changes all the time, in ways that none of us can ever fully anticipate. Whenever you're making a special trip to a special place, as opposed to merely wandering, always call ahead. Trust us on this.

And then, if something doesn't go quite right—as inevitably happens with even the best-laid plans—stay cool. Missed your train? Stuck in the airport? Use the time to study the people. Strike up a conversation with a stranger. Study the newsstands or flip through the local press. Take a walk. Find the silver lining in the clouds, whatever it is. And do send us a postcard to tell us what went wrong and what went right. You can e-mail us at editors@fodors.com (specify the name of the book on the subject line), or write the San Francisco editor at Fodor's upCLOSE, 201 East 50th Street, New York, NY 10022. We'll put your ideas to good use and let other travelers benefit from your experiences. In the mean time, bon voyage!

NORTHERN CALIFORNIA

OREGO

PACIFIC OCEAN

Crescent City
Redwood National Park
Klamath
KLAMATH NATIONAL FOREST
Yreka
Mt. Shasta
Mt. Shasta
Arcata
Eureka
Fortuna
Shasta Lake
TRINITY NATIONAL FOREST
Redding
Lassen Peak
Lassen Vol. National
Red Bluff
Guerneville
Leggett
Fel R.
MENDOCINO NATIONAL FOREST
Sacramento Valley
PLU
Paradise
Chico
Oroville
Fort Bragg
Willits
Mendocino
Ukiah
Clear Lake
Yuba City
Point Arena
Woodland
WINE COUNTRY
Santa Rosa
Vacaville
Davis
Sacramen
Napa
Elk Grov
Petaluma
Fairfield
Novato
Point Reyes National Seashore
Berkeley
Concord
Lodi
Stock
SAN FRANCISCO
Oakland
San Mateo
Fremont
Milpitas
Sunnyvale
San Jose
Santa Cruz

0   50 miles
0   75 km

N

OREGON

Goose Lake

MODOC NATIONAL FOREST

139 Alturas

299

139 395

44

Lassen Peak Lassen Volcanic National Park Susanville

NEVADA

Pyramid Lake

32 70 PLUMAS NATIONAL FOREST

70

Paradise 395

Chico 49

99 Oroville 89 Reno

80 Truckee

Yuba City Lake Tahoe Carson City

50

ELDORADO NATIONAL FOREST Tahoe Valley

Woodland 395 Walker Lake

Davis Sacramento

Elk Grove 88 4

5 Lodi NEVADA

STANISLAUS NATIONAL FOREST

Stockton 49 Mono Lake

Modesto Lee Vining

580 132 YOSEMITE NATIONAL PARK

remont 120 395

Milpitas Turlock

San Jose 33 99 140

101 Merced 41

152 Los Banos KINGS CANYON NATIONAL PARK

San Joaquin Valley

SIERRA

CASCADE RANGE

THE BAY AREA

Sonoma

Napa

TO SACRAMENTO
AND LAKE TAHOE

12

29 121

121

80

12

121

12

0   10 miles

29

37

0   15 km

37

101

Vallejo

San Pablo
Bay

Grizzly
Bay

Suisun
Bay

780

Benicia

Pittsburg

San
Rafael

MARIN
COUNTY

Richmond-
San Rafael
Bridge

Martinez

680

4

242

Concord

101

Richmond

Wildcat
Regional Park

Briones
Regional
Park

580

Mt. Tamalpais
State Park

El Cerrito

24

Muir
Woods

Mill Valley

Tilden
Regional Park

24

Mt. Diablo
State Park

Golden Gate
Natl.
Recreation
Area

Tiburon

Angel I.

Berkeley

Sausalito

SF-Oakland
Bay Br.

680

Treasure I.

Golden Gate
Bridge

80

580

TO PT. REYES
AND MARIN
HEADLANDS

Oakland

SAN
FRANCISCO

Yerba
Buena I.

880

San Ramon

35 1

280

Oakland
International
Airport

San Leandro

580

Daly
City

580

101

238

Hayward

TO YOSEMITE
NATIONAL PARK

Pacifica

San Francisco
International
Airport

San Francisco
Bay

92

238

Rockaway
Beach

35

880

1

San Mateo

92

San Mateo Br.

84

280

92

Dumbarton
Br.

84

Fremont

238

Montara

101

84

238

Half Moon Bay
State Beach

San Francisco Bay
National
Wildlife Refuge

92

Redwood City

35

680

Half Moon Bay

84

Milpitas

1

Palo Alto

101

237

Stanford
University

N

Mountain
View

San Jose
International
Airport

La Honda

280

880

San Gregorio

84

84

35

85

Santa Clara

101

TO SANTA CRUZ,
MONTEREY, AND
BIG SUR

Pescadero Creek
County Park

280

85

San Jose

x

BASICS

contacts and savvy tips to make your trip hassle-free

I f you've ever traveled with anyone before, you know that there are two types of people in the world—the planners and the nonplanners. Travel brings out the worst in both groups. Left to their own devices, the planners will have you goose-stepping from attraction to attraction on a cultural blitzkrieg, while the nonplanners will invariably miss the flight, the bus, and maybe even the point. This chapter offers you a middle ground; we hope it provides enough information to help you plan your trip to San Francisco and the Bay Area without nailing you down. Be flexible and remember that the most hair-pulling situations turn into the best travel stories back home.

AIR TRAVEL

MAJOR AIRLINE OR LOW-COST CARRIER?

Most people choose a flight based on price. Yet there are other issues to consider. Major airlines offer the greatest number of departures; smaller airlines—including regional, low-cost and no-frill airlines—usually have a more limited number of flights daily. Major airlines have frequent-flyer partners, which allow you to credit mileage earned on one airline to your account with another. Low-cost airlines offer a definite price advantage and fewer restrictions, such as advance-purchase requirements. Safety-wise, low-cost carriers as a group have a good history.

MAJOR AIRLINES • From the U.S.: **America West** (tel. 800/235–9292) to Oakland, San Francisco. **American** (tel. 800/433–7300) to Oakland, San Francisco. **British Airways** (tel. 800/247–9297) to San Francisco. **Continental** (tel. 800/231–0856) to San Francisco. **Delta** (tel. 800/241–4141) to Oakland, San Francisco. **Northwest** (tel. 800/225–2525) to San Francisco. **Southwest** (tel. 800/435–9792) to San Francisco. **TWA** (tel. 800/892–4141) to San Francisco. **United** (tel. 800/538–2929) to Oakland, San Francisco. **US Airways** (tel. 800/428–4322) to San Francisco. From the U.K.: **British Airways** (tel. 0345/222–111). **United** (tel. 0800/888–555). **Virgin Atlantic** (tel. 01293/747–747). **American** (tel. 0345/789–789) flies via New York or Chicago, and **Delta** (tel. 0800/414–767) flies via Los Angeles or Cincinnati. From Down Under: **United** (tel. 800/538–2929) to San Francisco.

SMALLER AIRLINES • **Midwest Express** (tel. 800/452–2022) to San Francisco. **Reno Air** (tel. 800/736–6247) to San Francisco.

DON'T STOP UNLESS YOU MUST

When you book, **look for nonstop flights** and **remember that "direct" flights stop at least once.** Try to **avoid connecting flights,** which require a change of plane. Two airlines may jointly operate a connecting flight, so ask if your airline operates every segment—you may find that your preferred carrier flies you only part of the way.

USE AN AGENT

Travel agents, especially those who specialize in finding the lowest fares (*see* Discounts & Deals, *below*), can be especially helpful when booking a plane ticket. When you're quoted a price, **ask your agent if the price is likely to get any lower.** Good agents know the seasonal fluctuations of airfares and can usually anticipate a sale or fare war. However, waiting can be risky: The fare could go *up* as seats become scarce, and you may wait so long that your preferred flight sells out. A wait-and-see strategy works best if your plans are flexible, but if you must arrive and depart on certain dates, don't delay.

GET THE LOWEST FARE

The least expensive airfares to San Francisco are priced for round-trip travel. Major airlines usually require that you **book in advance and buy the ticket within 24 hours,** and you may have to **stay over a Saturday night.** It's smart to **call a number of airlines, and when you are quoted a good price, book it on the spot**—the same fare may not be available on the same flight the next day. Airlines generally allow you to change your return date for a fee of $25–$50. If you don't use your ticket you can apply the cost toward the purchase of a new ticket, again for a small charge. However, most low-fare tickets are nonrefundable. To get the lowest airfare, **check different routings.** If your destination or home city has more than one gateway, compare prices to and from different airports. Flexibility is the key to getting a serious bargain on airfare. If you can play around with your departure date, destination, and return date, you will probably save money. Ask which days of the week are the cheapest to fly on—weekends are often the most expensive. Even the time of day you fly can make a big difference in the cost of your ticket.

To save money on round-trip flights originating in the United Kingdom, **look into an APEX or Super-PEX ticket.** APEX tickets must be booked in advance and have certain restrictions. Super-PEX tickets can be purchased at the airport on the day of departure—subject to availability.

AVOID GETTING BUMPED

Airlines routinely overbook planes, knowing that not everyone with a ticket will show up, but sometimes everyone does. When that happens, airlines ask for volunteers to give up their seats. In return these volunteers usually get a certificate for a free flight and are rebooked on the next flight out. If there are not enough volunteers the airline must choose who will be denied boarding. The first to get bumped are passengers who checked in late and those flying on discounted tickets, **so get to the gate and check in as early as possible,** especially during peak periods.

Always **bring a photo ID to the airport.** You may be asked to show it before you are allowed to check in.

ENJOY THE FLIGHT

For better service, **fly smaller or regional carriers,** which often have higher passenger-satisfaction ratings. Sometimes you'll find leather seats, more legroom, and better food.

For more legroom, **request an emergency-aisle seat**; don't, however, sit in the row in front of the emergency aisle or in front of a bulkhead, where seats may not recline. If you don't like airline food, **ask for special meals when booking.** These can be vegetarian, low-cholesterol, or kosher, for example. To avoid jet lag try to maintain a normal routine while traveling. At night **get some sleep.** By day **eat light meals, drink water (not alcohol), and move about the cabin** to stretch your legs.

COMPLAIN IF NECESSARY

If your baggage goes astray or your flight goes awry, complain right away. Most carriers require that you file a claim immediately.

AIRLINE COMPLAINTS • U.S. Department of Transportation **Aviation Consumer Protection Division** (C-75, Washington, DC 20590, tel. 202/366–2220). **Federal Aviation Administration (FAA) Consumer Hotline** (tel. 800/322–7873).

AIRPORTS & TRANSFERS

The major gateway to San Francisco is the San Francisco International Airport, just south of the city, off U.S. 101. Several domestic airlines serve the Oakland Airport, which is across the bay but not much farther away from downtown San Francisco (via I–880 and I–80), although traffic on the Bay Bridge may at times make travel time longer. Fourteen carriers, most notably American Airlines, fly into San Jose International Airport.

Flying time is six hours from New York, four hours from Chicago, and one hour from Los Angeles.

AIRPORT INFORMATION • San Francisco International Airport (tel. 650/761–0800). **Oakland Airport** (tel. 415/577–4000). **San Jose International Airport** (1661 Airport Blvd., off I–880 near U.S. 101, tel. 408/277–4759).

TRANSFERS

From the San Francisco International Airport you can take SamTrans Bus 7B (55 minutes, $2), Bus 7F (35 minutes, $2.50) to San Francisco's Transbay Terminal, or Bus 3X (20 minutes, $1) to the Colma BART station. From here you can catch a train to downtown San Francisco (20 minutes, $1.80) or Berkeley (45 minutes, $2.40). The buses run every half hour—Bus 3X from 6 AM to 11:30 PM, Buses 7B and 7F from about 5 AM to 12:45 AM. Bus 7F restricts you to one small carry-on bag. (Bus 7F will also tote you to Palo Alto, stopping near the Stanford Shopping Center.) Locals tend to rely on private shuttles for their convenience and reliability (*see* Airport Shuttles, *below*). Long-term parking is $11 per day up to seven days and then $14 for each additional day. The lot tends to fill up during peak travel times, especially three-day weekends; call the Parking Hotline to check on availability before you set out and plan for extra time to take the free shuttle from the lot to the terminal.

From the Oakland International Airport, the Air-Bart shuttle runs every 15–20 minutes to the Coliseum BART station. Buy tickets ($2) at the BART station or airport terminal before you board. AC Transit Bus 58 ($1.25) follows the same route, continuing on to downtown Oakland, a 50-minute trip. Another money-saving option is a van company (*see* Airport Shuttles, *below*). A taxi to downtown Berkeley from Oakland International costs about $30–$35. Long-term parking is $10 for 24 hours or $8 in the economy lot next to Terminal 1. A free shuttle will take you to the terminals.

From the San Jose International Airport, VTA Bus 65 ($1.10) departs every 30–60 minutes for downtown San Jose before continuing south to Almaden. To reach San Francisco or the East Bay, take a private shuttle (*see* Airport Shuttles, *below*). Short-term parking runs 75¢ per half hour and $17 per day; long-term is $8 per day.

RESOURCES • Parking Hotline (tel. 650/877–0227). **Air-Bart Shuttle** (tel. 510/562–7700).

AIRPORT SHUTTLES

Airport shuttles will pick you up at your doorstep at any time of day or night and whisk you to the airport. The fare from San Francisco to SFO runs a mere $10–$12; expect to pay $20–$35 from San Francisco to the Oakland Airport. There's often a reduced rate for a pickup of two or more people. You can save a few more bucks (up to $10) by boarding the shuttle at a major hotel.

The king of airport service is Super Shuttle, with service from San Francisco and the Peninsula to SFO and the Oakland airport. Quake City is a smaller, friendlier, employee-owned service: It runs to SFO and the Oakland Airport for a few dollars less than Super Shuttle. Yellow Shuttle Service and Airport Connection run from most Bay Area cities to SFO, Oakland International, and San Jose International. The BayPorter Express serves primarily the East Bay but also runs to SFO. The Marin Airporter will take you from Marin County to SFO.

RESOURCES • Super Shuttle (tel. 415/558–8500). **Quake City** (tel. 415/255–4899). **Yellow Shuttle Service** (tel. 415/282–7433). **Airport Connection** (tel. 510/841–0150). **BayPorter Express** (tel. 415/467–1800). **Marin Airporter** (tel. 415/461–4222).

BICYCLING

Though San Francisco's hills will undoubtedly give you thighs of steel and infinitely more respect for bike messengers, there are plenty of bicycle routes that can keep you away from traffic and get you around the larger hills. In 1996 the S.F. Bicycle Program began marking the most bicycle-friendly of its streets with numbered route signs. Follow them, and your biggest challenge may be to **keep an eye out for the opening doors of parked cars.** Berkeley TRiP (*see* Transportation, *below*) has great biking maps, including the *San Francisco Biking/Walking Guide* ($3), which shows street grades and bike routes. For suggested cycling routes around San Francisco and the Bay Area, *see* Hiking and Biking *in* Chapter 8.

Professional bike thieves abound in the Bay Area. **Always use U-shape locks to secure both the wheels and the frame** to a sturdy post. You can get a good bicycle for around $50 at any flea market or police bike auction, where unclaimed bikes are sold.

BIKES ON PUBLIC TRANSIT

You can take your bicycle on Bay Area transit systems with varying degrees of hassle. Caltrain allows bikes on all trains, save some express trains. All ferries, except the Blue and Gold Fleet's bay cruises, take on bicycles at any time of day.

Bikes on BART: In 1996 BART dropped its policy requiring a special permit for those who wish to bring their bike on board. The policy may be reinstated at a later date; for details call the BART Office of Passenger Service. Bikes are allowed in all but the first car of each train. Bikes are *not* allowed on BART during commuter rush hours, 6:30–9 and 3:30–6:30. During these hours a bike shuttle ($1) operates every 30–45 minutes between MacArthur BART and the Transbay Terminal; call CalTrans for more information. Bicycle lockers, available at some stations, rent for three months ($15) or one year ($30); call the BART Pass Office.

Taking your bike on Bay Area buses isn't easy. Often it depends solely on the discretion of the driver, with no more than two bikes allowed at once. In the East Bay AC Transit allows bikes on all lines from midnight to 5:30 AM and on Buses 65 (weekdays) and 67 (weekends) for transit to Tilden Park. During 1997 AC Transit hoped to install bike racks on buses covering several other popular routes; call for more information. Golden Gate Transit allows bikes (maximum two bikes per bus) on Buses 40 (to San Rafael) and 80 (to San Rafael and Santa Rosa) during non-commute hours. S. F. Muni allows bikes on Bus 76, which travels into the Marin Headlands. At press time Muni was experimenting with allowing buses on nine additional routes; call the general information number (*see* Bus and Streetcar Travel, *below*) for an update.

RESOURCES • BART Office of Passenger Service (tel. 510/464–7127). **CalTrans** (tel. 510/286–0669). **BART Pass Office** (tel. 510/464–7133). **AC Transit** (tel. 510/839–2882 for information on bike racks).

BUS & STREETCAR TRAVEL

Despite all the griping about graffiti and rising fares, most Bay Area residents will admit the city bus systems are actually quite good. Bus passes and discount tickets are available at most grocery stores and check-cashing venues. The only regional pass available is BART Plus (*see* Subway Travel, *below*).

SAN FRANCISCO

Muni's bus and streetcar service can put you within three blocks of anywhere you want to go. Buses are scheduled to run every 10–15 minutes, though regular Muni users will attest to chronic delays. Frequent breakdowns, disgruntled drivers, and belligerent passengers may also show you a side of the city you didn't plan on seeing. Between 1 AM and 5 AM, the owl service has nine lines running every 30 minutes.

The adult fare is $1. Your fare entitles you to one free transfer, good for 90 minutes. Passport passes allow unlimited access to Muni (including cable cars) for one day ($6), three days ($10), or seven days ($15). A special Weekly Pass ($9) is good only for Muni buses; with this you pay $1 for each cable car ride. The Fast Pass ($35) allows one month of unlimited travel on Muni buses, streetcars, and cable cars, as well as on BART and CalTrain routes within San Francisco. **Purchase passes at the Powell Street visitor center** (*see* Visitor Information, *below*).

If you don't mind crowds, cable cars are a great way to get the flavor of San Francisco's hills—or to feel like you're in a Rice-A-Roni commercial, depending on your point of view. They run at a pace straight out of the early 1900s (the cables that propel the cars move at 9.5 mph), so if you're a Type A, take the bus. For great views take the Hyde and Powell line, which travels from Fisherman's Wharf to Powell and Market streets downtown. Along the way you'll get a gander at Alcatraz and pass right by Lombard Street, the so-called crookedest street in the world. The line to board at the Hyde Street turnaround often requires a wait of more than an hour, making the less scenic California line from the Embarcadero BART station an attractive alternative. The fare is $2, and all passes except the $9 Weekly Pass are accepted.

INFORMATION • Muni (tel. 415/673–6864 or 415/923–6168 for lost and found).

EAST BAY

With more than 100 lines, AC Transit covers the East Bay from north of Richmond to south of Fremont. The fare is $1.25, and 25¢ transfers are good for two hours. Monthly passes run $45 for adults, $25 for youth. A book of 10 adult tickets costs $10; a book of 10 transfer tickets costs $2.50.

The AC Transit lines designated by letters rather than numbers cross the Bay Bridge to San Francisco's Transbay Terminal (1st and Mission Sts.). Most only run from dawn to dusk; exceptions include the F (Berkeley), T (Oakland, connecting to Berkeley on Bus 40), and N (Oakland) lines, which operate until midnight. The Transbay adult fare is $2.20. Monthly Transbay passes cost $75.

INFORMATION • AC Transit (1600 Franklin St., Oakland, tel. 510/817–1717).

NORTH BAY

Golden Gate Transit provides service almost everywhere in the North Bay. Buses connect San Francisco with Sausalito, Mill Valley, Tiburon, San Rafael, Novato, Rohnert Park, and Santa Rosa every half hour during the week. Many buses run weekdays only, from dawn to dusk, but some routes (including the 20 and 50, which stop in Sausalito) run on weekends until 1 AM. Within San Francisco, buses leave the Transbay Terminal and make stops throughout the city. Adult fare costs $1.25–$4.50, depending on the length of your trip; a Ride Value Discount Ticket Book, with 20 tickets at a 25% discount, is available for purchase at the Golden Gate Ferry Terminal (on the Embarcadero at the foot of Market St.); at the Golden Gate Transit Administration Office (1011 Andersen Dr., San Rafael); and at many bookstores, gas stations, and grocery stores.

"Flat" streets in San Francisco: Stockton, Polk, Broadway Tunnel, Geary/Post, Market, and Valencia.

INFORMATION • Golden Gate Transit (tel. 415/923–2000 or 415/257–4476 for lost and found).

SOUTH BAY

SamTrans runs buses regularly throughout San Mateo County, south of San Francisco. Buses depart from the Daly City BART station, from downtown San Francisco, and from the San Francisco International Airport (*see* Airports & Transfers, *above*) and go as far as Año Nuevo State Reserve, at the southern end of the county (*see* South Bay *in* Chapter 2). Bus 1L travels from Daly City BART along the coast to Half Moon Bay about five times daily. Most other buses run weekdays only, though some heavily trafficked routes are covered all week; **call SamTrans for help planning your trip.** The adult fare is $1; no transfers are issued. Monthly passes cost $36 for adults or $90 for an express route pass.

The Valley Transportation Agency (VTA) operates buses and one light-rail line throughout San Jose and the Silicon Valley. Basic fare is $1.10; express buses cost a flat $1.75. The VTA Information Center sells day passes (double the regular fare) and monthly passes ($33).

INFORMATION • Samtrans (tel. 800/660–4287). **VTA Information Center** (4 N. 2nd St., San Jose, tel. 408/321–2300 or 800/894–9908).

GREYHOUND LINES

Greyhound travels to and from Bay Area cities all day, to farther-flung destinations such as Tahoe (7–12 hours, $20 one way), Santa Cruz (2–4 hours, $15 one way), Los Angeles (7–12 hours, $32 one way), and Seattle (20–26 hours, $48 one way). In San Francisco Greyhound operates out of the third floor of the Transbay Terminal, where many Muni lines (*see above*) begin. Plan your departure for daytime, as this terminal is dicey at night. In the East Bay the Greyhound office is in Oakland; in the South Bay it's in San Jose; and in Marin County you'll find it in downtown San Rafael.

GREYHOUND INFORMATION • Greyhound (tel. 800/231–2222). In San Francisco: **Transbay Terminal** (1st and Mission Sts., tel. 415/495–1569). In the East Bay: **Oakland** (2103 San Pablo Ave., at 20th St., tel. 510/834–3213). In the South Bay: **San Jose** (70 Almaden Ave., at Santa Clara St., tel. 408/295–4151). In Marin County: **San Rafael** (850 Tamalpais St., at 3rd St., tel. 415/453–0795).

GREEN TORTOISE

Green Tortoise Adventure Travel is a cheap, funky alternative to humdrum bus travel. Buses come equipped with sleeping pads, kitchens, and stereos to make the ride enjoyable. The journey to Seattle (24 hrs, $49 one way) features a cookout ($4) and skinny-dipping. Regularly scheduled runs also go from the Bay Area to Los Angeles (12 hours, $30), Eugene, Oregon (17 hours, $39), and Portland (20 hours, $39), with select stops along the way. Make reservations before you show up at their pickup point

HALLIDIE'S SAN FRANCISCO TREAT

One rainy evening in 1873, young engineer Andrew Hallidie witnessed a horrible sight: One of four horses drawing a streetcar slipped and went barreling down a steep hill, dragging the other helpless horses behind it. This tragic incident inspired Hallidie to devise the era's most complex and industrious transportation system: the cable car—the world's first large-scale mechanized street transportation. In 1964 San Francisco's cable cars were declared a National Historic Landmark, the first moving entity to receive that honor.

in San Francisco (1st and Natoma Sts.) or Berkeley (Berkeley Marina, across from the bait shop). **Bring cash or traveler's checks** because you can't pay with plastic.

INFORMATION • Green Tortoise Adventure Travel (494 Broadway, San Francisco 94133, tel. 415/956–7500 or 800/867–8647).

CAR RENTAL

To fully experience the best of the Bay Area—the Wine Country, for example, or coastal beaches—a rental car is practically a necessity. Your best bet is to **rent a vehicle at one of the region's airports.** The cheapest rates are available to those who can present a plane ticket, but even residents can save as much as $15 a day over the rates at downtown rental franchises. If you absolutely can't make it to the airport, almost all rental-car agencies have pickup and drop-off spots in downtown San Francisco within five or six blocks of Union Square. No matter where you pick up your car, you'll always pay a heavy surcharge (starting at about $25) if you don't return it to the same spot.

Rates in San Francisco begin at $36 a day and $123 a week for an economy car with air-conditioning, an automatic transmission, and unlimited mileage. This does not include tax on car rentals, which is 8.25%. All Bay Area car-rental companies require a credit card for deposit purposes. Some cards—American Express, for example—provide liability and damage insurance, so check with your credit card company before paying for the rental agency's insurance policy. You'll usually pay less if you **reserve in advance, and always ask about specials and discounts**—some rental agencies, for example, offer 10%–20% discounts if you have AAA membership or frequent-flier miles on certain airlines. Small, independent agencies generally have cheaper daily rates than the national chains but usually impose mileage charges. However, if you're planning on going far, **consider using the national companies** (Avis, Hertz, Budget, etc.); they usually give you unlimited mileage, which may cut your total cost.

CUT COSTS

To get the best deal, **book through a travel agent who is willing to shop around.** When pricing cars, **ask about the location of the rental lot.** Some off-airport locations offer lower rates, and their lots are only minutes from the terminal via complimentary shuttle. You also may want to **price local car-rental companies,** whose rates may be lower still, although their service and maintenance may not be as good as those of a name-brand agency. They sometimes undercut the major agencies on daily or weekly rates, but you may not get unlimited mileage.

Be sure to **look into wholesalers,** companies that do not own fleets but rent in bulk from those that do and often offer better rates than traditional car-rental operations. Prices are best during off-peak periods.

Also **ask your travel agent about a company's customer-service record.** How has it responded to late plane arrivals and vehicle mishaps? Are there often lines at the rental counter, and, if you're traveling during a holiday period, does a confirmed reservation guarantee you a car?

No matter who you rent from, remember to ask about required deposits, cancellation penalties, and drop-off charges if you're planning to pick up the car in one city and leave it in another.

MAJOR AGENCIES • Alamo (tel. 800/327–9633, 0800/272–2000 in the U.K.). **Avis** (tel. 800/331–1212, 800/879–2847 in Canada). **Budget** (tel. 800/527–0700, 0800/181181 in the U.K.). **Dollar** (tel. 800/800–4000; 0990/565656 in the U.K., where it is known as Eurodollar). **Hertz** (tel. 800/654–3131, 800/263–0600 in Canada, 0345/555888 in the U.K.). **National InterRent** (tel. 800/227–7368; 0345/222525 in the U.K., where it is known as Europcar InterRent).

LOCAL AGENCIES • Enterprise (tel. 800/325–8007). **Reliable** (tel. 415/928–4414). **Flat Rate Rent-A-Car** (830 Huntington Ave., San Bruno, tel. 650/583–9232), near San Francisco International Airport, rents cars at bargain prices. **Sunbelt** (tel. 415/771–9191) specializes in BMWs and Corvette and Miata convertibles.

RENTAL WHOLESALERS • Auto Europe (tel. 207/842–2000 or 800/223–5555, fax 800–235–6321). The **Kemwel Group** (tel. 914/835–5555 or 800/678–0678, fax 914/835–5126).

NEED INSURANCE?

When driving a rented car you are generally responsible for any damage to or loss of the vehicle. You also are liable for any property damage or personal injury that you may cause while driving. Before you rent, **see what coverage you already have** under the terms of your personal auto-insurance policy and credit cards.

For about $14 a day, rental companies sell protection, known as a collision- or loss-damage waiver (CDW or LDW), that eliminates your liability for damage to the car; it's always optional and should never be automatically added to your bill. Some states, including California, have capped the price of CDW and LDW.

In most states you don't need CDW if you have personal auto insurance or other liability insurance. However, **make sure you have enough coverage to pay for the car.** If you do not have auto insurance or an umbrella policy that covers damage to third parties, purchasing CDW or LDW is highly recommended.

You wouldn't be the first driver to shudder as you sit at a stoplight on a steep San Francisco hill, hoping your stick shift car won't slide 200 feet backward as soon as you lift your foot off the brake and engage the clutch.

BEWARE SURCHARGES

Before you pick up a car in one city and leave it in another, **ask about drop-off charges or one-way service fees,** which can be substantial. Note, too, that some rental agencies charge extra if you return the car before the time specified on your contract. To avoid a hefty refueling fee, **fill the tank just before you turn in the car,** but be aware that gas stations near the rental outlet may overcharge.

MEET THE REQUIREMENTS

In the United States you must be 21 to rent a car, and rates may be higher if you're under 25. You'll pay extra for additional drivers (about $2 per day). Residents of the U.K. will need a reservation voucher, a passport, a U.K. driver's license, and a travel policy that covers each driver, in order to pick up a car.

CONSUMER PROTECTION

Whenever possible, **pay with a major credit card** so you can cancel payment if there's a problem, provided that you can provide documentation. This is a good idea whether you're buying travel arrangements before your trip or shopping at your destination.

If you're doing business with a particular company for the first time, **contact your local Better Business Bureau and the attorney general's offices** in your state and the company's home state, as well. Have any complaints been filed?

Finally, if you're buying a package, always **consider travel insurance** that includes default coverage (*see* Insurance, *below*).

LOCAL BBBS • Council of Better Business Bureaus (4200 Wilson Blvd., Suite 800, Arlington, VA 22203, tel. 703/276–0100, fax 703/525–8277).

CUSTOMS & DUTIES

ENTERING AUSTRALIA

If you're 18 or older, you may bring back A$400 worth of souvenirs and gifts, including jewelry. Your duty-free allowance also includes 250 cigarettes or 250 grams of tobacco and 1,125 ml of alcohol, including wine, beer, or spirits. Residents under 18 may bring back A$200 worth of goods.

RESOURCES • **Australian Customs Service** (Regional Director, Box 8, Sydney, NSW 2001, tel. 02/9213–2000, fax 02/9213–4000).

ENTERING NEW ZEALAND

Although greeted with a "Haere Mai" ("Welcome to New Zealand"), homeward-bound travelers with goods to declare must present themselves for inspection. If you're 17 or older, you may bring back $700 worth of souvenirs and gifts. Your duty-free allowance also includes 200 cigarettes or 250 grams of tobacco or 50 cigars or a combo of all three up to 250 grams; 4.5 liters of wine or beer and one 1,125-ml bottle of spirits.

RESOURCES • **New Zealand Customs** (Custom House, 50 Anzac Ave., Box 29, Auckland, New Zealand, tel. 09/359–6655, fax 09/309–2978).

ENTERING CANADA

If you've been out of Canada for at least seven days you may bring in C$500 worth of goods duty-free. If you've been away for fewer than seven days but more than 48 hours, the duty-free allowance drops to C$200; if your trip lasts 24–48 hours, the allowance is C$50. You may not pool allowances with family members. Goods claimed under the C$500 exemption may follow you by mail; those claimed under the lesser exemptions must accompany you.

Alcohol and tobacco products may be included in the seven-day and 48-hour exemptions but not in the 24-hour exemption. If you meet the age requirements of the province or territory through which you reenter Canada you may bring in, duty-free, 1.14 liters (40 imperial ounces) of wine or liquor or 24 12-ounce cans or bottles of beer or ale. If you are 16 or older you may bring in, duty-free, 200 cigarettes and 50 cigars; these items must accompany you.

You may send an unlimited number of gifts worth up to C$60 each duty-free to Canada. Label the package Unsolicited Gift—Value Under $60. Alcohol and tobacco are excluded.

INFORMATION • **Revenue Canada** (2265 St. Laurent Blvd. S, Ottawa, Ontario K1G 4K3, tel. 613/993–0534, 800/461–9999 in Canada).

ENTERING THE U.K.

From countries outside the EU, including the United States, you may import, duty-free, 200 cigarettes or 50 cigars; 1 liter of spirits or 2 liters of fortified or sparkling wine or liqueurs; 2 liters of still table wine; 60 milliliters of perfume; and 250 milliliters of toilet water; plus £136 worth of other goods, including gifts and souvenirs.

INFORMATION • **HM Customs and Excise** (Dorset House, Stamford St., London SE1 9NG, tel. 0171/202–4227).

ENTERING THE U.S.

Visitors age 21 and over may import the following into the United States: 200 cigarettes or 50 cigars or 2 kilograms of tobacco, 1 liter of alcohol, and gifts worth $100. Prohibited items include meat products, seeds, plants, and fruits.

DISABILITIES & ACCESSIBILITY

ACCESS IN THE BAY AREA

The Bay Area is an important national center for resources for people with disabilities, thanks mostly to Berkeley's Center for Independent Living—a group of people with disabilities who in the early '70s began fighting for their right to be accepted at UC Berkeley.

There are now more than 300 independent living centers nationwide, designed to help people with disabilities discover their potential; you'll find them throughout the Bay Area (*see below*). In addition, the American Foundation for the Blind has brochures and catalogs to help people access resources. Lighthouse Center for the Blind and Visually Disabled has assisting devices (canes, talking watches) and can direct people to support groups. Lion's Center for the Blind, in Oakland and San Jose, also has resources. Peninsula Center for the Blind has orientation and mobility specialists, social workers, and short-term counseling. For people with hearing impairments, the Hearing Society for the Bay Area provides social services, interpreting, vocational rehab, and referrals.

SAN FRANCISCO RESOURCES • Independent Living Center (70 10th St., tel. 415/863–0581). **American Foundation for the Blind** (111 Pine St., Suite 725, San Francisco, tel. 415/392–4845). **Lighthouse for the Blind and Visually Disabled** (214 Van Ness Ave., at Grove St., San Francisco, tel. 415/431–1481). **Hearing Society for the Bay Area** (870 Market St., Suite 330, tel. 415/693–5870, TDD 415/834–1005).

EAST BAY RESOURCES • Oakland's **Independent Living Center** (2539 Telegraph Ave., tel. 510/841–4776). Oakland's **Lion's Center for the Blind** (3834 Opal St., at 38th St., tel. 510/450–1580). In Marin County: San Rafael's **Independent Living Center** (710 4th St., tel. 415/459–6245).

SOUTH BAY RESOURCES • Santa Clara's **Independent Living Center** (1601 Civic Center Dr., Suite 100, tel. 408/985–1243). San Jose's **Lion's Center for the Blind** (101 N. Bascom Ave., tel. 408/295–4016). Palo Alto's **Peninsula Center for the Blind** (2470 El Camino Real, Suite 107, tel. 650/858–0202).

GETTING AROUND

Transit organizations in the Bay Area have joined ranks to create an ID card, called the Regional Transit Connection (RTC) Discount Card, which gives people with disabilities discounts on travel throughout nine Bay Area counties; each transit company decides what kind of a discount to give (*see* Bus Travel, *above, and* Subway Travel, *below*). You can **get a pass at any transit office** by filling out a form and getting proof of disability from your doctor.

The RTC Discount Card is available at the BART Customer Service Office, open weekdays 9–11:30 and 2–4:30. With the ID you may purchase a $16 BART ticket for $4. All BART stations have elevators; call for a daily update on which elevators are out of service. Most Muni buses are wheelchair accessible; with the discount ID you pay 35¢ instead of $1, and a monthly pass is $8; contact the Muni Discount Office for access information. All AC Transit buses are wheelchair accessible; contact AC Transit Customer Service for information on obtaining a disability ID card, which allows the bearer to pay 60¢ instead of the regular $1.25 bus fare. All Golden Gate Transit buses are wheelchair accessible, and riders with disabilities are entitled to 50% off the fare.

Some major car-rental companies are able to supply hand-controlled vehicles with a minimum of 24-hours advance notice. Avis will install hand-control mechanisms at no extra charge if given a day's notice. Hertz asks for 48-hour notice (except at San Francisco International Airport, where a day will suffice). Rental companies often can't install hand controls on economy cars.

Apria Healthcare rents manual wheelchairs starting at $10 per day or $80 per month. In the East Bay, Grand Mar rents and repairs wheelchairs. Manual wheelchairs rent for $15 the first day, $5 each subsequent day, or $50–$100 a month; power wheelchairs are $20 a day, $400–$500 a month.

RESOURCES • BART Customer Service Office (800 Madison St., at the Lake Merritt BART station, Oakland, tel. 510/464–2133, TDD/TTY 510/839–2220; 510/834–5438 for elevator information). **Muni Discount ID Office** (tel. 415/923–6070, TDD/TTY 415/923–6366). **AC Transit** (tel. 510/817–1717; 510/891–4706 for customer service). **Golden Gate Transit** (tel. 415/332–6600). **Avis** (tel. 800/331–1212). **Hertz** (tel. 800/654–3131, TDD 800/654–2280). **Apria Healthcare** (480 Carlton Ct., South San Francisco, tel. 415/864–6999). **Grand Mar** (1311 63rd St., at Doyle St., Emeryville, tel. 510/428–0441).

THE GREAT OUTDOORS

In San Francisco the nonprofit Environmental Traveling Companions organizes cross-country skiing, kayaking, and rafting trips for people with disabilities. Their prices are very reasonable: One-day trips start at about $40 per person. In the East Bay the Bay Area Outreach and Recreation Program organizes sports events and outdoor activities for people with disabilities, with programs for youth, adults, and senior citizens. California State Parks has a discount pass ($3.50) that gets you 50% off all parking and camping fees (provided the fees are more than $3). You can purchase the pass at any state park visitor center, or by mail.

RESOURCES • Environmental Traveling Companions (Fort Mason Center, Bldg. C, tel. 415/474–7662). **Bay Area Outreach and Recreation Program** (tel. 510/849–4663). **California State Parks** (Disabled Discount Pass Program, Box 942896, Sacramento 94296–0001).

TIPS & HINTS

When discussing accessibility with an operator or reservationist, **ask hard questions.** Are there any stairs, inside *or* out? Are there grab bars next to the toilet *and* in the shower/tub? How wide is the doorway to the room? To the bathroom? When possible, **opt for newer accommodations,** which are more likely to have been designed with access in mind. Older buildings may have more limited facilities. Be sure to **discuss your needs before booking.**

COMPLAINTS • Disability Rights Section (U.S. Department of Justice, Box 66738, Washington, DC 20035–6738, tel. 202/514–0301 or 800/514–0301, fax 202/307–1198, TTY 202/514–0383 or 800/514–0383) for general complaints. **Aviation Consumer Protection Division** (*see* Air Travel, *above*) for airline-related problems. **Civil Rights Office** (U.S. Department of Transportation, Departmental Office of Civil Rights, S-30, 400 7th St. SW, Room 10215, Washington, DC 20590, tel. 202/366–4648) for problems with surface transportation.

TRAVEL AGENCIES

Some agencies specialize in travel arrangements for individuals with disabilities.

BEST BETS • Access Adventures (206 Chestnut Ridge Rd., Rochester, NY 14624, tel. 716/889–9096), run by a former physical-rehabilitation counselor. **Hinsdale Travel Service** (201 E. Ogden Ave., Suite 100, Hinsdale, IL 60521, tel. 630/325–1335), which offers advice from wheelchair traveler Janice Perkins. **Wheelchair Journeys** (16979 Redmond Way, Redmond, WA 98052, tel. 206/885–2210 or 800/313–4751), for general travel arrangements.

DISCOUNTS & DEALS

While your travel plans are still in the fantasy stage, **start studying the travel sections of major Sunday newspapers**: You'll often find listings for good packages and incredibly cheap flights. Surfing on the Internet can also give you some good ideas. Travel agents are another obvious resource; the computer networks to which they have access show the lowest fares before they're even advertised. Agencies on or near college campuses, accustomed to dealing with budget travelers, can be especially helpful.

Always **compare all your options before making a choice.** A plane ticket bought with a promotional coupon may not be cheaper than the least expensive fare from a discount ticket agency. (For more on getting a deal on airfares, *see* Air Travel.) When evaluating a package, keep in mind that what you get is just as important as what you save. Just because something is cheap doesn't mean it's a bargain.

CREDIT CARDS & AUTO CLUBS

When you use your credit card to make travel purchases you may get free travel-accident insurance, collision-damage insurance, and medical or legal help, depending on the card and the bank that issued it. So **get a copy of your credit card's travel-benefits policy.** If you are a member of the American Automobile Association (AAA) or an oil-company-sponsored road-assistance plan, always **ask hotel or car-rental reservationists about auto-club discounts.** Some clubs offer additional discounts on admission to attractions. And don't forget that auto-club membership entitles you to free maps and trip-planning services.

DISCOUNTS BY PHONE

Don't be afraid to **check out "1-800" discount reservations services,** which use their buying power to get a better price on hotels, airline tickets, even car rentals. When booking a room, always **call the hotel's local toll-free number** (if one is available) rather than the central reservations number—you'll often get a better price. Always ask about special packages.

CHEAP AIRLINE TICKETS • Tel. 800/FLY–4–LESS. Tel. 800/FLY–ASAP.

CHEAP HOTEL ROOMS • Accommodations Express (tel. 800/444–7666). **Central Reservation Service (CRS)** (tel. 800/548–3311). **Hotel Reservations Network (HRN)** (tel. 800/964–6835). **Quickbook** (tel. 800/789–9887). **RMC Travel** (tel. 800/245–5738). **Steigenberger Reservation Service** (tel. 800/223–5652).

SAVE ON COMBOS

Packages and guided tours can both save you money, but don't confuse the two. When you buy a package your travel remains independent, just as though you had planned and booked the trip yourself. Fly-and-drive packages, which combine airfare and car rental, are often a good deal. In cities, **ask the local visitors bureau about hotel packages.** These often include tickets to major museum exhibits and other special events you'd be going to anyway.

DRIVING

Stick to public transportation if you want to avoid frustrations such as high tolls on the Golden Gate Bridge, traffic jams at any time, and a notable lack of parking.

From San Francisco I–80 heads east over the Bay Bridge to Oakland and Berkeley, then continues toward Sacramento and Lake Tahoe. Heading north across the Golden Gate are Highway 1 (19th Ave. and Park Presidio Blvd.) and U.S. 101 (Van Ness Ave. and Lombard St.). Highway 1 then splits off for a beautiful drive (complete with stunning views and treacherous curves) to Stinson Beach and north along the coast. U.S. 101 continues through Marin County toward the Wine Country. South along the peninsula, U.S. 101 (known here as the Bayshore Freeway) passes the San Francisco International Airport on the way to San Jose. I–280 heads south, going farther inland. This route is a bit longer milewise but sees less traffic and is fairly accurately called "The World's Most Beautiful Freeway." Highway 1 hugs the coastline south to Half Moon Bay and beyond. In the East Bay I–880 links San Jose with Oakland, where it connects with I–80 to San Francisco or Berkeley and Sacramento. AAA's "San Francisco Bay Region" road map will keep you on track.

PARKING

If you actually find a parking space in San Francisco, it may be on the side of a sheer precipice. Should you succeed in the hideous task of parallel parking on this 90-degree slope, **remember to curb your wheels.** Here's how: turn the wheels so they point toward the curb (to the left when facing uphill, to the right when facing downhill, set the emergency brake, and if you're in a stick shift, leave the car in gear. Not only will this keep you from rolling into other cars, it will also help you avoid a $23 ticket from the San Francisco Police Department.

Circled North Beach for half an hour? Ready to dump your car any place it fits? Think again. The city issues 2.4 million parking tickets a year—and the number is only expected to increase.

The large Sutter-Stockton Garage, at 444 Stockton Street, has reasonable rates and is within walking distance of Union Square, Chinatown, and North Beach. The cheapest lot near Fisherman's Wharf is the Wharf Garage, at 350 Beach St., between Taylor and Mason Streets. Parking in the East Bay is less difficult, though finding a spot near the UC Berkeley campus is no easy task. Try Sather Gate Garage, 2450 Durant Avenue, just west of Telegraph Avenue.

BRIDGE TOLLS

The toll on the Golden Gate Bridge is $3, collected only when you travel south into San Francisco. Discount ticket books are available at the toll office next to the bridge, at many city Safeway stores, and at some gas stations. For $16 you get six crossings (available at the toll office only); $40 gets you 15 crossings. Carpoolers (three or more people per car) pay no toll 5–9 AM and 4–6 PM weekdays. All the state bridges, including the Bay Bridge, San Mateo Bridge, Dumbarton Bridge, and Richmond/San Rafael Bridge, have the same toll ($1), collected in the westbound direction. A discount book ($34 for 40 crossings), good for four months from date of purchase, is available at the toll booths. Carpoolers cross free 5:30–10 AM and 3–6 PM weekdays in specially marked lanes.

EMERGENCIES

HOSPITALS

San Francisco General Hospital and the Medical Center at the University of California both have 24-hour emergency rooms. Physician Access Medical Center is a drop-in clinic in the Financial District. Access Health Care provides drop-in medical care at Davies Medical Center.

RESOURCES • San Francisco General Hospital (1001 Potrero Ave., tel. 415/206–8000). **Medical Center at the University of California, San Francisco** (505 Parnassus Ave., at 3rd Ave., near Golden Gate Park, tel. 415/476–1000). **Physician Access Medical Center** (26 California St., tel. 415/397–2881); open weekdays 7:30–5:00. **Access Health Care** (Davies Medical Center, Castro Street at Duboce Avenue, tel. 415/565–6600); open daily 8–8.

24-HOUR PHARMACIES • Walgreen Drug Stores (498 Castro, at 18th St., tel. 415/861–3136; 25 Point Lobos, near 42nd Ave. and Geary St., tel. 415/386–0736); 3201 Divisadero St. at Lombard St., tel. 415/931–6417.

FERRY TRAVEL

For a change of pace, pack a thermos of coffee and a warm jacket and hop aboard one of the many ferries plying the bay's waters. Ferries are comparable to other forms of transport in speed (though not in price), and you can drink your java while taking in a lovely view. Your ferry ticket acts as a free transfer to buses on both sides of the bay. In the city the main point of departure is the landmark San Francisco Ferry Building.

The Blue and Gold Fleet sends ferries to Tiburon, Sausalito, Angel Island State Park, and Alcatraz. The weekday commuter ferry to Tiburon (20 minutes) departs from the SF Ferry Building. All other departures are from Pier 41 at Fisherman's Wharf, including weekend service to Tiburon (30 minutes) and daily service to Sausalito (30 minutes), Angel Island (40 minutes), and Alcatraz. One-way adult fare to Sausalito or Tiburon is $5.50. To Angel Island, round-trip adult fare (including park admission) is $10. Bikes are allowed on board at no additional charge, though space is limited. To Alcatraz, the adult fare is $7.75, or $11 including a worthwhile audio tour. Call for current schedules.

The Blue and Gold Fleet's Oakland/Alameda Ferry leaves from Jack London Square (Embarcadero and Broadway) in Oakland or the Alameda Ferry Dock (2990 Main St., Alameda) for the San Francisco Ferry Building (30 minutes) or Pier 39 (40 minutes). Ferries run every 1–2 hours from 6 AM on weekdays, 10 AM on weekends and holidays, until 8:50 PM. This ride gives you great views of Oakland's harbor and the Bay Bridge. The fare is $4.

The Blue and Gold Fleet's Vallejo Ferry has a commuter run ($7.50) and an excursion fare to Marine World/Africa U.S.A. ($39 round-trip, which includes park admission and shuttle to and from the park). In San Francisco ferries leave from the San Francisco Ferry Building and Pier 39; call for a current schedule.

Golden Gate Ferry crosses the bay between the San Francisco Ferry Building and Larkspur (45–55 minutes; $2.50 weekdays, $4.25 weekends) or Sausalito (30 minutes, $4.25). Ferries depart hourly, from 7 AM to 8 PM.

INFORMATION • Blue and Gold Fleet's **Tiburon, Sausalito, Angel Island, and Alcatraz Ferries** (tel. 415/773–1188 for 24-hour recorded information or 415/705–5555 for tickets). Blue and Gold Fleet's **Oakland/Alameda Ferry** (tel. 415/705–5555 or 510/522–3300 for 24-hour recorded information). Blue and Gold Fleet's **Vallejo Ferry** (tel. 415/705–5444). **Golden Gate Ferry** (tel. 415/923–2000).

GAY & LESBIAN TRAVEL

San Francisco's gay community, particularly in the Castro district, is extremely supportive and close-knit. If you're trying to find your niche (be it a support group or a political organization), some friendly asking around at one of the Castro cafés or diners should get you helpful advice, if not a pal. Café Flore (see Castro District in Chapter 5), despite all the winking and whispering going on, is actually a great spot to start getting down to business with those in the know. If you're wired, the Gay Guys' Guide to San Francisco (www.niche.net/GayGuide2SanFran) is an excellent, humor-packed guide to gay life in the big city—and it lists dozens of local gay clubs, with interests from hiking to painting to political action.

Though the lesbian community doesn't center around a single district or neighborhood, Valencia Street in San Francisco's Mission District (see Mission District in Chapter 2) has several women's bookstores and organizations. Red Dora's Bearded Lady (see Mission District in Chapter 5) is a café and performance space frequented by young women, primarily in their twenties. In Berkeley the bookstore and coffeehouse Mama Bears (see Oakland in Chapter 5) hosts readings and social events in a warm, supportive environment. The lesbian-owned and -operated café Ann Kong's World-Famous Bleach Bottle Pig Farm is another happening spot—look in the papers for readings and other evening activities. For action of a more direct nature, contact Lesbian Avengers, a group of lesbian, bisexual, and transgendered women, for the lowdown on meetings and events.

INFORMATION • **Ann Kong's World-Famous Bleach Bottle Pig Farm** (2072 San Pablo Ave., between University Ave. and Addison St., Berkeley, tel. 510/848–7376). **Lesbian Avengers** (tel. 415/267–6195).

PUBLICATIONS

The weekly Bay Area Reporter (B.A.R.) and the bi-weekly Bay Times are the two main gay and lesbian papers. Both have excellent news (local, national, and international), though the B.A.R. is heavier on news coverage and lighter on events and listings. For a more conservative gay perspective, pick up the

Sentinel, which emphasizes national gay news. The section "168 Hours" is an excellent listing of arts, films, literary events, and social goings-on. The biweekly *Outnow* is a thin, San Jose–based forum for gay and lesbian news and community happenings; it also comes out in South Bay and East Bay editions. The monthly *Dykespeak: The Thinking Lesbian's Newspaper* is the best resource exclusively for lesbians. All these papers are free.

A Different Light (*see* Books *in* Chapter 3), the Bay Area's best gay bookstore, stocks a wide selection of "queerzines," including *Bear* ($6), which bills itself as "the magazine for hairy gay men"; *Girl Jock* ($4), the tongue-in-cheek magazine for girls who like sports; and *Drummer* ($6), for the leather fetishist. Also look for *On Our Backs* ($6) and *Girlfriends* ($5), two popular bimonthly lesbian pseudoporn mags, both based in San Francisco. The quarterly *Anything That Moves* ($6) is written specifically for bisexuals.

LOCAL ORGANIZATIONS

In San Francisco, Communities United Against Violence provides crisis counseling and referrals for gays and lesbians who are victims of antigay violence. The Lavender Youth Recreation and Information Center is a social and support organization for gays, lesbians, and transgenders 23 years old and younger. If you call Monday through Saturday 6:30 PM to 9 PM (Tuesday from 4 PM), you can talk to other young gays and lesbians or a counselor (during off hours you get recorded information). In Berkeley, the Pacific Center for Human Growth is a well-known gay and lesbian gathering place. The organization offers counseling, social gatherings, rap sessions, and support groups covering topics such as coming out. Check out the bulletin boards, which advertise everything from apartment rentals to social invitations. Drop-in hours are weekdays 10–10, Saturday noon–4, and Sunday 6 PM–10 PM. Their Lavender Line: Lesbian and Gay Switchboard and Counseling Services gives out information and referrals. In Palo Alto, the Stanford University Lesbian/Gay/Bisexual Community Center knows all about gay and lesbian happenings around campus and can refer you to a vast number of support groups and resources. During the school year the center is generally open weekdays from noon until 6; hours vary during summer.

INFORMATION • In San Francisco: **Communities United Against Violence** (973 Market St., Suite 500, tel. 415/777–5500 or 415/333–4357 for 24-hour emergency hot line). **Lavender Youth Recreation and Information Center** (Lyric; 127 Collingwood St., at 18th St., tel. 415/863–3636 or 800/246–7743). In Berkeley: The **Pacific Center for Human Growth** (2712 Telegraph Ave., at Derby St., tel. 510/548–8283). Pacific Center's **Lavender Line: Lesbian and Gay Switchboard and Counseling Services** (tel. 510/841–6224). In Palo Alto: **Stanford University Lesbian/Gay/Bisexual Community Center** (Fire Truck House, Santa Teresa St., Stanford Campus, Palo Alto, tel. 650/725–4222).

AIDS SUPPORT GROUPS & ACTIVISM

The San Francisco AIDS Foundation is an umbrella organization that will refer you to whichever of the city's AIDS-related group best suits you. They also operate a trilingual AIDS Hotline. For late-night counseling or information, call the AIDS/HIV Hotline, open nightly 5 PM–5 AM. The newly opened AIDS Health Project (AHP) Castro Center, run in conjunction with UCSF's AIDS Health Project, provides emotional support and counseling; every Friday they offer free, confidential HIV testing.

San Francisco has two chapters of the AIDS Coalition To Unleash Power (ACT UP), a national organization that advocates "militant, nonviolent, direct action" for increased AIDS research and an end to discrimination against those living with AIDS. ACT-UP rallies in San Francisco have frequently made headlines because of their confrontational tactics. ACT UP SF meets every Monday at 7:30 PM at the Epicenter Zone (475 Valencia St., at 16th St.). ACT UP Golden Gate holds meetings in its offices every Tuesday at 7:30 PM.

INFORMATION • San Francisco AIDS Foundation (10 United Nations Plaza, Market St., between 7th and 8th St., tel. 415/487–3000; for hotline, 415/863–2437 or 800/367–2437 in northern California). **AIDS/HIV Nightline** (tel. 415/434–2437 or 800/273–2437 in northern California). **AIDS Health Project** (AHP) **Castro Center** (400 Castro St., at Market St., tel. 415/476–3902). **ACT UP SF** (tel. 415/522–2907). **ACT UP Golden Gate** (592B Castro St., tel. 415/252–9200).

INSURANCE

Organizations such as STA Travel and the Council on International Educational Exchange (*see* Students, *below*) sell the International Student ID card, which includes health-and-accident coverage when purchased in the United States and used to travel abroad. Citizens of the United Kingdom can buy an annual travel-insurance policy valid for most vacations during the year in which it's purchased. For Australians, the Insurance Council of Australia recommends buying travel insurance whenever you go

ALTERNATIVE AIRWAVES

A number of alternative broadcasters air political back-and-forths, eclectic music playlists, and radical chitchat from undisclosed (sometimes mobile) locations on unoccupied frequencies. Due to their low broadcasting power, you need to be nearby to pick up the following stations' broadcasts. Radio Libre (103.3 FM) is heard in the Mission, parts of Noe Valley, and in the SoMa area; San Francisco Liberation Radio (93.7 FM) can be picked up in the Richmond and Sunset districts; North Beach Radio (88.1 FM) transmits in the area between Columbus Avenue and Pier 39 in San Francisco; and Free Radio Berkeley (104.1 FM) can be heard in north Oakland and Berkeley.

abroad. Most policies sold in Australia are comprehensive and cover trip interruption and cancellation, lost luggage, and medical treatment.

TRAVEL INSURERS • In the U.S., **Access America** (6600 W. Broad St., Richmond, VA 23230, tel. 804/285–3300 or 800/284–8300), **Carefree Travel Insurance** (Box 9366, 100 Garden City Plaza, Garden City, NY 11530, tel. 516/294–0220 or 800/323–3149), **Travel Guard International** (1145 Clark St., Stevens Point, WI 54481, tel. 715/345–0505 or 800/826–1300), **Travel Insured International** (Box 280568, East Hartford, CT 06128–0568, tel. 860/528–7663 or 800/243–3174). In Canada, **Mutual of Omaha** (Travel Division, 500 University Ave., Toronto, Ontario M5G 1V8, tel. 416/598–4083, 800/268–8825 in Canada). In the U.K., **Association of British Insurers** (51 Gresham St., London EC2V 7HQ, tel. 0171/600–3333). Down under, **Insurance Council of Australia** (tel. 03/9614–1077, fax 03/9614–7924).

MAIL

San Francisco's Civic Center post office will hold letters addressed to general delivery for 10 days. In Berkeley the main post office also holds mail for 10 days. A passport or valid ID is required to pick up general delivery mail. The Postal Answer Line is a 24-hour automated service that provides post office hours, postal rates, and more.

INFORMATION • **General Delivery:** Recipient's name, General Delivery, San Francisco, CA 94142). **Postal Answer Line** (tel. 800/725–2161). **San Francisco's Civic Center post office** (101 Hyde St., at Golden Gate Ave., tel. 800/275–8777). **Berkeley's main post office** (2000 Allston Way, Berkeley 94704, tel. 510/649–3100).

MEDIA

NEWSPAPERS & MAGAZINES

The Bay Area's two big dailies, the *San Francisco Chronicle* (morning) and the *San Francisco Examiner* (afternoon), are equally unremarkable. The *Chron* does have some great columns, and it has strangely endeared itself to local readers despite its lightweight coverage. The combined *Chronicle-Examiner* Sunday paper comes with the "Pink Section," useful for its extensive movie reviews and listings of all sorts of upcoming events.

The *Oakland Tribune,* formerly one of the country's premier African-American-owned dailies, has been reduced to a small-town rag. Many Berkeleyans read the student-produced *Daily Californian,* but it, too, wavers in the quality department. The *Marin Independent Journal* focuses mainly on Marin County but also tackles some more general issues. The big surprise in Bay Area dailies is the *San Jose Mercury News,* a paper that's read throughout the area and is highly respected in the journalism community.

You'll find better local coverage (and often better writing) in the Bay Area's many free weekly newspapers. The *San Francisco Bay Guardian* has run daring investigative pieces that the dailies don't dare print; also look for the *Guardian*'s "Best of the Bay Area" special in late July or early August and the "Insider's Guide" issue in February. The *SF Weekly* occasionally comes up with great cover stories and also has extensive cultural events listings. You'll find a lot of good information in the Bay Area's many gay and lesbian publications (*see* Gay & Lesbian Travel, *above*).

The *East Bay Express* comes in two parts: The front section has the East Bay's best local coverage of politics and issues, and the varied front-page articles (which may discuss Oakland history, highlight current issues, or showcase active locals) are usually well written and researched. The "Billboard" section has the best events listings in the East Bay as well as a huge classified section. Marin County's *Pacific Sun* has an events calendar and decent (if scant) local news. The much better *Metro* covers the whole South Bay, with high-quality feature articles and events listings.

ON-LINE RESOURCES

Your first stop for Bay Area information on the World Wide Web should be the San Francisco Bay Resource Net, which has up-to-date links with more than a hundred Web sites covering Bay Area government, transportation, media, entertainment, museums and other points of interest, the arts, sports, restaurants, and more. Yahoo has a whole subsection devoted to San Francisco and is chock-full of links to entertainment, art, housing, travel—you name it. Equally useful is the Bay Area Transit Info Project, which offers maps, schedules, and fares for all Bay Area transport lines (a total of nine counties). The current issue of the *Bay Guardian* is yours to peruse at Guardian Online, while KUSF (*see* Radio, *below*) runs a Web site with information on Bay Area clubs, upcoming shows, and other goodies. The *San Jose Mercury News* has received praise as one of the best on-line newspapers in the country, and it's chock-full of local reports. The Gay Guys' Guide to San Francisco (*see* Gay & Lesbian Travel, *above*) is a humor-packed guide to gay life in the city.

If you're in the mood to hear a good yarn, call the Public Library's Dial-a-Story (tel. 415/437-4880), where the tale changes once a week.

What about when you're in town without a laptop computer? Most public libraries have terminals, but those at the San Francisco Main Library, at 100 Larkin Street, are brand-new and state-of-the-art, with net and web access; check out its on-line catalog. For on-line access in cafés, *see box* SF NET: A Café Connection *in* Chapter 5.

WEB SITES • San Francisco Bay Interactive (www.sftoday.com). **Yahoo** (sfbay.yahoo.com). **Bay Area Transit Info Project** (www.transitinfo.org). **Guardian Online** (www.sfbg.com). **KUSF** (web.usfca.edu/kusf). *San Jose Mercury News* (www.sjmercury.com). **San Francisco Main Library** (sfpl.lib.ca.us).

RADIO

The Bay Area radio scene is largely dominated by Top 40, classic rock, and soft rock megastations. Set your dial to live 105 (105.3 FM) or KOME (98.5 FM) for modern rock, for classical music tune to KDFC (102.1 FM), and for country tunes, KSAN (94.9 FM). Browse the far left end of the FM range to find some less conventional programming. And keep in mind that the Bay Area's many hills mean that not all the stations listed here will be in range all the time. A few of the Bay's best: UC Berkeley's KALX (90.7 FM), a cool, alternative college station run by an all-volunteer staff, can be counted on for the eclectic, the avant-garde, and the noisy. The regular program *Women Hold Up Half the Sky* (Saturday 11–noon) features interviews with fierce and fabulous women from around the country; *Straightjackets* (Monday noon–12:30) deals with issues of gender and (homo)sexuality. KUSF (90.3 FM) comes out of the University of San Francisco, playing new music, ethnic music, and specialty shows. *Spotlight* (Sunday 4 PM–6 PM) is a two-hour tribute to a particular musical artist, label, or genre; *Shoestring Radio Theatre* (Wednesday 9:30 PM–10 PM) takes you back to pre-TV days with original comedy or mystery radio plays.

Berkeley-based KPFA (94.1 FM), a much-loved listener-sponsored station, broadcasts classical, reggae, rap, soul, folk, and blues music as well as national news. Also tune in for interviews with artists and members of special-interest groups you didn't know even existed. At San Francisco–based KPOO (89.5 FM) tunes range from Coltrane to salsa, with great DJs spinning all day. Listener-sponsored KCSM (91.1 FM), out of San Mateo, is 100% jazz. In the South Bay Foothill Junior College's KFJC (89.7 FM) beams out all kinds of music plus some outstanding shows. The award-winning *Norman Bates Memorial Soundtrack Hour* plays your favorite TV and movie themes (Saturday 9–noon), *Phil's Garage* features grungy garage-band music (Saturday 7 PM–10 PM), and *One Step Beyond* (Sunday 7 PM–11 PM) is an alternative news show.

News junkies have a few options. On the AM dial, San Francisco–based KCBS (740 AM) has rapid-fire news bites around the clock. They may not have the most in-depth coverage, but they certainly have the fastest. For higher-quality reporting, try San Francisco's public radio station KQED (88.5 FM), which broadcasts a lot of National Public Radio programming. *All Things Considered* starts at 4:30 PM weekdays and is repeated at 11 PM (weekends 2 PM and 5 PM). The *BBC News Hour* airs weekdays at 9 PM and is repeated at 1 AM (weekends 11:30 AM and 3 PM). San Francisco–based KALW (91.7 FM) also plays NPR and BBC throughout the day.

MONEY

ATMS

Virtually all U.S. banks belong to a network of ATMs. Before leaving home, **make sure that your credit cards have been programmed for ATM use.**
ATM LOCATIONS • Cirrus (tel. 800/424–7787). **Plus** (tel. 800/843–7587).

PACKING FOR THE BAY AREA

When packing for a vacation in the San Francisco Bay Area, **prepare for temperature variations.** An hour's drive can take you up or down many degrees, and the variation from daytime to nighttime in a single location is often marked. The city can be chilly at any time of year, especially in summer when the fog is apt to descend and linger. Bring sweaters, jackets, and clothes for layering; you'll also want shorts or cool cottons for summer. Always tuck in a bathing suit, since many lodgings have pools and hot tubs.

LUGGAGE

In general you are entitled to check two bags on flights within the United States. A third piece may be brought on board, but it must fit easily under the seat in front of you or in the overhead compartment. If your bag is too bulky, be prepared for the humiliation of rejection and last-minute baggage check.

Airline liability for baggage is limited to $1,250 per person on flights within the United States. On international flights it amounts to $9.07 per pound or $20 per kilogram for checked baggage (roughly $640 per 70-pound bag) and $400 per passenger for unchecked baggage. Insurance for losses exceeding these amounts can be bought from the airline at check-in for about $10 per $1,000 of coverage; note that this coverage excludes a rather extensive list of items, which is shown on your airline ticket.

At check-in, **make sure that each bag is correctly tagged** with the destination airport's three-letter code. If your bags arrive damaged or not at all, file a written report with the airline before leaving the airport. If you're traveling with a pack, tie all loose straps to each other or onto the pack itself, so that they don't get caught in luggage conveyer belts.

PASSPORTS & VISAS

AUSTRALIAN CITIZENS

Australian citizens need a valid passport to enter the United States. If you are staying for fewer than 90 days on vacation and have a return or onward ticket, you probably will not need a visa. However, you will need to fill out the Visa Waiver Form, 1-94W, supplied by the airline.
INFORMATION • Australian Passport Office (tel. 008/131–232).

CANADIANS

A passport is not required to enter the United States.

NEW ZEALAND CITIZENS

New Zealand citizens need a valid passport to enter the United States. If you are staying for fewer than 90 days on vacation and have a return or onward ticket, you probably will not need a visa. However, you will need to fill out the Visa Waiver Form, 1-94W, supplied by the airline.
INFORMATION • New Zealand Passport Office (tel. 04/494–0700 for information on how to apply, 0800/727–776 for information on applications already submitted).

U.K. CITIZENS

British citizens need a valid passport to enter the United States. If you are staying for fewer than 90 days on vacation and have a return or onward ticket, you probably will not need a visa. However, you will need to fill out the Visa Waiver Form, 1-94W, supplied by the airline.

INFORMATION • London Passport Office (tel. 0990/21010) for fees and documentation requirements and to request an emergency passport. **U.S. Embassy Visa Information Line** (tel. 01891/200–290) for U.S. visa information; calls cost 49p per minute or 39p per minute cheap rate. **U.S. Embassy Visa Branch** (5 Upper Grosvenor St., London W1A 2JB) for U.S. visa information; send a self-addressed, stamped envelope. Write the **U.S. Consulate General** (Queen's House, Queen St., Belfast BTI 6EO) if you live in Northern Ireland.

SAFETY

It's a wise idea to carry all cash, traveler's checks, credit cards, and your passport in a money belt or some other inaccessible place, such as a front or inner pocket or a bag that fits underneath your clothes. Waist packs are safe if you keep the pack part in front of your body. Even if you're only planning to be gone for only a minute, **never leave your belongings unguarded.**

STUDENTS

DEALS

To save money, **look into deals available through student-oriented travel agencies** and the various other organizations involved in helping out student and budget travelers. Typically, you'll find discounted airfares, rail passes, tours, lodgings, or other travel arrangements, and you don't necessarily have to be a student to qualify.

STUDENT IDS AND SERVICES • Council on International Educational Exchange (CIEE, 205 E. 42nd St., 14th floor, New York, NY 10017, tel. 212/822–2600 or 888/268–6245, fax 212/822–2699), for mail orders only, in the United States. **Travel Cuts** (187 College St., Toronto, Ontario M5T 1P7, tel. 416/979–2406 or 800/667–2887) in Canada.

HOSTELS

Hostelling International (HI), the umbrella group for a number of national youth hostel associations, offers single-sex, dorm-style beds and, at many hostels, "couples" rooms and family accommodations. Membership in any HI national hostel association, open to travelers of all ages, allows you to stay in HI-affiliated hostels at member rates (one-year membership about $25 for adults; hostels about $10–$25 per night). Members also have priority if the hostel is full; they're eligible for discounts around the world, even on rail and bus travel in some countries.

INFORMATION • Hostelling International–American Youth Hostels (HI–AYH; 733 15th St. NW, Suite 840, Washington, DC 20005, tel. 202/783–6161, fax 202/783–6171).

SUBWAY TRAVEL

Relatively clean and quiet, Bay Area Rapid Transit (BART) is a smooth subway and commuter rail system that's better at moving you from one town to another than getting you around town. Its four lines serve San Francisco, Daly City/Colma, and the East Bay from Richmond to Fremont and out to North Concord. In 1997 BART opened a spur line expanding South Bay service to new stations, Castro Valley and Dublin/Pleasanton. The long-anticipated BART extension to San Francisco International Airport has yet to get off the ground. Trains run every 10–20 minutes until midnight, with service starting up again at 4 AM weekdays, 6 AM Saturday, and 8 AM Sunday. Evenings, Sunday, and holidays only the North Concord–Colma and Richmond–Fremont lines operate. For information on the Air-BART Shuttle to the Oakland Airport, *see* Airports & Transfers, *above*.

FARES & DISCOUNTS

The cost of a BART ticket ranges from $1.10 to about $4 depending on the length of the journey. Machines at each station allow you to buy tickets worth between $1.10 and $40; new machines allow purchases with ATM cards and credit cards as well as cash. Insert your ticket into the fare gate, then hold onto it when it pops out the top—you'll need it to exit. The fare is automatically deducted from your ticket at the gate. Any amount left unused can be used on your next ride, as you can add value to old tickets. A 15-minute ride from San Francisco's Embarcadero station to Oakland's MacArthur station costs $2.35; from downtown San Francisco to Berkeley (20–25 minutes) you'll pay $2.65.

BART is seriously lacking in discount fares. Adults can purchase one of two high value tickets: $48 worth of rides for $45 or $32 worth of rides for $30. A bus transfer to Muni or AC Transit is available from the white machines near the BART gate. The two-part ticket gets you on the bus and is also good for a ride back to the same station within three days. In San Francisco put four quarters in the machine—both bus rides are then free. In the East Bay the transfer reduces the fare to $1 for each trip. The BART Plus ticket gives a discount on local bus systems: A $28–$61 ticket entitles you to unlimited rides on any Bay Area bus system for either the first two or last two weeks of the month, plus $15–$50 worth of BART rides.

SCHEDULES & INFORMATION • BART (tel. 650/992–2278 or 510/465–2278, 510/464–7090 for lost and found).

TAXIS

You can occasionally hail a cab in San Francisco, but this is not New York City: **Phone for faster service.** The metered rates for Bay Area taxis are set by each city; you may be able to negotiate a flat rate to the airport or for travel between San Francisco and the East Bay. In San Francisco the rate is $1.70, plus 30¢ each additional sixth of a mile and 30¢ for every minute of waiting time or traffic delay. In the East Bay you'll pay a $2 base fee plus $2 a mile; a ride to San Francisco can cost $25 or more. Don't forget to tip the driver (15% is typical).

CAB COMPANIES • Veteran's Cab (tel. 415/552–1300) or **Yellow Cab** (tel. 415/626–2345). In the East Bay: **Friendly Cab** (tel. 510/536–3000) or **Yellow Cab** (tel. 510/841–8294).

TELEPHONES

The area code for Oakland, Berkeley, and the East Bay is 510; for San Francisco and Marin County it's 415; for Palo Alto and San Mateo County, 650; and for San Jose and Santa Cruz, 408. Beginning in July 1998, the new area code for Carmel, Monterey, and Santa Cruz will switch from 408 to 831.

CALLING LONG DISTANCE

Calling home? Pre-paid phone cards are good for long-distance and international calls, can be used at any time and from any phone, and offer rates slightly cheaper than regular long-distance companies. Buy them at any convenience store. AT&T, MCI, and Sprint long-distance services make calling home relatively convenient and let you avoid hotel surcharges. In the United States, you typically you dial an 800 number.

TO OBTAIN ACCESS CODES • AT&T USADirect (tel. 800/874–4000). **MCI** Call USA (tel. 800/444–4444). **Sprint** Express (tel. 800/793–1153).

TOUR OPERATORS

Buying a vacation package can make your trip to the Bay Area less expensive. The tour operators who put them together may handle several hundred thousand travelers per year and can use their purchasing power to give you a good price. Their high volume may also indicate financial stability. But some small companies provide more personalized service; because they tend to specialize, they may also be more knowledgeable about a given area.

A GOOD DEAL?

The more your package includes, the better you can predict the ultimate cost of your vacation. Make sure you know exactly what is covered, and **beware of hidden costs.** Are taxes, tips, and service charges included? Transfers and baggage handling? Entertainment and excursions? These add up.

If the package you are considering is priced lower than in your wildest dreams, **be skeptical.** Ask about the hotel's location, room size, beds, and whether it has a pool, room service, or programs for children, if you care.

BUYER BEWARE

Each year consumers are stranded or lose their money when tour operators—even large ones with excellent reputations—go out of business. So **check out the operator.** Find out how long the company has been in business, and ask for references that you can check. And **don't book unless the firm has a consumer-protection program.**

Members of the National Tour Association and United States Tour Operators Association are required to set aside funds to cover your payments and travel arrangements in case the company defaults. Nonmembers may carry insurance instead. Look for the details, and for the name of an underwriter with a solid reputation, in the operator's brochure. When it comes to tour operators, **don't trust escrow accounts.** Although there are laws governing charter-flight operators, no governmental body prevents tour operators from raiding the till. For more information, *see* Consumer Protection, *above*.

TOUR-OPERATOR RECOMMENDATIONS • National Tour Association (NTA, 546 E. Main St., Lexington, KY 40508, tel. 606/226–4444 or 800/755–8687). **United States Tour Operators Association** (USTOA, 342 Madison Ave., Suite 1522, New York, NY 10173, tel. 212/599–6599, fax 212/599–6744).

USING AN AGENT

A good travel agent is an excellent resource. When shopping for one, **collect brochures from several sources** and remember that some agents' suggestions may be skewed by promotional relationships with tour and package firms that reward them for volume sales. If you have a special interest, **find an agent with expertise in that area** (*see* Travel Agencies, *below*).

SINGLE TRAVELERS

Remember that prices for vacation packages are usually quoted per person, based on two sharing a room. If traveling solo, you may be required to pay the full double-occupancy rate.

PACKAGES

The companies listed below offer vacation packages in a broad price range.

AIR/HOTEL/CAR • American Airlines Fly AAway Vacations (tel. 800/321–2121). **Continental Vacations** (tel. 800/634–5555). **Delta Dream Vacations** (tel. 800/872–7786). **United Vacations** (tel. 800/328–6877). **US Airways Vacations** (tel. 800/455–0123).

HOTEL ONLY • SuperCities (139 Main St., Cambridge, MA 02142, tel. 800/333–1234).

CUSTOM PACKAGES • Amtrak's Great American Vacations (tel. 800/321–8684). **Budget World-Class Drive** (tel. 800/527–0700, 0800/181181 in the U.K.) for self-drive itineraries.

FROM THE U.K. • British Airways Holidays (Astral Towers, Betts Way, London Rd., Crawley, West Sussex RH10 2XA, tel. 01293/723–121). **Jetsave** (Sussex House, London Rd., East Grinstead, West Sussex RH19 1LD, tel. 01342/312–033). **Key to America** (1–3 Station Rd., Ashford, Middlesex TW15 2UW, tel. 01784/248–777). **Kuoni Travel Ltd.** (Kuoni House, Dorking, Surrey RH5 4AZ, tel. 01306/742–222). **Premier Holidays** (Premier Travel Center, Westbrook, Milton Rd., Cambridge CB4 1YG, tel. 01223/516–688). **Trailfinders** (42–50 Earls Court Rd., London W8 6FT, tel. 0171/937–5400; 58 Deansgate, Manchester, M3 2FF, tel. 0161/839–6969).

FOR CHEAP FARES • Trailfinders (42–50 Earls Court Rd., London W8 6FT, tel. 0171/937–5400), specialists in around-the-world fares and independent travel. **Travel Cuts** (295A Regent St., London W1R 7YA, tel. 0171/637–3161), the Canadian Students' travel service. **Flight Express Travel** (77 New Bond St., London W1Y 9DB, tel. 0171/409–3311).

THEME TRIPS

ADVENTURE • Trek America (Box 189, Rockaway, NJ 07866, tel. 201/983–1144 or 800/221–0596, fax 201/983–8551).

BALLOONING • Above the West Hot Air Ballooning (Box 2290, Yountville, CA 94599, tel. 707/944–8638 or 800/627–2759). **Bonaventura Balloon Company** (133 Wall Rd., Napa, CA 94558, tel. 707/944–2822 or 800/359–6272, fax 707/944–2220).

BICYCLING • Backroads (801 Cedar St., Berkeley, CA 94710-1800, tel. 510/527–1555 or 800/462–2848, fax 510/527–1444).

GOLF • Golf Pacific Coast (1267 Saratoga Ave., Ventura, CA 93003, tel. 800/335–3534).

WALK THIS WAY

Wok Wiz Chinatown Tours and Cooking Company (654 Commercial St., San Francisco 94111, tel. 415/981–8989) leads several culinary/historic tours, including the popular "I Can't Believe I Ate My Way Through Chinatown" tour ($65). Despite the cheesy name, this is a great way to single out some great restaurants and learn about Chinese cuisine from cookbook author Shirley Fong-Torres. Tours usually start on Saturday morning at 10 and end, according to Shirley, "when the first person explodes."

Trevor Hailey (tel. 415/550–8110), a prominent member of the San Francisco lesbian community, leads a highly recommended tour of the city's famous gay neighborhood called Cruisin' the Castro ($30). The 3½-hour tour includes brunch; call for reservations.

To be led around San Francisco for free (donations appreciated), call City Guides (tel. 415/557–4266), whose guided walks are sponsored in part by the San Francisco Public Library. They offer 25 tours each week covering almost every corner of town: Roof Gardens and Open Spaces, the Telegraph Hill Hike, Art Deco Marina, History of Haight-Ashbury, and the Mission Murals are just a few tour topics.

LEARNING • Earthwatch (Box 9104, 680 Mount Auburn St., Watertown, MA 02272, tel. 617/926–8200 or 800/776–0188, fax 617/926–8532) for research expeditions. **Oceanic Society Expeditions** (Fort Mason Center, Bldg. E, San Francisco, CA 94124, tel. 415/441–1106 or 800/326–7491).

MUSIC • Dailey-Thorp Travel (330 W. 58th St., Suite 610, New York, NY 10019-1817, tel. 212/307–1555 or 800/998–4677, fax 212/974–1420).

SAILING • Bay & Delta Yacht Charters (3020 Bridgeway, #271, Sausalito, CA 94965, tel. and fax 415/332–7187 or 800/762–6287).

TRAIN TRAVEL

CALTRAIN

CalTrain offers regular service from San Francisco (4th and Townsend Sts.) to downtown San Jose (65 Cahill St.). A one-way trip costs $4.75 and takes 1½ hours; trains leave hourly between 5 AM and 10 PM, more frequently during commuter hours. Along the way the trains stop at a number of peninsula cities, including Burlingame (30 minutes, $2.50), Palo Alto (1 hour, $3.75), Mountain View (70 minutes, $3.75), and Santa Clara (80 minutes, $4.25). Prices are lower during off-peak (midday) hours. Not all trains stop at all stations, so **check schedules carefully.**

INFORMATION • CalTrain (tel. 800/660–4287).

AMTRAK

Amtrak trains stop at five Bay Area stations: in Richmond; Berkeley, where you can board but can't buy tickets; Oakland; Emeryville; and San Jose. From the Emeryville and Oakland stations, ticket holders can catch a free Amtrak bus to the San Francisco Ferry Building, on Embarcadero at the foot of Market Street. Amtrak's fares vary according to the time of year and other factors; a Bay Area–Seattle round-trip

(24 hours each way) runs from $180 to $330, while Bay Area–Los Angeles round-trips (12 hours each way) are from $78 to $155.

AMTRAK STATIONS • Richmond (16th St. and MacDonald Ave.). **Berkeley** (3rd St. and University Ave.). **Oakland** (245 2nd St., at Jack London Sq.). **Emeryville** (5885 Landregan St.). **San Jose** (65 Cahill St.).

TRANSPORTATION

The San Francisco Bay Area has one of the most comprehensive public transportation systems of any U.S. region, making it easy for commuters and travelers to get around without contributing to traffic jams. For the lowdown on public transit, call the TravInfo hot line, which has up-to-the-minute information on public transit lines, highway traffic conditions, carpooling, parking, and airport transit for all nine Bay Area counties. Additionally, the *Regional Transit Guide* ($5) is an excellent resource listing Bay Area transportation agencies, lines, and frequency. It's available in bookstores as well as at the San Francisco Visitor Information Center and the Berkeley TRiP Commute Store. You can buy public transit passes for the whole Bay Area at the latter; or send a check for $5.50 to the Department of Technical Services. For information on how to maneuver through the city and its public transit system with a bicycle, *see* Bicycling, *above*.

INFORMATION • TravInfo hot line (tel. 415/817–1717, 510/817–1717, or 408/817–1717). **Berkeley TRiP Commute Store** (2033 Center St., 1 block west of Berkeley BART, tel. 510/644–7665). **MTC, Department of Technical Services/Regional Transit Guide** (101 8th St., Oakland 94607).

TRAVEL AGENCIES

A good travel agent puts your needs first. **Look for an agency that specializes in your destination, has been in business at least five years, and emphasizes customer service.** If you're looking for an agency-organized package, choose an agency that's a member of the National Tour Association or the United States Tour Operator's Association (*see* Tour Operators, *above*).

Historic Black Landmarks: A Traveler's Guide (Visible Ink Press; $18) and African American Historic Places (Preservation Press; $26) are two solid travel books that include information on African-American landmarks in California.

LOCAL AGENT REFERRALS • American Society of Travel Agents (ASTA, 1101 King St., Suite 200, Alexandria, VA 22314, tel. 703/739–2782, fax 703/684–8319). **Alliance of Canadian Travel Associations** (Suite 201, 1729 Bank St., Ottawa, Ontario K1V 7Z5, tel. 613/521–0474, fax 613/521–0805). **Association of British Travel Agents** (55–57 Newman St., London W1P 4AH, tel. 0171/637–2444, fax 0171/637–0713).

TRAVEL GEAR

Travel catalogs specialize in nifty items that can **save space when packing.**

MAIL-ORDER CATALOGS • Magellan's (tel. 800/962–4943, fax 805/568–5406). **Orvis Travel** (tel. 800/541–3541, fax 540/343–7053). **TravelSmith** (tel. 800/950–1600, fax 800/950–1656).

U.S. GOVERNMENT

The U.S. government can be an excellent source of inexpensive travel information. When planning your trip, **find out what government materials are available.**

ADVISORIES • U.S. Department of State American Citizens Services Office (Room 4811, Washington, DC 20520); enclose a self-addressed, stamped envelope. **Interactive hot line** (tel. 202/647–5225, fax 202/647–3000). **Computer bulletin board** (tel. 202/647–9225).

PAMPHLETS • Consumer Information Center (Consumer Information Catalogue, Pueblo, CO 81009, tel. 719/948–3334) for a free catalog that includes travel titles.

VISITOR INFORMATION

For general information, there are dozens of chambers of commerce and convention and visitors bureaus in the San Francisco Bay area. For information about the Wine Country, redwood groves, and northwestern California, contact the Redwood Empire Association Visitor Information Center. For $3 they'll send you a visitor guide; or pick up one at the center for $1. You can get information about Silicon Valley from the San Jose Visitor Information Center.

IN SAN FRANCISCO • San Francisco Convention and Visitors Bureau (201 3rd St., Suite 900, 94103–3185, tel. 415/974–6900). **SFCVB Visitor Information Center** (900 Market St., at Powell St., Hallidie Plaza, San Francisco 94102, tel. 415/391–2000 or 415/391–2001 for 24-hour recorded information).

IN GREATER BAY AREA • Berkeley (1834 University Ave., Berkeley 94703, tel. 510/549–7040). **Oakland** (550 10th St., Oakland 94607, tel. 510/839–9000 or 800/262–5526). **San Jose** (333 W. San Carlos St., Suite 1000, San Jose 95110, tel. 408/295–9600 or 800/726–5673). **Santa Clara** (Box 387, Santa Clara 95052, tel. 408/296–7111).

WINE COUNTRY & SILICON VALLEY • Redwood Empire Association Visitor Information Center (2801 Leavenworth St., 94133, tel. 415/394–5991 or 888/678–8507, fax 415/394–5994). **San Jose Visitor Information Center** (150 W. San Carlos, Santa Clara, 95110, tel. 408/283–8833).

STATEWIDE • California State Office of Tourism (801 K St., Suite 1600, Sacramento, CA 95814, tel. 916/322–2882 or 800/862–2543) has a free visitor's guide.

IN THE U.K. • California Tourist Office (ABC California, Box 35, Abingdon, Oxfordshire OX14 4TB, tel. 0891/200–278); calls cost 50p per minute peak rate or 45p per minute cheap rate; send £3 for brochure.

WHEN TO GO

CLIMATE

San Francisco is often cold and windy, even in summer. Things warm up in September and October, the Indian summer months, and in May. The yearly average high temperature is 69°F, the average low 46°F. The East Bay tends to be a few degrees warmer than San Francisco: Highs average 72°F, lows 43°F. Marin County's weather varies from town to town: The coast is usually fogged in, the bay-side towns of Tiburon and Sausalito get a cool breeze, and San Rafael checks in at a solid few degrees warmer than most of the Bay Area, with an average summer high of 82°F. In the South Bay average summer highs, both on the coast and inland, hover in the 80s. In winter things cool down to a medium rare, with lows dipping to 40°F.

What follows are the average daily maximum and minimum temperatures for San Francisco.

Jan.	56F	13C	May	64F	17C	Sept.	70F	21C
	46F	8C		51F	10C		56F	13C
Feb.	60F	15C	June	66F	19C	Oct.	69F	20C
	48F	9C		53F	11C		55F	13C
Mar.	61F	16C	July	66F	19C	Nov.	64F	18C
	49F	9C		54F	12C		51F	10C
Apr.	63F	17C	Aug.	66F	19C	Dec.	57F	14C
	50F	10C		54F	12C		47F	8C

INFORMATION • Weather Channel Connection (tel. 900/932–8437), 95¢ per minute from a Touch-Tone phone. **National Weather Service** (tel. 650/364–7974). For ski conditions in northern California, Tahoe, or the Sierras: **California State Automobile Association's Ski Report Hotline** (tel. 415/864–6440).

FESTIVALS

JANUARY • The whale-watching season runs through April. Patient watchers bundle up and pull out their binoculars at Point Reyes (*see* Hiking and Biking *in* Chapter 8). The rangers at the Point Reyes lighthouse (tel. 415/669–1534) can tell you how many whales have swum past in the days before your visit.

In case you want to see the world.

In case you want to be welcomed there.

We're here to see that you're always welcomed at establishments everywhere. That's why millions of people carry the American Express® Card – for peace of mind, confidence, and security, around the world or just around the corner.

do more ®

Cards

In case you're running low.

We're here to help with more than 118,000 Express Cash locations around the world. In order to enroll, just call American Express before you start your vacation.

do more

Express Cash

And just in case.

We're here with American Express® Travelers Cheques and Cheques *for Two*.® They're the safest way to carry money on your vacation and the surest way to get a refund, practically anywhere, anytime.

Another way we help you…

do more ®

AMERICAN EXPRESS

Travelers Cheques

The one-day **Tet Festival** street fair (tel. 415/391–8050) is held on the Saturday nearest the Vietnamese New Year (the first new moon after January 20). The streets around the Civic Center come alive with performances by Vietnamese, Cambodian, and Laotian singers and dancers, and numerous booths sell Southeast Asian delicacies.

FEBRUARY • North America's oldest Chinese community celebrates the **Chinese New Year and Golden Dragon Parade** (tel. 415/982–3000) with cultural events, fireworks, and costumes. Festivities take place around January 28; this year, they'll celebrate the dawn of the Year of the Tiger (year 4696 on the lunar calendar).

MARCH • During the two-week **Tulipmania** (tel. 415/705–5500) more than 40,000 tulips bloom around Pier 39 at Fisherman's Wharf. You can walk around on your own or join one of the free guided tours.

With shamrocks, Guinness stout, and enough green to make even Mother Nature envious, the **St. Patrick's Day Parade** (tel. 415/661–2700) on March 15 at 12:30 PM is a party in motion. Despite the recent politicization of the parade, with "Gaylic Pride" and "IRA All the Way" banners popping up, the emphasis for San Francisco's Irish community is still firmly on green beer and folk tunes.

APRIL • Japantown's **Cherry Blossom Festival** (tel. 415/563–2313) features nearly 400 Japanese performers along with numerous exhibits of Japanese art. The most popular attractions are the *taiko* drum performance and the 2½-hour parade. For a schedule of events, send a self-addressed, stamped envelope to Cherry Blossom Festival, Box 15147, San Francisco 94115.

Don't miss the huge week-long Chinese New Year's festival, held during the first new moon in February. Come early to get a spot for the final parade—a riotous celebration of Asian culture, featuring firecrackers, lion dancers, and painted dragons.

San Francisco International Film Festival (tel. 415/929–5000), the nation's oldest, features two full weeks of seminars and films ranging from the almost-mainstream (Pedro Almódovar, Wayne Wang) to the truly obscure. Screenings take place near the end of April at the Kabuki 8 and the Castro Theatre in San Francisco, the Pacific Film Archive in Berkeley, and other locations in the South Bay and Marin.

If your energy needs to be rechanneled, come to the **Whole Life Expo,** an annual, weekend-long New Age fest, held at San Francisco's Fashion Design Center (8th and Brannan Sts., tel. 415/721–2484). More than 250 booths display energy pyramids, massage tools, and healing crystals. Another exposition is held the third week in October, when the emphasis is on food and health.

MAY • Vibrant mariachi bands and colorful Mexican folklórico dancers congregate in the Mission District the weekend nearest May 5 to celebrate **Cinco de Mayo** (tel. 415/826–1401), the anniversary of Mexico's defeat of the French at the Battle of Puebla. On Sunday floats, bands, and salsa dancers wearing little more than feathers parade through the Mission, starting at 24th and Bryant streets and ending with a festival at the Civic Center.

The weekend-long **Festival of Greece,** at the Greek Orthodox Cathedral (4700 Lincoln Ave., at Hwy. 13, Oakland, tel. 510/531–3710), emphasizes food—moussaka, dolmas, baklava—and wine, though music and Greek crafts also make an appearance. Costumed dancers perform for the crowds, but when the bands pull out their bouzoukis, everyone gets in on the action.

Listed in the *Guinness Book of World Records* as the world's largest footrace, the zany 100,000-person **Bay to Breakers** (tel. 415/777–7770) pits world-class runners against costumed human centipedes and huge safe-sex condom caravans in a 7½-mile race from the Financial District to Ocean Beach. The race takes place the third Sunday of May (May 17 in 1998). Entry forms start appearing in the *San Francisco Examiner* (*see* Media, *above*) on March 1.

On Memorial Day weekend, long after Mardi Gras and Carnaval celebrations in New Orleans and Rio de Janeiro are over, the Mission District revives the party with **Carnaval** (tel. 415/826–1401). Dozens of Latin American musical groups, including the Caribbean All-Stars and Xiuhcoatc Danza Azteka, keep the energy at top levels. The parade along Mission Street starts at 10 AM Sunday and terminates near the fair on Harrison Street (between 16th and 22nd streets), with food, craft booths, and performances.

JUNE • Summer brings out the neighborhood festivals. On the first weekend in June the **Union Street Spring Festival** (tel. 415/346–9162), near the upscale Marina district, features big bands, wine and food, tea dancing, and a waiters' race. The following weekend the **Haight-Ashbury Street Fair** (tel. 415/661–8025) has two stages, both featuring mostly local bands playing rap, jazz, and rock. Come see the "worlds biggest salami" at the **North Beach Festival** (tel. 415/403–0666), the country's oldest urban street fair, held in mid-June. There's chalk street painting, small-press booksellers, and music (flamenco, jazz, and more).

Free Folk Festival takes place for two days every June at the John Adams campus of City College (1860 Hayes St., at Masonic Ave., San Francisco). Bring your guitar, harmonica, or fiddle to the workshops and impromptu jam sessions that spring up between concerts of folk, blues, and international music. It's a very loosely organized event, and participants change yearly; check newspaper entertainment listings for details.

The East Bay's largest urban fair, **Festival at the Lake** (tel. 510/286–1061), has gotten so big it has expanded from its Lakeside Park home to include sites at Laney College and at the Henry J. Kaiser Convention Center, across Lake Merritt (ferries and trams shuttle you among the sites). The fair takes place the first weekend in June and features crafts, international food, storytelling, and world music.

Juneteenth, the day Lincoln's Emancipation Proclamation was read in Texas, is celebrated in nearly every city in the Bay Area. One of the larger events is the **Oakland Juneteenth Celebration** (tel. 510/238–3866), held at Lakeside Park at Lake Merritt. Show up at the park June 16 between noon and 6 to enjoy big-name blues and R&B acts, ethnic food booths, arts and crafts, and lots of activities for the kids.

On June 21, the longest day of the year, the streets vibrate with the sounds of more than 250 bands during the annual rendition of **Making Waves** (tel. 415/391–0370), when every kind of music—from local funk to zydeco to jazz to African indigenous sounds—entertains listeners at 25 downtown San Francisco stage sites.

Come see free music (classical, jazz, world music, and more) in a beautiful park setting at the **Stern Grove Music Festival** (tel. 415/252–6252), held throughout the summer on the first Sunday of every month, beginning the second weekend in June. Stern Grove is in the southwest corner of San Francisco, at 19th Street and Sloat Boulevard.

Known as San Francisco Pride for short (and formerly known as the Gay and Lesbian Freedom Day Parade), the **San Francisco Lesbian, Gay, Bisexual, Transgender Pride Celebration** parade (tel. 415/864–3733) traditionally attracts huge names in the gay community; one of 1995's grand marshals was Candice Gingrich, Newt's out half-sister. Check local newspapers or call for location and date. June also brings the much-loved and internationally famous **International Lesbian and Gay Film Festival** (*see* Movie Houses *in* Chapter 6).

JULY • Summer heat keeps the festivals coming. In mid-July you can groove your way down Polk Street between Jackson and Bush streets during the festival of **Blues and Art on Polk** (tel. 415/346–9162).

Fourth of July Waterfront Festival (tel. 415/777–7120), the biggest Independence Day celebration in the Bay Area, takes place along the San Francisco waterfront (between Aquatic Park and Pier 39), with music in the afternoon and fireworks at night. The show is impressive even when the waterfront is fogged in.

In the 1940s, '50s, and '60s the Fillmore area was famous for its sizzling jazz and blues clubs. Old-time musicians (and younger ones, too) revive those heady days on the first weekend of every July with **Jazz and All That Art on Fillmore** (tel. 415/346–9162); on Fillmore Street between Post and Jackson streets, arts-and-crafts booths fill the sidewalks, and outdoor cafés serve everything from barbecued ribs to knishes.

Join 5,000 San Franciscans at the Concourse Exhibition Center (Brannan and 8th Sts.) in early July to sample 250 beers at the **KQED International Beer and Food Festival** (tel. 415/553–2200), the largest international beer festival in the nation. There's live music on two stages, and food booths hand out everything from Thai cuisine to pizza. Free cable car shuttles run from the Civic Center BART station. Get tickets ($35) in advance by calling the number above; profits support public TV.

Taking place during the last two weeks of July, the **Jewish Film Festival** (tel. 510/548–0556) is the largest of its kind in the world. Films are shown at theaters in Berkeley and San Francisco. Call for admission prices.

Oakland's large Chinatown celebrates its diversity on the fourth weekend in August during the **Oakland Chinatown Streetfest** (tel. 510/893–8979), with food and cultural activities representing all East Asian cultures.

AUGUST • The **Festival of the Sea** (tel. 415/929–0202) celebrates San Francisco's maritime tradition with sail- and rope-making demonstrations, seafaring music, and a parade of tall ships and yachts along the San Francisco waterfront. The free festival takes place at San Francisco's Hyde Street Pier, usually late in the month.

SEPTEMBER • Shakespeare in the Park (tel. 415/666–2221) brings free outdoor performances of a selected Shakespeare play to San Francisco's Golden Gate Park, beginning Labor Day weekend. In October the festival continues at Lakeside Park in Oakland and at St. James Park in San Jose. Shows take place at 1:30 PM weekends.

The San Francisco Opera kicks off the opera season with **Opera in the Park** (tel. 415/861–4008), a free concert in Golden Gate Park's Sharon Meadow on the Sunday after the first performance of the season, usually the week after Labor Day.

Even in San Francisco, the **Folsom Street Fair** (tel. 415/861–3247) has created controversy with its past displays of leather and bondage gear. People crowd the blocks of Folsom Street between 7th and 12th Streets strutting their latest leather ware, usually the last or next-to-last Sunday in September.

Festival de las Americas (tel. 415/826–1401) celebrates the independence of Mexico and seven other Latin American countries. More than 80,000 people flock to 24th Street between Mission and Hampshire streets for this socially responsible, alcohol-free, family-oriented event that promotes pride in the Latino community. There are Latino musicians, ethnic food, and booths selling original crafts.

Big-name musicians like B. B. King and Robert Cray perform at the **San Francisco Blues Festival** (tel. 415/979–5588), the country's oldest, usually held the last weekend of the month at Justin Herman Plaza (Market St. at Embarcadero) and at Fort Mason's Great Meadow (Marina Blvd. and Laguna St.). Tickets average $20–$30 and advance purchase is recommended.

Taste home-brewed beer at Berkeley's Civic Center Park at the **Berkeley Beer and Music Festival** (tel. 510/843–7625), held on the first or second weekend in September, and you may never drink anything else. A $15 tasting kit includes a beer mug and 10 drink coupons.

OCTOBER • The Black Cowboys Parade (tel. 510/531–7583) takes place the first Saturday in October and honors the role of minorities in the Old West.

On the first Sunday of the month, the **Castro Street Fair** (tel. 415/467–3354) brings out crafts vendors; booths run by community, health, and social organizations; and musical entertainment.

In mid-October San Francisco salutes its sailors with activities and booths on Fisherman's Wharf and a Blue Angels air show—all part of the annual **Fleet Week** (tel. 415/705–5500).

San Francisco's flamboyant **Halloween parade** (tel. 415/777–5500) recently relocated from the Castro district to Civic Center. About 300,000 revelers attend each year.

San Francisco International Accordion Festival (tel. 415/775–6000) brings food, dancing, and booths to the Anchorage Shopping Center in Fisherman's Wharf on the third weekend in October. Perennial faves Zydeco Flames and Those Darn Accordions often compete in the "I'm San Francisco's Main Squeeze" contest, which chooses the accordionist with the wildest costume to be next year's poster child.

NOVEMBER • Bibliophiles eagerly await the **San Francisco Book Festival** (tel. 415/908–2833), held the first weekend in November at the Concourse exhibition center, at 8th and Brannan Streets. More than 300 booths represent small, alternative presses as well as big publishing houses; many sell books at a discount. Some 250 authors also show up to read and sign their books; Isabel Allende, Tony Hillerman, and June Jordan are just a few who have appeared in recent years.

Día de los Muertos, or Day of the Dead, derived from Aztec rituals and the Catholic All Souls' Day, is celebrated in early November in San Francisco's Mission District with art exhibitions and a parade starting from the Mission Cultural Center (2868 Mission St., tel. 415/821–1155).

On the Sunday after Thanksgiving more than 13,000 people dressed like their favorite Gary Larson characters compete in the **Run to the Far Side** (tel. 415/564–0532), a 5-kilometer walk or 10-kilometer run through Golden Gate Park. The event benefits the California Academy of Sciences' environmental education programs.

DECEMBER • In celebration of the season, the San Francisco Ballet (tel. 415/865–2000) presents *The Nutcracker* every year. In Oakland the Mormon Temple (4766 Lincoln Ave., tel. 510/531–0704) holds a **tree-lighting ceremony** early in the month and offers musical entertainment during the evenings until Christmas Eve.

Celebration of Craftswomen (tel. 415/821–6480), held during the first two weekends of December at Fort Mason, features leather works, wearable art, and glassworks along with gourmet food and live entertainment.

EXPLORING THE BAY AREA

REVISED BY JENNIFER BREWER AND KATHLEEN DODGE

Y ou'll never run out of opportunities for adventure in the Bay Area, no matter how long you stay. San Francisco is a densely populated cosmopolitan city, yet its historic Victorian homes, wide-open parks, and miles of waterfront render it anything but claustrophobic. The best way to explore is by walking its dozen distinct neighborhoods; along the way you'll encounter shops, parks, and cafés that invite you to stop and soak up the atmosphere. On days when you desire something more rugged, head for Marin County's stunning cliffs, forests, and beaches—an impressive backdrop to the multi-million-dollar homes that dot the landscape. The East Bay offers acres of hilly parks with incredible views of the city and the bay beyond. The East Bay's two major cities are Berkeley, known for its university, its radical politics, and its antic street scene; and Oakland, a sprawling, unpretentious city with a strong African-American identity. In the South Bay you'll find one of California's most renowned universities as well as Silicon Valley and the striking, wind-swept San Mateo County coast.

SAN FRANCISCO

San Francisco's eclectic history has left plenty for modern explorers to discover. In nooks and crannies all over the city, you'll find reminders of everything from the drinking and whoring of the gold prospectors to the living and loving of the country's largest lesbian and gay population. Weathered brick and iron warehouses of the Barbary Coast are now the sites of antiques shops in the Financial District, while huge Victorian mansions that survived the 1906 quake are still standing proud in the Mission. One minute you're marveling at the frenetic pace of Financial District workers, and the next you're strolling through Chinese herb shops and produce markets. You down a cappuccino and *biscotti* at a noisy Italian café, and 10 minutes later you're gazing at the Golden Gate Bridge from the water's edge. Bored? You should be ashamed of yourself.

You can spend countless days (and almost no money at all) just kicking around the city's hilly streets. Discover the latest artistic trend as you gallery-hop; get your exercise climbing Russian Hill's narrow, hidden stairway streets; gawk at the mansions that dominate the peaks of Pacific Heights and the Presidio; or get lost for a day in Golden Gate Park. When you tire, as you inevitably will on the dizzying hills in some parts of the city, hop a bus for a higher-speed version of the San Francisco experience. You can get a Muni Street and Transit Map for $2.50 at most liquor and grocery stores. If you want enthusiastic locals to show you their fair city, tag along on one of San Francisco's quirky tours (*see box* Walk This Way *in* Chapter 1).

MAJOR SIGHTS

San Francisco's major sights are considered major for a reason. Even the most jaded natives can't help but inhale a reverent breath at the sight of the majestic Golden Gate Bridge. The Alcatraz tour explores such a fascinating place—on such a genuinely stark, scary island—that for all the hype, it is utterly compelling. Coit Tower and Golden Gate Park will forever be places to get a feel for quintessential San Francisco. Even Fisherman's Wharf, despite its saccharin-sweet carnival atmosphere, never fails to attract hordes of people with its dazzling waterside location and nonstop activity.

GOLDEN GATE BRIDGE

The bridge to end all bridges has come to symbolize San Francisco more than any other monument. This masterpiece of design and engineering, which links San Francisco to its wealthy neighbor, Marin County, has endured wind, fog, a daily load of 100,000 cars, the ignominy of more than 1,000 suicides, and the weight of the more than 200,000 people who showed up to celebrate its 50th birthday in 1987. More than a mile long, the bridge is painted international orange for visibility in fog (so the seagulls don't crash into it). Engineer Joseph Strauss designed the bridge to withstand winds of more than 100 mi. per hour and to swing nearly 27 ft at its center. The cables that support it are more than 3 ft in diameter, and the combined lengths of the individual strands would wrap around the earth three times.

To catch a glimpse of the bridge, you'll have to scale a hill or two or head to the waterfront near Fisherman's Wharf. Bus 28 will drop you at the toll plaza, at the northern tip of the Presidio (*see* Neighborhoods, *below*); the walk across and back takes about an hour, and the wind can be freezing. Bicycling across the bridge is a thrill; Lincoln Boulevard in the Presidio is a gorgeous way to get there (to reach Lincoln, take a gentle ride west down Lombard Street or have a screaming downhill adventure by approaching from the south on Presidio Boulevard). The pedestrian walkway and the bicycle path are both open 5 AM–9 PM.

Below the bridge on the San Francisco side is historic **Fort Point** (tel. 415/556–1693). The massive fort, built between 1853 and 1861 by the U.S. Corps of Engineers, is an enduring symbol of the commercial and strategic military importance of San Francisco. Though it was designed to hold 500 soldiers and 126 cannons, it was never called on to fire a single shot. All the soldiers packed up and left around 1900, but the public can still drop by for guided tours, free movies on Fort Point history, and "cannon drills" (where you do everything *but* fire the cannon), daily 10–5. From U.S. 101N take Lincoln Boulevard (the last San Francisco exit), then follow the signs. Admission is free.

ALCATRAZ ISLAND

Known as the Rock, Alcatraz Island served for 59 years as the nation's most notorious federal penitentiary, holding high-risk prisoners in its isolated maw. Al Capone, Robert "the Birdman" Stroud, and Machine Gun Kelly were among the more famous bad guys who got "Rock fever" gazing out day after day at the bittersweet sight of San Francisco.

Since the prison closed in 1963, people have been trying to get *onto* Alcatraz Island, not off it. In 1969 a group of Native Americans attempted to reclaim the land, saying that an 1868 federal treaty allowed Native Americans to use all federal territory that the government wasn't actively using. After almost two years of occupation, the U.S. government forced them off, none too gently. The bloody incident is recounted in the island's small museum, and graffiti still reminds visitors that "this is Native American Land."

Today the island is part of the National Park System, and tourists visit the grounds in hordes—though even heavy weekend crowds don't alter the lonely, somber, abandoned feel of the place. Rangers on Alcatraz give a variety of free talks; subjects include escape attempts, the island's history as a 19th-century military fort, the Native American occupation, and Alcatraz's unique properties as part of an

PACIFIC OCEAN

Golden Gate Bridge

Fort Point
National
Historic Site

Wav

101

Golden Gate
National
Recreation
Area

1

The Presidio

Lincoln Blvd.

W. Pacific Ave.

Presid

Baker
Beach

China
Beach

Lands
End

Lincoln
Park

Palace of
the Legion
of Honor

SEACLIFF

Lake St.

Clement St.

Park Presidio Blvd.

8th Ave.

Arguello Blvd.

Geary Expre

Masonic

Point
Lobos

Cliff
House

43rd

Ave.

34th

Ave.

Geary Blvd.

25th

Ave.

19th

Ave.

Balboa St.

Turk

RICHMOND

McLaren
Lodge

HAI
ASH

Fulton St.

Kennedy Dr.

Golden Gate Park

Jr.

Stanyan St.

Clayton Jr.

Martin

Middle Dr.

Luther

King

Dr.

COLE
VALLEY

Lincoln Way

Judah St.

28th
Ave.

Funston Ave.

7th Ave.

Lawton St.

1

Clarendon Ave.

Noriega St.

Ortega St.

19th
Ave.

SUNSET

Quintara St.

TV
P.

41st Ave.

Sunset Blvd.

McCoppin
Square

14th
Ave.

Dewey Blvd.

Taraval St.

Larsen
Park

Dr.

Mt.
Davidson

Vicente St.

Stern Grove

Portola

Yerba Buena Ave.

Monterey

Blvd.

Miramar
Ave.

Great

Highway

Ocean Beach

San Francisco
Zoo

Sloat Blvd

STONESTOWN

Ocean Ave.

Mont

Junipero Serra Blvd.

Harding
Park

San Francisco
State Univ.

Holloway Ave.

Plymouth Ave.

Skyline Blvd.

Lake Merced

Lake Merced Blvd.

Font Blvd.

Garfield St.

280

N

0   1 mile

0   1 km

Fort
Funston

35

Brotherhood
Way

San Francisco Bay

Organ ■ · Marina
Green
Fort
Mason
TO ALCATRAZ
ISLAND
Pier
39

MARINA
Bay St.
Aquatic
Park
Fisherman's
Wharf
NORTH
BEACH
Coit
Tower

alace of Fine Arts
nd Exploratorium
Lombard St.
Columbus
Ave.
TELEGRAPH
HILL

COW
HOLLOW
Union St.
RUSSIAN
HILL
(tunnel)

PACIFIC
HEIGHTS
Broadway
Washington St.
Hyde St.
CHINATOWN
FINANCIAL
DISTRICT

Sacramento St.
California St.
Powell St.
Grant Ave.
NOB HILL

Pine St.
Bush St.
Gough St.
Van Ness Ave.
Post St.
Geary St.
UNION
SQUARE
1st St.
2nd St.

Divisadero St.
Laguna St.
Franklin St.
Steiner
JAPAN
TOWN
Turk St.
CIVIC
CENTER
Market St.
SOMA
Mission St.
3rd St.
4th St.
5th St.
6th St.

ssway
Golden Gate Ave.
Fulton St.
HAYES
VALLEY
6th St.
5th St.
4th St.
Folsom
Harrison
Bryant
Brannan St.
Townsend St.

Alamo
Square
Oak St.
WESTERN
ADDITION
9th St.
10th St.
7th St.

HT-
URY
Haight St.
Buena
Vista
Park
Castro St.
Duboce Ave.
Central
Freeway
7th St.

17th St.
Potrero Ave.
Mariposa St.
Arkansas St.
Indiana St.
3rd St.

Market St.
CASTRO
Mission
Dolores
Park
MISSION
20th St.
Harrison St.
South Van Ness Ave.
Mission St.
Valencia St.
Guerrero St.
Dolores St.
POTRERO
HILL
San Francisco
General
Hospital

in
aks
25th St.
NOE
VALLEY
Diamond St.
César Chavez (Army) St.

en
nyon
ark
Bosworth
St.
rey Blvd.
Fwy.
Silver Ave.
Felton Ave.

GLEN
PARK
Excelsior Ave.
Alemany Blvd.
Mission St.
Persia St.
Moscow St.
John
McLaren
Park
Mansell St.

Southern
Ave.
alboa
Park
n Jose
France Ave.
Geneva
Ave.
TO COW
PALACE
TO SAN FRANCISCO
INTERNATIONAL AIRPORT
Gilman Ave.
Jamestown Ave.
3Com Park
(Candlestick)

San Francisco-Oakland
Bay Bridge

China
Basin

Central Basin

Islais Cr. Channel

India
Basin

Quesada Ave.

Hunters
Point

South
Basin

island chain in San Francisco Bay. Check for schedules at the ranger station at the ferry landing when you arrive or call the dock office at 415/705–1042.

The **Blue and Gold Fleet** (tel. 415/773–1188 for information or 415/705–5555 for tickets) ferries you to the island from San Francisco's Pier 41. The price ($11) includes the ferry ride and an audiocassette tour of the prison itself; tapes are available in several languages, and the average tour takes about 2½ hours. You can skip the cassette tour and pay only $7.75, but the tape, which features former inmates and guards talking about their experiences on Alcatraz, is one of the best parts of the experience. Ferries leave Pier 41 9:30–2:30 year-round (until 4:15 June–August). You can use a credit card to reserve tickets by phone (there's a $2 per ticket service charge). If you're buying tickets in person, go to the ferry ticket office (open 8:30–5) at Pier 41. You should reserve or purchase tickets *several* days in advance. Bus 32 will get you to Pier 41 from the Ferry Building downtown.

COIT TOWER

Built to memorialize San Francisco's volunteer firefighters, the 210-ft concrete observation tower atop Telegraph Hill is named for the colorful woman who willed the funds to build it, Lillie Hitchcock Coit (1843–1929). Heiress Coit was a cross-dresser (she could gain access to the city's more interesting realms in men's clothes) who literally chased fire engines around town. Most people agree the building resembles a fire nozzle—supposedly, that's not intentional.

The walls inside the lobby are covered with Depression-era murals in the style of Diego Rivera, painted by local artists on the government dole. **City Guides** (tel. 415/557–4266) runs free descriptive tours of the tower every Saturday at 11, including the second-floor murals that are normally closed to the public. For $3 the elevator inside the tower will take you to the top for a drop-dead 360-degree view of the Golden Gate Bridge, the Bay Bridge, and Alcatraz.

One of the best (albeit tiring) ways to reach Coit Tower is via two old-fashioned stairways: The historic **Filbert Steps** are narrow wooden walkways that wind through gardens, while the concrete **Greenwich Stairs** are a prime vantage point for a full cityscape. It's best to tackle the Filbert Steps on the way up and marvel at magnificent views as you head down the Greenwich Stairs. To start, take Bus 42 from Market Street north to Filbert Street. At the base of the cliff, you will see a set of concrete steps; take a deep breath and start climbing. The concrete will eventually yield to a rickety wooden path. When the path meets Montgomery Street, look to your left and check out Lauren Bacall's apartment in the 1947 classic, *Dark Passage.* Cross the street and continue up the steps to Coit Tower. Start your descent under the GREENWICH STREET sign near the parking lot. Brick steps will lead you back to Montgomery Street. Head south about half a block; on your left you'll find the second half of the stairway. The stairs bottom out at the site of a 1966 Janis Joplin concert hosted by a nearby drug halfway house—now a trendy health club. *Tel. 415/362–0808., From Market and 3rd Sts. downtown, Bus 30 or 45 to Washington Sq.; walk 2 blocks east on Union St., left on Kearny St. Or Bus 39 from Fisherman's Wharf to top of Telegraph Hill. Tower open daily 10–6:30.*

GOLDEN GATE PARK

The pride of San Francisco is Golden Gate Park: a thousand acres of manicured gardens, museums, playing fields, and bridle paths, not to mention a pair of Dutch windmills and a paddock full of bison. Wooded areas, wide swaths of open field, formal flower beds, and a zillion varieties of vegetation are all packed into an area that is 4 mi long and less than a mile wide. And if you make it all the way to the west end of the park, you'll hit blustery Ocean Beach and the Pacific Ocean. The park's eastern boundary, lying close to Haight Street, has always been a natural hangout for the countercultural denizens of that neighborhood: Hippie historians should note that Ken Kesey and friends celebrated the first **Human Be-In** here on January 14, 1966. Fittingly, a devotional shrine was erected in tribute to Jerry Garcia after his death in 1995. The park has hosted rock concerts ranging from the Grateful Dead and Jefferson Airplane to Pearl Jam and the Beastie Boys' Tibetan Freedom benefit.

Once a lonely stretch of sand dunes, Golden Gate Park was designed in 1868 by William Hammond Hall, a 24-year-old civil engineer with no prior experience (his bid was lowest), and landscaped by John MacLaren. Its dramatic beauty debunks the claim of Frederick Law Olmsted—who designed the Stanford University campus and Central Park in New York City—that "beautiful trees could not be made to grow in San Francisco." Today blue-gum eucalyptus, Monterey pine, and Monterey cypress, not to mention one of the world's foremost horticulture displays, are scattered throughout the park. Bordered by

Stanyan Street, the Great Highway, Lincoln Way, and Fulton Street, Golden Gate Park is one of the largest urban parks in America. Several places near the park rent bikes and in-line skates; **Park Cyclery** (1749 Waller St., at Stanyan St., tel. 415/752–8383) rents mountain bikes for $5 an hour or $25 a day (for skate rentals, see In-Line Skating in Chapter 8). For park information and maps, drop by the **McLaren Lodge** (John F. Kennedy Dr. near Stanyan St., tel. 415/666–7200) weekdays 8–5. A second visitor center is in the charming, historic **Beach Chalet,** at the western edge of the park. The building's upper level houses the Beach Chalet Brewery and Restaurant (1000 Great Hwy., tel. 415/386–8439), where you can enjoy a fine microbrew as you gaze out to sea. Both the visitor center and brew pub opened in 1997 as part of a $6 million renovation of the park.

Strybing Arboretum and Botanical Gardens (tel. 415/661–1316), near the intersection of 9th Avenue and Lincoln Way, has a dazzling 70-acre display of plants, featuring some 5,000 specimens arranged by country of origin, genus, and fragrance. A $1 donation is suggested. Another star attraction is the **Japanese Tea Garden** (tel. 415/752–4227), originally built for the 1894 Mid-Winter Fair, the first world's fair held in San Francisco. During the week or on a rainy day, the garden is well worth the $2.50 admission (free before 9:30 and after 5:30); at other times crowds spoil any chance at serenity. The meticulously designed garden, open daily 9–6:30 (with shorter hours in winter), has an exquisite 18th-century Buddha and a scant number of koi in the fishponds—survivors of raids by local raccoons and hawks. The Hagiwara family took care of the garden until World War II, when they, along with other Japanese-Americans, were forced into internment camps. In 1994, on the garden's 100th anniversary, a cherry blossom tree was planted in their memory. While you're there, treat yourself to a pot of green tea and cookies to complete the experience.

On Sunday, John F. Kennedy Drive, the park's main thoroughfare, is closed to car traffic between Stanyan Street and 19th Avenue, and flocks of bicyclists, in-line skaters, and skateboarders take over.

The park's many free gardens include the **Shakespeare Garden,** which has every type of plant mentioned in Shakespeare's works (don't eat the nightshade) and quotations engraved in bronze; the 15-acre **National AIDS Memorial Grove** (tel. 415/750–8340), established in 1991, the only one of its kind in the country; and the **Rose Garden,** which explodes with color, especially in June. There's also the **Rhododendron Dell,** the **Fuchsia Garden,** and the **Queen Wilhelmina Tulip Garden,** with its two nearby Dutch windmills. A herd of **bison** lives in a large paddock near the park's northwest corner.

Park fixtures also include three world-class museums: the **Asian Art Museum;** the **M. H. de Young Memorial Museum,** notable for its collection of American art; and the **California Academy of Sciences** (see Museums, below). Or head to the **Laserium** (at the California Academy of Sciences, tel. 415/750–7138), where high-tech music and light shows are projected onto the planetarium's dome; Pink Floyd's *Dark Side of the Moon* is a favorite. Shows are held three or four times daily Thursday–Sunday. Admission is $7 (matinee $6); the special 3-D show, Friday–Sunday at 7:30 PM, costs $8. To reach the park from downtown or the Civic Center, take Bus 5, 71, or 73.

FISHERMAN'S WHARF

Once the domain of Italian fishermen, the wharf is now San Francisco's prize tourist trap, whose sole purpose is to get you to spend money. You won't see many fishermen here unless you arrive in the misty early morning hours (around 5) to watch the fishing boats unload. Jefferson Street, the wharf's main drag, is packed with expensive seafood restaurants, tacky souvenir shops, and rip-off "museums" like the Wax Museum, Ripley's Believe It or Not!, the Guinness Museum of World Records, the Haunted Gold Mine, and the Medieval Dungeon (featuring graphic re-creations of torture devices from the Middle Ages). Each can be yours for the low admission price of $6–$10. The only thing that remains fairly authentic on the wharf (albeit rather pricey) is the array of seafood stands along Jefferson Street. If the weather's nice, buy clam chowder ($3–$4) or a half pound of shrimp ($7) from one of the sidewalk vendors and a loaf of sourdough bread ($2.50–$3.25) from **Boudin Bakery** (156 Jefferson St., tel. 415/928–1849) and eat on one of the piers, watching cruise ships and fishing boats glide in and out of the harbor. Then catch a ferry to Alcatraz (see above) or Angel Island (see Tiburon and Angel Island in Marin County, below) or walk over to Fort Mason (see The Presidio and Marina in Neighborhoods, below) to check out the museums.

GOLDEN GATE PARK

PACIFIC OCEAN

Ocean Beach · Great Highway

Dutch Windmill

Murphy Windmill

Golf Course

J.F. Kennedy Dr.

47th Ave.

43rd Ave.

41st Ave.

North Lake

South Lake

Middle Lake

Bison Paddock

Sunset Blvd.

Mt. King Dr.

Golden Gate Park Stadium (Polo Field)

Lindley Meadow

Spreckels Lake

Speedway Meadow

Mars Meadow

Metson Lake

Middle Dr.

Elk Glen Lake

Lloyd Lake

Mallard Lake

Fulton St.

Cabrillo St.

Geary Blvd.

Anza St.

R I C H M O N D

25th Ave.

Balboa St.

S U N S E T

Kirkham St.

Judah St.

Irving St.

Lincoln Way

25th Ave.

19th Ave.

9th Ave.

7th Ave.

3rd Ave.

Cross Over Dr.

Stow Lake

Boat House

Park Presidio Blvd.

10th Ave.

8th Ave.

6th Ave.

J.F. Kennedy Dr.

Arguello Blvd.

Music Concourse

Children's Playground Pavilion

Kezar Stadium

Kezar Tennis Courts

Stanyan St.

N

0 · 500 meters

0 · 1/2 mile

32

Three shopping complexes girdle the wharf: **Pier 39,** the **Cannery,** and **Ghirardelli Square.** Owned by the billionaire Bass brothers of Texas, Pier 39 (off Jefferson St., tel. 415/981–7437) is a bland imitation of a turn-of-the-century New England seaport village. A former Del Monte peach-canning factory, the **Cannery** (2801 Leavenworth St., between Beach and Jefferson Sts., tel. 415/771–3112) is now a gallery of chic boutiques. Chocolate is no longer made on-site at **Ghirardelli Square** (900 N. Point St., tel. 415/775–5500), but you can buy it here in bars or atop a huge, tasty ice cream sundae ($6). To reach Fisherman's Wharf, take Bus 32 from the Ferry Building downtown. Or fulfill your other tourist obligation by taking a cable car from Powell Street (*see* Bus Travel *in* Chapter 1) to the end of the line.

If you lack the stamina or credit rating to shop Fisherman's Wharf, for $5 you can set a course for the **USS *Pampanito* submarine** (Pier 45, tel. 415/929–0202), or visit the **Maritime Museum** (Beach St. at foot of Polk St., tel. 415/556–3002), housed in an Art Deco building that displays all sorts of artifacts from the maritime history of San Francisco. Admission to the museum is free, but if you have $3 to spare, you might have more fun walking around on one of the old ships at the Hyde Street Pier, between the Cannery and Ghirardelli Square. Docked there are the ***Balclutha,*** a 100-year-old square-rigged ship; the ***Eureka,*** a newly restored turn-of-the-century paddlewheel ferry; and the ***C. A. Thayer,*** an equally venerable schooner. Comedian Jonathan Winters was once briefly institutionalized after he climbed the mast of the *Balclutha* and hung from it, shouting, "I am the man in the moon!"

At the other end of the wharf, **UnderWater World** (Beach St. just east of Pier 39, tel. 415/623–5300) is a 707,000-gallon "diver's-eye view" aquarium, where visitors listen to a taped 30-minute tour as they glide through a 300-ft transparent tunnel. Though the two main tanks are full of sharks, rays, anemones, and 10,000 types of fish, many visitors seem more amused by the scuba divers who scrub the tanks each morning. It's entertaining in a surreal sort of way, but the $12.95 admission price is mighty steep for an attraction that you can breeze through in under an hour.

A few years ago a swarm of sea lions took over several of the marina docks at Pier 39 and have refused to leave. The owners wanted them removed (killed if necessary) until they realized the barking sea mammals were attracting more tourists.

NEIGHBORHOODS

Though the city of San Francisco is a compact 49 sq mi, its neighborhoods guard their individuality like medieval fiefdoms. Each district is a distinct entity culturally, socially, and often politically, and they are all fascinating grounds for urban exploration. The best way to experience the city's neighborhoods is on foot: Plan your walk with a map or just start off in an interesting spot and surrender to the whims of the streets.

DOWNTOWN

For better or worse, downtown is grand old San Francisco—that of tea dances and cocktail hours. Looking up at the beautiful architectural details, you might forget what decade it is. Noteworthy architectural stops include the 1930 Art Deco **Shell Building** (100 Bush St., between Battery and Sansome Sts.) and the 1926 Romanesque château-style **Hunter-Dulin Building** (111 Sutter St., between Montgomery and Kearny Sts.). Today the downtown area has the major concentration of money-making businesses. It's typical cosmopolitan walking territory, with all the elements—both fascinating and horrifying—of urban American life.

UNION SQUARE • Union Square is the physical heart—though not the soul—of the city, especially for tourists who come to shop, browse the galleries, attend the theater, and then sleep in the finer hotels. The square, bordered by Powell, Post, Stockton, and Geary streets, was named in honor of pro-Union rallies held prior to the Civil War. Some San Franciscans will tell you the name more appropriately refers to the huge demonstrations held here in the 1930s by labor organizations, which at one point effectively shut down the city for a week.

Today Union Square consists of a park (where a few palm trees remind you that you're still in California) encircled by a ring—make that a solid-gold band—of the city's ritziest stores and boutiques, including Neiman Marcus, Saks Fifth Avenue, Chanel, Tiffany, Cartier, Hermès, Giorgio Armani, Gumps, Ralph

COW
HOLLOW

RUSSIAN
HILL

PACIFIC
HEIGHTS

Alta
Plaza

Lafayette
Park

Ina Coolbrith
Park

NO
HIL

POLK
GULCH

JAPANTOWN

Geary Expressway

TENDERLOIN

WESTERN
ADDITION

Alamo
Square

CIVIC
CENTER

Civic Center
BART Station

HAYES
VALLEY

Lombard St.

Octavia St.

Gough St.

Franklin St.

Van Ness Ave.

Polk St.

Larkin St.

Hyde St.

Leavenworth St.

Greenwic

Filbert St

Union St.

Russell St.

Macondray Ln.

Green St.

Vallejo St.

Broadway

Broadway Tunnel

Pacific Ave.

Jackson St.

Washington St.

Clay St.

Sacramento St.

California St.

Pine St.

Bush St.

Sutter St.

Post St.

Geary St.

O'Farrell St.

Ellis St.

Eddy St.

Turk St.

Golden Gate Ave.

McAllister St.

Fulton St.

Grove St.

Hayes St.

Market St.

7th St.

8th St.

Pierce St.

Steiner St.

Fillmore St.

Webster St.

Buchanan St.

Laguna St.

Gough St.

Franklin St.

Van Ness Ave.

Polk St.

Larkin St.

Hyde St.

Leavenworth St.

Jones St.

Taylor St.

Ansel Adams Center, **53**	Center for African and African-American Art and Culture, **13**
Bank of America World Headquarters, **51**	Center for the Arts, **55**
Bella Union Building, **38**	Chinatown Gate, **43**
Belli Building, **46**	Chinese Historical Society of America, **49**
Cable Car Museum, **25**	Chinese Telephone Exchange, **39**
Capp Street Project, **65**	City Lights Bookstore, **36**
Cartoon Art Museum, **52**	City Hall, **18**
	Civic Center Plaza, **20**

Coit Tower, **28**	Herbst Theatre, **17**
Coleman House, **7**	Hunter-Dulin Building, **57**
Embarcadero Center, **58**	Jackson Square Historical District, **45**
Fairmont Hotel, **31**	Japan Center, **9**
Ferry Building, **59**	Jewish Museum, **61**
Glide Memorial Methodist Church, **23**	Justin Herman Plaza, **60**
Golden Gate Fortune Cookie Factory, **35**	Kabuki 8 Theatres, **11**
Grace Cathedral, **24**	Kabuki Hot Springs, **12**
Haas-Lilienthal House, **6**	
Hallidie Plaza, **41**	

San Francisco
Bay

KEY
----- Cable Car
ℹ Tourist Information
AE American Express Office

NORTH
BEACH

Lombard St.

TELEGRAPH
HILL

Grant Ave.

Columbus Ave.

Mason St.

Powell St.

The Embarcadero

Davis St.

Front St.

FINANCIAL
DISTRICT

Battery St.

Sansome St.

Montgomery St.

Stockton St.

CHINATOWN

Waverly Pl.

Kearny St.

Halleck St.

Front St.

Davis St.

Drumm St.

**Embarcadero
BART Station**
ba

DOWNTOWN

Maiden
Ln.

AE

Union
Square

Market St.

SOMA

New Montgomery St.

2nd St.

1st St.

Fremont St.

Beale St.

Main St.

Spear St.

Steuart St.

**Montgomery St.
BART Station**
ba

**Powell St.
BART Station**
ℹ ba

Mission St.

4th St.

3rd St.

Howthorne St.

Moscone
Center

Folsom St.

5th St.

6th St.

Howard St.

Harrison St.

Bryant St.

Brannan St.

Townsend St.

The Embarcadero

80

WELCOME
ALL YE SINNERS

Ever been to church and come away humming and tapping your toes? Enjoy religion (with none of the guilt) at Glide Memorial United Methodist Church, presided over by a beaming Reverend Cecil Williams. Instead of organ music, a funky band and choir give parishioners reason to stand up and groove. Celebrations occur every Sunday morning at 9 and 11. It gets crowded and hot—arrive early (330 Ellis St., at Taylor St., tel. 415/771-6300). To get there, from the Powell Street BART/Muni station, walk one block on Powell Street, then go left on Ellis Street.

Lauren, Macy's, Bulgari, Brooks Brothers, Coach, Williams-Sonoma, Mark Cross, Versace, and a brand-new three-story **NikeTown** (278 Post St., tel. 415/392-6453). Combined, Union Square merchants ring up an estimated $1 billion in sales annually. Even so, the park tends toward seediness at night; linger elsewhere.

Heading south on Powell Street from Union Square, you'll come to the intersection of Market and Powell streets. Everyone passes through here: proselytizers, street musicians, artists, punks, young professionals, vendors, protesters, dogs, pigeons, and tourists in matching jogging suits. All converge around the **cable car turnaround,** the Powell Street BART station, and the **San Francisco Visitor Information Center** (see Visitor Information *in* Chapter 1), tucked below street level on **Hallidie Plaza.** Across Market Street from the cable car turnaround is the ritzy **San Francisco Shopping Centre** (see Chapter 3), which is built around a dizzying four-story atrium.

MAIDEN LANE • This short alley off the east side of Union Square was home to the "cribs" (brothels) that formed the center of a notoriously rowdy red-light district. Now it's a shopping arcade for the thick-walleted and the site of San Francisco's only Frank Lloyd Wright–designed building, **140 Maiden Lane,** which served as the prototype for the Guggenheim Museum in New York.

FINANCIAL DISTRICT

San Francisco is the financial capital of the West Coast. The center of the city's Financial District is **Montgomery Street,** the "Wall Street of the West," where the towers of wealth blot out the sun at street level. This part of town is built on landfill comprising the remains of hundreds of abandoned ships and docks; on the corner of Sacramento and Clay streets you'll find a plaque dedicated to the *Niantic*—a trading ship buried at this site. Nowadays it's a monument to the type A personality, where traffic lights stop vehicles in all four directions to allow harried office workers to cross diagonally and to let kamikaze bicycle messengers cheat death.

Begin your exploration at the glowering **Bank of America World Headquarters,** at the corner of California and Kearny streets. Its north plaza is graced with a black-granite shard of public art officially called *Transcendence,* but popularly known as "The Banker's Heart." In the elegant **Carnelian Room** (tel. 415/433-7500), on the building's 52nd floor, you can nurse a $6 cocktail and gaze in wonder at the city below. Bank of America's archrival, Wells Fargo Bank, lures you in with the free **Wells Fargo History Museum** (420 Montgomery St., tel. 415/396-2619), detailing the history of California's oldest bank and celebrating the short-lived but picturesque Pony Express. The museum is open weekdays 9–5 (except for bank holidays).

TRANSAMERICA PYRAMID • The Pyramid (600 Montgomery St., between Clay and Washington Sts.) is *the* distinguishing feature of the San Francisco skyline. Adjacent to the Pyramid is a small, peaceful redwood park (open weekdays 8–6), complete with fountain.

BARBARY COAST • In the 1850s San Francisco was home to the Barbary Coast, one of the most infamous red-light districts ever to exist. It was not uncommon to enter a bar; get drugged, clubbed, or fall through a trap door; and find yourself an involuntary sailor heading for Asia the next morning. The strip of Pacific Street between Sansome Street and Columbus Avenue, once called Terrific Pacific, was the heart of the action: Every building along this street was a saloon, a gambling hall, or a brothel, often featuring shows of women dancers engaged in acts of bestiality. To the chagrin of Bible-thumping reformists, many of these buildings survived the 1906 earthquake and fire. Today you can still visit the remains of the Barbary Coast in the **Jackson Square Historical District,** just north of the Financial District. One of the most notable structures in the area is the **Belli Building** (722 Montgomery St.), which once served as a musical saloon and was later the famed office of notorious San Francisco attorney Melvin Belli, the "King of Torts" (who represented the likes of the Rolling Stones, Mae West, and Jim Bakker and his then-wife, Tammy Fay). Belli, who died in July 1996, used to shoot cannons off the roof after winning big cases. Also worth a look are the nude nymphs carved on the entrance gateway to the **Bella Union** building (555 Pacific St.), as well as the **Little Fox Theatre** (535 Pacific St.), which was once a saloon and went on to illegally house a 60-ft distillery tank during Prohibition.

EMBARCADERO

The Embarcadero, Spanish for "wharf," looks more like a string of office buildings than anything vaguely maritime. One exception is the **Ferry Building,** at the end of Market Street. The 230-ft clock tower, modeled after Venice's Campanile, is an attractive landmark that can be seen along much of Market Street. Ferries still depart from here for Oakland, Sausalito, Larkspur, and Vallejo (see Ferry Travel in Chapter 1).

Embarcadero Center (tel. 800/733–6318) is a set of neatly stacked concrete buildings along Sacramento Street between Battery and Drumm streets. Its monolithic architectural style is no draw, but it *is* one of the few shopping malls that offer free parking on weekends for buying customers. The center is a conglomeration of four nearly identical towers housing offices, restaurants, boutiques that cater to the corporate crowd, and the **Embarcadero Center Cinema,** which features foreign and independent films (see Movie Houses in Chapter 6). Opened in 1996, the **Skydeck** (Embarcadero Center, 41st floor, tel.

Shanghai Kelly was one of the nastiest bar owners along the Barbary Coast. He was famed for serving the occasionally deadly Mickey Finn: a whiskey, gin, brandy, and opium concoction named for the chemist who invented it.

888/737–5933) is an indoor-outdoor observation area ($4) with impressive views. Views from the fancy Equinox restaurant, at the **Hyatt Regency Hotel** (5 Embarcadero Center, tel. 415/788–1234), are dizzying (literally!): The rooftop bar revolves 360 degrees.

JUSTIN HERMAN PLAZA • Between Embarcadero Center and the Ferry Building stretches Justin Herman Plaza, a favorite haunt of the office bag-lunch crowd and daredevil young skateboarders. Here, Jean Dubuffet's mammoth stainless-steel sculpture La Chiffonière poses like a Napoleonic Pillsbury Dough Boy. Nearby, Armand Vaillancourt's huge building-block fountain looks a little too much like prehistoric plumbing, but you can gambol among its girders even when the water is streaming through. Around the winter holidays, Justin Herman Plaza converts to an ice-skating rink. At other times of year it hosts free concerts, usually on a Wednesday or Friday at noon. During a free, unannounced concert by the band U2 in the plaza in 1988, U2 member Bono spray-painted the fountain, earning the ire of city officials, who were waging a war against graffiti at the time (Bono later apologized). This anarchist-type gesture is recorded for posterity in the concert movie Rattle and Hum.

RINCON CENTER • Rincon Center, which houses shops, offices, and apartments, was formerly the city's main post office. The outside of the building is unassuming—you'll recognize it by the raised blue dolphins on its sides—but inside you'll find a recently restored 1940s lobby and a stately atrium into which a tall, shimmering column of water descends. The socialist-realist-type murals in the lobby depict the history of California, including the oppression of Native Americans and the exploitation of workers by capitalist overlords. *101 Spear St., at Mission St., tel. 415/243–0473.*

CIVIC CENTER AREA

The Civic Center is the locus of San Francisco government and home of many of the city's cultural events, including dance and opera. The area immediately surrounding the center is also where a good percentage of San Francisco's homeless have camped since the 1940s. To reach the area, take BART to the Civic Center station or catch any of a thousand buses plying Market Street.

CITY HALL

The offices of San Francisco's mayor and board of supervisors are in this building, built in classic beaux arts style with a prominent bronze rotunda that can be seen blocks away. City hall has a fascinating history: Joe DiMaggio and Marilyn Monroe got married here on January 15, 1954. In 1960 civil rights and freedom of speech protesters were washed down city hall's central stairway with giant fire hoses, while the hearings of the House Un-American Activities Committee went on inside—all depicted in the amusing government propaganda effort (now a cult film) *Operation Abolition.* Mayor George Moscone and Supervisor Harvey Milk were murdered here on November 27, 1978. And on February 14, 1991, scores of gay couples lined up to get "married" in celebration of the passage of San Francisco's Domestic Partners Act the previous November. *Between Van Ness Ave. and Grove, McAllister, and Polk Sts.*

Surrounding city hall are many of the city's cultural mainstays. On Van Ness Avenue the **Louise M. Davies Symphony Hall** and the more stately **War Memorial Opera House** offer San Franciscans their fill of high culture (*see* Classical Music *in* Chapter 6). You can catch a variety of cultural events, including concerts, readings, and lectures at **Herbst Theatre,** just north of the Opera House. Volunteers conduct 75-minute tours of the three buildings every Monday on the hour from 10 to 2, leaving from the Grove Street entrance of Davies Symphony Hall. Tickets cost $3; call 415/552–8338 for information. The sparkling new **San Francisco Main Library** (Larkin St. at Grove St., tel. 415/557–4400) is one of the most technologically advanced in the country. It houses a fine collection of books, records, CDs, and San Francisco memorabilia, as well as 300 computer terminals, many with free Web access and CD-ROMs. In addition to books, you'll find a café, a rooftop garden, an incredible children's library, an excellent video library, an African-American center, the nation's first Gay and Lesbian Archive Center, an Asian-American center, and more, more, more! If you're walking around the area, head to Hayes Street between Franklin and Webster streets; dubbed **Hayes Valley,** this area is loaded with specialty shops, art galleries, cafés, and restaurants (*see* Chapters 4 and 5).

Just east of city hall is the sprawling **Civic Center Plaza,** which has seen its share of protest marches, political rallies (those during the Persian Gulf War drew crowds of more than 200,000), and riots. Continue east to the intersection of Market and 7th streets to find **United Nations Plaza,** commemorating the founding of the United Nations, in San Francisco in 1945. The plaza is presided over by a dramatic statue of Latin American revolutionary hero Simón Bolívar. It is also home to an excellent farmers' market (tel. 415/558–9455) on Sunday and Wednesday.

POLK GULCH

Once the gay heart of San Francisco, Polk Gulch (Polk Street between Geary and California streets) now takes second place to the even gayer Castro. The Gulch is part yuppie neighborhood, part urban blight: a good place to buy roast coffee, watch a drug bust, browse a bookstore, and get solicited for prostitution. There are more than a dozen small and special-interest bookstores here, including **Acorn Books** (*see* Books *in* Chapter 3). For coffee, try one of two **Royal Ground** locations (2216 Polk St., near Vallejo St., tel. 415/474–5957; 1605 Polk St., at Sacramento St., tel. 415/749–1731).

Once you get past the sleaze, Polk Street makes a pleasant 15-minute walk to Fisherman's Wharf. The street is lined with shops and cafés, including **Rainbow Café** (1406 Polk St., between Pine and California Sts., tel. 415/922–3286), a popular place to drink coffee, eat sandwiches, and loiter. On the more gentrified stretch of Polk Street, at the foot of Russian Hill, you'll find **Pure T** (2238 Polk St., at Green St., tel. 415/441–7878), a full-service teahouse with exotic teas from Asia such as monkey-picked Ti Kuan Yin blend and 15 delicious homemade tea-flavored ice creams. Bus 19 from the Civic Center BART station runs along Polk Street on its way to Ghirardelli Square at Fisherman's Wharf.

THE TENDERLOIN

The **Tenderloin** encompasses portions of O'Farrell, Geary, Post, and Sutter streets. For decades it's been considered a dangerous area: In the early days policemen got higher wages for working these streets, which enabled them to buy more tender cuts of meat—hence the name. The area still has the highest reported incidence of rape in the city—a particularly seedy triangle is formed by Larkin, Market, and Post streets. When the Tenderloin's call of cheap beer, live music, and inexpensive Vietnamese and Thai food beckons, you're best off visiting by cab.

CHINATOWN

The best way to experience San Francisco's Chinatown—possibly the most famous immigrant community in the world—is to arrive hungry and energetic. Skip the souvenir shops and instead wander the back alleys, soaking up the atmosphere and snacking on takeout bundles of dim sum. One of the largest Chinese populations outside Asia has made this district its home for 140 years. The original immigrants were refugees from the Opium Wars who came to San Francisco to seek their fortune during the gold rush; most ended up working on the railroad. To learn more about the history of Chinese immigration to San Francisco and the development of Chinatown, visit the **Chinese Historical Society of America** (*see* Museums, *below*).

If Chinatown's pagoda-heavy architecture looks contrived, that's because it is. In the late 1800s many right-wing groups blamed the shortage of jobs on the Chinese and wanted to bulldoze Chinatown. Indeed, in the wake of the destructive 1906 earthquake, it looked as if Chinatown wouldn't survive. But thanks to the persuasive powers of some local real estate barons, Chinatown was saved and rebuilt on the premise that it could attract tourists. Soon American and European architects were put to work, constructing their stereotypes of Asian building styles into a Chinese theme park.

To reach Chinatown, take Bus 45 from Market and 3rd streets downtown. You'll know you're in the 16-block neighborhood when you see street signs in Chinese. The best way to enter is through the dragon-crowned **Chinatown Gate** (Grant Ave. at Bush St.), where the sense of being in a different world is suddenly palpable. Or enter through **Portsmouth Square** (Washington and Kearny Sts.), where elderly Chinese men gather to gamble and shoot the breeze. If you are coming from the North Beach area, check out the **Imperial Tea Court** (1411 Powell St., at Broadway, tel. 415/788–6080), where you can relax and enjoy full tea service in an elegant Chinese tearoom.

During the late 1850s public hangings took place at Portsmouth Square (at the corner of Kearny and Clay streets), now part of Chinatown.

GRANT AVENUE

The main tourist thoroughfare in Chinatown, Grant Avenue, also reigns as the oldest street in San Francisco—dating to 1834. The Chinese characters above the Chinatown Gate read ALL UNDER HEAVEN IS GOOD FOR THE PEOPLE; decide if that's the case as you wander by gimmicky souvenir shops, restaurants, and flocks of wide-eyed visitors clutching $1.50 bamboo back-scratchers. Formerly known as Dupont Street, Grant Avenue once teemed with opium dens, bordellos, and gangs, especially in the sections near the Barbary Coast (*see* Financial District *above*). Today the real Chinatown can be better found by exploring the numerous small alleys that branch off of Washington, Clay, and Sacramento streets, where you're more likely to see locals shopping for groceries and carrying grandchildren down the street on their backs. The old **Chinese Telephone Exchange** building, now the Bank of Canton, stands at 743 Washington Street, at Grant Avenue. It's both architecturally and historically interesting: Operators here had to memorize the names of all their customers and speak English and five Chinese dialects.

STOCKTON STREET

The crowded shops and sidewalks of Stockton Street are the spitting image of the barter and trade district in Hong Kong. Between Sacramento and Green streets you'll find meat and produce shops letting it all hang out (vegetarians might wince at the pigs hanging from hooks). The friendly staff at **Ellison Enterprises Co. USA Ltd.** (805 Stockton St., tel. 415/982–3886) will happily explain the secrets and powers of herbal medicine—and may show you a dried human placenta. Also worth seeing is the **Kong Chow Temple** (855 Stockton St., tel. 415/434–2513), a Taoist temple where you can light incense offerings to representations of 17 gods sitting on the altar.

WAVERLY PLACE

One of the most colorful streets in Chinatown is Waverly Place, off California and Clay streets, between Grant and Stockton streets. You may recognize the name from Amy Tan's *The Joy Luck Club*; it's also known as the "street of painted balconies." There are a number of Chinese temples along Waverly Place, including the **Tin Hou Temple** (125 Waverly Pl., top floor), purportedly the oldest in the city. Don't miss nearby **Ross Alley,** between Grant and Stockton and Jackson and Washington streets, the home of the **Golden Gate Fortune Cookie factory** (56 Ross Alley, tel. 415/781–3956), where you can watch old women fold cookies—then pick up a bag (40 for $2) to take home. At the end of Ross Alley is **Jackson Street,** where you'll find several Chinese herbal medicine shops with drawers that contain medicines made from the therapeutic plants that line the walls.

THE ROOT OF
THE PROBLEM

Chinese roots and herbs are widely believed to be highly effective in promoting good health. Some, like ginger and ginseng, are widely used in teas; you can pick these up in one of the many stores along Stockton and Washington streets. Besides tasting good, ginger prevents motion sickness and may also help prevent blood clots, which can cause heart attacks and strokes. Ginseng stimulates the immune system, helps defend the liver against toxins, and acts as a stimulant. Some people believe it also increases sexual potency. You be the judge.

NORTH BEACH

Walk north on Columbus Avenue from the Columbus and Broadway intersection (one of San Francisco's best-known red-light districts), and you'll find yourself in the heart of the legendary Italian district, where the beat movement was born. (Nowadays, North Beach is better known for its many trattorias, cafés, and delis.) Poets and writers including Jack Kerouac, Lawrence Ferlinghetti, and Allen Ginsberg came to North Beach around 1953 to write, play music, and generally promote a lifestyle that emphasized Eastern religions, free love, drugs, and crazy new means of artistic expression. Ferlinghetti's **City Lights Bookstore** (*see* Books *in* Chapter 3) continues to publish and sell works by little-known alternative authors, as well as the writings of the beats (who have been anthologized to high heaven and hardly qualify as alternative anymore). In the late 1980s Ferlinghetti led a movement to rename a number of small San Francisco streets after authors who had lived here; **Jack Kerouac Lane** is right next to the store. In 1994 Ferlinghetti received the same honor: An alley off Union Street, near Stockton Street, was renamed **Via Ferlinghetti,** though the short dead-end street is barely longer than its new name.

Although the beats had their day in the 1950s and the number of Italian-Americans living in North Beach is diminishing, the neighborhood remains one of San Francisco's most interesting. Many of North Beach's shops and watering holes look the same as they did during the bohemian era: At **Vesuvio** (*see* Chapter 6), a bar just across the alley from City Lights, the poets undoubtedly consumed more than one glass of red. **Caffè Trieste** (*see* Chapter 5) fueled the beats with their favorite legal amphetamine, espresso; the clientele, some 35 years later, still looks pretty beat. Newly arrived in the neighborhood but following in its offbeat tradition is the **UFO, Bigfoot, and Loch Ness Monster Museum** (*see* Museums, *below*).

Continue to **29 Russell Street,** a hefty walk on Russian Hill (between Larkin and Hyde streets and Union and Green streets), where Kerouac crashed with Neal and Carolyn Cassady for a time in the early '50s. (His relationship with Neal is immortalized in his popular novel *On the Road,* though *The Subterraneans* better evokes Kerouac's North Beach days.) The **North Beach Museum,** on the mezzanine level of EurekaBank (1435 Stockton St., at Columbus Ave., tel. 415/391–6210), contains a handwritten manuscript of Ferlinghetti's "The Old Italians Dying," a poem about the old men of North Beach.

But real San Franciscans come to North Beach for the food, not a history lesson. Stop in at **Liguria Bakery** (1700 Stockton St., at Filbert St., tel. 415/421–3786) for focaccia right out of the oven. The **Molinari Delicatessen** (373 Columbus Ave., at Vallejo St., tel. 415/421–2337) has an extensive selection of salamis, olive oils, cheeses, pastas, wines, chocolates, and breads—perfect for a splendid picnic at **Washington Square** (*see* Parks, *below*). Bus 30 or 45 will get you to North Beach from Market and 3rd streets.

NOB HILL AND RUSSIAN HILL

The most elitist of San Francisco's districts is **Nob Hill** (between California, Powell, Broadway, and Leavenworth streets), the locus of San Francisco high society for more than a century. "Snob Hill," as it's called by some residents of the valley below, has great views that even the downtrodden will enjoy, though it's a strenuous walk to the top. North of Nob Hill lies **Russian Hill,** originally the burial ground for Russian seal hunters and traders, which today houses a combination of old Victorian homes, new high-rises, and more of San Francisco's moneyed class. On your way from Nob Hill to Russian Hill, check out the small **Cable Car Museum** (*see* Museums, *below*).

A steep walk (or a $2 cable car ride) up Powell Street from Union Square brings you to what once were the hilltop estates of the Big Four railroad kings: Leland Stanford, Mark Hopkins, Collis Huntington, and Charles Crocker. Now the city's most luxurious hotels are here, including the **Fairmont Hotel,** at California and Mason streets, and the **Stanford Court Hotel,** at California and Powell streets. Across California Street from the Fairmont is the plush Mark Hopkins Hotel, whose **Top of the Mark** (tel. 415/392–3434) is the perfect place for high tea (daily 3–5), cocktails (daily 5–midnight), and breathtaking views of the city. The mansion that belonged to silver magnate James Flood is one of the few that survived the 1906 quake; it now houses the **Pacific Union Club** (1000 California St.).

GRACE CATHEDRAL

A pseudo-Gothic structure that took 53 years to build, the cathedral is essentially a poured-concrete replica of an old European-style cathedral. The gilded bronze doors at the east entrance were taken from casts of Ghiberti's *Gates of Paradise* on the Baptistery in Florence. For a truly sublime experience, come for the singing of **vespers** every Sunday at 3:30 or Thursday at 5:15; an all-male choir will leave you feeling uplifted. If this doesn't do the trick, take a walk through the marble labyrinth to the right of the east entrance—it's a replica of France's Chartres Cathedral.

Fittingly, Nob Hill derives its nomenclature from the term nabob, meaning "anyone of great worth or wealth."

Guided tours of the cathedral are free (donations accepted). *1100 California St., at Taylor St., tel. 415/749–6310. From Embarcadero BART/Muni, Bus 1 west to corner of Sacramento and Jones Sts.*

LOMBARD STREET AND ENVIRONS

The most famous of Russian Hill's manicured streets is undoubtedly Lombard Street, a block of which is known as the **crookedest street in the world.** It descends the east side of Russian Hill in eight switchbacks between Hyde and Leavenworth streets.

Steep Russian Hill has a number of funky little stairways that wind through trees or lead to miniature parks. The steps at Lombard and Larkin streets eventually reach a small rest spot with an incredible view of the Golden Gate Bridge. On the east side of Russian Hill, the steps at Vallejo and Mason streets will transport you to **Ina Coolbrith Park,** which offers shady trees and views of Oakland and the Bay Bridge. When you reach Taylor Street, you can tackle an additional set of stairs across the street or visit **Macondray Lane.** To reach the lane, go right on Taylor Street and stroll two blocks to a set of wooden stairs between Green and Union streets (this is an official path, not someone's private entrance). These steps will bring you to a tiny cobblestone alley—Macondray Lane—the thinly veiled setting of Armistead Maupin's *Tales of the City.* Also look for the dark, wood-shingled houses designed by Willis Polk before the 1906 earthquake. One lies on the **1000 block of Green Street,** which also contains one of the city's two remaining eight-sided houses, built in the 1850s, as well as a firehouse dating from 1907. The more strenuous route from Coolbrith Park continues straight through the intersection of Taylor and Vallejo streets: The flower-lined path ends at **San Simone Park,** which has a prime view of Alcatraz and the East Bay. Coming down Vallejo Street, you will pass by a few side alleys; notable are **Florence Place** and the beautiful English cottages of **Russian Hill Place.**

THE PRESIDIO AND MARINA

Stretching over a gorgeous swath of waterfront between Fort Mason and the Presidio and bordered to the south by **Union Street,** the Marina provides a home—or rather, a series of multi-million-dollar Mediterranean-style homes—for San Francisco's young professionals. Ironically, all these folks with stable incomes live on decidedly unstable property: The Marina is built on landfill and is dangerously susceptible to the whims of Mother Earthquake. Recent college grads come to the Marina's main drag, **Chestnut Street,** from all over the city to chow down and drink up at innumerable restaurants and bars and to engage in mating rituals at singles bars. This is also the most convenient area to get a bite or a drink after visiting Fort Mason.

THE $1 TOUR BUS

For a quick $1 tour of some of the city's most varied neighborhoods, hop aboard Muni's 30 Stockton bus. From the Montgomery Street BART station, the bus takes you through downtown and North Beach, then past the lavish Victorian mansions of Russian Hill. Next, you'll go through the Marina and Ghirardelli Square, and finally you'll wind right past the Palace of Fine Arts, the Exploratorium, and the eastern edge of the Presidio. On the return route, you'll go through the heart of Chinatown before ending up on Market Street, near the Powell Street BART station.

A well-stocked **Safeway** supermarket (15 Marina Blvd., between Laguna and Buchanan Sts., tel. 415/563–4946), right across the street from Fort Mason, provides cheap food for guests of the **Fort Mason International Hostel** (*see* Hostels *in* Chapter 7). This particular store is nicknamed Singles Safeway because of the "meat market" opportunities. If you're in a picnicking mood, **Marina Green,** directly west of Fort Mason, provides the necessary lawn as well as stunning views of the bay and the Marin Headlands.

FORT MASON

A series of warehouses built atop piers on the Marina's eastern border, Fort Mason was once an army command post. Now it's a nexus of artistic, cultural, and environmental organizations: The African-American, Mexican, and Italoamericano museums (*see* Museums, *below*) are all housed here. Most days it's fairly quiet, so you can enjoy fantastic views of the bay in peace and solitude. Worth picking up is the Fort Mason monthly newsletter (available free at any of the museums), which details classes, lectures, concerts, and special exhibitions.

Tucked into one of the Fort Mason warehouses is the renowned vegetarian restaurant **Greens** (*see* Chapter 4). At the **Book Bay Bookstore** (Fort Mason Center, Bldg. C, tel. 415/771–1076), run by the Friends of the San Francisco Public Library, you can still get a book for 50¢. It's open Tuesday–Sunday 11–5. From Fisherman's Wharf Fort Mason is a 10-minute walk west: Follow Beach Street past the Municipal Pier and climb the forested hill past the AYH Hostel; as you descend on the other side, you'll see Fort Mason spread out along the waterfront. *Tel. 415/979–3010 for general information. Buses 22, 28, 30, 42, 47, and 49.*

PALACE OF FINE ARTS

At the far western edge of the Marina is the Palace of Fine Arts, built to resemble a classic colonnaded Roman temple, with attractive landscaping and a pond out front. Several similar structures were erected for the 1915 Panama Pacific Expo, but this is the only one that remains. Adjacent you'll find the **Exploratorium** (*see* Museums, *below*), a hands-on museum devoted to making science interesting for common folk. *Baker and Beach Sts., tel. 415/563–6504. Buses 28, 29, 30, and 43.*

THE PRESIDIO

The Presidio, a 1,480-acre chunk of prime waterfront land stretching from the west end of the Marina all the way to the Golden Gate Bridge, was originally a fort, founded by the Spanish in 1776. The flags of Mexico, the Bear Flag Republic, and the U.S. Army have all flown over the Presidio—one of the oldest military installations in the United States. On October 1, 1994, it became part of the National Park System, though the army will remain here in a reduced capacity for a while longer.

The ambitious 15-year plan for the Presidio is to turn it into the country's first self-sustaining national park, equal parts commerce and nature. A handful of nonprofit organizations have already moved into vacant army buildings—but since this is some of the most desirable real estate in the city, money-hungry developers are fighting with conservationists over its future. How much of the park will remain open space and how much will be developed is still up for debate—but for now you can count on finding rolling hills crossed by plenty of trails (for specifics on hiking, *see* Chapter 8); historic military buildings; and terrific views of the bay. A few paths lead through a man-made **forest** of 400,000 pine, cypress, and eucalyptus trees; these were planted in the 1880s by schoolchildren and soldiers to make the post seem larger. The **Officer's Club,** on Moraga Avenue, contains one adobe wall reputed to date from 1776, the year the base was founded. The free **Presidio Museum** has a collection relating to the Presidio's history. *Funston Ave. at Lincoln Blvd., tel. 415/561–4331. Open Wed.–Sun. 10–4.*

The easiest way to get to the Presidio is to drive north toward the bay on Van Ness Avenue, turn left on Lombard Street, and then follow the signs. Otherwise, take Bus 38 from the Montgomery Street BART/Muni station to Geary Boulevard and Presidio Avenue, then switch to Bus 43, which travels into the Presidio.

UNION STREET

Union Street competes with Chestnut Street (*see above*) with its abundance of specialty boutiques and expensive coffee bars. The neighborhood around it is known as **Cow Hollow,** so named because it used to house a dairy-farming community. Its rows of sparkling refurbished Victorian houses are undoubtedly beautiful, but the area clobbers you over the cranium with quaintness.

Don't miss the **Wedding Houses** (1980 Union St., near Buchanan St.), two identical houses built side by side as wedding presents for two sisters who were marrying at the same time. The brides' father had the houses stationed next to each other so he could keep an eye on them. These days all he'd see are two stunning Victorians filled with upscale shops. **Carol Doda's Champagne and Lace Lingerie Boutique** (*see* Specialty Items *in* Chapter 3) is owned by the woman who led the movement to legalize topless dancing in the 1960s, when she became the first woman to bare her breasts as part of a nightclub show. A block north of Union Street, the Vedanta Society of Northern California's **Old Temple** (2963 Webster St., at Filbert St.) combines the best elements of Victorian architecture and the Taj Mahal's design. The Hindu temple (built in 1905) is closed to tourists. Bus 41 from the Embarcadero BART/Muni station runs along Union Street.

THE WAVE ORGAN

A visit to the wave organ, built by artists with help from the Exploratorium, is a unique and peaceful San Francisco experience. The funky sea-powered organ, decorated with recycled bits of marble and granite, consists of a set of pipes that run along the waterfront and extend into the bay. Take a seat at one of the stone benches, place your ear on one of the pipes, and listen to the soothing musical tones of lapping waves. Acoustics are best at high tide. To get to the wave organ from the Exploratorium, walk north on Baker Street across Marina Boulevard to Yacht Road (Lyon Street); follow the road past the St. Francis and Golden Gate Yacht clubs to the end of the jetty.

PACIFIC HEIGHTS

Pacific Heights is the posh neighborhood of Victorian mansions that rises up from Van Ness and over to the Presidio, between California and Union streets. The district's stately homes were fortunate to survive the great 1906 fire; houses east of Van Ness Avenue were utterly destroyed, and those along the avenue were dynamited to create a firebreak. **Upper Fillmore**—the stretch of Fillmore Street from Bush Street to Jackson Street—is a picturesque area in which to stroll, browse the neighborhood's ritzy boutiques, and have a cup of espresso. To get to Pacific Heights, take Bus 1 California from the Embarcadero BART/Muni station or Bus 22 Fillmore from the Marina.

HAAS-LILIENTHAL HOUSE

A good place to start your tour of Victorian Pacific Heights is at the Haas-Lilienthal House, the city's only Victorian mansion open to the public. The 1886 Queen Anne–style house, considered modest in its day, is now the pride and joy of the **Foundation for San Francisco's Architectural Heritage,** headquartered here. You must join an hour-long docent-led tour ($5) to see the house's interior. Tours depart Wednesday noon–3:15 and Sunday 11–4 whenever a small group has gathered. Meet here at 12:30 on Sunday for a two-hour walking tour ($5) covering the surrounding blocks of Victorians and Edwardians—and learn once and for all that these terms refer to periods (1837–1901 and 1901–1910, respectively), not architectural styles. *2007 Franklin St., between Washington and Jackson Sts., tel. 415/441–3000.*

LAFAYETTE PARK

From the Haas-Lilienthal House, walk three blocks south to the corner of California Street to get to the **Coleman House** (1701 Franklin St.), which is now filled with law offices and closed to the nonlitigious public. This a Queen Anne tower house—you'll see the aforementioned tower prominently displayed on the corner. Turn right on California Street and right again on Octavia Street to reach **Lafayette Park.** Visited by dog walkers, picnickers, and sunbathers, the park's expansive lawns slope to a wooded crest, just as a well-behaved English-style garden should. On the north side of the park, behold the **Spreckels Mansion** (2080 Washington St.), an imposing 1913 French baroque structure now owned by author Danielle Steele and her husband. You can see the effects of San Francisco's moist and salty air on the ill-chosen Utah limestone, which has noticeably eroded. Blame architect George Applegarth, who also designed the California Palace of the Legion of Honor (*see* Museums, *below*).

JAPANTOWN

Modern Japantown, which spans the area north of Geary Expressway between Fillmore and Laguna streets, unfortunately is dominated by the massive, somewhat depressing shopping complex called Nihonmachi, better known as **Japan Center.** The city's Japanese community was much larger prior to World War II, when California "relocated" Japanese-Americans into concentration camps. There are a number of good restaurants (*see* Chapter 4) here and some import shops.

Japan Center's **Peace Plaza** and five-story **Pagoda** were designed by architect Yoshiro Taniguchi as a gesture of goodwill from the people of Japan. The plaza is landscaped with traditional Japanese-style gardens and reflecting pools and is the site of many traditional festivals throughout the year. The **Nihonmachi Street Fair** (tel. 415/771–9861), held in early August, is a two-day festival celebrating the contributions of Asian-Americans in the United States. The popular **Cherry Blossom Festival** (*see* When to Go *in* Chapter 1), held in late April, features *taiko* drumming, martial arts, food, music, dance, and a parade.

To relax after a tough day of sightseeing, try a Japanese steam bath at the **Kabuki Hot Springs** (1750 Geary Expressway, tel. 415/922–6000 for recorded information or 415/922–6002 for appointments), where you can use the steam room, sauna, and hot and cold baths for $10, no reservations necessary. A 25-minute shiatsu massage (with unlimited communal bath use) costs $35, appointment required. The communal baths are reserved for women on Sunday, Wednesday, and Friday; men get to use it the rest of the week. Hours are weekdays 10–10, weekends from 9. Also in the Japan Center, the **AMC Kabuki 8** theater (*see* Movie Houses *in* Chapter 6) shows first-run films in a high-tech complex. From the Montgomery Street BART/Muni station, Buses 2, 3, 4, and 38 will deposit you in Japantown.

RICHMOND DISTRICT

The Richmond District, north of Golden Gate Park, is a sprawling, largely uninteresting neighborhood of bland town houses. A bit of color comes from the large number of Southeast Asian and Chinese families who have moved here in recent years, escaping the cramped conditions of Chinatown. **Clement Street,** the main shopping boulevard, contain a dizzying array of produce markets, Chinese herb shops, and Asian restaurants, as well as a smattering of Irish pubs and a couple of good used bookstores. Bus 2 from the Montgomery Street BART/Muni station downtown will get you here.

Clement Street between Arguello Boulevard and 8th Avenue is a great place to refuel after a day at Ocean Beach or in Golden Gate Park. **Haig's Delicacies** (642 Clement St., at 8th Ave., tel. 415/752–6283) is a one-of-a-kind market and delicatessen, importing interesting food items from the Middle East, India, and Europe. **New May Wah Supermarket** (547 Clement St., no phone) has special ingredients (sauces, teas, noodles, and more) for Chinese, Vietnamese, Thai, and Japanese dishes. **Green Apple Books** (*see* Books *in* Chapter 3) has a huge selection of new and used books—you could lose yourself in this store for days.

HAIGHT-ASHBURY

East of Golden Gate Park sits the Haight-Ashbury district—a name that still strikes fear in the hearts of suburban parents everywhere. The Haight, nicknamed "Hashbury" by Hunter S. Thompson, began its career as a center for the counterculture in the late 1950s and early '60s, when some beat writers, several illustrious fathers of the drug culture, and bands like the Grateful Dead and Jefferson Airplane moved in. Attracted by the neighborhood's ensuing liberal atmosphere, several hundred thousand blissed-out teenagers soon converged on the Haight to spend their savings on acid, play music, and sing days-long renditions of "Uncle John's Band"; the first **Human Be-In** was held blocks away in Golden Gate Park on January 14, 1966. But like the '60s themselves, Haight-Ashbury's atmosphere of excitement and idealism was pretty much washed up by the mid-1970s. Nowadays the Haight is a punk-rock haven where '90s kids do things that frighten their formerly hippie parents.

Since the 1970s the stretch of **Haight Street** between Divisadero and Stanyan streets—often called the Upper Haight to distinguish it from the Lower Haight (*see below*)—has gone through various stages of increasing and decreasing seediness and gentrification. With no little irony, its countercultural spirit survives largely in terms of the goods you can buy: rock star T-shirts, bumper stickers, necklaces made with "healing crystals," and such. Neohippies still play guitar on the street corner, but the revolution is nowhere in sight. What *is* in sight is the gleaming Gap store now standing on the famed corner of Haight-Ashbury. The youthful slackers who live here now wear black, ride motorcycles, pierce body parts, and listen to dissonant music at bars like the **Thirsty Swede** (1821 Haight St., no phone) or to live jazz and swing at **The Deluxe** (*see* Bars *in* Chapter 6). The attraction is probably less the neighborhood's historical legacy than its bars, cafés, and breakfast joints, like the **Pork Store Café** (*see* Chapter 4).

As a tourist in Haight-Ashbury, you'll find there's little to do besides people-watching (while dodging panhandlers) and exploring the jewelry and secondhand clothing stores lining the blocks between Masonic and Clayton streets. For secondhand threads try **Aardvark's Odd Ark, Buffalo Exchange,** or **Wasteland** (*see* Secondhand and Vintage Clothing *in* Chapter 3). The Grateful Dead, Speed Racer, Alfred E. Newman, and Bob Marley are all represented on the walls of **Haight-Ashbury T-Shirts** (1500 Haight St., at Ashbury St., tel. 415/863–4639). Down the street, the **Haight-Ashbury Free Medical Clinic** (*see* Emergencies *in* Chapter 1) is one of the last vestiges of hippie idealism on the street; it's been offering free medical care ever since the '60s. When the weather is warm, head down the street to **Buena Vista Park** (*see* Parks, *below*). Buses 6, 7, 66, and 71 will get you to Haight-Ashbury from downtown's Market Street.

LOWER HAIGHT AND THE WESTERN ADDITION

The hip, alternative Haight of the '60s isn't dead; it's just relocated. Today's young urban nihilists congregate in the Lower Haight—between **Divisadero** and **Webster streets.** As in the Upper Haight, consumerism and counterculture go hand in hand here; the street is full of head shops, record stores, underground cafés, and nightclubs. This colorful haven of new subcultures is itself subverted, however, by the very real poverty of its neighboring district to the north, the Western Addition.

LOWER HAIGHT

Full of disaffected youths and battered Victorian houses, the Lower Haight is a new breeding ground for a community of angry youth, eccentrics of all ages, mental cases, and—perhaps an amalgam of all three—aspiring artists and writers. At night the street is loud with the din of '70s funk or '90s hip-hop blaring from the doorway of **Nickie's BBQ** (*see* Clubs *in* Chapter 6), which overflows with sweaty dancing youth of all races. If you're looking for a more laid-back scene, skirt the ornery drunks and drug dealers and head for **Mad Dog in the Fog,** an English-style pub (*see* Bars *in* Chapter 6). During daylight the **Horse Shoe Coffee House** (*see* Chapter 5) is a meeting place for neopsychedelic artists and poetry-writing trust-fund kids, while **Café International** (*see* Chapter 5) plays those old Donovan songs you thought you'd finally escaped. Join the neobeatniks and punks for brunch at **Kate's Kitchen** (*see* Chapter 4) or head to **Naked Eye News and Video** (533 Haight St., between Fillmore and Steiner Sts., tel. 415/864–2985) for alternative comics and 'zines or avant-garde, foreign, and obscure videos.

WESTERN ADDITION

Best explored during daylight hours, the Western Addition is a community struggling with a legacy of poverty and discrimination. During World War II, African-Americans migrated here in droves to fill vacated factory jobs; after the war most lost their jobs to returning white GIs, and the neighborhood became a nest of brothels and gambling joints. In the 1960s many older buildings were torn down as part of a city "urban renewal" program. Today the main commercial drag is Fillmore Street between Oak Street and the Geary Expressway. Among the highlights of the neighborhood is **Marcus Books** (*see* Books *in* Chapter 3), which sells an outstanding range of works on African-American literature and his-

HOME SWEET HOME

Haight-Ashbury has had its share of famous (and infamous) residents. You probably won't run into Jimi today, but you can certainly check out the home where he once lived.

Janis Joplin: 112 Lyon St., between Page and Oak Sts.

The Grateful Dead: 710 Ashbury St., at Waller St.

The Manson Family: 636 Cole St., at Haight St.

Jefferson Airplane: 2400 Fulton St., at Willard St.

Sid Vicious: 26 Delmar St., at Frederick St.

Jimi Hendrix: 142 Central Ave., at Haight St.

Hunter S. Thompson: 318 Parnassus Ave., at Willard St.

tory. The **Center for African and African-American Art and Culture** (762 Fulton St., at Webster St., tel. 415/928–8546) has a modest library of books and magazines on African-American themes; Internet and computer databases; and an archive room full of rare pamphlets, magazines, and publications. Call for information on poetry workshops and other events. At the corner of **Octavia** and **Bush streets,** a half-dozen eucalyptus trees and a memorial plaque mark the former residence of Mary Ellen Pleasant (1816–1904), a heroine of the Western Addition. Rumored to be a madam, a murderer, a witch, or some combination thereof, Pleasant was most renowned for her business savvy—her profits financed the western leg of the Underground Railroad.

PAINTED LADIES • The most famous row of houses in San Francisco is across from Alamo Square, a block west of Fillmore Street. Featured on hundreds of postcards and the opening credits of several TV shows set in San Francisco, the Painted Ladies—six beautifully restored, brightly painted Victorians—sit side by side on a steep street with the downtown skyline looming majestically behind. To snap the obligatory picture, take Bus 6, 7, 66, or 71 from downtown Market Street to Haight and Steiner streets and walk north on Steiner to Hayes Street.

CASTRO DISTRICT

You'll know you're in the Castro when you see rainbow flags adorning businesses and homes and pink-triangle bumper stickers on cars. Since the early 1970s this neighborhood has been attracting gay men and women from around the world. Before the AIDS epidemic it was known as a spot for open revelry, with disco music pumping on Castro Street 24 hours a day. Today the community is less carefree than in the first years of open gay pride, but on weekends it still bustles with people socializing on the streets, in the bars, and at the gyms.

The heart of the district is **Castro Street** between Market and 19th streets. At the southwest corner of Market and Castro, where the K, L, and M Muni streetcar lines stop, is **Harvey Milk Plaza,** named in honor of California's first openly gay elected official. On November 27, 1978, Milk and then-mayor George Moscone were assassinated by Dan White, a disgruntled former supervisor. During his trial White claimed the high sugar content of his junk-food diet altered his mental state—the so-called Twinkie defense—and was convicted of voluntary manslaughter by reason of diminished capacity. The night of the verdict 40,000 San Franciscans gathered at the plaza and proceeded to city hall in a candlelight march. The procession is repeated every year on the anniversary of the event.

One block away, where 18th and Castro streets meet, you'll find the gayest four corners in the world: All of the shops, bars, and cafés cater to the gay community. On weekends people hand out advertisements for gay clubs, marches, lectures, and political causes. Travel agencies bill themselves as gay and lesbian vacation experts, and card shops have names such as **Does Your Mother Know . . .** (4079 18th

St., tel. 415/864–3160), which stocks coming-out and same-sex love cards. A block from the intersection is the **Castro Theatre** (see Movie Houses in Chapter 6), the grand Art Deco repertory house that hosts the much-loved International Lesbian and Gay Film Festival each summer.

Everywhere, the Castro abounds with unique shops and services. The offerings at **Man Line** (516 Castro St., tel. 415/863–7811) include Keith Haring earrings and rainbow-striped robes and flags. **Under One Roof** (see Specialty Items in Chapter 3), adjacent to the NAMES Project Foundation (see below), carries license plate holders marked with pink triangles, red-ribbon pins, and a good selection of soaps, lotions, books, and cards. It donates 100% of its profits to AIDS organizations. The renowned **A Different Light** (see Books in Chapter 3) stocks an extensive collection of lesbian, gay, and transsexual literature. **Gauntlet** (2377 Market St., at Castro St., tel. 415/431–3133), a friendly neighborhood piercing studio, has a knowledgeable staff and a photobook of piercing possibilities.

The social hub of the neighborhood is east of Harvey Milk Plaza, at **Café Flore** (see Chapter 5), where heads turn and the gossip mills churn. Closer to Castro Street, **The Café** (see Bars in Chapter 6) is the only bar in the area where women are a majority of the clientele, although even the Café has shifted toward a more male crowd in recent years. At the intersection of Castro and Market streets, **Twin Peaks** (see Bars in Chapter 6) has the distinction of being the first gay bar in the city with clear glass windows.

You can watch a nonmainstream film, admire the Art Deco architecture and fabulous ceiling decorations, and listen to a live organist—all at the beloved Castro Theatre.

NAMES PROJECT FOUNDATION

For a sobering reminder of the continuing crisis facing the gay community, drop by the NAMES Project Foundation's **Visitor Center and Panelmaking Workshop,** where panels from the now-famous *NAMES Quilt*—a tribute to many who have died of AIDS—are displayed. The project started in 1987 when gay rights activist Cleve Jones organized a meeting with several others who had lost friends or lovers to AIDS, hoping they could create a memorial. They decided on a quilt, each panel to be created by loved ones of individuals who have succumbed to the disease. The idea caught on, and people from all over the country sent in quilt panels. To date, the entire quilt (more than 30,000 panels) has been displayed in front of the White House four times. There are always some panels on display in the San Francisco office, as well as in other offices all over the world. For those who are interested in creating a panel, the foundation provides sewing machines, fabric, and support at their weekly quilting bee, on Wednesday 7 PM–10 PM. *2362A Market St., at Castro St., tel. 415/863–1966. Visitor center open daily noon–7.*

TWIN PEAKS

When the Spanish came to this area in the 18th century, they named the pair of peaks looming over the bay *Los Pechos de la Choca* (the Breasts of the Indian Maiden). The name has changed, but the Twin Peaks remain spectacular: From here you can see both the bay and the ocean and everything in between. To reach Twin Peaks, take Bus 37 west from Market and Castro streets. Bring a picnic and allow at least 30 minutes to walk up and around.

One of San Francisco's most beautiful staircases, **Pemberton Place,** is worth a visit if you're in the Twin Peaks area. Take Bus 33 to Corbett Avenue and start climbing the stairs off Clayton Street. You will be rewarded with incredible views—and a workout to boot!

NOE VALLEY

Lying one major hill away from the hectic Mission and Castro districts, Noe Valley seems like a sedate older sister, one who traded the glitz and glamour and hard edges of city life for a more settled arrangement. It's a sunny, neighborly venue for eco-conscious types, their babies, and their dogs. Decades ago this was strictly an enclave of Irish and German immigrants; these days you can still find grandmotherly types gossiping in German on Noe Valley's street corners. **Lehr's German Specialties** (1581 Church St., at 28th St., tel. 415/282–6803) stocks Old Country favorites, from bottled bitters to Bavarian tunes. **Speckmann's** (1550 Church St., between 27th and 28th Sts., tel. 415/282–6850) serves up delicious, embarrassingly outsized platefuls of kraut, wurst, and goulash soup. Their adjacent deli stocks your favorite German specialties—even *bloodwurst.*

GAY AND LESBIAN
SAN FRANCISCO

San Francisco promotes itself as not only a gay city but the gayest in the world. Some neighborhood populations are as much as 95% gay; it is possible here for lesbians and gay men to go about their lives dealing almost exclusively with other gays and lesbians, both in business and in pleasure. And although gay bashing is still a reality, at least here many such cases are fully prosecuted.

San Francisco's most concentrated gay neighborhood is the Castro District, followed closely by Polk Gulch. Although there isn't a lesbian neighborhood per se, many young lesbians gravitate to the Mission. Bernal Heights attracts slightly older gay women, while the more upwardly mobile lesbian set heads to Noe Valley. Valencia Street in the Mission is home to the greatest concentration of women-oriented shops, though it is not nearly the lesbian enclave it was in the 1980s.

Until the early 1970s the Castro was a neighborhood of middle-class heterosexual families. When the countercultural fervor in nearby Haight-Ashbury came too close for comfort, whole blocks of families fled for more suburban digs. Houses stood vacant, rents plummeted, and young single men moved in. By 1967 the first gay bars opened on Castro Street, and in the '70s the scene exploded. Lured by national publicity, gay men and lesbians from all over the country migrated to the Castro and Polk Street, and the community became a serious force in city politics. Many gays and lesbians hold public office, ranging from sitting on the Board of Supervisors to being Police Commission members to being judges on the Municipal Court.

Noe Valley's main drag, **24th Street,** is a comfortable mixture of old-timey restaurants and trendy new clothing stores, of hardware stores and chic cafés. The blocks surrounding its intersection with **Noe Street** are best for exploring. **Global Exchange** (*see* Charitable Causes *in* Chapter 3) satisfies the neighborhood's social conscience: It's an international organization that promotes exchange between the United States and developing countries. At the end of the day grab a cup of espresso at **Spinelli** (3966 24th St., near Noe St., tel. 415/550–7416), relax on one of the benches outside, and contemplate which Brie you're going to bring home from the **24th Street Cheese Company** (3893 24th St., at Sanchez St., tel. 415/821–6658).

MISSION DISTRICT

The Mission District, named after the historic Mission Dolores (*see below*) and stretching south along Mission Street from Market Street to César Chavez (Army) Street, is blessed with an unbelievable climate: Although the city's other districts are shrouded in fog, the Mission is usually basking in sun. For centuries it was considered San Francisco's prime real estate, first by Ohlone Native Americans and then by Spanish missionaries. Over the years various populations, primarily European, have given way to immigrants from Central and South America, though the neighborhood also currently includes a significant contingent of artists and radicals of all ethnicities. In all, the Mission is a colorful, friendly place, but it can also be dangerous. Be particularly careful on Mission Street between 14th and 20th streets, 24th Street near Treat Avenue, and on South Van Ness Avenue. Most women won't feel comfortable walking alone here at night, and when you actually find a parking space, you might think twice about leaving your car. Luckily, public transportation is a snap: Two BART stations (one at Mission and 16th streets, the other at Mission and 24th streets) put you right in the heart of things.

The Mission is the place to go for cheap food, especially huge burritos and succulent tacos made fresh in the numerous storefront *taquerías*. The area is also full of specialty bookstores (*see* Books *in* Chapter 3), inexpensive alternative theater companies, and an increasing variety of bars, which often have live music, poetry readings, and dance spaces. The architecture is worth noting, too, since many of the Mission's large Victorians survived the 1906 quake. For a listing of neighborhood culture stops, pick up *A Booklover's Guide to the Mission,* a free foldout map available at most bookstores in the area.

The Mission's art scene is concentrated in the northern half of the neighborhood. A notable collection of cafés, bars, thrift shops, and cheap restaurants are gathered at the intersection of **16th** and **Valencia streets** (*see below*), which is also the site of an independent movie theater, the **Roxie Cinema** (*see* Movie Houses *in* Chapter 6). A few blocks north, **Red Dora's Bearded Lady** (*see* Chapter 5), a lesbian-owned café, is the only full-time lesbian-oriented space around. The southern half of the Mission is densely Mexican and Latin American, especially **24th Street** between Mission and Potrero streets. Here you'll find produce stands, *dulcerías* (sweets shops), and *panaderías* (bakeries) like **La Mexicana Bakery** (2804 24th St., at York St., tel. 415/648–2633). The **St. Francis Soda Fountain and Candy Store** (*see box* Sweet Treats *in* Chapter 4) has been serving homemade ice cream since 1918.

VALENCIA STREET

A good place to discover the offbeat side of the Mission is on Valencia Street (a block west of Mission Street) between 16th and 24th streets. The shops here are unusual, to say the least: **Yahoo Herb'an Ecology** (968 Valencia St., between 20th and 21st Sts., tel. 415/248–1840) specializes in worm boxes for composting, plus herbal teas, organic seeds, and products made of hemp fiber. **Botanica Yoruba** (998 Valencia St., at 21st St., tel. 415/826–4967) has incense, candles, herbs, and oils, as well as hour-long *limpieza* (spiritual cleansing) sessions, performed by a member of the Santeria religion (reservations required). For leftist books, try **Modern Times** (*see* Books *in* Chapter 3); for indie music, drop by **Epicenter** (*see* Records, Tapes, and CDs *in* Chapter 3); and for avant-garde videos, head to **Leather Tongue** (*see* Specialty Shops *in* Chapter 3).

Neighborhood landmarks include the **Women's Building** (3543 18th St., between Valencia and Guerrero Sts., tel. 415/431–1180), a meeting place for progressive and radical political groups. Note the mural *Women's Wisdom Through Time,* completed in 1995 with the help of more than 500 artists. You'll see Audre Lorde, Georgia O'Keeffe, and Rigoberta Menchú among many other women's names woven into the fabric of the mural (*see box* Murals with a Mission, *below*). The 1906 **Levi Strauss factory** (250 Valencia St., tel. 415/565–9159), the oldest jeans-making facility in the West, conducts free, 1½-hour tours every Tuesday and Wednesday at 10:30 and an additional tour Wednesday at 1. Reservations are required.

DOLORES STREET AND THE MISSION DOLORES

West of Valencia Street, the Mission becomes green, hilly, and residential. Dolores Street, its median graced with a row of stately old palm trees, marks the district's western border. Although many gay men live in the Castro, just west of here, Dolores Street and the surrounding residential area are quietly, though not exclusively, lesbian. **Mission Dolores Park** (*see* Parks, *below*) is a favorite with locals on warm, sunny days—if you stop by, be sure to look for the **gold fire hydrant** at the park's southwest corner (20th and Church streets). When all the other hydrants went dry during the firestorm that followed the 1906 earthquake, this one kept pumping.

Though it's made of humble adobe, **Mission Dolores,** the oldest building in San Francisco, has survived some powerful earthquakes and fires. It was commissioned by Junípero Serra to honor San Francisco de Asís (St. Francis of Assisi) and completed in 1791. The Spanish nicknamed it Dolores after a nearby stream, *Arroyo de Nuestra Señora de los Dolores* (Stream of Our Lady of the Sorrows), and the name stuck long after the river dried up and disappeared. Architecturally, Mission Dolores is the simplest of all the California missions—it's also seen the fewest modifications over the centuries. Look up at the ceiling and you'll see traditional Native American designs, hand-painted by local Costanoan Indians. The mission bells still ring on holy days, and the cemetery next door is the permanent home of a few early rancheros, including San Francisco's first mayor, Don Francisco de Haro. The small admission fee gives

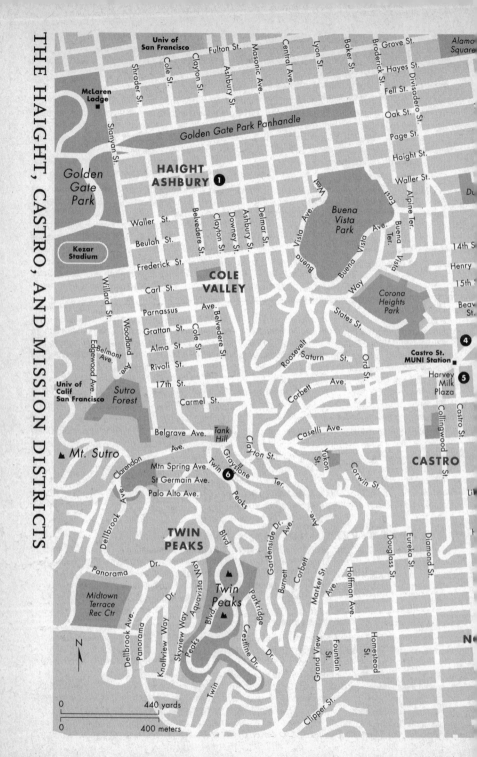

Univ of
San Francisco

Fulton St.

Alamo
Square

Grove St.

Hayes St.

Broderick St.

Baker St.

Lyon St.

Central Ave.

Masonic Ave.

Ashbury St.

Clayton St.

Cole St.

Shrader St.

McLaren
Lodge

Stanyan St.

Fell St.

Oak St.

Page St.

Haight St.

Waller St.

Divisadero St.

Golden Gate Park Panhandle

**HAIGHT
ASHBURY** ❶

Golden
Gate
Park

Alpine Ter.

Du

Buena
Vista
Park

Waller St.

Buena Vista Ave. East

Buena Vista Ave. West

Buena
Vista
Ter.

Buena Vista

14th

Henry

15th

Beav
St.

Belvedere St.

Delmar St.

Ashbury St.

Downey St.

Clayton St.

Waller St.

Beulah St.

Kezar
Stadium

Buena
Vista
Way

Corona
Heights
Park

Frederick St.

**COLE
VALLEY**

Willard St.

Carl St.

Parnassus Ave.

Belvedere St.

Cole St.

Grattan St.

States St.

Woodland Ave.

Roosevelt

Saturn

St.

Alma St.

Rivoli St.

Ord St.

Castro St.
MUNI Station ❹

Univ of
Calif
San Francisco

Edgewood Ave.

Belmont
Ave.

17th St.

Corbett

Ave.

Harvey
Milk
Plaza ❺

Sutro
Forest

Carmel St.

Collingwood St.

Caselli Ave.

Castro St.

▲ Mt. Sutro

Belgrave Ave.

Tank
Hill

Ave.

Clarendon Ave.

Clayton St.

Yukon St.

CASTRO

Mtn Spring Ave.

Graystone Ter.

Corwin St.

Li

St Germain Ave.

Twin
Peaks
Blvd.

Palo Alto Ave.

Dellbrook Ave.

Gardenside Dr.

Corbett Ave.

Douglass St.

Eureka St.

Diamond St.

**TWIN
PEAKS**

Panorama Dr.

Aquavista Way

Burnett Ave.

Market St.

Hoffman Ave.

Midtown
Terrace
Rec Ctr

▲
Twin
Peaks
▲

Parkridge Dr.

Grand View Ave.

Fountain St.

Homestead St.

N

Dellbrook Ave.

Panorama

Skyview Way

Knollview Way

Twin Peaks Blvd.

Crestline Dr.

N

Clipper St.

0 _____ 440 yards

0 _____ 400 meters

Café Flore, **3**
Castro Theatre, **5**
Collision Gallery, **9**
Four Walls, **10**
Gold Fire Hydrant, **14**
Haight-Ashbury Free Medical Clinic, **1**
The Lab, **12**
Levi Strauss Factory, **8**
Mission Cultural Center, **15**
Mission Dolores, **7**
NAMES Project, **4**
Painted Ladies, **2**
Pemberton Place Stairway, **6**
Precita Eyes Mural Arts Center, **16**
Roxie Cinema, **11**
Women's Building, **13**

MURALS WITH A MISSION

Following in the tradition of Mexican muralist Diego Rivera (1886–1957), various San Francisco artists have been painting huge, vibrant works on walls all over the city for the past 25 years—especially in the Mission District. Pick up a "Mission Mural Walk" map ($1.50 donation) at the Precita Eyes Mural Arts Center (348 Precita Ave., between Folsom and Harrison Sts., tel. 415/285–2287), or sign up for one of their mural walks ($4), Saturday at 1:30. Take Bus 27 from 5th and Market streets downtown and get off at 27th and Harrison streets; the center is across the park.

you access to the mission, the cemetery, and a small display of artifacts; or opt for a worthwhile 45-minute audio tour ($5). *16th and Dolores Sts., tel. 415/621–8203. Admission $2. Open daily 9–4.*

POTRERO HILL

Just east of the Mission and South of SoMa, Potrero Hill is a sunny, quiet, and untouristed community where you can feast your eyes on spectacular views of the Financial District skyline and the East Bay. The main strip of Goat Hill, as it's also known, is along 18th Street between Arkansas and Connecticut streets, where you'll find an assortment of mellow restaurants, cafés, and a bookstore, as well as the **Daily Scoop** (1401 18th St., at Missouri St., tel. 415/824–3975), an old-fashioned ice cream parlor. Come on a Monday, and your trek will be rewarded with pizza galore at **Goat Hill Pizza** (300 Connecticut St., at 18th St., tel. 415/641–1440). The waitstaff circles around the restaurant with different slices, and $7.95 buys you all you can stuff in your mouth—plus a salad. There's live piano Thursday and Friday, jazz on Saturday. At **Bottom of the Hill** (*see* Live Music *in* Chapter 6), you can enjoy a great selection of local bands and occasional surprise visits by big-timers. And finally, don't tell Lombard Street enthusiasts (*see* Nob Hill and Russian Hill, *above*), but **Vermont Street,** at 20th Street, is *more* crooked—and without a tourist in sight. To get to Potrero Hill, take Bus 9 south from Civic Center to 16th Street and Potrero Avenue and then transfer to Bus 22 heading east.

SOUTH OF MARKET

Until recently SoMa—the area bordered by Mission Street, Townsend Street, the Embarcadero, and 12th Street—was merely a flat, nondescript stretch of abandoned factories. Only in the last decade or so has the region come alive, filling those rows of empty warehouses with art galleries, alternative theaters, and dusk-to-dawn nightclubs. The SoMa nightlife scene centers around **Folsom Street,** a heathen's haven of dance clubs (*see* Chapter 6). SoMa is also home to the city's outlet stores and bargain warehouses (*see* Chapter 3): At **Six Sixty Center** (660 3rd St., between Brannan and Townsend Sts., tel. 415/227–0464) you'll find 22 outlet stores under one roof. Closer to the water it's strictly a suits-and-heels crowd, but you'll find several sort-of-hip, sort-of-yuppie cafés and restaurants around surprisingly green **South Park** (*see* Parks, *below*).

The brand-new Yerba Buena Gardens and the San Francisco Museum of Modern Art (*see* Museums, *below*) are the stars of the SoMa arts scene. Smaller, edgier galleries are relocating to the neighborhood as fast as they can, using light from the big names to draw attention to themselves; there are dozens of warehouse-cum-gallery spaces within a three-block radius of SFMOMA. One such venture, the **Capp Street Project** (525 2nd St., between Bryant and Brannan Sts., tel. 415/495–7101), sponsors three controversial murals in the South of Market area: *Inner City Home,* at 6th and Brannan streets; *One Tree,* at 10th and Brannan streets; and *Extinct,* at 5th and Folsom streets.

YERBA BUENA GARDENS

This 8½-acre arts and performance space opened to much fanfare in 1993, after more than 30 years of planning and bureaucratic disputes. On the east side of the garden complex, the **Center for the Arts** houses galleries (*see* Museums, *below*) and a theater (*see* Multimedia Performance Spaces *in* Chapter 6) whose purpose is to celebrate the multicultural nature of the Bay Area. However, critics point out that the multicultural emphasis may be to the exclusion of mainstream arts. Others smirk at the money spent building the center: a whopping $41 million. *Mission St. at 3rd St., tel. 415/978–2787.*

Yerba Buena isn't just about high-concept art: Its manicured lawns provide a down-to-earth respite from the frenzy of downtown—just a couple of blocks southeast of the Montgomery Street BART station. Walk along the grassy, spacious esplanade to find the Martin Luther King, Jr., Memorial: 12 glass panels, all behind a shimmering waterfall, engraved with quotes from Dr. King in English and in the languages of each of San Francisco's sister cities.

The **San Francisco Museum of Modern Art** (*see* Museums, *below*), the **California Historical Society Museum** (678 Mission St., at 3rd St., tel. 415/357–1848), with an admission of $3, and the **Cartoon Art Museum** (*see* Museums, *below*) are all new neighbors of Yerba Buena Gardens. The **Mexican Museum** (*see* Museums, *below*), now in cramped quarters at Fort Mason, will make its new home here in late 1998 or early 1999.

PARKS

Along with Golden Gate Park (*see* Major Sights, *above*), the city has an abundance of smaller strips of greenery where you can cavort or sprawl on a blanket with the Sunday paper.

Folsom Street is the center of the hypermacho leather-oriented gay circuit. At no time is this more obvious than during September's Folsom Street Fair (tel. 415/861–3247), when studded bikers, cowboys, and construction workers choke the strip.

BUENA VISTA

They named this Buena Vista (good view) for a reason: It's set on a steep hill covered with cypress and eucalyptus, and from the summit, the views of the Golden Gate Bridge, the ocean, the Bay Bridge, and downtown create a mystical backdrop. The park has a reputation for being dangerous at night, but in the daytime it's a largely undiscovered escape from the asphalt chaos below. Entrance to the park is at the intersection of Haight and Lyon streets; from Market Street downtown, take Bus 6, 7, 66, or 71.

GLEN CANYON

Glen Canyon Park is hidden in part of the southwest corner of the city that isn't crawling with tourists; a visit is a total escape from city life. Eucalyptus trees and a few climbing boulders loom above you, and grass-covered slopes lead down to a shady path, equal parts poison oak and soothing stream. Take BART to the Glen Park station, then walk about five blocks uphill (west) on Bosworth Street.

MISSION DOLORES PARK

In a sunny residential area between the Mission and Castro, beautiful Dolores Park attracts picnickers, dog owners, and families of all sorts. On warm days there's usually a contingent of sunbathing men wearing Speedos—they are Castro residents who've dubbed the park "Castro Beach." The park, set on a gently sloping hill, has tennis courts, a basketball court, a playground, and wide expanses of grass, not to mention spectacular views of the city and the Bay Bridge. The thoroughfare down the park's center is where prostitutes transact business: Avoid this area at night. On July 4 weekend and Labor Day, the San Francisco Mime Troupe (*see* Theater *in* Chapter 6) gives free performances here. The park is between Dolores, Church, 18th, and 20th streets. From downtown take the J Church streetcar to 18th Street.

SAN FRANCISCO ZOO

Northern California's largest zoological park is home to 1,000 species of birds and animals, more than 120 of which have been designated endangered. In recent years zoo caretakers have gone to great lengths to create natural environments for their charges: **Gorilla World,** a $2 million exhibit, is one of the largest and most natural gorilla habitats of any zoo in the world. Nearby, the $5 million **Primate Discovery Center** is home to 14 endangered species of monkeys. The **Feline Conservation Center** was designed with rare ocelots and jaguars in mind, while the new **South American Gateway** exhibit con-

GREAT SF VIEWS

Baker Beach. The bridge looms to your right, the ocean extends to your left, and the Marin Headlands rise before you.

Treasure Island. See the familiar San Francisco skyline from a different angle. By car, take the Treasure Island exit from the Bay Bridge and park at the water's edge.

Upper Market Street. Where Portola Street ends and Market Street begins, near Twin Peaks, you'll find a view of the city and the East Bay.

Tank Hill. Drive south on Stanyan Street to Belgrave Avenue, turn left, and continue to the road's end. A footpath leads to a high, craggy overlook.

tains 7 lush acres of rain forest that tapirs and howler monkeys call home. Other enclosures worth a look include Koala Crossing, Otter River, the Lion House, and the Australian Walkabout. And don't forget to say hello to **Prince Charles,** a rare white tiger (the first of its kind to be exhibited in the West). A children's zoo ($1) houses 300 cuddly mammals, and there's also a 1921 carousel ($1). Feeding time for the big cats is 2 Tuesday–Sunday; feeding time for the penguins is 3 daily. *Sloat Blvd. at 45th Ave., tel. 415/753–7080. From any downtown Muni station, take L Taraval streetcar to last stop (45th Ave. and Wawona St.), then walk 1 block south. Admission $7; free 1st Wed. of month. Open daily 10–5; children's zoo open weekdays 11–4, weekends 10–4:30.*

SOUTH PARK

Set in the middle of the warehouse-laden and utterly ungreen SoMa District is a welcome surprise: South Park, a tree-filled square that looks like it was airlifted in from Paris. With a playground, several cafés and restaurants, and dozens of inviting benches, it's an old-fashioned antidote for postmodern angst. Its proximity to the newly designated Multimedia Gulch—the first cousin of Silicon Valley—has earned it the moniker South Park; on weekdays you'll see plenty of harried graphic artists, writers, architects, and attorneys guiltily gulping a midmorning latte. *South Park Ave. off 2nd and 3rd Sts., between Bryant and Brannan Sts.*

SUTRO FOREST

Sutro Forest is that big patch of trees, visible from almost anywhere in the city, that *isn't* Golden Gate Park. This wild, dense forest is just off Stanyan Street, above the more famous Golden Gate Park and behind the UCSF Medical Center (in fact, most hiking trails lead to UCSF residence halls). Take the N Judah streetcar to Willard Street, head south on Willard, right on Belmont Avenue, and left on Edgewood Avenue.

WASHINGTON SQUARE

This tiny urban park at the north end of North Beach is a perfect example of the blending of cultures within San Francisco. Old Italian men chew on long-dead cigars as the bells of a Romanesque church ring the hour. Early mornings, Chinese women engage in the graceful movements of tai chi, surrounded by lingering wisps of fog. Grab an Italian-style picnic at one of the nearby markets and watch the show. From Market Street (at Kearny Street) Bus 15 or 30 will bring you to the intersection of Powell and Union streets, the heart of Washington Square.

BEACHES

Step off the bus at Ocean Beach in your bikini and flip-flops, and you might be in for a shock. San Francisco's beaches are not the kind of sunny, sandy expanses you see on *Baywatch;* locals prefer to use city beaches for activities like meditating, kite flying, and exercising their dogs. At **Fort Funston,** San

Francisco's southernmost beach, watch hang gliders soar overhead, then take a 7-mi stroll north to Ocean Beach (*see below*). From the Balboa Park BART station, take Bus 88 west.

BAKER BEACH

One end of Baker Beach sees families, tourists, anglers, and wealthy homeowners walking their dogs, while the other end sees a lot of skin as one of the city's most popular nude beaches. Beautiful views of the Marin Headlands, the Golden Gate Bridge, and the bay make this a great place to sunbathe. From Clay and Drumm streets (near Embarcadero Center), take Bus 1 to 25th Avenue in the Richmond, then transfer to Bus 29 heading north into the Presidio.

CHINA BEACH

Named after a Chinese fisherman who camped here in the 1870s, China Beach (also known as Phelan Beach) is one of the city's safest swimming beaches *and* the most convenient, with its free changing rooms and showers. (Watch out for the occasional deadly rip currents.) The beach is tucked between Lands End and the Presidio, just off Seacliff Avenue (home to actor Robin Williams and many other multimillionaires). Take Bus 1 from Clay and Drumm streets (near Embarcadero Center) to 30th Avenue in Richmond, then walk north.

LANDS END

The mile-long Lands End loop trail is popular with mountain bikers, hikers, and picnickers—largely because of its amazing views of the Golden Gate Bridge, the ocean, and the Marin Headlands. Lands End Beach, just off the main trail, is a nude beach that's no longer exclusively gay. It's rocky and unsafe for swimming—but at least there's sand. From downtown go west on Geary Street, right on El Camino del Mar, park at the Sutro Baths (*see* Ocean Beach, *below*) main parking lot, and look for trail signs. Or take Bus 38 west from Union Square.

OCEAN BEACH

This is the surfers' beach, the family beach, the walkers' beach. It's also the tourists' beach: The **Cliff House** (1090 Point Lobos Ave., tel. 415/386–3330) is a historic landmark restaurant; on its lower level is a National Park Service office (tel. 415/556–8642), open daily 10–5. Across the road is the offbeat Musée Méchanique (*see* Museums, *below*). Just west of the Cliff House lie the ruins of the **Sutro Baths,** a huge complex of fresh and saltwater pools modeled after ancient Roman baths. Opened in 1896, the baths had five saltwater tanks and one freshwater tank, as well as restaurants, art exhibits, and an amphitheater. Alas, the baths fell victim to budget problems and were torn down in 1966. Offshore, look for **Seal Rock,** so named because seals used to sun themselves here—before they relocated to cozier digs by Fisherman's Wharf. Take the N Judah streetcar from any downtown underground Muni station to reach Ocean Beach.

MUSEUMS

Although San Francisco has recently trumpeted itself as a city of big, impressive institutions of art—like the newly relocated Museum of Modern Art and the renovated California Palace of the Legion of Honor—the buzz has also been a boon to smaller, more avant-garde spaces that fit more naturally into the city's eclectic cultural landscape.

AFRICAN AMERICAN MUSEUM

A contemporary art gallery displays works by African and African-American artists, and an intriguing gift shop sells jewelry and artifacts. There's also a historical archive and research library. Call for information on lectures and performing arts classes. The Center for African and African-American Art and Culture (*see* Western Addition, *above*) is an affiliate of the museum. *Fort Mason Center, Bldg. C, tel. 415/441–0640. Admission $3. Open Tues.–Sun. noon–5.*

ANSEL ADAMS CENTER

If you're even remotely interested in serious photography, this is the place. The largest repository of art photography on the West Coast, the center has five rotating exhibits, one of which is devoted to Adams's work (despite the name, there aren't that many works by Adams); the other exhibits range from traditional portraiture to computer-altered images. For serious photographers there are educational programs and competitions. The center's 1993 Annie Leibovitz retrospective put it on the pop-culture map.

The bookstore alone is worth a trip. *250 4th St., between Howard and Folsom Sts., tel. 415/495–7000. Admission $5. Open Tues.–Sun. 11–5 (until 8 on 1st Thurs. of month).*

ASIAN ART MUSEUM

Housed in the same building as the M. H. de Young (*see below*), this is the West Coast's largest Asian museum. The first floor is devoted to Chinese and Korean art; the second floor holds treasures from Southeast Asia, India and the Himalayas, Japan, and Persia. The collection of more than 12,000 pieces from 40 Asian countries is rotated periodically, so everything comes out of storage once in a while. Highlights of the permanent collection include the oldest known Buddha image (AD 338) and superb collections of carved jade and ancient Chinese ceramics. *John F. Kennedy and Tea Garden Drs., Golden Gate Park, tel. 415/379–8801. Admission $6; free 1st Wed. of month. Open Wed.–Sun. 9:30–5 (until 8:45 on 1st Wed. of month).*

CABLE CAR MUSEUM

Between Nob Hill and Russian Hill is this small museum chockablock with photographs, scale models, vintage cars, and other memorabilia devoted to the cable car's 125-year history. From the adjacent overlook you can gander at the brawny cables that haul the cars up and down the city's hills or watch the cables turn from an underground room. *1201 Mason St., at Washington St., tel. 415/474–1887. Admission free. Open daily 10–5 (Apr.–Oct. until 6).*

CALIFORNIA ACADEMY OF SCIENCES

This huge natural history complex is subdivided into blockbuster sights, including the **Morrison Planetarium,** the **Steinhart Aquarium,** and the **Natural History Museum.** Wander the complex's labyrinthine corridors until you find the aquarium's **Fish Roundabout,** which places you in an underwater world of 14,500 different creatures. The living coral reef, with its fish, giant clams, and tropical sharks, is one of the academy's most fascinating sights. The Space and Earth Hall has an Earthquake Room, where you can experience the vibrations of an 8.0-magnitude quake. Also worth visiting are the Life through Time Hall, which chronicles evolution from the dinosaurs through early mammals, and the Birds of a Feather exhibit, which explores the languages, physical features, and learning habits of birds. To see the *Sky Show* on the 65-ft dome at the Morrison Planetarium, you'll need to pay a separate admission fee ($2.50). For information on **Laserium** shows ($6–$8) at the academy, *see* Golden Gate Park *in* Major Sights, *above. Between John F. Kennedy and Martin Luther King Jr. Drs., Golden Gate Park, tel. 415/ 750–7145. Admissions: Natural History Museum and Steinhart Aquarium $7, Morrison Planetarium $2.50; all exhibits (except Laserium) free 1st Wed. of month. Open daily 10–5 (until 8:45 on 1st Wed. of month).*

CALIFORNIA PALACE OF THE LEGION OF HONOR

This landmark building now has an underground gallery complex and a full-service restaurant overlooking the Pacific Ocean. On display are San Francisco's European fine arts; though the collection isn't stunning, it does include some fine pieces from the late 19th century. Among them are several Rodin sculptures, including a cast of *The Thinker,* and one of Monet's *Water Lilies. Lincoln Park, Richmond District, tel. 415/750–3600. From Union Square, Bus 38 Geary west to 33rd Ave., then transfer to Bus 8 north; park entrance at 34th Ave. and Clement St. Admission $7; free 2nd Wed. of month. Open Tues.–Sun. 9:30–5.*

CARTOON ART MUSEUM

This tiny gem, near Yerba Buena Gardens, is the only museum on the West Coast devoted to the funnies. Its 10,000-piece collection includes everything from political cartoons of the 1700s to the *Far Side* and *New Yorker* cartoons of the present day. You'll find special exhibitions in the main rooms, plus an interactive CD-ROM room, a children's gallery, and a gift shop overflowing with your favorite comic books. *814 Mission St., between 4th and 5th Sts., tel. 415/227–8666. Admission $4. Open Wed.–Fri. 11–5, Sat. 10–5, Sun. 1–5.*

CENTER FOR THE ARTS

Part of Yerba Buena Gardens (*see* South of Market, *above*), this cultural complex houses three spacious galleries in its Visual Arts Building, plus a media screening room for video and film and a multiuse forum. Exhibits focus on contemporary works, usually of emerging local and regional artists. The center's goal is to reflect San Francisco's multicultural community in a welcoming, unpretentious, and appealing space to as large a community as possible. *701 Mission St., at 3rd St., tel. 415/978–2700 or 415/978–2787. Admission $4; free 1st Thurs. of month 6 PM–8 PM. Open Tues.–Sun. 11–6 (until 8 on 1st Thurs. of month).*

CHINESE HISTORICAL SOCIETY OF AMERICA

This nonprofit organization houses a modest museum in its basement headquarters. Historical photos and graphics accompanied by moving explanations trace the experiences of Chinese-Americans from the 1850s to the present. Among other artifacts the small museum contains opium pipes, a *queue* (the long braid men wore as a symbol of allegiance to the Manchu emperor of China before the 1911 Revolution), an altar built in the 1880s, and a parade dragon's head from 1909. *650 Commercial St., between Kearny and Montgomery Sts., tel. 415/391–1188. Admission free, donations accepted. Open weekdays 10–2.*

EXPLORATORIUM

The Exploratorium is a cavernous warehouse with more than 650 hands-on exhibits, many computer-assisted, about science and technology. It's a fun place for children—and grown-ups—to overcome their fear of science. Advance reservations ($12, includes Exploratorium admission) are required for the enormously popular **Tactile Dome** (tel. 415/560–0362), a series of small rooms, each with a different texture, in which you walk, crawl, and slither through the darkness. Adjacent to the Exploratorium is the **Palace of Fine Arts** (*see* The Presidio and Marina, *above*). *3601 Lyon St., between Marina Blvd. and Lombard St., tel. 415/563–7337 or 415/561–0360 for recorded information. Admission $9; free 1st Wed. of month. Open winter, Tues.–Sun. 10–5 (Wed. until 9:30); Memorial Day–Labor Day, Tues.–Sun. 10–6.*

Save $1 on admission at the Asian Art Museum, California Academy of Sciences, or M. H. de Young Museum by presenting a valid Muni pass or transfer ticket. . . . Here's to public transportation!

JEWISH MUSEUM

Here you'll find works by Jewish artists—contemporary ones as well as old masters—and revolving exhibits that trace important moments in Jewish history. *121 Steuart St., between Mission and Howard Sts., tel. 415/543–8880. Admission $5; free 1st Mon. of month. Open Sun. 11–6, Mon.–Wed. noon–6, Thurs. noon–8.*

MEXICAN MUSEUM

It has long been the bittersweet curse of the Mexican Museum to have an enormous permanent collection (including works by Rodolfo Morales and Diego Rivera), a strong reputation as a national center for Mexican and Chicano culture, and only a few tiny rooms to move around in. Fortunately, the museum will relocate to more spacious quarters at Yerba Buena Gardens (*see* South of Market, *above*) in late 1998 or early 1999. Meanwhile, come and enjoy the few pieces on display, usually focusing on 20th-century artists. *Fort Mason Center, Bldg. D, tel. 415/441–0404. Admission $3; free 1st Wed. of month. Open Wed.–Fri. noon–5 (until 7 on 1st Wed. of month), weekends 11–5.*

M. H. DE YOUNG MEMORIAL MUSEUM

The de Young is best known for its substantial survey collection of American art, which includes paintings, sculpture, decorative arts, textiles, and furniture dating to 1670. There are works by Sargent, Whistler, Church, and Wood; look for George Caleb Bingham's *Boatmen on the Missouri* and Georgia O'Keeffe's *Petunias*. The de Young also houses impressive collections of art from Africa, Oceania, and the Americas. There are docent-led tours on the hour; call for information on lectures and other events (tel. 415/750–3636). *Golden Gate Park, between John F. Kennedy Dr. and 8th Ave., tel. 415/750–3600. Admission $6; free 1st Wed. of month. Open Wed.–Sun. 9:30–5 (until 8:45 on 1st Wed. of month).*

MUSEE MECHANIQUE

This quirky museum is at the end of Geary Boulevard near the Cliff House (*see* Ocean Beach, *above*). It's stuffed with antique carnival attractions like player pianos, marionettes, and a truly frightening mechanical laughing lady (bring plenty of coins in order to play with all the gadgets). Don't miss the miniature amusement park—complete with a Ferris wheel—built out of toothpicks by San Quentin inmates. *1090 Point Lobos Ave., tel. 415/386–1170. Admission free. Open Oct.–Apr., weekdays 11–7, weekends 10–7; May–Sept., daily 10–8.*

MUSEO ITALOAMERICANO

If this modest collection of 20th-century Italian and Italian-American art seems out of place at Fort Mason, consider that it was founded two decades ago in North Beach. Though throngs of Italian Americans do not seem to be pouring in, the museum has stuck to its mission to research, collect, and display new works by Italians and Italian Americans in an effort to restore appreciation of contemporary Italian art and culture. The one important work of the rotating permanent collection is Arnaldo Pomodoro's 1961 bronze sculpture *Tavola della Memoria* (Table of Memory). *Fort Mason Center, Bldg. C, tel. 415/673–2200. Admission $2; free 1st Wed. of month. Open Wed.–Sun. noon–5 (until 7 on 1st Wed. of month).*

PACIFIC HERITAGE MUSEUM

On display are rare works from private collections representing China, Taiwan, Japan, Thailand, and many other Asian nations. Past exhibitions have featured Chinese classical furniture, paintings, vases, and ceramics. Call for the latest exhibition information. *608 Commercial St., at Kearny St., tel. 415/399–1124. Admission free. Open weekdays 10–4.*

SAN FRANCISCO MUSEUM OF MODERN ART

Designed by Swiss architect Mario Botta, the new brick-and-stone home of the SFMOMA is dominated by a huge cylindrical skylight trimmed with black and white stripes of stone. The interior is just as impressive: The stately entrance hall and galleries provide a sleek setting for the museum's sprawling exhibits. The space doubles that of the museum's prior home at the War Memorial Veterans Building, where it opened in 1935 as the West Coast's first museum devoted to 20th-century art. The permanent collection includes works by Jackson Pollock, Jasper Johns, Frida Kahlo, Henri Matisse, and Frank Stella, as well as a healthy representation of contemporary photography and Bay Area figurative movement works. *151 3rd St., tel. 415/357–4000. Admission $7; free 1st Tues. of month, ½ price Thurs. 6–9. Open Mon.–Tues. 11–6, Thurs. 11–9, Fri.–Sun. 11–6.*

UFO, BIGFOOT, AND LOCH NESS MONSTER MUSEUM

San Francisco's newest museum is also its oddest. Curator-owner Erik Beckjord, a former president of the San Francisco Star Trek Fan Club, calls it "a museum of the unknown, of the tentative, of the unproven." Translation? You'll learn about crop circles and Martian "artifacts," as well as signs of Sasquatch, a.k.a. Bigfoot. Check out photos, news clips, videos, artists' conceptions, and testimonials straight out of *The X-Files. 709 Union St., at Columbus Ave., tel. 415/974–4339. Admission $3. Open Tues.–Fri. 1–6, weekends noon–6.*

GALLERIES

The best time to wade into the gallery world is the first Thursday evening of each month, when many art houses host receptions with free drinks and snacks and occasionally some interesting new art. It's a great and fairly casual scene. For current happenings keep an eye on publications like the *San Francisco Arts Monthly* and *San Francisco Gallery Guide,* both available at galleries throughout town.

DOWNTOWN

No fewer than 30 galleries, most relatively mainstream and high-end, are in this area, a stone's throw from ritzy Union Square. The thickest concentrations are along the first three blocks of Grant Street, the 100 block of Geary, the 100 and 200 blocks of Post, and the 200 block of Sutter. At **49 Geary Street,** each of the second through fifth floors claims a separate swank gallery. On the fifth floor the **Robert Koch** gallery (tel. 415/421–0122) explores traditional and experimental photography; other floors focus on painting or multimedia art. All galleries within the building are open at least Tuesday–Saturday 11–5.

MISSION DISTRICT

The Mission is the undisputed center of the city's Latino arts scene; it's also the place for experimental art by up-and-coming female artists. **Galeria de la Raza** (2857 24th St., at Bryant St., tel. 415/826–8009), founded in 1970 by members of the Chicano Arts Movement, was the first Mexican museum in the United States; it remains an influential cultural resource, with its exhibits of local Latin American art and community arts programs. The **Women's Building** (*see* Mission District, *above*) occasionally hosts visual arts installments by San Francisco women. Check out local and traveling artists and performances at the following up-and-coming Mission galleries: **Southern Exposure** (401 Alabama St., at 17th St., tel. 415/863–2141); **Collision Gallery** (417 14th St., at Valencia St., tel. 415/431–4074); **Four**

Walls (3160-A 16th St., between Valencia and Guerrero Sts., entrance on Albion St., tel. 415/626–8515); and the **Lab** (2948 16th St., at Capp St., tel. 415/864–8855).

Mission Cultural Center. This Mission District landmark has gallery space as well as classrooms, dance spaces, painting studios, and a theater, all devoted to promoting the Latino arts community. Current budget woes are keeping performance arts to a minimum, but visual arts exhibits continue, often featuring neighborhood artists, and the center is a great place to find out what's going on in the neighborhood. Call or stop by for a complete rundown of events, including exhibits, performances, lectures, and classes. *2868 Mission St., between 24th and 25th Sts., tel. 415/821–1155. Donation requested. Open Tues.–Sat. 10–4.*

SOUTH OF MARKET

In SoMa plain old paintings won't draw a crowd anymore; everyone who's anyone is jumping on the mixed-media and multimedia bandwagons. Two galleries that are old hands at the multimedia game are **SOMAR** (934 Brannan St., at 8th St., tel. 415/552–2131), which is known more for its theater than its visual arts, and **New Langton Arts** (1246 Folsom St., between 8th and 9th Sts., tel. 415/626–5416), the granddaddy of the city's mixed-media centers.

By day the endearingly awkward **Gallery 111** (111 Minna St., between New Montgomery and 2nd Sts., tel. 415/974–1719) is a gallery showcasing contemporary California artists; at night it's a performance space, with musical and multimedia events. Drink specials during happy hour (weekdays 4–7) bring a sociable crowd. **Theatre Concrete** (550 Natoma St., tel. 415/621–4068) offers unusual performances, often involving music and robots. **Acme** (667 Howard St., near 3rd St., tel. 415/777–2263) is another good, tiny space to see a strange creation or two. **SF Camera Work** (115 Natoma St., between New Montgomery and 2nd Sts., tel. 415/764–1001) is a good photography gallery with strong alternative shows in an airy warehouse space.

EAST BAY

The funk and soul of San Francisco extend beyond the city limits: Only a bridge away are Berkeley and Oakland, each with its own flavor and its own set of unmatchable attractions. Sample the hip-hop beat of Oaktown (as it's called), join in Berkeley's hippie parade. . . Whether you're looking for a New Age healing session or a good blues band, odds are good that you'll find it somewhere in the East Bay.

BERKELEY

Berkeley and the University of California campus there may not be synonymous, but they're so interdependent it's difficult to tell where one stops and the other begins. You won't find many backpack-toting students in the upscale neighborhoods that buffer the north and east sides of campus, but for the most part Berkeley is a student town, dominated by the massive UC campus and its 30,000 undergraduate and post-graduate enrollees. Because of its offbeat, countercultural reputation, the university attracts every sort of person imaginable—from artists, anarchists, and hypergenius intellectuals to superjocks and fashion slaves, not to mention the stubbornly apathetic and the piously ideological. Recent campus celebrities have included former math professor Theodore Kaczynski (the alleged Unabomber) and the former student known as the Naked Guy (expelled for attending classes in the nude). But anyone who has watched the documentary *Berkeley in the Sixties* might be surprised to find out that the city isn't what it used to be. Berkeley *is* still a breeding ground for alternative social trends both important and inane, for posers and protesters. But ever since the 1994 election of a more conservative mayor, Shirley Dean, there has been a reaction by some Berkeley residents against the city's free-for-all reputation. Those who continue their love affair with the '60s still influence the city, but others want to drag Berkeley kicking and screaming into the '90s.

Berkeley's University of California **campus** is surprisingly beautiful, with walking paths, a creek, and eucalyptus and redwood groves. Southside, or the area south of campus, is dominated by chaotic **Telegraph Avenue,** and just east of it, **College Avenue** is the heart of the Elmwood District, lined with boutiques and cafés with a bohemian flair. North Berkeley, a more sedate and residential area, is where you'll find the **Gourmet Ghetto,** home of the famed restaurant Chez Panisse (*see* Chapter 4) and a number of excellent organic food markets. The Berkeley Hills, rising north and east of campus, shelter the huge **Tilden Regional Park** and acres of densely forested slopes. Farther west, around **University** and **San Pablo avenues,** you'll find working-class Berkeley, a gritty neighborhood that is also among the city's most ethnically diverse. No matter what part of town you're in, you're never far from movie houses, bookstores, restaurants, and cafés geared toward counterculture tastes and student budgets.

WORTH SEEING

TELEGRAPH AVENUE

Whether you love it or hate it, the first five blocks of this congested and colorful avenue—which begins at the campus and runs south into Oakland—form the spiritual heart of Berkeley. It's a jumble of cafés, bookstores, used clothing stores, and cheap restaurants populated by harried students, long-haired hippies, homeless people and street entertainers, metaphysical warriors, street vendors, and wide-eyed tourists. Telegraph today is a unique fusion of '60s and '90s counterculture, and the two elements blend nicely. This is especially evident on Sunday between 11 and 3, when students, hippies, former hippies, and yuppies with a penchant for organic produce gather on Telegraph around Haste Street for the weekly farmers' market. Most Fridays a Peruvian band sets up on the corner of Telegraph and Bancroft avenues, while other afternoons bring folks hammering on dulcimers, drumming on buckets, and strumming on acoustic guitars. The first or second Sunday in October, Telegraph hosts a **jazz festival,** and authors, bookmakers, and musicians fill the street during the avenue's annual **book festival,** in late July or early August. Call the Telegraph Area Association (tel. 510/649–9500) for news of upcoming events.

Shops along Telegraph come and go, but neighborhood landmarks include **Amoeba** and **Rasputin Music,** both of which feature a huge selection of vinyl, tapes, and CDs (*see* Records, Tapes, and CDs *in* Chapter 3). Book lovers should check out **Cody's** and **Moe's** (*see* Books *in* Chapter 3). Cody's hosts regular readings and has probably the largest selection of new books, magazines, and 'zines in the area, while Moe's specializes in used and rare books. For candles, incense, black-light posters, hookahs, and decorative pipes (for tobacco, of course), stop by Southside's infamous **Annapurna** (2416 Telegraph Ave., between Haste and Channing Sts., tel. 510/841–6187). One block south, **Mediterraneum Caffè** (*see* Chapter 5), alleged to once be the workplace of beat poet Allen Ginsberg, opened in 1957 and was immortalized by an anxious Dustin Hoffman in the film *The Graduate.*

PEOPLE'S PARK

In 1969 the now-defunct *Berkeley Barb* urged people to "bring shovels, hoses, flowers, soil, colorful smiles, laughter, and lots of sweat" to convert a 2.8-acre vacant lot owned by the university into a park for the people. Thousands of people showed up at the newly green space, and People's Park was born. Conflict began when the university decided to build a dormitory on the spot. Protests ensued, ending in a 17-day occupation of Berkeley by the National Guard (ordered by then-governor Ronald Reagan), thousands of arrests, and the dropping of tear gas on Sproul Plaza. Over the years the park has decayed as activists and university officials continue to struggle over its future. In 1991 the university tried to beautify the park by installing volleyball courts, but many people saw the courts as a scheme to dislocate the homeless and hippies who call the park home. Still, the anniversary of People's Park is celebrated annually on the last Sunday in April, with music, arts and crafts, and food. **People's Park Annex** (Telegraph Avenue at Dwight Way) is another vacant, fenced-in lot with witty graffiti and art displays made out of recycled material. *Between Haste St. and Dwight Way, just east of Telegraph Ave.*

UNIVERSITY OF CALIFORNIA CAMPUS

Established in 1868 as the first branch of the statewide University of California system, the UC Berkeley campus retains some of the beauty and gentility of its early years, particularly in the old brick and stone buildings scattered about campus. On a walk through campus you'll find peaceful glades and imposing academic buildings in the architectural style known as brutalism, as well as battalions of musicians, zealots, and students "on their way to class" (i.e., napping in the sun). Free student-led tours of campus leave from the **visitor center** (University Hall, Room 101, 2200 University Ave., at Oxford St., on the west side of campus, tel. 510/642–5215) weekdays at 10. Tours depart Saturday at 10 from a small visitor center (tel. 510/642–4636) on the second floor of the Student Union Building, on the west side of Sproul Plaza (*see below*). You can pick up a map or brochure outlining a self-guided walking tour from either office.

SPROUL PLAZA • UC Berkeley's Sproul Plaza, just north of the Telegraph and Bancroft intersection, is where the Free Speech Movement began in 1964. Look inside imposing **Sproul Hall** for a display of photographs from this first demonstration in which 3,000 students surrounded a police car containing a UC Berkeley student arrested for distributing political flyers. Both the man and the car were released after 32 hours, but the students famously continued to battle university head Clark Kerr. Today Sproul Plaza is a source of endless entertainment for locals and tourists, where some of Berkeley's most famous loonies congregate: Look out for the Hate Man (the man in a bra, high heels, long skirt, and lipstick), who professes hatred for everything. **Lower Sproul Plaza,** just west of Sproul Plaza, is the site of occasional free noon concerts during the school year on Wednesday (usually rock) and Thursday (usually the Cal jazz band). Nearby **Zellerbach Hall** (*see* Classical Music *in* Chapter 6) hosts professional theater and concerts; check the box office for upcoming events.

SATHER GATE AND DOE LIBRARY • North of Sproul Plaza, pass through Sather Gate, the main entrance to campus until expansion in the 1960s. The second building on your right, Doe Library, is worth a look for its cavernous and beautiful reference room, and the cozy oak-paneled **Morrison Reading Room** (open weekdays 9–5 during school year, noon–5 in summer). Anyone is welcome to peruse the Morrison Room's international newspapers and magazines, listen to its collection of compact discs and records with headphones, or just kick back in a cushy leather easy chair.

The Doe Library building also contains the **Bancroft Library** (accessible from the east side of the building-ing), which houses a vast collection of historical documents, rare books, and old photographs. Anyone with a photo ID can get access to the huge, noncirculating collection. On permanent display in the administrative office is a gold nugget purported to have started the California gold rush when it was discovered on January 24, 1848, at Sutter's Mill.

CAMPANILE AND AROUND • Directly east of Bancroft Library is **Sather Tower** (more commonly known as the Campanile), a 307-ft clock tower modeled after the one in Venice's Piazza San Marco. The carillon is played daily (except during final exams), weekdays at 7:50, noon, and 6; Saturday at noon and 6; and Sunday at 2 for an extended 45 minutes. At the top of the Campanile is an observation deck, open Monday–Saturday 10–3:30 and Sunday 10–1:45 and accessible by elevator (50¢); the view of the bay is spectacular. Southwest of the Campanile, the redbrick South Hall is the only one of the original university buildings still standing. Or walk northeast from the clock tower to check out the **Hearst Mining Building,** a masterpiece of Beaux Arts architecture designed by John Galen Howard.

If you're lucky you may cross paths with the Bubble Lady (poet and bubble maker Julia Vinograd), Rare (a lunatic and sports-trivia fiend), Pink Man (hot-pink-unitard-wearing unicyclist), or any of the other wacky denizens who give Berkeley its odd appeal.

UNIVERSITY AVENUE AND ENVIRONS

University Avenue stretches from I–80 along the bay to the UC campus in the Berkeley foothills. It teems with cheap ethnic restaurants, cafés, and offbeat clothing stores—as well as car-repair shops and seedy motels. The area can be dangerous at night, and most things worth seeing are too few and far between to be conducive to exploration on foot. Near the university campus, the **UC Theatre** (*see* Movie Houses *in* Chapter 6) shows a diverse range of classics, along with Saturday midnight performances of *The Rocky Horror Picture Show.* A few miles west of campus, University Avenue intersects **San Pablo Avenue,** which recently has been colonized by a smattering of funky shops, bars, and cafés. Within a few blocks of each other, you'll find the hip female-owned restaurants **Brick Hut Café** (*see* Chapter 4) and **Ann Kong's World-Famous Bleach Bottle Pig Farm** (2072 San Pablo Ave., between University Ave. and Addison St., Berkeley, tel. 510/848–7376); the ultracasual pub the **Albatross;** the folk music club **Freight and Salvage;** and the world-music emporium **Ashkenaz** (for more on Berkeley nightlife, *see* Chapter 6).

Upscale shops abound on **4th Street,** in a former warehouse district near the bay just north of University Avenue. The street is a fine place to browse for overpriced goodies like sleigh beds, hummingbird feeders, and organic cotton bathrobes; for real bargains head to the **Crate and Barrel Outlet Store** (*see* Specialty Items *in* Chapter 3). **Vivarium** (1827 5th St., at Hearst St., tel. 510/841–1400) stocks exotic pets like pythons, giant tortoises, and iguanas. **Takara Sake** (708 Addison St., at 4th St., tel. 510/540–8250), one of only three makers of sake (Japanese rice wine) in the United States, offers a slide show and free samples of their product daily noon–6. From here it's a short drive to the **Berkeley Marina** (*see* Parks and Gardens, *below*).

BERKELEY

Z

0
0

1/2 mile

500 meters

TO CESAR
CHAVEZ PARK

Berkeley
Marina

Shorebird
Nature Center

Emeryville
Marina

San Francisco
Bay

Powell
St.

80

TO SAN
FRANCISCO

EMERYVILLE

123

Hollis St.

Amtrak
Depot

65th St.

Stanford Ave.

Adeline St.

MLK Jr. Way

Shattuck Ave.

TO DOWNTOWN
OAKLAND

ROCKRIDGE

TO ROCKRIDGE
BART

13

Claremont

Tunnel Rd.

Ave.

Ashby

Aquatic
Park

Ave.

San Pablo Ave.

San Pablo
Park

13

Sacramento St.

California St.

Alcatraz Ave.

Woolsey St.

Telegraph Ave.

Ashby
BART
Station ba

Stuart St.

Derby St.

Milvia St.

MLK Jr. Way

Fulton St.

Ellsworth St.

Ashby
Ave.

Hillegass Ave.

College Ave.

Willard
Park

ELMWOOD
DISTRICT

People's
Park

Piedmont
Ave.

4th St.

6th St.

7th St.

9th St.

Bancroft Way

Channing Way

Dwight Way

Porter St.

Sacramento St.

University Ave.

Delaware St.

Francisco St.

Ohlone
Park

Hearst Ave.

Cedar St.

BERKELEY
BART
Station ba

Bancroft Way

Channing Way

Haste St.

Durant Ave.

Bancroft Way

University
Art Museum

Harmon
Arena

Sather
Gate

Sproul
Plaza

Campanile

Greek
Theatre

Campus
Visitor Center

Shattuck Ave.

Oxford St.

Arch St.

LeConte Ave.

Euclid Ave.

Vine St.

Rose St.

GOURMET
GHETTO

TO INDIAN
ROCK PARK

Rose
Garden

Codornices
Park

Memorial
Stadium

Phoebe Hearst
Museum of Anthropology

UNIVERSITY
OF
CALIFORNIA

Lawrence
Hall of
Science

Botanical
Gardens

Grizzly

Peak

Shasta Rd.

Tilden
Park

Blvd.

North Berkeley
BART Station ba

123

80

Amtrak
Depot

University Ave.

KEY

i Tourist Information

80

62

COLLEGE AVENUE/ELMWOOD DISTRICT

The heart of the Elmwood District is the intersection of College Avenue (which runs south from campus) and Ashby Avenue. This neighborhood has some well-preserved examples of California Craftsman homes, as well as a plethora of upscale cafés, specialty stores, and gourmet restaurants, including **Nabolom Bakery** (2708 Russell St., at College Ave., tel. 510/845–2253), a co-op that produces great breads and pastries. Hotshot composer John Adams has been known to quaff caffeine at stylish **Espresso Roma** (see Chapter 5), while just about everyone in the neighborhood goes to **Slash** (see Chapter 3) to buy fashionably pre-owned Levi's jeans.

NORTH BERKELEY

Grad students, professors, and folks with steady jobs frequent Northside, lending it a calmer atmosphere than you'll find on the campus's Southside. Homes in the hilly neighborhoods here date from the 1920s and are in a variety of architectural styles. The area's crowning glory is the so-called **Gourmet Ghetto** (Shattuck Avenue and Vine Street). It's lined with dozens of tantalizing restaurants, including **Chez Panisse** (see Chapter 4), as well as specialty stores, clothing boutiques, and bookstores. Of note are **Black Oak Books** (see Books in Chapter 3) and the original **Peet's Coffee & Tea** (2124 Vine St., at Walnut St., tel. 510/841–0564), now part of a caffeine empire. Cafés and restaurants also line a block-long section of **Euclid Street**, where it dead-ends at the campus. Continue north on Euclid to reach the Berkeley Rose Garden (see below).

Shattuck Avenue becomes **Solano Avenue** about 2 mi north of University Avenue. The small shopping district here is worth a trip simply because of **Zachary's Pizza** (see Chapter 4), which sells heavenly Chicago-style pies ($11 and up). The **Bone Room** (1569 Solano Ave., at Peralta Ave., tel. 510/526–5252) is a one-of-a-kind shop selling dinosaur bones, live tarantulas, and other living or fossilized paleontological delights.

The Berkeleyan, a campus newspaper published every Wednesday, has a long list of free events and lectures—everything from "Double-Strand Break Repair and the Specific Cloning of Human DNA in Yeast" to "Spatialization of Violence."

PARKS AND GARDENS

TILDEN REGIONAL PARK

Tilden Park's more than 2,000 acres of forests and grasslands are a wonderful escape from the gridlocked lowlands. Follow the signs to **Inspiration Point** for a view of reservoirs and of rolling hills where cows laze. There are plenty of picnic spots (call 510/636–1684 to reserve a group picnic area) and miles of hiking and biking trails (see Chapter 8).

Tilden Nature Area Environmental Education Center (EEC; tel. 510/525–2233), at the north end of the park, sponsors a number of naturalist-led programs throughout the year. Independent types can borrow or buy a self-guided trail booklet ($2) at the center, which is open Tuesday–Sunday 10–5. For a nice, easy walk (about a mile), take the **Jewel Lake Trail** loop from the EEC office—and look out for the salamanders. To make friends with domestic animals, detour to the nearby **Little Farm.**

Other destinations in the park include **Lake Anza** (tel. 510/848–3028), which is open for swimming mid-May to mid-October, daily 11–6; pony rides ($2.50); a vintage carousel ($1); a botanical garden of California plants, open daily 8:30–5, with no admission charge; the 18-hole **Tilden Park Golf Course** (tel. 510/848–7373 for reservations); and a miniature steam train ($1.50). Rides operate on weekends and holidays when school is in session and daily during spring and summer vacations; call 510/843–2137 for specific hours.

To reach Tilden Park from the Berkeley BART station, take Bus 8, 65, or 67. If you're driving, take University Avenue east from I–80 to Oxford Street, go left on Oxford, right on Rose, and left on Spruce to the top of the hill, cross Grizzly Peak Boulevard, make an immediate left on Canon Drive, and follow the signs. The park is open 5 AM–10 PM.

BERKELEY MARINA

Warm days were meant to be spent at the Berkeley Marina, at the end of University Avenue approximately half a mile west of I–80. Head for the ¾-mi pier jutting out into the bay to enjoy the unbeatable views of the Golden Gate Bridge and Alcatraz Island. Winds along the bay can be quite chilly, which makes nearby **César E. Chávez Park** (formerly North Waterfront Park) a perfect retreat. The hilly 92-acre park is Berkeley's only open space without a leash law for dogs and is also one of the most popular kite-flying areas in the Bay Area.

The **Shorebird Nature Center** (160 University Ave., tel. 510/644–8623) has maps of the marina and runs all sorts of educational and environmental programs. For information on renting boats or hooking up with one of the sailing clubs stationed at the marina, stop by the **Marina Office** (201 University Ave., tel. 510/644–6376). To get to the marina, drive west on University Avenue across I–80 or take Bus 51M from the Berkeley BART station.

BERKELEY ROSE GARDEN/CODORNICES PARK

Built during the Depression, the rose garden is an attractive spot for a picnic or to watch the sunset. There are a multilevel rose garden, an amphitheater with roses and more roses, and a panoramic view of the bay. It's north of campus on Euclid Avenue, between Bayview Place and Eunice Street. Across the street is Codornices Park, where you'll find basketball courts, a baseball diamond, swings, grass and sand, and picnic areas. Hiking paths lead up the hill from Codornices Park, along Codornices Creek. To reach the rose garden and the park, walk north from campus on Euclid Street for 20 minutes or take Bus 65 from the Berkeley BART station.

U.C. BOTANICAL GARDEN

Nestled in the hills east of Strawberry Canyon, the garden is a valuable research and education center with a diverse collection of plants—more than 10,000 neatly labeled species from around the world. In addition to regional areas with habitats ranging from South African deserts to Himalayan forests, there are also specialized plots, like the Chinese Medicinal Herb Garden and the Garden of Economic Plants, as well as three indoor exhibits and a slew of paths to explore. Relax on a rock along Strawberry Creek in the shady Asian Garden, on a bench near the sunny Cactus Garden, or head uphill for a lovely green-framed view of the bay. The garden is especially colorful in spring when the extensive rhododendron collection is in full bloom. Check the visitor center for bulletins on various plant seminars and public education programs, then take home some plants, for sale at bargain prices. *200 Centennial Dr., tel. 510/642–3343. From the Berkeley BART station, take Bus 8 or take Hill Service Shuttle (50¢) from Hearst Mining Circle, on campus. Admission $3; free Thurs. Open daily 9–4:45; tours weekends at 1:30.*

BERKELEY HILLS FIRE TRAIL

One of Berkeley's best semiurban hiking trails begins at a small dirt parking area just uphill from the Strawberry Canyon Recreational Facility, on Centennial Drive (and just downhill from the UC Botanical Garden). Peppy joggers, thoughtful ramblers, and dog walkers come to enjoy this wide dirt path; though sometimes crowded, it's a wonderful and accessible escape for nature seekers. The path climbs steeply at first, then levels off to meander along the hillside, with stellar views of Berkeley and the bay. *Off Centennial Dr. Follow directions to UC Botanical Garden (see above).*

INDIAN ROCK PARK

Head north on Shattuck Avenue to reach Indian Rock Avenue, where you'll see enormous volanic-rock outcroppings jutting from the hillside. As there was no way for developers to sandblast the stone, the city eventually set it aside as a park. The view of Solano Avenue far below, Albany Hill in the distance, and the Marin Headlands is humbling. Rock climbers both awkward and nimble converge here to practice their sport on the north side of the boulder, making it a great place to find climbing buddies. Steps are available for those who would prefer to saunter up the rock. The park is open from dawn to dusk.

MUSEUMS

LAWRENCE HALL OF SCIENCE

Perched on a cliff overlooking the East Bay, the museum is a memorial to Ernest O. Lawrence, UC Berkeley's first Nobel laureate, who helped design the atomic bomb. The exhibits here are mostly hands-on and geared toward children, with an emphasis on the life sciences. On weekends and daily during summer, you can catch films, lectures, laboratory demonstrations, and planetarium shows. On the hillside outside the museum's rear patio, look for a set of 36 long, slender pipes sticking out of the ground, part of a wind organ. If you walk among them when the wind is blowing, you'll hear their music; you can play with the tones by turning one of six moveable pipes. On clear Saturday nights employees and local amateur astronomers break out their telescopes from about 8 to 11 to give interested visitors a free peek at the moon, planets, star clusters, galaxies, and whatever else the universe has on tap that night. Call the hall's

Astronomy and Night Sky Info Line (tel. 510/642–5132) for details. *Centennial Dr. near Grizzly Peak Blvd., tel. 510/642–5132. Drive east on Hearst Ave., which borders campus on the north, and follow signs; or Bus 8, 65, or 67 from Berkeley BART station (ask driver for a transfer, 25¢, redeemable for $1 off museum admission); or Hill Service Shuttle (50¢) from Hearst Mining Circle, on campus. Admission $6, free Thurs.; planetarium show an additional $2. Open daily 10–5.*

PHOEBE HEARST MUSEUM OF ANTHROPOLOGY

This is one of Berkeley's best museums, with rotating exhibits that cover everything from ancient America to neolithic China. Also on display are artifacts used by Ishi, the last survivor of California's Yahi tribe, who was brought to live on the UC campus in 1911 after gold miners slaughtered the rest of his tribe. Frequent talks by artists, anthropologists, and other scholars shed light on the artifacts on display; call for a schedule. *Kroeber Hall, Room 103, UC Berkeley campus, tel. 510/642–3681. Admission $2; free Thurs. Open Wed.–Sun. 10–4:30 (Thurs. until 9 during school year).*

UNIVERSITY ART MUSEUM

The UAM houses the largest university-owned art collection in the country. Though the low concrete building may not look like much from the street, the galleries inside are surprisingly airy. Displays may include anything from a 16th-century altar panel to a passel of Bibles made of sugar candy by a Berkeley MFA candidate. One of the most impressive permanent installations is a room full of violently colorful paintings by the abstract expressionist Hans Hofmann. On the ground floor of the museum is the **Pacific Film Archive** (*see* Movie Houses *in* Chapter 6). Pick up a schedule of upcoming exhibits and movies at the museum entrance. A sculpture garden to the rear of the museum is pleasant during summer. *2626 Bancroft Way, tel. 510/642–0808. Admission $6; free Thurs. 11–noon and 5–9. Open Wed.–Sun. 11–5 (Thurs. until 9).*

The Berkeley History Center and Museum (1830 Center St., tel. 510/848–0181) has changing exhibits of community interest such as the Berkeley literary scene. It's open Thursday–Saturday 1–5; admission is free.

OAKLAND

Oakland doesn't have the same dazzling effect on visitors as San Francisco, so if you're looking for glitz, you might want to save the $2 BART fare and use it for another cable car ride through Union Square. Voted All-American City in 1993, predominantly working-class Oakland is a typical example of American cities built after 1850—with a diverse cultural landscape, a struggling downtown, some great architecture, some crime-ridden areas, and high hopes for community renewal. Oakland also has its own special flair as home to the West Coast blues; the Oaktown school of rap (heard in the music of local-artists-made-good MC Hammer, Digital Underground, Too Short, Tony! Toni! Toné!, Oaktown 3-5-7, and the late Tupac Shakur); and a vibrant art scene from the many artists who live in the city's plentiful, low-rent warehouse spaces.

Present-day Oakland was founded in the mid-1800s by three unsuccessful gold miners who leveled the area's oak groves and set up a town. Oakland prospered thanks to a thriving port, profitable manufacturing industries, and the arrival of the railroad. By the early 1990s the city was home to a large number of businesses, an electric streetcar system, and an ever-swelling population lured from around the country by job prospects and cheap housing. Wealthy families crossed the bay to escape San Francisco's urban blight, and still others migrated after damage wrought by the 1906 earthquake. Encouraged by this rapid growth, a group of powerful citizens spearheaded a beautification plan with the hope of changing Oakland's image from a suburb of San Francisco into a thriving metropolis in its own right. These boom days saw a flurry of new buildings downtown (many of which are now empty); a bigger, better city hall (once the tallest building west of Chicago); and the creation of Lake Merritt Park. Unfortunately, the growing downtown was shattered by the Depression, the flight of wealthy citizens to the hills, and a poor development plan. Another blow to the city's fabric was the freeway built in the 1960s, which resulted in the fracturing of neighborhoods and conflict between the haves and have-nots. Controversies continue to this day.

But there's plenty to explore in Oakland. The neighborhoods around **Grand, College,** and **Piedmont avenues** are lined with cafés, reasonably priced and upscale restaurants, bookstores, and boutiques. Wander through **Chinatown** for lively restaurants and markets selling produce, pungent spices, and

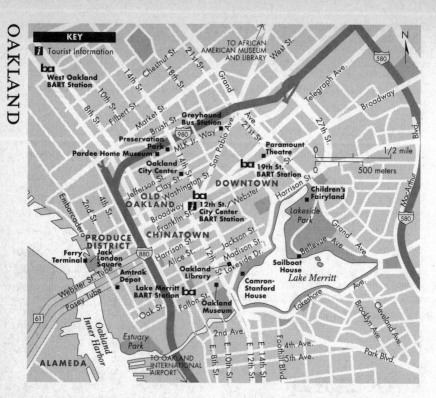

KEY

i Tourist Information

ba West Oakland BART Station

meats. Check out the downtown revitalization efforts around **Jack London Square** and **City Center,** or if the city is fraying your nerves, head for the parks in the hills to the east (*see* Chapter 8). Though some residential areas in these hills were devastated by a fire in October 1991, most of the multi-million-dollar homes have been rebuilt in a variety of interesting architectural styles. You'll need a car or bike to explore Oakland's hills, but most everything else is within reach of a BART station.

WORTH SEEING

DOWNTOWN

Downtown Oakland, occupying 10th through 20th streets along Broadway, is an odd conglomeration of Art Deco, Beaux Art, and Victorian buildings in various states of repair, interspersed with shiny office complexes and the grimy concrete facades of abandoned businesses (the last remaining department store left downtown in 1996). Though it's not a place you should visit alone at night, it's definitely worth a trip during the day to see some surprisingly impressive late-19th- and early 20th-century architecture. One of the most impressive Art Deco buildings in the Bay Area is the 1931 **Paramount Theatre** (*see* Movies Houses *in* Chapter 6), home to the Oakland Symphony and the Oakland Ballet. Two-hour tours ($1) of the historic building are held at 10 on the first and third Saturday of the month; no reservations are required. Next to the Paramount is the emerald green Art Deco I. Magnin Building; as if symbolizing downtown's problems, it now stands empty. Though many downtown businesses have moved, the **De Lauer Super Newsstand** (1310 Broadway Ave., at 14th St., tel. 510/451–6157) has been selling "your hometown newspaper" for years, as well as maps, paperbacks, foreign-language and domestic newspapers, and an overwhelming number of magazines; it's open 24 hours daily.

Farther south, the new federal building at **Oakland City Center** (between Clay, Jefferson, 12th, and 14th Sts.) has a 70-ft-high glass rotunda and a courtyard full of funky modern sculptures. During business hours you can enter the building—which houses the IRS as well as the Bureau of Alcohol, Tobacco, and

Firearms—to visit the two-tiered glass-enclosed walkway that connects the building's two towers. Security has tightened in the wake of the 1995 Oklahoma City bombing, so be prepared to show picture ID.

Old Oakland, between 8th and 10th streets just west of Broadway, is a slice of the city from the days when houses were Victorian and sidewalks were made of hand-placed red bricks. This was a bustling business district during the 1870s, and slowly it's beginning to regain some of the old buzz and hum. Recently opened eateries include **Café 817** (817 Washington St., at 9th St., tel. 510/271–7965), the snazzy **Café Chenéville** (499 9th St., at Washington St., tel. 510/893–5439), and the **Pacific Coast Brewing Company** (*see* Bars *in* Chapter 6), which makes its own delicious brews. **Pro Arts Gallery** (461 9th St., at Broadway, tel. 510/763–4361) hangs work by artists in the neighborhood. Gallery staff can also provide information about **East Bay Open Studios,** in which artists' work spaces are opened to the public for two weekends in June.

PRESERVATION PARK • In the shadow of Oakland City Center (*see above*), Preservation Park is a recreation of an idyllic 19th-century Oakland neighborhood, complete with decorative wrought-iron fences and period street lamps. Forty years of architectural history can be seen in the 16 restored houses here (five are in their original location; the others were condemned houses that were transplanted here), including Queen Anne and Italianate cottages, as well as colonial revival and Craftsman homes. The buildings are private office spaces and aren't open to visitors, but you can stroll the grounds, then visit the **Pardee Home Museum** (672 11th St., at Castro St., tel. 510/444–2187). The home of former Oakland mayor and California governor George C. Pardee now houses family and historical relics and is only open for guided tours, which cost $5, no reservations required. They take place Saturday at 11, 1, and 2:30. *Martin Luther King Jr. Way at 13th St.*

LAKE MERRITT

Lake Merritt was built in the early 1900s as part of a city beautification program. Formerly swamp, it is now a 155-acre oasis

A much-loved feature of downtown Oakland's skyline is the Tribune Tower; built in 1923, it was the city's first landmark building. Its original tenant, the Oakland Tribune, has since moved to new digs in Jack London Square.

in the middle of urban Oakland. By day the 3½-mi paved path around the lake is filled with sun seekers, joggers, business types on lunch break, and old men feeding the ducks. The 1876 **Camron-Stanford House** (1418 Lakeside Dr., near 14th St., tel. 510/836–1976), near the southwestern edge of the lake, is the only remaining Victorian building in this formerly bourgeois neighborhood. Tours of the meticulously refurbished interior are offered Wednesday 11–4 and Sunday 1–5. They cost $4 and are free the first Sunday of the month. **Lakeside Park** (tel. 510/238–3091), on the north shore, has picnic facilities, Japanese and herb gardens, the oldest urban bird sanctuary in the United States (1879), and frequent music events. Nearby, the **Sailboat House** (568 Bellevue Ave., tel. 510/444–3807) rents rowboats, paddleboats, kayaks, and sailboats for $6–$12 an hour, plus deposit. It's open year-round; call for hours. The **Children's Fairyland** (Grand and Bellevue Aves., tel. 510/238–6876) is a storybook theme park with rides, puppet shows, strange mushroom-, whale-, and shoe-shaped buildings, and other miniature delights. Walt Disney reputedly visited Fairyland to gather ideas for his own theme parks. Admission to Fairyland is $3.25 for adults, who are allowed inside only if they bring a child ($2.75).

Grand Avenue, which begins at the north tip of the lake, is also a good place for a stroll, with a number of reasonably good ethnic restaurants and cafés, including the **Grand Bakery** (3264 Grand Ave., tel. 510/465–1110), which makes great breads, pastries, and kosher treats, and the **Coffee Mill** (3363 Grand Ave., tel. 510/465–4224), which claims to be Oakland's oldest coffeehouse. Across the street is **Walden Pond** (3316 Grand Ave., tel. 510/832–4438), a cozy bookstore with frequent poetry readings. On your way back to the lake, peek inside the **Grand Lake Theatre** (*see* Movie Houses *in* Chapter 6), an Art Deco movie palace where an enormous chandelier and grand staircase remain from the 1920s. The theater now shows first-run movies on four screens. For information on local summer events like the **Festival at the Lake** and the **Juneteenth Festival,** *see* Festivals *in* Chapter 1. To reach the south end of the park, walk three blocks northeast from the Lake Merritt BART station. To reach the north end of the lake and Grand Avenue, take BART to 19th Street and walk east.

JACK LONDON SQUARE

Although born in San Francisco, Jack London spent his early years in Oakland before shipping out on the adventures that inspired *The Call of the Wild, The Sea Wolf,* and *The Cruise of the Snark*. In an effort to cash in on this legacy, Oakland created Jack London Square on the waterfront west of downtown, at the foot of Broadway. Though several years ago the project resembled a ghost town with more FOR LEASE

MARCHING TO A DIFFERENT BEAT

Oakland has a legacy of revolutionary politics. In the 1960s the militant Black Panther Party began here. In the 1970s the city was headquarters for the Symbionese Liberation Army, which kidnapped Patty Hearst and demanded as part of her ransom that food be distributed to Oakland's poor. Most recently, the Oakland school board set off national controversy by recognizing Ebonics (black English) as a distinct language. Even the city's most famous literary figure, Jack London, was an ardent socialist who wanted California to secede from the United States.

signs than tenants, the buildings have slowly been filled by boutiques, pricey eateries, a massive Barnes and Noble bookstore, and the **Jack London Cinema** (100 Washington St., tel. 510/433–1320), which features first-run films. The 1997 relocation of the enormously popular Berkeley jazz club **Yoshi's** (*see* Live Music *in* Chapter 6) has been a boon to the area; these days weekends at the square can be downright bustling. There's a swell Sunday Farmers' Market (10–2), often in conjunction with free live theater and concert events on the square.

Somewhat scant remnants of the square's namesake include **Heinhold's First and Last Chance Saloon** (56 Jack London Sq., tel. 510/839–6761), the former hangout of Jack London, as well as Robert Louis Stevenson and Joaquin Miller. The proprietors will proudly tell you about the memorabilia on the walls and the crazily sloping floor (a result of the 1906 earthquake). Next door you can look through the window of a reassembled (and often litter-strewn) cabin in which Jack once spent a winter (the cabin was transplanted here from Alaska). Also near the saloon is the tiny **Jack London Museum** (Suite 104, tel. 510/451–8218), open Wednesday–Sunday 10:30–6, displaying a small collection of London-related artifacts ($1 donation requested).

MUSEUMS

Oakland has a number of excellent museums, including the **Ebony Museum of Art** (30 Jack London Sq., Suite 208–209, tel. 510/763–0745), with work by African and African-American artists. It's open Tuesday–Saturday 11–6, Sunday noon–5, and admission is free. The **Creative Growth Art Center** (355 24th St., at Valdez St., tel. 510/836–2340), also free, displays arts and crafts by artists with disabilities. It's open weekdays 10–4, but closes one week out of every five for installation, so call ahead.

AFRICAN AMERICAN MUSEUM AND LIBRARY

This branch of the Oakland public library focuses on the history of people of African descent in North America, with a special emphasis on Oakland and the Bay Area. The collection includes original manuscripts, photos, journals, audiotapes, and photographs of Bay Area residents, as well as special exhibits and a reference library for those interested in learning more about the history of Black Americans. *5606 San Pablo Ave., at 56th St., tel. 510/597–5053. From downtown, Bus 72 north on Broadway. Admission free. Open Tues. 11:30–7, Wed. 10–5, Thurs. and Sat. 10–5:30, Fri. noon–5:30.*

OAKLAND MUSEUM

This well-designed building, a few blocks from Lake Merritt, houses collections on the environment, history, and art of California. On the ground floor is the **Gallery of Natural Sciences,** where a simulated walk takes you through the state's eight biotic zones, with their various plants and animals. If the stuffed animals don't intrigue you, perhaps the quotes by eminent scientists and writers hanging overhead will. The **Cowell Hall of California History,** on the second floor, puts today's multicultural population in context, with documents on the rise and fall of the Ohlone Native American people (the region's first inhabitants), the Spanish settlers, the suburban California dreamers, and the 1967 "Summer of Love," and tackles present-day issues of urban violence. The third-floor **Gallery of California Art** showcases paintings, sculpture, crafts, and installations by international and local artists; the art of the gold rush and the clothing of Chinese-American women are among the current (and past) exhibits. Spend some time walking around the museum's terraced gardens and the nearby **Sculpture Court** (1111 Broadway, at Oakland City Center) for a look at some surprisingly beautiful assemblages. *1000 Oak St., at 10th St., 1 block east of Lake Merritt BART, tel. 510/238–2200. Admission $5, free Sun. 4–7. Open Wed.–Sat. 10–5, Sun. noon–7.*

MARIN COUNTY

Marin, just across the Golden Gate Bridge from San Francisco, is one of the richest counties in California, an upscale playground for children old enough to remember Woodstock. Everywhere you turn, you'll see an odd combination of hippie idealism and yuppie wealth: expensive estates buffered by rugged log cabins, Porsches and BMWs parked next to aging VW microbuses. The reason so many '60s-refugees-turned-'80s-success-stories want to live here—and the reason you'll want to visit despite the price tag—is Marin's incredible natural beauty. The stunning ocean views of western Marin give way to thick redwood forests of **Mt. Tamalpais** (*see below*). On the steep east side of the mountain are perched small, woodsy towns, including **Mill Valley.** You could spend a lifetime describing the pleasures of hiking in **Muir Woods** and the **Point Reyes National Seashore,** and it's hard to act blasé about the view from **Coastal Highway 1,** no matter how many times you've driven that road.

Even the most bucolic corners of Marin County are little more than two hours from San Francisco (except during rush hour, when it can take nearly an hour just to cross the bridge). It's possible to bike across the Golden Gate Bridge from San Francisco, then take a ferry (*see* Ferry Travel *in* Chapter 1) back from Sausalito or Tiburon. A final note: If you opt for public transportation in this area, be forewarned that service is infrequent and travel times long.

MARIN HEADLANDS

For a quick taste of Marin County's natural beauty, cross the Golden Gate Bridge, exit at Alexander Avenue, and drive up Conzelman Road to the Marin Headlands. This undeveloped 1,000-acre area consists of several small but steep bluffs overlooking San Francisco Bay and the Pacific Ocean. Thick fog often whips across the headlands, obscuring everything but the top of the towers of the Golden Gate Bridge; on a sunny day, however, the views of downtown San Francisco, the East Bay, and Point Reyes to the north are stunning. Hundreds of hiking and biking trails meander along the wind-carved hills and cliffs (*see* Chapter 8).

The headlands were used as a military camp in the late 19th century, and during World War II emplacements were dug for huge naval guns to protect the approaches to the bay. The guns are long gone, but several overgrown concrete batteries still stand watch along the coast. One of the most impressive, Battery Wallace, is off Conzelman Road before you reach the Point Bonita Lighthouse. The two forbidding concrete structures you see today, once the site of 12-inch guns aimed 17 mi out to sea, are only part of the structure: They are connected by an inaccessible series of underground rooms used to hold troops and supplies. Stop by the **Marin Headlands Visitor Center** (Field and Bunker Rds., tel. 415/331–1540) to pick up the free "Park Events" brochure or the almost indispensable "Marin Headlands Map and Guide to Sights, Trails, and Wildlife" ($1.60).

About a mile past the visitor center (follow signs from Bunker Rd.) is the **Marine Mammal Center.** The center rehabilitates and rescues suffering marine mammals, including sea lions, dolphins, and whales. One of the more famous rescuees was Humphrey, an endangered humpback who was stuck in the mud for three days. More than 600 volunteers help operate the center alongside veterinary and medical staff. Visitors are welcome year-round, but call first to find out which animals are in residence. *Tel. 415/289–7325. $1 donation suggested. Open daily 10–4.*

MARIN COUNTY

TO SANTA ROSA

Rohnert Park

SONOMA COUNTY

Dillon Beach

Tomales

Two Rock

Petaluma

Petaluma R.

Marshall

Tomales Bay

Bay

Tomales Bay State Park

Soulajule Res.

Olompali State Park

POINT REYES

Inverness

NATIONAL

Pt. Reyes Station

MARIN COUNTY

Nicasio Res.

Novato

Drakes Beach

SEASHORE

Olema

Nicasio

Bear Valley Visitors Center

Samuel P. Taylor State Park

San Pablo Bay

Point Reyes Lighthouse

Drakes Bay

Lagunitas

China Camp State Park

Kent Lake

Fairfax

San Anselmo

San Rafael

GOLDEN

Alpine Lake

Point Reyes Bird Observatory

Audubon Canyon Ranch

Larkspur

Bolinas

GATE

Corte Madera

Duxberry Reef

Mt. Tamalpais State Park

Stinson Beach

Muir Woods Nat'l. Mon.

Mill Valley

NATIONAL

Green Gulch Farm Zen Center

SF Bay Model

Tiburon

Muir Beach

Marin City

Angel Island State Park

Tennessee Valley Beach

RECREATION

Marin Headlands

Sausalito

San Francisco Bay

Headlands Visitor Center

AREA

N

PACIFIC OCEAN

San Francisco

0   10 miles
0   6 km

SAUSALITO

Only a few miles north of San Francisco is Sausalito, which flourished during the 1880s and '90s as a whaling town infamous for its unruly saloons, gambling dens, and bordellos. Even after the town became suburbanized in the 11940s, it continued to attract an offbeat and raffish element, becoming by midcentury a well-known artists' colony. Over the last several decades, however, Sausalito's wharf rats have been replaced by lawyers and investment bankers escaping the San Francisco rat race. Today this is a wealthy resort town, popular with yachters and tourists. Parking is next to impossible, and shops and restaurants are shockingly expensive. Still, if you can arrange to arrive by bike or by ferry, the views of the bay make Sausalito a worthwhile excursion.

Bridgeway is Sausalito's main thoroughfare, bordered on one side by waterfront restaurants and the bay, on the other by shops hawking pricey antiques or tacky pelican paperweights. At the south end of Bridgeway is the Sausalito Ferry Terminal, where the commuter ferry from San Francisco docks (*see* Ferry Travel *in* Chapter 1). Farther south on Bridgeway is Sausalito's oldest restaurant, built in 1893 and originally known as Valhalla. It was used as a backdrop in the classic Orson Welles film *The Lady From Shanghai*; today it's the **Sausalito Chart House Restaurant** (201 Bridgeway, tel. 415/332–0804), part of an upscale seafood-and-steak chain, with one of the best views in town.

About a mile north of Sausalito on Bridgeway, look for signs advertising the **Bay Model,** an enormous working model of San Francisco Bay and the Sacramento–San Joaquin Delta, housed in a vaulted building the size of a city block. Don't expect a cute replica of Coit Tower—this is strictly a scientific tool, used by the U.S. Army Corps of Engineers to study the tides and other forces affecting the bay. *2100 Bridgeway, tel. 415/332–3871. Admission free. Open summer, Tues.–Fri. 9–4, weekends 10–6; fall–spring, Tues.–Sat. 9–4.*

TIBURON AND ANGEL ISLAND

Some folks come to Tiburon with picnic baskets in hand and set out their spread on the harbor-front lawns. Others dock their boats at the harbor and head to one of the many waterside restaurants. Do both these things, and you'll have just about exhausted the possibilities of this tiny, peninsula-tip town north of Sausalito. The atmosphere is relaxed, and the views of Angel Island and San Francisco are superb, but since it's really no more that a cluster of waterfront gift shops and pricey boutiques, it can quickly become cloying. Escape uphill to **Old St. Hilary's Landmark and Wildflower Preserve,** which protects both a simple 1889 Carpenter Gothic church (now a historical and botanical museum) and the windswept field of rare black-jewel wildflowers in which it stands. The flowers bloom in May and June. *At top of Esperanza St., tel. 415/435–2567. Admission free. Open Apr.–Oct., Wed. and Sun. 1–4.*

During the Great Depression, a local grocer graciously honored his customers' credit, preventing countless Sausalito residents from going hungry. Today, where Bridgeway meets the bay, the eponymous Yee Tock Chee Park stands as a monument to him.

Most of Tiburon's restaurants and boutiques are on Main Street or on tree-lined **Ark Row,** which veers west at the end of Main Street. For less expensive delis and grocery stores, try Tiburon Boulevard, a few blocks up from the waterfront. **Windsor Vineyards** (72 Main St., tel. 415/435–3113) gives out samples of their 30 or so red, blush, white, sparkling, and dessert wines, all grown in Sonoma County. Bottles run $7–$25.

From Tiburon take the 15-minute ferry ride to **Angel Island,** a 750-acre state park where you can explore sandy beaches and old military installations. The island used to be thickly forested with Australian eucalyptus trees, but in June 1996 the park set in motion a controversial effort to eradicate all nonnative flora. With the imminent completion of this project, park officials assure visitors that the island will soon return to having only native species, and eucalyptus or no, the surrounding view is stunning. **Ayala Cove,** the area around the ferry landing, is congested with picnickers taking advantage of tables and barbecue grills (bring your own charcoal, as wood gathering is not allowed). The **Ayala Cove Visitor Center** (tel. 415/435–1915) distributes a brochure that details the history and geography of the island ($2). Nearby you can rent day-use lockers (50¢).

The 5-mi perimeter road that rings the island offers access to plenty of scenic and historic sites (*see* Hiking and Biking on Angel Island *in* Chapter 8), as well as plenty of tourists. To escape the crowds, tote your picnic fixings about a mile from Ayala Cove to **Camp Reynolds,** which functioned as an army camp from the Civil War to World War II. Plenty of people linger at the Commanding Officer's House along the road, but about a quarter mile past the old army barracks, at the water's edge, you'll find some isolated picnic tables and an outstanding close-up view of the Golden Gate Bridge. You can also camp on the island (*see* Chapter 7).

On the other side of the island is an **immigration station** once known as "the Ellis Island of the West," where immigrants (mostly Asian) were detained when trying to enter the United States between 1910 and 1940. A few poems written by despairing detainees are still etched into the walls.

COMING AND GOING

To get to Tiburon, exit U.S. 101 at Tiburon Boulevard and drive 3 mi to the tip of the peninsula, where Main Street curves to the right. The **Tiburon–Angel Island Ferry** (tel. 415/435–2131) leaves for Angel Island from Tiburon's Main Street Pier (21 Main St.) at 10, 11, 1, and 3 on spring and summer weekdays, and every hour from 10 to 5 on spring and summer weekends (schedules are subject to change; call ahead). Boats depart from Angel Island 20 minutes after they dock. Round-trip fares, which include entry fees for the island state park, are $6, plus $1 for bicycles. Cars are not allowed. Ferries also leave from Fisherman's Wharf in San Francisco (*see* Ferry Travel *in* Chapter 1). For information on bike rental on the island, *see* Hiking and Biking *in* Chapter 8.

MILL VALLEY

Nestled among California redwoods on the eastern flank of Mt. Tamalpais, Mill Valley is a community of millionaires and mountain bikers, where people have paid enormous sums of money for their solitude. Sneak up on them by taking the East Blithedale exit from U.S. 101.

On weekends all the action is on the plaza at the corner of Miller Street and Throckmorton Avenue; here people play Hacky Sack and drink coffee bought at one of the three nearby coffeehouses. The best of the lot is the **Depot Bookstore & Café** (87 Throckmorton Ave., at Miller St., tel. 415/383–2665), a favorite of mountain bikers after a run down Mt. Tam, as the locals call it. Another Mill Valley institution is 25-year-old **Village Music** (9 E. Blithedale Ave., at Throckmorton Ave., tel. 415/388–7400), where the collection is almost exclusively vinyl. The store has become a landmark on the international music map, attracting big-name customers like Mick Jagger. Consider sticking around Mill Valley after sunset to pay a visit to **Sweetwater** (153 Throckmorton Ave., at Miller Ave., tel. 415/388–2820), where on any given night local resident Huey Lewis or bluesman Roy Rogers might show up to jam. Covers range from about $5 to $20 (plus a two-drink minimum).

If you've come to enjoy more pastoral pursuits, take a "walk around the block," Mill Valley–style: The short **Three Wells** and **Cascade Falls** walks follow a gentle uphill route through the redwoods, along a creek, and past a few frigid swimming holes to a small waterfall. To get here, walk or drive up Throckmorton and turn left on Cascade Drive until you see the THREE WELLS sign nailed to a tree. Follow the path starting at the sign for about a quarter mile, cross the street, and continue uphill at the CASCADES FALLS sign.

SAN RAFAEL

Unassuming San Rafael, set between the foot of Mt. Tamalpais and San Rafael Hill, would attract more day-trippers from foggy San Francisco if people realized it's almost always warmer here than elsewhere in the Bay Area. In fact, that's exactly why the town was founded in the first place: In 1817, when Native Americans at San Francisco's Mission Dolores started dying at an alarming rate, missionaries built a hospital here so the sick could receive care in a more hospitable climate. The original buildings of the Mission San Rafael Archangel were torn down in the 1870s, but a replica of the **chapel** (corner of 5th and A Sts.), built of stuccoed concrete instead of the original adobe, now sits next to a gift shop selling Catholic kitsch. A block away from the chapel, **4th Street** is the town's main drag, lined with used bookstores, a large contingent of department stores, and some good cafés and clubs, including **New George's** (842 4th St., at Cijos St., tel. 415/457–1515) and **Cafe Kaldi** (835 4th St., at Cijos St., tel. 415/457–6562). Both have won Bay Area polls for "best nightlife in Marin." At New George's check out the live jazz, R&B, and acoustic entertainment; airy Cafe Kaldi stays open late—until midnight Sunday through Thursday and until 2 AM Friday and Saturday—and serves sandwiches and espresso to the local skater contingent. San Rafael's **Farmers' Market** (4th and B Sts., tel. 415/457–2266) takes place April–October, Thursday 6 PM–9 PM. The market is more like a weekly block party than a simple produce sale; locals come in droves to buy handicrafts, listen to live music, and let the kids take pony rides.

North of downtown—take the North San Pedro Road exit off U.S. 101—the enormous pink-and-blue **Marin Civic Center** (3501 Civic Center Dr., tel. 415/499–7407) offers guided tours (reserve ahead) of its impressive complex, designed by architect Frank Lloyd Wright. Concerned with preserving the natural contours of the site, Wright integrated the buildings into the surrounding landscape. The inside has been called one of the most functional and offbeat office spaces ever conceived. For information on dance and drama performances in the adjoining theater, call the Marin Center box office (tel. 415/472–3500).

Four miles east of San Rafael on North San Pedro Road is **China Camp State Park,** a pristine 1,600-acre wilderness area. Remnants of an old Chinese fishing village are still visible, and the oak knolls and saltwater marshes are great for hiking and camping (*see* Chapter 7). Park ($3) at China Camp Point for the 5-mi hike along the well-marked **Shoreline Trail.** The steeper **Bay View Trail** is a favorite of park rangers (it's also much less crowded). Pick up a trail map from the **ranger station** (tel. 415/456–0766), about a mile from the park entrance on North San Pedro Road.

MUIR WOODS AND MT. TAMALPAIS

MUIR WOODS NATIONAL MONUMENT

If you judge only by the crowded parking lot and tacky gift shop, the Muir Woods National Monument looks like just another overtouristed attraction to be avoided. This 550-acre park, however, contains one of the most impressive groves of coastal redwoods in the world, some more than 250 ft tall and over 800 years old. It's crowded, to be sure, but you can find rugged, unpopulated trails that meander along cool, fern-filled ridges high above the clogged canyon. The **Ocean View Trail,** one of the best for beating the crowds, ascends for 1⅓ mi before connecting with the **Lost Trail,** which descends through forests of Douglas fir before returning to the redwood groves. The Lost Trail hooks up with the **Fern Creek Trail,** which takes you back to the parking lot. The moderate hike is 3 mi round-trip and passes some of the park's most impressive stands of redwoods. (For more trail tips, *see* Hiking and Biking *in* Chapter 8.)

Neither picnicking nor camping is allowed in the park, but snacks are available at the gift shop, along with every type of redwood souvenir imaginable. The **visitor center** (tel. 415/388–2595) organizes free nature walks through the woods; call for the current schedule. From U.S. 101 take the Stinson Beach/Highway 1 exit and follow the signs. The monument is open daily 8 AM–sunset, and parking is free, though on sunny weekends Muir Woods is so crowded you may have to park a mile or more from the lot.

MUIR BEACH

If you continue on Highway 1 instead of following the turnoff to Muir Woods, you'll come to **Muir Beach,** a quiet strip of sand punctuated by hundreds of tidal pools. The strikingly scenic beach, the site of the first coastal settlement north of San Francisco, attracts folks looking to relax—not the Budweiser-and-volleyball crowd you'll find at Stinson Beach (*see below*), 6 mi farther north.

If you really want to get a feel for Marin's landscape, park your car at Muir Beach and hike the **Coastal Trail** (*see* Hiking and Biking *in* Chapter 8), which leads up a steep hill overlooking the ocean and then winds through a series of deserted coves and valleys. Return the same way and reward yourself with a pint of Guinness in front of the fire at the **Pelican Inn** (10 Pacific Way, at Hwy. 1, tel. 415/383–6000). You can eat lunch here for less than $10; the adjoining pub has a dartboard and a healthy sampling of British ales and bitters. Ask the innkeeper about renting horses from the nearby stables.

Less than a mile south of Stinson Beach, the **Green Gulch Farm Zen Center** (1601 Shoreline Hwy., tel. 415/383–3134) offers seven-week Zen training sessions, with everything from walking meditation to Japanese tea ceremonies—as well as less intensive programs for visitors. On Sunday you can sign up for instruction, meditation, a lecture, tea, a discussion period, and optional lunch ($5 for instruction, $6 for lunch); you may also wander the idyllic grounds and gardens any day of the week. Expect to pay a $5 parking fee on Sunday between 8:45 AM and 10:30 AM unless you have three or more people in your car. Another option is to carpool, as many people do, from the Shoreline Shopping Center (Miller Ave. exit, Hwy. 1, near U.S. 101); look for someone holding a GREEN GULCH CARPOOLING sign.

MT. TAMALPAIS STATE PARK

There are several theories about the origin of the name *Tamalpais,* but it's most commonly believed to be a combination of the Miwok words *tammal* (bay country) and *plis* (mountain). Begin your exploration of Mt. Tamalpais State Park at the **Pantoll ranger station** (tel. 415/388–2070), where you can pick up one of several topographical maps ($1–$6) describing all the trails and roads. If you're going mountain biking, take care to distinguish the fire trails (where biking is allowed) from the walking trails (where biking nets you an $80–$120 fine). One strenuous and popular hike, the 2-mi **Steep Ravine Trail** (*see* Hiking and Biking *in* Chapter 8), starts from the Pantoll station and takes you down a series of ladders to the Steep Ravine cabins (*see* Chapter 7). Parking is $5 in the Pantoll parking lot, but you can park for free anywhere along the road. The place is packed on weekends, so you'll have trouble parking if you arrive after noon.

The **summit** of Mt. Tam can be reached by car (look for the turnoff opposite the Pantoll station), and the gates are open dawn to dusk. Unfortunately, the military owned the summit until recently and left the kind of squat buildings and strange towers that only the military seems to build. Also near the summit is the open-air **Mountain Theater,** where for six consecutive summer Sundays, a play or musical is produced. For performance and ticket information ($15–$18) contact the Mountain Play Association (tel. 415/383–1100). Plays do sell out, so it's wise to purchase tickets well in advance.

STINSON BEACH

Six treacherous miles north of Muir Beach on Highway 1 lies Stinson Beach, one of northern California's most popular coastal towns. It's loaded with weather-beaten wooden houses and neighborly general stores, and its 3-mi beach—the longest in Marin County—has a beach-bum appeal that's hard to find north of Santa Cruz. Despite Stinson's isolated location, chilly waters, and lurking sharks, hordes of surfers and sun worshipers descend on this town of 1,200 every spring and summer weekend. Even if you're not planning to surf or swim, the 20-minute (10-mi) drive from Muir Woods to Stinson, past towering cliffs and jagged granite peaks, is incredible. For groceries, stop by **Beckers by the Beach** (101 Calle del Mar, tel. 415/868–1923), next to the stop sign on Highway 1. Traffic can be a problem on summer weekends, but there are plenty of scenic overlooks along the way to cushion the blow of bumper-to-bumper traffic. Bus service from San Francisco to Stinson Beach operates on weekends and holidays only: From the Transbay Terminal (1st and Mission Sts.), take Golden Gate Transit Bus 20 to Marin City, then transfer to Bus 63. For information on surfboard rentals, *see* Water Sports *in* Chapter 8.

Along Bolinas Lagoon, just north of Stinson on Highway 1, you'll find **Audubon Canyon Ranch** (tel. 415/868–9244), a 1,000-acre nesting ground for blue herons, snowy egrets, and other shore birds. The sanctuary and its hiking trails are open to the public March 15–July 15, weekends 10–4 (additional hours Tuesday–Thursday 2–4 by appointment only). There's a small museum ($5 donation suggested) with geological and natural history displays, a bookstore, a gift shop, and a picnic area.

For an encounter with a different sort of wildlife, walk down to **Red Rocks Beach,** where during extremely low tides, caves containing hot springs are revealed—as well as the bare buns of bathers. Even when the caves are concealed by water, the beach is peopled by nudists: Leave your inhibitions in the car. To get here, drive ¾ mi south of Stinson Beach and park in the big gravel lot you'll see on the right. A path leads down to the beach.

BOLINAS

A few miles north of Audubon Canyon Ranch (*see above*) lies Bolinas, a town dedicated to discouraging tourism: Locals are perpetually taking down the sign marking the Bolinas/Olema Road (it's the first left after you curve around the lagoon to your left). If you breeze into town to wander Main Street and do some shopping, you'll feel tolerated at best. The **Fourth of July** brings out the town's friendliest faces; past festivities have included outrageous parades and a tug-of-war with Stinson Beach (the loser ended up in the muddy mouth of the estuary between the two towns).

Though the Bolinas of the '90s looks much like any of Marin's wealthy towns, you'll still find a few bearded radicals hanging out on street corners, strumming their guitars or fixing their VW microbuses, and a handful of '60s-style establishments. The **Bolinas People's Store** (14 Wharf Rd., at Brighton Ave., tel. 415/868–1433) is famous for its fresh, high-quality local produce, grown by the same sweaty hippies who once gave Bolinas so much of its character. For a bite to eat, go next door to the **Bolinas Bay Bakery and Café** (20 Wharf Rd., tel. 415/868–0211), stocked with freshly baked goods, pasta salads, and pizzas. The only nightlife in town is **Smiley's Schooner Saloon** (41 Wharf Rd., at Brighton Ave., tel. 415/868–1311), ostensibly the oldest continually operated saloon in California. Huddled around the pool table and jukebox are an odd combination of suit-and-tie professionals and tie-dyed hippies.

A worthwhile detour is the **Point Reyes Bird Observatory** (tel. 415/868–0655), which harbors 225 species of birds. From the second stop sign on Bolinas/Olema Road, take Mesa Road 4½ mi north. It's open year-round dawn to dusk, and admission is free (donations requested). On your way you'll pass a turnoff for **Duxberry Reef,** a peaceful breaker that's dotted with hundreds of tidal pools. To reach the reef from Mesa Road, go left on Overlook Drive and right on Ocean Park Way. For hikes in this area, see Chapter 8.

POINT REYES NATIONAL SEASHORE

Explore the Point Reyes National Seashore—a 66,500-acre mosaic of marshes, ferocious cliffs, and undisturbed beaches—and you'll feel a lot farther than 40 mi away from San Francisco. And with good reason: Point Reyes is on the Pacific tectonic plate, while most of the rest of California is on the North American plate. As a result, its bedrock, plants, and the terrain are all very different from the rest of the Bay Area. Even though it's isolated, Point Reyes is a manageable day trip from San Francisco, a drive of about 90 minutes each way. There are hundreds of hiking trails on the peninsula (see

With its lush grazing land and rambling farms, Point Reyes—a hammerhead-shaped peninsula that juts 10 mi into the ocean— could easily pass for western Ireland, minus the pubs.

Chapter 8), along with four backpackers-only campgrounds and an excellent hostel (see Chapter 7), if you want to spend the night.

Twelve miles north of Bolinas on Highway 1, past the block-long town of Olema, look for a sign marking the turnoff for Point Reyes and the **Bear Valley Visitor Information Center** (Bear Valley Rd., tel. 415/663–1092), open weekdays 9–5, weekends 8–5. Here you can see a short orientation film, sign up for ranger-led tours, explore a small museum of cultural and natural history, or pick up trail maps and camping permits. A short walk away, look for the replica of a typical Miwok village, built on the ruins of a 400-year-old Native American farming settlement. Also nearby is the **Bear Valley Trail,** a lightly traveled 4-mi hike that wanders through the woods and down to a secluded beach with a view of the peninsula.

Two miles farther down Bear Valley Road (which turns into Sir Francis Drake Boulevard), you'll pass through the quiet town of **Inverness.** Coming across this town's Czech architecture (it's full of oddly colored, intricately carved wooden houses) can be disorienting after miles of empty coastline, but the town's Eastern European flavor is genuine. In 1935, after a freighter ran aground in San Francisco Bay, a number of its Czech deckhands jumped ship and settled here. Since then dozens of Czech families have immigrated to Inverness, bringing their culture, language, and cuisine.

Continue west through Inverness on Sir Francis Drake Boulevard, then take Drakes Beach Road to a massive stretch of white sand fittingly called **Drakes Beach**—supposedly Sir Francis himself landed here on his world tour. It's often windy and too rough for swimming (unless you're a great white shark— they love it here), but the beach is terrific for sunning.

A quarter mile north of Drakes Beach, a sign directs you to the **Point Reyes Lighthouse** (tel. 415/669–1534), 6 mi to the west. It's open Thursday–Monday 10–5, except during particularly stormy or windy weather. Admission is free. From the parking lot a steep trail leads down to the lighthouse, and a dozen or so trails are carved into the surrounding cliffs. The ¾-mi hike to **Chimney Rock** is one of the most scenic; look for the trailhead in the parking lot. On clear days you can see San Francisco, but usually thick fog provides little visibility. From mid-December to April, and especially in January and March, this is a great place to look for the gray whales on their 12,000-mi round-trip migration along the Pacific coast.

To reach Point Reyes from San Francisco, cross the Golden Gate Bridge on U.S. 101. If speed is more important than scenery, exit at Sir Francis Drake Boulevard and follow it 21 mi to the coast. Eventually you'll end up 2 mi north of Olema on Highway 1. Otherwise, take the Stinson Beach/Highway 1 exit and enjoy the 30-mi curvy, scenic drive along the coast. Bus service from San Francisco to Point Reyes operates on weekends and holidays only: From the Transbay Terminal (1st and Mission Sts.) take any Golden Gate Transit bus to the San Rafael Transit Center (Bus 80 is the most direct), then transfer to Bus 65.

There aren't too many places to eat in Point Reyes, so stock up in San Francisco or at the **Bovine Bakery** (11315 Hwy. 1, 2 mi north of Olema, tel. 415/663–9420). They have excellent, reasonably priced sandwiches, pastries, and breads—the perfect makings for a picnic. The most popular picnic stop is Inverness's **Perry's Delicatessen** (12301 Sir Francis Drake Blvd., near Vallejo Ave., tel. 415/663–1491). For less than $6, you can brown-bag one of their crab sandwiches and a pasta salad. Also in Inverness is the **Gray Whale Inn** (12781 Sir Francis Drake Blvd., tel. 415/669–1244), good for home-style pizzas, pastries, sandwiches, coffee, and beer. It's more expensive than Perry's, but the sunny patio is a good place to watch day fade into night.

SOUTH BAY

Heading south on U.S. 101 brings a change of both scenery and pace. As the cosmopolitan frenzy of San Francisco fades, you sense the quiet blandness of industrial parks, shopping malls, and tract housing. To its credit, the South Bay has its own interesting, amusing, or just plain weird attractions that San Francisco snobs thoroughly underrate (or don't know about). The cities that stretch south from San Francisco to San Jose lie on what locals refer to as the **Peninsula**, a finger of land wedged between the San Francisco Bay on the east and the Pacific Ocean on the west; a number of cities, including Palo Alto—home to acclaimed Stanford University—make for easy day trips from San Francisco. Geographically near but seemingly worlds away from the urban commotion of the San Jose area and the Peninsula, the secluded **San Mateo County coast** is a long stretch of windswept coastline punctuated by quiet coastal communities.

PALO ALTO

Palo Alto, about 30 mi south of San Francisco, is mostly known as the home of **Stanford University,** and it's certainly worth the drive just to check out the beautiful 8,200-acre campus. However, contrary to popular Bay Area opinion (held particularly by UC Berkeley students, Stanford's arch rivals), the town of Palo Alto itself has some cultural attractions that are worth a look, as well as a downtown area with a few good cafés and restaurants. Off U.S. 101, **University Avenue,** between Middlefield Road and High Street, is Palo Alto's main drag; west of El Camino Real it metamorphoses into **Palm Drive,** Stanford's entrance and main thoroughfare. University Avenue travels through Palo Alto's oldest and wealthiest neighborhood—keep your eyes peeled for mansions. In the downtown area University Avenue and its side streets are loaded with restaurants, cafés, galleries, boutiques, and bookstores. All are rather upscale for a student shopping district, but the streets are pleasantly punctuated by plazas with benches and plants.

STANFORD UNIVERSITY

Sometimes called the Ivy League university of the West Coast, Stanford opened its doors to scholars in October 1891. The land it occupies was once a stud farm, hence the school's popular nickname, the Farm. Today its mustard-color buildings combine Romanesque and Spanish-mission styles to achieve a look that's described alternately as Western Ivy League and Giant Taco Bell.

From downtown enter the campus along the aptly named Palm Drive, which will take you to the **quad,** the heart of campus and a popular hangout. At the **visitor center** (tel. 650/723–2560) in Memorial Hall you can pick up free maps or take an hour-long guided walking tour (departures at 11 and 3:15 daily). Standing in the center of the quad is the stately Romanesque **Memorial Church,** best known for its Venetian mosaic. Organ recitals take place in the church; ask at the visitor center for a schedule. Near the entrance to the quad, the grassy **Memorial Court** has a couple of Auguste Rodin statues including *The Burghers of Calais,* depicting 14th-century French martyrs at the moment of painful departure from their families and other citizens. A less traditional New Guinean **sculpture garden,** installed in 1995, can be found near the intersection of Lomita Drive and St. Theresa Street. Just to the south of the quad, the 280-ft **Hoover Tower** thrusts mightily into the sky. It's home to the famed Hoover Institution for the Study of War, Revolution, and Peace. To get the classic view of campus and parts of Palo Alto, pay $2 to climb to the tower's observation deck; it's open daily 10–4:30.

The **Stanford Museum of Art** has been closed since 1989 due to damage from the Loma Prieta earthquake (it's scheduled to reopen in January 1999), and the **Rodin Sculpture Garden,** a collection of 20 or so works by French sculptor Auguste Rodin (1840–1917), will be closed from October 1998 until April 1999. If you can make it to the sculpture garden when it's open, do so. Most pieces depict nudes in various stages of introspection, ecstasy, or anguish. Check out the particularly intense *Gates of Hell*— the subject of innumerable art history lectures and descriptive tours (held at 2 every Wednesday and on weekends; call for details). The sculptures are clustered in a small area to the left of the art museum. *Museum Way and Lomita Dr., tel. 650/723–3469. From Palm Dr. turn right on Museum Way, 1 block past Campus Dr.*

The huge, sprawling campus is best explored by bike (the cycling is even better in the foothills west of the university). For rentals, try **Campus Bike Shop** (551 Salvatierra St., on campus, tel. 650/325–2945), which can get you rolling on a mountain bike for $15 a day or a three-speed for $8. Either kind of bike requires a cash, check, or credit card deposit.

STANFORD LINEAR ACCELERATOR

Even if you're only vaguely interested in science, make the trek up Sand Hill Road (west from campus toward I-280) to see this masterpiece of modern ingenuity. The 2-mi-long atom smasher is truly amazing—thousands of house-size machines, dials, and diodes, as well as scientists who get excited when you mention n-orbits and electrons. Reserve space for the free two-hour tour, held twice a week, which includes a slide show and lecture (days and times vary); it's geared toward lay people and is extremely interesting. The accelerator is only open to the public during tour times. *2575 Sand Hill Rd., Menlo Park, tel. 650/926–2204. From I-280, exit east at Sand Hill Rd.*

BARBIE HALL OF FAME

"Barbie mimics society; whatever we've done, she's done," says Evelyn Burkhalter, founder of the Barbie Hall of Fame. She's put together the largest collection of Barbie dolls on public display in the world, with 16,000 plastic figures in residence. Evelyn says just about every fashion and lifestyle trend of the past few decades can be seen in these halls. Don't miss the infamous Talking Math Barbie, who says, "Math is *so hard*"—Mattel took a lot of heat from feminists for that one. *433 Waverly St., at University Ave., tel. 650/326–5841. Admission $6. Open Tues.–Fri. 1:30–4:30, Sat. 10–noon and 1:30–4:30.*

NEAR PALO ALTO

NASA AMES RESEARCH CENTER

For a true technological trip, visit this 140-acre research center devoted to the design of all types of flying machines, at Moffett Field in Mountain View (about 5 mi southeast of Palo Alto). Though the research facility is normally closed to the general public, you can check out the aviation and space-flight paraphernalia at the **NASA Visitors Center Museum,** which is open weekdays 8–4:30. Better yet, call two weeks ahead and sign up for an escorted tour of the main plant. Depending on what's available that day, the free two-hour tour may take you around flight simulators, design centers, retired research crafts, or construction hangars. *Tel. 650/604–6274. From U.S. 101, exit at Moffett Field, left on Moffett Blvd. at main gate, and head toward space shuttle.*

SAN JOSE

Too sprawling to have cultivated any sort of cohesive identity, northern California's largest city wallows in misunderstanding. To many, San Jose is another faceless component of **Silicon Valley**—the conceptual land of whirring computer chips and complex equations. In reality, San Jose is part high-tech wonderland and part minimall suburbia. It's encircled by mountain ranges, buffered by city parks and gardens, and home to museums, symphonies, and wineries as well as industrial parks, computer companies, and corporate headquarters.

The new billion-dollar **downtown** is a good place to start exploring. Hop on the **light rail** (tel. 408/321–2300) that connects San Jose State University on one end with the Center for Performing Arts on the other (fare is $1.10); its numerous stops should give you a good overview of the city center, which is architecturally interesting in its attempt to meld existing Old West themes with modern styles and materials (note the traditional small-town clock tower built from marble and stainless steel). Around the intersection of Market and San Carlos streets you'll find a number of pedestrian plazas and a host of museums, including the **Tech Museum of Innovation** (145 W. San Carlos St., across from Convention Center, tel. 408/279–7150), a hands-on technology museum that inspires admiration for the wizardry of the computer age; it's well worth the $6 admission. **Plaza de César Chávez** (S. Market St., in front of Fairmont Hotel) is a pleasant grassy strip that runs for two blocks, complete with benches and a fountain great for splashing around (the water shoots straight up out of grates in the ground).

Though it's known more for its corporate image than anything else, San Jose is becoming increasingly recognized for its cultural diversity. You can get the full flavor in July, when the three-day **San Jose America Festival** (tel. 408/534–4414) brings live entertainment and crafts booths to town. Other festivals to look for: June 19's **Juneteenth Festival** (tel. 408/292–3157) showcases the achievements of African-Americans through lecture, cinema, art, and cultural foods. For some hip action (literally) catch the **Tahiti Fête** (tel. 408/486–9177), a three-day dance competition in July that brings together Tahitian dance groups (*halaus*) from all over the Bay Area and even draws dancers from as far as Hawaii. August nights heat up (as if it weren't already scorching) when the **San Jose Jazz Festival** (tel. 408/457–1141) rolls into town.

The **Rosicrucian Egyptian Museum and Planetarium** houses one of the most impressive collections of Egyptian, Assyrian, and Babylonian artifacts west of the Nile. Standouts are the animal and human mummies, the underground tomb, and the decorative wall reliefs. Sign up for a guided tour of the walk-through replica of a pyramid tomb or catch a planetarium show (tel. 408/947–3634 for show times and ticket prices). *1342 Naglee Ave., at Park Ave., tel. 408/947–3636. Get off I–880 at Alameda East exit, turn right at Naglee Ave. Admission $7. Open daily 9–5 (last entry at 4:30).*

The student population of San Jose State has gradually encouraged the growth of a trendier side of downtown, which has become known as **SoFA** (South of First Area)—a small section roughly between East Carlos and West Reed streets. Make a beeline here if you find yourself in San Jose after dark (*see* South Bay *in* Chapter 6).

NEAR SAN JOSE

GARBAGE MUSEUM

Californians generate more garbage per capita than any other group of people in the world, and this museum gives you some dramatic ways to feel guilty about it. The massive 100-ft Wall of Garbage exhibit represents merely one second's worth of what the country is continually throwing out. At least there's the Recycling Hall, where a huge magnet separates steel and iron from a mountain of tin cans.

1601 Dixon Landing Rd., Milpitas, tel. 408/262–1401. Take Dixon Landing exit off I–880, 5 mi north of San Jose. Admission free. Open weekdays 7:30–5.

GREAT AMERICA

Favorite rides here include the occasionally drenching water ride called **Logger's Run** and the stand-up **Vortex** roller coaster, which cost a whopping $5 million to build. Newest is the **Drop Zone**—the world's tallest free fall, at 22 stories. If you'd rather not eat amusement park food, bring your own, leave it in a locker near the front gate, and eat in the picnic area outside. *Great America Pkwy., Santa Clara, tel. 408/988–1776. Take Great America Pkwy. exit off U.S 101, about 10 mi north of San Jose. Admission $28. Open spring, weekends only 10–9; fall, weekends only 10–9; summer, Sun.–Fri. 10–9, Sat. 10–11.*

WINCHESTER MYSTERY HOUSE

The continuous construction of this 160-room Victorian mansion occupied Sarah Winchester's life for 38 years until her death. Apparently Mrs. Winchester was told by a fortuneteller to begin nonstop construction to placate the ghosts of those killed by Winchester guns; according to the seer, if she followed through with the project, she would have eternal life. (Luckily, her $20 million inheritance was enough to fund her venture!) The end result was a floor plan so bizarre and complex that she and her servants used maps to get around. On March 5, 1996, the San Jose City Council designated the Winchester Mansion a city landmark. General building manager Keith Kittle was quoted in the *San Francisco Chronicle* as saying, "I think Sarah Winchester would be proud. We're going to have a seance and talk to her and see." *525 S. Winchester Blvd., tel. 408/247–2101. From I–280, take Stevens Creek exit to Winchester Blvd. Admission $13. Open daily 9–5.*

SAN MATEO COUNTY COAST

PACIFICA AND MONTARA

Highway 1 and the secluded San Mateo County coast consist of more than 75 mi of winding shoreline and gently undulating hills that seem a world away from the overdeveloped inland communities. Along the highway are long, sandy beaches frequently devoid of any life aside from the local sea lions, surfers, and gulls; small towns just beginning to awaken to their potential as tourist destinations; and redwood groves filled with great hiking trails. At the north end of the coast, about 20 minutes south of San Francisco along Highway 1, Pacifica and Montara are sleepy seaside towns that offer an easy escape from urban chaos.

The "historic" section of Pacifica, on the northernmost outskirts of town, is full of unpretentious bungalow-style homes that once served as weekend retreats for wealthy San Franciscans but today house a majority of the town's locals. Pacifica's small commercial district, to the south, is an eclectic combination of old mom-and-pop stores and upscale specialty shops, the latter suggesting the town is growing a little weary of its backwater authenticity and wants to start attracting some yuppie weekend tourists. Linking past and present are the recently renovated paved promenade and old fishing pier. Come here to smell the saltwater, feed the pigeons, and watch fishermen ply their trade; the pier also affords brilliant views of San Francisco and Marin County.

In addition to some fine hiking trails (*see* Chapter 8), Pacifica harbors a number of dark-sand beaches. About 2 mi south of old Pacifica, **Rockaway Beach** consists of two large dollops of sand on either end of a gorgeous cove—just large enough for half a dozen sunbathers and a handful of surfers and fishermen (swimming is not advised here as the waves are rough). Immediately south of Rockaway you'll come to the more popular **Pacifica State Beach,** a longer stretch of sand favored by surfers and a fair number of local sun worshipers.

Just a few miles farther south of San Francisco, Montara consists almost entirely of beach—its commercial district is virtually nonexistent. **Montara State Beach,** in the north end of town, is a wide, picturesque stretch of sand, less crowded than Pacifica's beaches. It's a good place to catch some rays, play Frisbee, have a picnic, or walk along the beach. Half a mile farther north, **Gray Whale Cove State Beach** (tel. 650/728–5336) is an American anomaly: a government-supported clothing-optional beach. Entrance to the spectacular, secluded cove is $5. Immediately south of Montara, in Moss Beach, the rich tide pools of the **James V. Fitzgerald Marine Reserve** (tel. 650/728–3584) stretch along the coast for 4 mi. Go at low tide (call ahead to find out when) to check out abalone, barnacles, kelp, shells, and maybe an octopus or two; but remember, this is a reserve, so look but don't touch. Pick up a tidal timetable at the Point Montara Lighthouse Hostel (*see* Chapter 7); from there you can reach the reserve by taking Highway 1 south to California Avenue and turning right. The beaches and reserve are open from dawn to dusk.

For a meal in Pacifica, head straight to Francisco Boulevard, paralleling Highway 1 to the west. Here you'll find **Pacifica Thai Cuisine** (1966 Francisco Blvd., tel. 650/355–1678)—good for traditional specialties like chicken curry in coconut milk ($7)—and the oddly named **Pacifica Harry** (1780 Francisco Blvd., tel. 650/738–8300), an upscale Chinese restaurant with enticing entrées like cashew-nut shrimp. Both restaurants have vegetarian options. In Montara, **A Coastal Affair** (Hwy. 1 at 8th St., tel. 650/728–5229), ⅓-mi north of the Point Montara Lighthouse Hostel (*see* Chapter 7), is a combination craft gallery and café, with excellent espresso and freshly made sandwiches. Half a mile south of the hostel, in Moss Beach, **El Gran Amigo** (2448 Hwy. 1, at Virginia Ave., tel. 650/728–3815) serves up a wide variety of authentic Mexican specialties including enchiladas and nachos. Across the street, **Coastside Market** (501 Virginia Ave., tel. 650/728–3142) is an amply stocked spot to buy picnic supplies.

Get to Pacifica and Montara via public transportation by taking BART to the Daly City or Colma station. From Daly City take SamTrans Bus 1L, and from Colma take Bus 1C. Both bus lines will take you down Highway 1. Fares are $1.

HALF MOON BAY

Twenty-eight miles south of San Francisco, Half Moon Bay is the closest thing to a major town along the San Mateo County coast. In the late 1800s this was a sleepy agricultural hamlet called Spanish Town—until Prohibition paved the way for Canadian bootleggers to seek refuge (and a good time) in the town's then-untrafficked streets. The festive spirit still lives on: These days Half Moon Bay hosts a variety of festivals and events and is famous for growing pumpkins, Christmas trees, and flowers. It's also a mecca for surfers, with its immense waves (*see* Water Sports *in* Chapter 8). The revitalized downtown area centers around **Main Street,** which parallels Highway 1; the cozy street is cluttered with crafts stores, produce markets, gardens, cafés, and straightforward burger joints. If lolling on the beach is more your speed, follow Kelly Avenue west from Highway 1 to the popular **Half Moon Bay State Beach,** actually a series of beaches covering more than 2 mi. To avoid the $5 parking fee, walk from downtown. Before too long it will get a little chilly as you near the water, a perfect excuse to trek 2 mi inland along Highway 92 and sample—for free—the local wines at **Obester Winery** (12341 San Mateo Rd., tel. 650/726–9463), open daily 10–5.

Half Moon Bay hosts literally dozens of annual festivals, any of which you could plan a visit around. The largest and most popular is the **Art and Pumpkin Festival,** held the weekend after Columbus Day. The high-spirited fall celebration includes live music, local foods, crafts, vendors, a children's parade, and outrageous pie-eating and pumpkin-carving contests. Also popular is the aptly named **Coastal Flower Market,** which takes place on the third Saturday of each month from May through September. Other yearly events include the riotous **Human Race** every May, in which entrants use every wacky scheme they can devise to carry other contestants along the course; the **Brew Ha-Ha** beer- and sausage-tasting festival each spring; and the daring **California Coast Air Show,** which takes place at Half Moon Bay's tiny airport in the fall. For more information on any of these festivals, contact the **Half Moon Bay Chamber of Commerce** (520 Kelly Ave., at Hwy. 1, tel. 650/726–8380 or 650/726–5202). Traffic can be overwhelming during the festivals; avoid gridlock headaches by visiting on a weekday when activity is more subdued. Better yet, leave your car behind and take SamTrans Bus 1L from the Daly City BART station (Bus 1C from Colma BART).

For a meal, Half Moon Bay offers everything from health food markets to overpriced seafood restaurants. The best of the former is **Healing Moon Natural Foods Market** (523 Main St., tel. 650/726–7881); if you're not looking for groceries, serve yourself a cup of soup and eat it on the peaceful outdoor patio. At **La Di Da** (500C Purissima St., tel. 650/726–1663) you can sip a cherry mocha while getting your palm read—or come for $2 movie night. At the **Half Moon Bay Bakery** (514 Main St., tel. 650/726–4841) watch piping hot muffins emerge from a 19th-century brick oven. You'll find reasonably priced seafood—a rarity in this area—at the **Flying Fish Grill** (99 Hwy. 92, at Main St., tel. 650/712–1125), closed Monday.

SAN GREGORIO TO ANO NUEVO

Day-trippers seeking sand, sea, and forest in quiet solitude are likely to find it along the desolate stretch of coastline south of Half Moon Bay. With the exception of Año Nuevo State Reserve during the elephant seals' mating season, this area is nearly deserted year-round. Though the beaches are usually cold and the choice of affordable food and lodging limited, the area is rich with natural assets: tide pools at Pescadero State Beach, the sky-high trees lining Highway 84 through La Honda—and the cliff-hugging Pigeon Point Lighthouse Hostel (*see* Chapter 7) is nothing short of spectacular.

SAN GREGORIO

Although not much of a destination in itself, San Gregorio is a worthwhile stop if you're traveling up or down the coast between Santa Cruz and Half Moon Bay. Half the fun is the drive in from the coast to this hitching-post of a town, at the junction of Highways 1 and 84—even if you don't come by the spectacular coast road. **Highway 84,** the east–west road running to San Gregorio from I–280 (also known as La Honda Road), is not for the car-sickness-prone; but if you can take it, the highway is so thick with redwoods you'll barely believe it's daytime. Best of all, the road spits you out at the isolated **San Gregorio State Beach,** where you can lie back and soak up some rays or, more likely, throw on a sweater and battle the wind as the fog comes rolling in. If you get too cold, the bluff north of the parking lot is a good place for a brisk, blood-warming walk.

Don't miss the **San Gregorio General Store** (Stage Rd., tel. 650/726–0565), open daily 9–6, Friday until 7, a mile east of Highway 1 on Highway 84. This eclectic Old West–style store, which has served the ranching and farming community since 1889, sells everything from used books and stuffed animals to cast-iron pots and antiques (it also doubles as the town saloon and community center). Weekends bring live bands playing bluegrass and Grateful Dead covers; locals, bicyclists, and tourists gather round to stomp their heels and drink local brews.

LA HONDA

For an interesting contrast to coastal scenery, head inland about 11 mi east of Highway 1 to the densely forested community of La Honda—a town that seems almost lost in the shadows of countless giant redwoods. If you don't have time to head north to California's redwood country, this is a surprisingly good substitute. Before you head out into the wilds, stop at the **Pioneer Market** (La Honda Center, tel. 650/747–0551), where you can stock up on camping supplies and sandwiches; the **Cool Water Café** (8725 La Honda Rd., tel. 650/747–9600), offering barbecued chicken sandwiches and espresso drinks, open daily until 8; and **Apple Jack's Tavern** (La Honda Rd., tel. 650/747–0331). The last is a scruffy bar, open weekdays noon–2 AM and weekends 10 AM–2 AM, where men drink their whiskey straight up, the women are loud and boisterous, and a brawl seems ready to erupt any minute.

Ringing the tiny town are four state and county parks whose forested hills provide excellent terrain for hiking and biking (*see* Chapter 8). Take Highway 84 about a mile west of La Honda, make a left on Alpine Road, and 4½ mi later you'll come to the parking lot of **Pescadero Creek County Park** (tel. 650/879–0212), a secluded expanse of fir- and pine-covered hills crisscrossed by a series of gentle streams. From the parking lot follow the **Tarwater Trail Loop** in either direction for a moderate hike of about 2 mi, which will take you from a ridge with ocean views down through the scrub and into the redwoods. For yet another encounter with towering redwoods, Douglas fir, and pine trees, drive a bit farther along Alpine Road and you'll reach the turnoff for **Portola Redwood State Park** (Portola State Park Rd., tel. 650/948–9098), 2,400 acres of even more remote and scenic forest—the only drawback is the $5 parking fee. Just past the entrance to the park, the visitor center sells trail maps ($1) and wood ($3) for camping (*see* South Bay *in* Chapter 7). For information on hikes here, *see* Chapter 8.

Two more woodsy parks lie on Pescadero Road, which meets up with Alpine Road a mile south of Highway 84. The first is **Sam McDonald County Park** (for information call Memorial County Park, tel. 650/879–0238), a small, almost deserted redwood forest good for short hikes and complete solitude. A bit farther along Pescadero Road you'll come to **Memorial County Park** (tel. 650/879–0238), the most developed of the four parks—with a freshwater swimming hole, picnic areas, fire roads popular with mountain bikers, and a number of short- and medium-length hiking trails through the redwoods (*see* Hiking and Biking *in* Chapter 8). To avoid the $4 parking fee at Memorial, park on the side of the road just outside the entrance.

THE MERRY PRANKSTERS

In the early 1960s La Honda was home to one of the hippie era's most renowned groups of psychedelic crazies, the Merry Pranksters. Led by Ken Kesey, author of "One Flew Over the Cuckoo's Nest," the pranksters spent several years on a La Honda farm exploring "states of nonordinary reality"— dropping acid and smoking dope. When La Honda became too limiting, they outfitted an old school bus with Day-Glo paintings and filming and recording equipment and set off to travel across the country, a journey made famous by Tom Wolfe in his popular chronicle "The Electric Kool-Aid Acid Test."

PESCADERO

In the flatlands 1 mi inland from the coast on Pescadero Road is the small fishing village of Pescadero. More than 100 years ago all the wooden buildings here were painted white with paint that washed up when the clipper ship *Carrier Pigeon* crashed into the rocks off Pigeon Point, a few miles south of town. Today the bakery, general store, bank, local post office, and other shops that populate Pescadero still retain their whitewashed uniformity, giving this town, in the flatlands a mile inland from the coast on Pescadero Road, a calming, subdued ambience.

After you've rambled around the three blocks that make up Pescadero's commercial district, head to **Duarte's Tavern** (202 Stage Rd., at Pescadero Rd., tel. 650/879–0464), open 7 AM–9 PM daily, a combination bar and restaurant. Duarte's has been run by four generations of Duartes since 1894, and they're in no big hurry to serve you before the next generation takes over. The homey restaurant serves everything from peanut butter and jelly sandwiches to lamb chops, but it's most famous for its cream of artichoke soup, made with local produce, as well as fresh seafood plates and homemade pies.

On the coast just west of town, you'll find **Pescadero State Beach,** a long, sandy expanse rich with tide pools. Just north of the beach, the **Pescadero Marsh Reserve** (tel. 650/879–2170) is a protected area favored by ornithologists. Free guided walks leave from the parking lot just south of Pescadero Creek on Saturday at 10:30 and Sunday at 1 year-round, weather permitting. If you prefer to take to the hills, **Butano State Park** (tel. 650/879–0173), 5 mi south of Pescadero on Cloverdale Road, has 20 mi of trails on 2,700 acres (*see* Chapter 8). You can reach the park from Gazos Creek Road, off Highway 1 near Año Nuevo State Reserve (*see below*), or take Pescadero Road a couple miles east from town and head south on Cloverdale; there's a $5 parking fee.

ANO NUEVO STATE RESERVE

Named by explorer Sebastian Viscaino on New Year's Day 1603, the Punta del Año Nuevo is one of the few places in the world where you can safely view live elephant seals up close. Not only that, if you're here between December and March, you get to watch them do the wild thing. During mating season you'll need to make reservations up to eight weeks in advance through Destinet (tel. 800/444–7275), and you can only visit the reserve on one of the 2½-hour guided walks ($4, plus a $4 parking fee). If you're lucky, you may catch sight of migrating gray whales at the same time. Sea lions, sea otters, and harbor seals have also been known to make appearances, mostly off the coast and on Año Nuevo Island, inhabited only by seals and birds.

Though not as thrilling as the fighting and preening of mating season, the elephant seals come ashore from April through September to shed their old, furry brown skin for a sleek new one; the yearlings stick around until November, gaining strength for the upcoming months spent entirely in the water. At these times you can gain access to the reserve by obtaining a free permit from the visitor center (tel. 650/879–

2025), open April through September, daily 8–6, October through November, daily 8–4. To avoid the $4 parking fee, continue about a quarter mile south past the main reserve entrance and park on the west side of Highway 1 (where you'll also find an alternate trail to the reserve). The path to the elephant seals' beach from the main parking lot is 1½ mi long; and if you come in spring, you'll be treated to the sight of thousands of colorful wildflowers along the trail. The reserve, about 40 mi south of San Francisco, can be reached on SamTrans Bus 96C (*see* Bus Travel *in* Chapter 1).

SHOPPING

REVISED BY JENNIFER BREWER

I n the Bay Area, your challenge won't be finding something to buy, but deciding how much you're willing to spend. On trendy **Haight Street** neohippies will find wall-to-wall sellers of secondhand and vintage clothing, alternative music shops, tie-dye boutiques, costume jewelry shops, and radical bookstores—all selling their wares at a premium. A cheaper option is the **Mission District,** rife with warehouses for secondhand clothing, books, and furniture, with *botanicas* and other magic shops for those who want to flirt with the occult. **Chinatown** has tons of inexpensive electronic goods and silk items; the **Castro** abounds with places catering to gay lifestyles; and the **South of Market** area has bargain warehouses that stock slightly flawed brand-name threads at good prices. **North Beach** has unique (and often expensive) specialty stores, mostly boutiques selling fabulous women's fashions. Tony **Union Street,** at the foot of Pacific Heights, is off-limits to budget travelers—though the shops full of beautiful clothing and antiques make for pleasant window-shopping.

Downtown San Francisco is a shopper's paradise in and of itself—providing you have the credit cards to pay. The **Embarcadero Center** (Clay and Battery Sts. between Drumm and Sacramento Sts., tel. 800/733–6318) is an eight-block complex with 175 chichi shops catering to harried Financial District types on their lunch breaks. **San Francisco Shopping Centre** (865 Market St., between 4th and 5th Sts.) houses a Nordstrom department store and dozens of other upscale shops, built around a dizzying four-story atrium. The city's ritziest emporiums (*see box* Tony Shopping in Union Square, *below*) are clustered around **Union Square** and adjacent **Post Street.** On Post alone you'll find Giorgio Armani, Ralph Lauren, Bulgari, Brooks Brothers, Coach, Williams-Sonoma, Mark Cross, Versace, Cartier, Gumps, Eddie Bauer, and a brand-new, three-story NikeTown. This is first-class shopping at its finest.

In the East Bay, Oakland's few viable shopping districts, like **Piedmont Avenue** and **Rockridge** (College Ave. between Alcatraz Ave. and Broadway), are chock-full of boutiques and antiques stores. Head to **Berkeley** if you're looking for political consumerism, eco-friendly products, abundant bookstores, or used clothing to fit cheapskate student budgets. **Telegraph Avenue,** next to the UC Berkeley campus, is a rollicking seven-day street fair, with stands selling tie-dye clothing, cheap silver jewelry, handmade pottery, and New Age crystals.

NEW CLOTHES

Bay Area clothing stores stock everything from Armani suits to vinyl pants. The trick is knowing where to look and when to buy. Almost all clothing stores slash prices by 30%–50% January–February and July–August to make way for next season's fashions. Year-round, discount outlets like **Loehmann's** (*see below*) offer amazing bargains—if you have the stamina to paw through racks of flowered dresses in search of a Calvin Klein. This section steers you toward some of the cheaper clothing stores, as well as some of the most cutting edge. If you're looking for mainstream, stick with the department stores—or the Gap.

SAN FRANCISCO

Behind the Post Office. Come here for the latest and greatest hip-hop gear, including in-your-face T-shirts, skate-girl dresses, and phat baggy pants. On weekends local DJs spin tunes. *1510 Haight St., at Ashbury St., tel. 415/861–2507.*

Betsey Johnson. Postmodern designer-goddess Betsey Johnson brings you outrageous women's fashions in a campy neon-lighted shop. The often silly clothes aren't cheap, but half-off sales are frequent. *2031 Fillmore St., between Pine and California Sts., tel. 415/567–2726; 160 Geary St., between Stockton and Grant Sts., tel. 415/398–2516.*

Esprit Factory Outlet. In-season clothing from Esprit women's and children's lines, as well as shoes and accessories, are sold with deep discounts at this enormous, airy outlet store. For best results check the bins in the back. *499 Illinois St., at 16th St., tel. 415/957–2550.*

Although many stores in San Francisco and Berkeley stay open seven days a week until 8 PM or 9 PM, stores in Oakland tend to close by 7 PM, and they remain shuttered on Sunday.

European Menswear Outlet. Quality suits, shirts, ties, and belts—mostly Italian—sell at up to 60% off. *393 Sutter St., at Stockton St., tel. 415/788–0340.*

J. Crew. The popular preppy mail-order company has a shop at San Francisco Centre, and although nothing is particularly cheap, at least you won't have to pay shipping and handling costs. *865 Market St., at 5th St., tel. 415/546–6262.*

Joshua Simon. This Noe Valley shop stocks unusual women's garments: flowing pants, romantic dresses, woven vests, hand-painted shirts. Many items are by local designers. *3915 24th St., near Sanchez St., tel. 415/821–1068.*

Loehmann's. Some of the city's best-dressed women swear by this discount store, which stocks labels like Karl Lagerfeld and Krizia at drastically reduced prices. *222 Sutter St., near Union Sq., tel. 415/982–3215.*

Na Na. The San Francisco branch of this national chain sells clothes and shoes to ultrahip Gen-Xers. The sales rack (up to 50% off) guarantees you won't go broke looking cool. *2276 Market St., near Noe St., tel. 415/861–6262.*

New West. Spruce up your wardrobe with big-name seconds and samples of a practical (yet stylish) nature at markdown prices. *426 Brannan St., between 3rd and 4th Sts., tel. 415/882–4929; 2967 College Ave., at Ashby Ave., Berkeley, tel. 510/849–0701.*

The Outlaw. Bikers and wanna-be bikers won't want to miss the chance to stock up on leather jackets, T-shirts, hats, and other Harley-Davidson fashions. *900 N. Point St., between Polk and Larkin Sts., tel. 415/563–8986.*

Rolo. This San Francisco minichain is wildly popular with club goers. The store on Market is heavy on flamboyant, expensive menswear; the Howard Street store features a flashy women's selection; Castro Street caters to style-conscious men; and the downtown branch targets the more conservative crowd. *1301 Howard St., at 9th St., tel. 415/861–1999; 2351 Market St., tel. 415/431–4545; 450 Castro St., tel. 415/626–7171; 25 Stocktown St. (downtown), tel. 415/989–7656.*

Shoe Biz. The latest European styles are here, in neon pink glitter or on 4-inch platforms. Check the sale corner labeled LAST SIZE for high-quality shoes at fantastic discounts. *1446 Haight St., at Masonic Ave., tel. 415/864–0990.*

TONY SHOPPING
IN UNION SQUARE

To the diehard shopper there's nothing more pleasurable than an afternoon spent drifting through the perfumed halls of San Francisco's venerable department stores, all grouped conveniently within walking distance of Union Square. Macy's (Stockton and O'Farrell Sts., tel. 415/397–3333) will complete extensive remodeling by spring 1998, creating glamorous new display areas for its men's, women's, and housewares departments. (Foodies flock to the Cellar, the food department downstairs.) Nordstrom (865 Market St., at 5th St., tel. 415/243–8500), though much smaller, is famous for its excellent customer service. Designer fashions, shoes, accessories, and cosmetics are the specialties. Saks Fifth Avenue (384 Post St., at Powell St., tel. 415/986–4300) stocks designer fashions both conservative and trendsetting; the opulent jewelry and accessories departments are not to be missed. As you pass through the main entrance of Neiman Marcus (150 Stockton St., at Geary St., tel. 415/362–3900), look up at the spectacular glass dome. Eclectic designer clothing, top-brand cosmetics, and fancy household wares are what you'll find here.

X-Large. Part of a chain financed by Beastie Boy Mike D, X-Large brings cool clothes and hip-hop beats to the Haight and to Berkeley. Sonic Youth bassist Kim Gordon designed some of the threads—so you *know* they're cool. *1415 Haight St., at Masonic St., tel. 415/626–9573; 2422 Telegraph Ave., Berkeley, tel. 510/849–9242.*

Yerba Buena Square. The square is a collection of 10 shops selling discount apparel, shoes, and toys. Spend a few hours weeding through the racks, and you'll find gems by Armani, Calvin Klein, and Dior. *899 Howard St., at 5th St., tel. 415/974–5136.*

EAST BAY

Deep Threads. Deep Threads sets up hip-hop fans with baggy jeans, baseball caps, beanies, and parkas. And they'll give you the latest on Oakland's hip-hop scene. *5243 College Ave., at Broadway, Oakland, tel. 510/653–4790.*

Futura. A whimsical blend of new and used clothes for men and women includes vintage jackets, bowling shirts, baby Ts, and baggy pants. Futura's outlet store (De Haro St. at Mariposa St.) rivals Goodwill for low prices. *2350 Telegraph Ave., near Durant Ave., Berkeley, tel. 510/883–9050.*

SECONDHAND AND
VINTAGE CLOTHING

The cheapest clothes in the Bay Area are someone else's castoffs, though many secondhand shops carry expensive vintage fashions as well. The big-name stores **Buffalo Exchange** (1555 Haight St., tel. 415/431–7733; 1800 Polk St., tel. 415/346–5726; 2512 Telegraph Ave., Berkeley, tel. 510/644–9202; 3333 Lake Shore Ave., Oakland, tel. 510/452–4464) and **Wasteland** (*see below*) are dependable sources for flannel, polyester shirts, and basic black dresses, often with inflated prices. For a better selection at cheaper prices, try the smaller shops in the **Mission** and **Haight** districts or in the East Bay along **College Avenue** in Rockridge and **Telegraph Avenue** near the UC Berkeley campus.

Looking for a vintage silk Chanel suit or a 1930s beaded satin gown? Head to **Divisadero Street** (between Pine and Bush streets) or **Fillmore Street** (between Bush and Sacramento streets), where ritzy vintage shops and high-end secondhand stores carry designer labels tossed aside by wealthy Pacific Heights matrons. The stretch of Hayes Street between Franklin and Buchanan streets, known as **Hayes Valley,** is another happy hunting ground.

SAN FRANCISCO

Aardvark's Odd Ark. Aardvark's enthralls thrift store shoppers with a wide selection of used clothing: men's basics, cotton dress shirts, hats, and vintage Levi's. *1501 Haight St., at Ashbury St., tel. 415/621–3141.*

American Rag. This store stocks old and new, and precious little is cheap. But they do have the best selection of black vintage dresses in San Francisco, plus racks of stylish suits and classy jackets. *1305 Van Ness Ave., between Sutter and Bush Sts., tel. 415/474–5214.*

Clothes Contact. You really can't go wrong, as just about everything here—used, vintage, old jeans, jackets—is $8 per pound. On the occasional bargain days the price is reduced to $4. *473 Valencia St., near 16th St., tel. 415/621–3212.*

Crossroads Trading Co. The Fillmore store tends to carry early '80s wear, while the other two branches are better for jeans (under $25) and unusual vintage dresses. *2231 Market St., between Sanchez and Noe Sts., tel. 415/626–8989; 1901 Fillmore St., at Bush St., tel. 415/775–8885; 5636 College Ave., near Keith St., Oakland, tel. 510/420–1952.*

If outlet malls are your gig, the Peninsula is the place to go. Worth checking out are the Metro 280 Center (Colby Blvd. at I–280 in Colma) and Marina Square (Marina Blvd. at I–880 in San Leandro).

Departures from the Past. It's exclusively vintage clothing here, including costumes, formal attire, and some casual wear. Tuxedos sell for $100–$160 or rent for $40–$60 per night. A partner store, **Costumes on Haight** (735 Haight St., tel. 415/621–1356), rents costumes and has some vintage items for sale. *2028 Fillmore St., between California and Pine Sts., tel. 415/885–3377.*

560 Hayes Vintage Boutique. Vintage, one of a cluster of boutiques in Hayes Valley, stocks an assortment of used clothing, mostly women's. You'll find pants, coats, and dresses that reek deliciously of the '70s. *560 Hayes St., between Laguna and Octavia Sts., tel. 415/861–7993.*

Wasteland. Wasteland brings you trendy and outrageous treasures, like bell-bottoms, as well as vintage gowns, suits, and costume jewelry. It's one of the city's most popular—but priciest—secondhand stores. *1660 Haight St., between Belvedere and Clayton Sts., tel. 415/863–3150.*

Worn Out West. This Castro District store sells secondhand Western wear and leather goods to budget-conscious cowboys. *582 Castro St., near 19th St., tel. 415/431–6020.*

EAST BAY

Madame Butterfly. Vintage hats and gloves, summer dresses, and a small selection of men's jackets go for $15–$40. Fancy dresses cost $30–$80. *5474 College Ave., at Taft St., Oakland, tel. 510/653–1525.*

Mars Mercantile. The most reliable used- and vintage-clothing store on Telegraph Avenue has racks of vintage dresses, acrylic men's shirts, genuine leather jackets, and '50s-era jeans ($300!). *2398 Telegraph Ave., at Channing Way, Berkeley, tel. 510/843–6711.*

Rockridge Rags. Here racks of secondhand clothing are conveniently arranged by size and often include upscale items like Anne Klein suits or Polo chinos—at bargain basement prices. *5711 College Ave., near Rockridge BART, Oakland, tel. 510/655–2289.*

Slash. This tiny shop deals exclusively in used denim and corduroy, including Levi's ($15–$30) and overalls ($20). Owners Carla Bell and Ocean Edgars are always happy to help you rummage for the perfect pair of 5-0-whatevers. *2840 College Ave., at Russell St., Berkeley, tel. 510/841–7803.*

BOOKS

For some a trip to the Bay Area is not complete without an evening spent browsing the shelves at **City Lights** (*see below*), San Francisco's most famous bookshop. However, the city has more than 200 other bookstores—new and used, tiny and huge, nonprofit and corporate—for every language, political bent, and cultural interest. The best browsing grounds are around the **Upper Haight**, in **Polk Gulch** (Polk Street between Ellis and Union streets), and in the **Mission District,** particularly along Valencia Street.

East Bay intellectuals don't have to trek to San Francisco to look for quality new and used books. With a huge university in its midst and more ambitious scholars per square mile than anywhere outside the Académie Française, you'll find enough bookstores here to keep you occupied for a year. **Telegraph Avenue,** in Berkeley, has the highest concentration of bookstores.

SAN FRANCISCO

Abandoned Planet Bookstore (518 Valencia St., near 16th St., tel. 415/861–4695) has music, theater, and art history books at rock-bottom prices. It's a homey place, with an old piano in one corner and a pair of pet cats. **Dog Eared Books** (900 Valencia St., at 20th St., tel. 415/282–1901) is another Mission favorite.

Acorn Books. Customers in search of an antiquarian, out-of-print, or used book know that the dedicated staff at Acorn would scour the earth's four corners to find it—although the well-stocked store probably already has it somewhere on the shelves. Acorn is one of a dozen bookstores in Polk Gulch. *1436 Polk St., between Pine and California Sts., tel. 415/563–1736.*

Adobe Book Shop. Adobe specializes in used and rare books (particularly art and modern philosophy); it's probably the cheapest in the city for those categories. The staff is erudite and affable. *3166 16th St., between Valencia and Guerrero Sts., tel. 415/864–3936.*

Bound Together Book Collective. For more than 20 years budding anarchists have come here for their bomb-making manuals, underground magazines, controversial political tracts, and all-around subversive materials. *1369 Haight St., near Masonic St., tel. 415/431–8355.*

City Lights. The city's most famous bookstore, opened in 1955 by poet Lawrence Ferlinghetti, is *the* source for beat literature—much of it published under the store's own imprint. The upstairs room is stocked with poetry, beat literature, and a few used books; a "little press" alcove contains local journals and 'zines; and there's nonfiction downstairs. *261 Columbus Ave., at Broadway, tel. 415/362–8193.*

A Different Light. This renowned Castro District bookstore stocks an extensive collection of lesbian, gay, and transgender literature; T-shirts and knicknacks; and "queerzines" (*see* Gay & Lesbian Travel *in* Chapter 1) to suit every taste. Book signings and readings take place weekly. *489 Castro St., near 18th St., tel. 415/431–0891.*

Eastwind Books and Arts, Inc. Eastwind deals exclusively in new books on Asian-American themes, and on Asia itself—particularly China. There are both Chinese- and English-language sections. *1435 Stockton St., 2nd floor, at Columbus St., tel. 415/772–5899.*

European Book Company. Come here for French-, German-, and Spanish-language books, magazines, and newspapers, as well as foreign-language dictionaries and travel guides. *925 Larkin St., between Post and Geary Sts., tel. 415/474–0626.*

Green Apple Books. Consistently voted the Bay Area's best bookstore by *SF Bay Guardian* readers, this ramshackle Richmond District institution is not for neat freaks. New, used, and rare books are jumbled together in a space reminiscent of grandma's attic. Ask for help from the knowledgeable and friendly staff. *506 Clement St., between 6th and 7th Aves., tel. 415/387–2272.*

Modern Times. Modern Times is collectively run, carries underground papers and 'zines, and hosts readings and forums with a politically progressive, multicultural focus. It's best for Spanish-language titles, art, current affairs, gay and lesbian issues, and cultural theory. *888 Valencia St., between 19th and 20th Sts., tel. 415/282–9246.*

San Francisco Mystery Bookstore. This Noe Valley shop stocks everything imaginable for the armchair Sherlock Holmes: new and used books and a few gay and lesbian mysteries. *4175 24th St., between Castro and Diamond Sts., tel. 415/282–7444. Closed Mon.–Tues.*

Sierra Club Bookstore. Come here for new books on all aspects of environmentalism, including political tomes and nature poetry. In addition, there are environment-themed children's books, practical guides for hiking and camping, and topographical maps. A bulletin board lists area hikes, meetings, and events. *85 2nd St., at Mission St., tel. 415/977–5600; 6014 College Ave., Oakland, tel. 510/658–7470.*

William Stout Architectural Books. Books and periodicals on architecture and design are what you'll find here, including an impressive out-of-print collection. *804 Montgomery St., between Jackson and Pacific Sts., tel. 415/391–6757.*

EAST BAY

Black Oak Books. This well-stocked north Berkeley shop is popular with UC professors for its rare books, or possibly for its collection of cheap paperback fiction ($1 and up). Weekly author readings and book signings include occasional big-name writers. *1491 Shattuck Ave., at Vine St., Berkeley, tel. 510/486–0698.*

Cody's. A Berkeley institution if there ever was one, Cody's stocks every imaginable genre, from poetry and philosophy to self-defense and women's studies. It also has an impressive newsstand, a cheery children's room, and an extensive selection of foreign-language books. Readings by local and nationally known authors are always crowded; arrive early if you want a shot at a seat. *2454 Telegraph Ave., at Haste St., Berkeley, tel. 510/845–7852.*

City Lights, the legendary home of the beat generation, was once charged with obscenity for selling Allen Ginsberg's poem "Howl."

Diesel—A Bookstore. In Rockridge near the College of Arts and Crafts, Diesel has an excellent collection of fiction, history, political, and art books. Weekly readings and book signings run the gamut from local history to poetry. *5433 College Ave., at Kales St., Oakland, tel. 510/653–9965.*

Gaia Books, Music, and Crafts. Books on spirituality, ecology, holistic health, and sexuality fill this bright, airy space. Readings and lectures are held regularly. *1400 Shattuck Ave., at Rose St., Berkeley, tel. 510/548–4172.*

Marcus Books. Marcus specializes in books by and about African-Americans: fiction, history, religion, art, children's literature, and more. Readings are held twice a week. *3900 Martin Luther King Jr. Way, between 39th and 40th Sts., Oakland, tel. 510/652–2344; 1712 Fillmore St., near Post St., San Francisco, tel. 415/346–4222.*

Moe's. Gruff, cigar-chomping Moe Moskowitz knows how to run a successful bookstore. His shop has five floors of new, used, and antique books, with a strong emphasis on the used and antique. *2476 Telegraph Ave., between Haste St. and Dwight Way, Berkeley, tel. 510/849–2087.*

Shambhala Booksellers. Shambhala stocks new and used books on Eastern religions, alternative medicine, mysticism, psychology, and theology. *2482 Telegraph Ave., between Haste St. and Dwight Way, Berkeley, tel. 510/848–8443.*

University Press Books. Here you'll find titles from more than 100 university presses, representing all disciplines. Pick up the latest treatise on cultural theory and read it next door at the Musical Offering Café (tel. 510/849–0211). *2430 Bancroft Way, near Telegraph Ave., Berkeley, tel. 510/548–0585.*

RECORDS, TAPES, AND CDS

The **Upper Haight** is a good place to look for obscure titles and classic punk, while the **Mission District** is great for Latin music. And Berkeley's **Telegraph Avenue** boasts no fewer than four mammoth record stores within five blocks of the UC campus. You can find virtually any new CD at the gargantuan **Virgin Megastore** (2 Stockton St., at Market St., tel. 415/397–4525), but your friendly neighborhood store is bound to be cheaper, with more used goods and vinyl. Most places guarantee their records against scratches; check to make sure.

For Middle Eastern music, try **Samiramis Imports** (2990 Mission St., tel. 415/824–6555). If it's gospel you're craving, make a trip to **Reid's** (3101 Sacramento St., at Prince St., Berkeley, tel. 510/843–7282).

SAN FRANCISCO

Groove Merchant. Groove Merchant's owners run the highly recommended Luv 'n Haight and Ubiquity labels, both of which put the spotlight on the local acid jazz scene. The store has plenty of great finds for the collector, DJ, or serious amateur. *687 Haight St., between Pierce and Steiner Sts., tel. 415/252–5766.*

Reckless Records. A reliable source for used cassettes and CDs, Reckless also carries new music, T-shirts, posters, and used videos. They specialize in independent and mainstream rock, hip-hop, and soul. *1401 Haight St., at Masonic St., tel. 415/431–3434.*

Recycled Records. Vinyl junkies will find their fix among the great selection of new and used (mostly used) records. The collection focuses on rock, but other genres are well represented. *1377 Haight St., at Masonic St., tel. 415/626–4075.*

Reggae Runnins Village Store. This reggae wonderland carries records, tapes, videos, T-shirts, jewelry, and other paraphernalia in red, gold, black, and green. *505 Divisadero St., between Fell and Hayes Sts., tel. 415/922–2442.*

Ritmo Latino. This colorful, Carnaval-esque store in the heart of the Mission sells an enormous variety of Latin music: *ranchero,* mariachi, salsa, Tex-Mex, merengue, *norteño,* and more. Best of all, the store has listening stations where you can sample CDs before buying. *2401 Mission St., at 20th St., tel. 415/ 824–8556.*

Star Classics. Star stocks classical CDs and cassettes (new, not used). The adjoining Star Classics Recital Hall hosts vocal and musical performances every Friday and Sunday. *425 Hayes St., at Gough St., tel. 415/552–1110.*

Street Light Records. Because they buy and sell at great prices to a diverse clientele, Street Light's selection of records, tapes, and CDs is usually offbeat and always fresh. The Noe Valley store is smaller but has a better selection of vinyl. *3979 24th St., between Noe and Sanchez Sts., tel. 415/282–3550; 2350 Market St., near Castro St., tel. 415/282–8000.*

EAST BAY

Amoeba. The Bay Area's widest and choicest selection of new and used 7-inch records—and used CDs—includes jazz, international, indie, hip-hop, import rock, and more. The experienced staff will show you the newest artists and dig out their rarest records. *2455 Telegraph Ave., at Haste St., Berkeley, tel. 510/549–1125.*

Groove Yard. Venture out to this cozy shop, halfway between Berkeley and downtown Oakland, for acid jazz, funk, blues, Latin and Brazilian discs, and plenty of used jazz and soul records. *4770 Telegraph Ave., at 48th St., Oakland, tel. 510/655–8400.*

Mod Lang. At Mod Lang shipments of ambient, indie, and psychedelic '60s music arrive from the United Kingdom every week—and sell at amazingly low prices. *2136 University Ave., near Shattuck Ave., Berkeley, tel. 510/486–1880.*

Rasputin Music. Rasputin had the lock on Telegraph Avenue cool until Amoeba showed up in 1990. Still, Rasputin has miles of new and used CDs and regularly hosts live performances. *2403 Telegraph Ave., at Channing Ave., Berkeley, tel. 510/848–9005.*

Saturn Records. The wall-to-wall racks here contain excellent and extensive selections of rock, jazz, blues, oldies, show tunes, and soundtracks in hard-to-find vinyl and on new or used CDs. *5488 College Ave., at Lawton St., Oakland, tel. 510/654–0335.*

FLEA MARKETS

Bay Area flea markets often swallow up entire fairgrounds, parking lots, or football fields, all full of good deals on antique furniture, clothes, toys, books, bikes. . . anything remotely old, quirky, or dusty. In all cases, you'll find the best selection if you arrive just after dawn, but prices are lower late in the day, when vendors are tired and anxious to avoid reloading their trucks. For complete, up-to-date listings, pick up a copy of the free *Classified Flea Market,* available at most newsstands and convenience stores. On summer weekends Noe Valley, particularly Church Street between 19th and 27th streets, is garage-sale paradise. So, too, are Dolores and Guerrero streets between 16th and 24th, and 18th Street between Church and Castro.

SAN FRANCISCO

Alemany Flea Market. San Francisco's newest flea market is a fairly mellow affair. Funky knickknacks are plentiful; you'll also find small selections of clothing, household appliances, furniture, and some antiques and collectibles. Best of all, prices are low. *100 Alemany Blvd., at Crescent Ave., Bernal Heights, no phone. From I–280, take Alemany Blvd. exit; market is under exit ramp at the Hwy. 101 and I–280 interchange. Open Sun. 8–3.*

Geneva Swap Meet. Get down and dirty at this anything-sells market, held in the parking lot of the Geneva drive-in theater, next to the Cow Palace. New things like T-shirts and polyester underwear can be found near the entrance; the real finds lurk in the stalls at the back. *607 Carter St., at Geneva Ave., Daly City, tel. 415/587–2884. From I–280 or Hwy. 101, take Cow Palace exit and follow signs on Geneva Ave. Open weekends 7–4.*

Pier 29 Antique and Collectible Market. A cut above the city's other flea markets, Pier 29 has dozens of indoor booths selling antique furniture, rare books, vintage clothing, kitchenware, costume jewelry, and other collectibles. Unlike other markets, it charges hefty admission: $2, or $10 before 9:30 AM. *Pier 29, The Embarcadero, between Sansome and Battery Sts., no phone. Open Sun. 7–5.*

San Francisco Flea Market. Vendors at this South of Market parking lot hawk mostly junk, like plastic toys, Chinese-made batteries, and used clothes that were never in fashion. But if you're in the market for new or used kitchen appliances, clock radios, and other small electronics, it's worth a look. *1651 Mission St., between S. Van Ness Ave. and 12th St., no phone. Open weekends 6–4:30.*

EAST AND SOUTH BAY

Ashby BART Flea Market. Vendors of used furniture and clothing always have some funky desks or a good vintage coat they're willing to lower the price on, as well as "manly man" tools, kitchen appliances, African-American jewelry, used bikes, and secondhand (or thirdhand) books. To top it off, there's fresh produce from local farmers. *Ashby BART station, corner Ashby Ave. and MLK Jr. Way, Berkeley, tel. 510/644–0744. Open weekends 8–7.*

Coliseum Swap Meet. This vast flea market sprawls across the drive-in movie theater parking lot, next to the Oakland Coliseum. You'll find furniture, clothing, electronic goods, and more. *5401 Coliseum Way, tel. 510/534–0325. I–880 and Coliseum Way, near Coliseum BART station. Open weekends 8–4.*

NorCal Swap Meet. Larger than Ashby but smaller than the Coliseum, this market at Laney College, in Oakland, is especially good for wacky, off-the-wall items and lots of fresh produce. Although there are plenty of organized stands, the best finds require digging through the vendors' piles. *7th and Fallon Sts., near Lake Merritt BART station, tel. 510/769–7266. Open weekends 7–4.*

San Jose Flea Market. One of the world's largest, this market-to-end-all-markets houses around 2,600 vendors on a 120-acre selling area. Everything from furniture to car parts to clothes to farm-fresh produce is up for grabs. *1590 Berryessa Rd., tel. 408/453–1110. 13th St. exit from U.S. 101; or from College Park CalTrain station, Bus 36 toward East San Jose. Open Wed.–Sun. 7–5:30.*

SPECIALTY ITEMS

If you're looking for a gift, souvenir, or shopping experience unique to the Bay Area, poke your head into one of the city's many New Age or herbal medicine shops, make a purchase at a store that donates its proceeds to charity, or patronize a purveyor of alternative or avant-garde posters, toys, or videos.

ART AND PHOTOGRAPHY

Adolph Gasser. Your best source for photography and video equipment, Gasser has the largest inventory of such items in northern California. *181 2nd St., between Howard and Mission Sts., tel. 415/495–3852; 5733 Geary Blvd., tel. 415/751–0145.*

Amsterdam Art. A favorite of local artists for years, Amsterdam Art stocks supplies for painting, printmaking, ceramics, and more. There's also a full selection of frames, as well as a helpful staff. *1013 University Ave., near San Pablo Ave., Berkeley, tel. 510/649–4800; 5424 Geary Blvd., San Francisco, tel. 415/751–6248.*

Art Rock Gallery. Handmade silk-screened posters—many in an artsy vintage style—run $15–$20. The gallery frequently holds exhibitions of rare and vintage posters. *1155 Mission St., between 7th and 8th Sts., tel. 415/255–7390.*

Looking Glass. This small store sells tripods, paper, film, books, and other photographic supplies. They also offer classes and darkroom space ($6 per hour). *2848 Telegraph Ave., at Oregon St., Berkeley, tel. 510/548–6888.*

CHARITABLE CAUSES

Global Exchange Fair Trade Center. With a mission to foster economic self-sufficiency for Third World communities, this nonprofit shop specializes in handmade crafts, from African jewelry to Guatemalan backpacks. Call for information about lectures, tours, and seminars. *2840 College Ave., at Russell St., Berkeley, tel. 510/548–0370; 3900 24th St., at Sanchez St., San Francisco, tel. 415/648–8068.*

Planet Weavers Treasure Store. Indulge your socially conscious side at this UNICEF-run store, stocked with handcrafted gifts, toys, and an international selection of musical instruments, from bongos to Australian didgeridoos. A portion of the proceeds goes to the UN Children's Fund. *1573 Haight St., between Ashbury and Clayton Sts., tel. 415/864–4415.*

Under One Roof. Under the same roof as the NAMES Project (*see* Castro District *in* Chapter 2), this shop sells goods gathered from 62 AIDS organizations—gay pride T-shirts, greeting cards, and more. *2362B Market St., between Noe and Castro Sts., tel. 415/252–9430.*

EROTICA

Carol Doda's Champagne and Lace Lingerie Boutique. Let the legendary and alluring Carol Doda, who led the effort to legalize topless dancing in the 1960s, help you find just the right bra, teddy, bustier, corset, garter belt, slinky dress, or bikini. *1850 Union St., No. 1, at Laguna St., tel. 415/776–6900.*

Good Vibrations. This self-described "clean, well-lighted place to shop for sex toys, books, and videos" is a friendly woman-owned-and-operated enterprise. If you think all sex shops are sleazy, you haven't been here. *1210 Valencia St., at 23rd St., tel. 415/974–8980; 2504 San Pablo Ave., at Dwight Way, Berkeley, tel. 510/841–8987.*

GAMES AND TOYS

FAO Schwarz Fifth Avenue. At the lavish San Francisco branch of this famed toy store, you'll find dancing bears, singing dolls, motorized cars, and toys galore—including a reproduction of that giant keyboard used by Tom Hanks in the movie *Big. 48 Stockton St., at O'Farrell St., tel, 415/394–8700.*

Gamescape. They've got a splendid selection of new and used board, computer, and role-playing games, from old favorites like Monopoly to the latest high-tech offerings from Nintendo. *333 Divisadero St., between Page and Oak Sts., tel. 415/621–4263.*

Scary Hairy Toy Company. The kooky shop of underground cartoonists Bruce Helvitz and Flower Frankenstein is your source for unique gifts like the Miss PMS Fun Action Toy or the Super Cool Fufu Café People finger puppets. *3804 17th St., at Sanchez St., tel. 415/864–6543.*

HANDICRAFTS

African Outlet. Handmade goods from all over Africa include Zulu spears and shields, Berber and Tuareg jewelry, cowrie-shell necklaces, brilliant West African textiles, and plenty of other artifacts and accessories. *524 Octavia St., between Hayes and Grove Sts., tel. 415/864–3576.*

Asakichi. When you're exploring Japantown, stop by this tiny shop for wind chimes, teapots, handmade chopsticks, simple Japanese furniture, and other delights. *Japan Center, on the bridge between Kinokuniya and Kintetsu Bldgs., tel. 415/921–3821.*

F. Dorian. F. Dorian specializes in cards, jewelry, and crafts from Mexico, Peru, Indonesia, the Philippines, Sri Lanka, and Japan, as well as works by local craftspeople. *388 Hayes St., at Gough St., tel. 415/861–3191.*

HOME FURNISHINGS

Butterfield West. At the low-key annex of San Francisco's premier auction house, you can occasionally bid for bargain pieces of furniture and art. Call for an auction schedule. *164 Utah St., at 15th St., tel. 415/861–7500, ext. 308 or 888.*

Cookin': Recycled Gourmet Appurtenances. Why buy new kitchen appliances when Cookin' carries quality used fondue makers, espresso machines, food processors, cookie cutters, Jell-O molds, pots, and pans. . . for so much less? *339 Divisadero St., between Oak and Page Sts., tel. 415/861–1854.*

Crate and Barrel Outlet. This is the only Crate and Barrel outlet in California, stocking kitchenware, decorative items, and some furniture. Most items are irregular or discontinued, priced 30%–50% off. *1785 4th St., near Hearst St., Berkeley, tel. 510/528–5500.*

Greenhaven. Formerly known as Super Thrift, this is more than a thrift store—it routinely wins praises by *SF Bay Guardian* readers as the city's "Best Vintage Furniture Store." There's a mixture of old and new, all reasonably priced. *560 Valencia St., between 16th and 17th Sts., tel. 415/255–4877.*

Urban Ore. You could outfit your entire house with the choice of sofas, chairs, tables, and dressers from this giant warehouse. Don't be put off by the junkyard feel of the place; it's full of great bargains. Couches start around $15. *7th St., at Gilman St., Berkeley, tel. 510/559–4450.*

Whole Earth Access. True to its name, this longtime local favorite is a one-stop shop carrying everything from computers to love seats, all at hard-to-beat prices. *2990 7th St., at Ashby Ave., Berkeley, tel. 510/845–3000.*

Worldware. Recycling is art at Worldware: Picture frames and candlesticks are made from aluminum cans; purses and wallets are cut from discarded inner tubes. The owner, Shari Sant, also designs her own line of clothing made from organic hemp, wool, or cotton. *336 Hayes St., between Franklin and Gough Sts., tel. 415/487–9030.*

JEWELRY

Gallery of Jewels. Gallery of Jewels stocks rhinestone, glass, and silver jewelry crafted by local artisans. The styles are eclectic, and the prices are well below Tiffany & Co.'s. *1400 Haight St., at Masonic Ave., tel. 415/255–1180.*

Gargoyle Beads. Why buy jewelry when you can make your own from Gargoyle's exotic beads, seeds, and polished stones? *1310 Haight St., at Central St., tel. 415/552–4274.*

Zeitgeist Timepieces & Jewelry. The owners repair and restore clocks, jewelry, and fine watches. They also sell beautiful vintage wrist and pocket watches from the likes of Grüen and Bulova. *437B Hayes St., at Gough St., tel. 415/864–0185.*

NEW AGE AND HERBAL MEDICINE

Lady Luck Candle Shop. The friendly proprietor of this tiny shop can convince even the most bitter cynic to buy a hope candle. The wide selection of incense, devotional candles, and love potions will thrill your favorite mystic. *311 Valencia St., between 14th and 15th Sts., tel. 415/621–0358.*

Lhasa Karnak Herb Co. This place is an excellent source for herbs and herbal information, with a knowledgeable and friendly staff. *2513 Telegraph Ave., at Dwight Way, Berkeley, tel. 510/548–0380; 1938 Shattuck Ave., Berkeley, tel. 510/548–0372.*

ONE-OF-A-KINDS

Binky's. Relive your lost childhood at Binky's: They've got all your old favorites from the '60s and '70s, like the *Charlie's Angels* board game, the Bionic Woman lunch box, and plenty of Barbies. *1009 Guerrero St., at 22nd St., tel. 415/285–4876.*

Capezio. At San Francisco's best costume shop you'll find fake hands, clown ruffles, vampire teeth, ball gowns, sinister capes, and other miscellany. *126 Post St., 2nd floor, at Kearny St., tel. 415/421–5657.*

Dudley Perkins Harley-Davidson. This is the oldest Harley-Davidson dealership in the world, selling new and vintage Harley motorcycles. The **Dudley Perkins Gift Shop** (2595 Taylor St., at N. Point St., tel. 415/776–7779), on Fisherman's Wharf, stocks a mind-boggling array of Harley-Davidson T-shirts, caps, key chains, and tool kits. *66 Page St., between Franklin and Gough Sts., tel. 415/703–9494.*

Red Desert. Hundreds of species of cacti are for sale here, big and small, rare and common, for indoors or out. *1632 Market St., at Franklin St., tel. 415/552–2800.*

PAPER, CARDS, AND STATIONERY

Kozo Bookbinding. For beautiful Japanese stationery, blank books, and other exotic paper goods, come here. The poster-size silk-screened wall hangings range from $4 for a basic print to $40 for an elaborate design on handmade paper. *531 Castro St., between 18th and 19th Sts., tel. 415/621–0869.*

Tilt. A wide and whimsical selection of postcards includes old snapshots of San Francisco, bits of Americana, and images from the '50s. Tilt is also the exclusive distributor of posters by Frank Kozik, whose psychedelic art has advertised bands like Green Day, among others. *1441 Grant St., between Green and Union Sts., tel. 415/986–8866; 507 Columbus Ave., near Stockton St., tel. 415/788–1112; 1427 Haight St., near Masonic St., tel. 415/255–1199.*

VIDEO

Leather Tongue. This Mission institution sells and rents cult films, film noir, sci-fi, and more, but its greatest claim to fame is an extensive collection of films by local and independent filmmakers. *714 Valencia St., at 18th St., tel. 415/552–2900.*

Le Video. Le Video wins the *SF Bay Guardian*'s reader poll every year, possibly because of its exhaustive collection of more than 30,000 titles spread among all genres. *1239 9th Ave., at Lincoln Ave., Sunset District, tel. 415/566–3606. Le Video Too: 1231 9th Ave., same phone.*

Movie Image. Film buffs will appreciate the great selection of film noir and American classics here, as well as the foreign and independent sections. The racks at the center of the store are arranged alphabetically according to director. *64 Shattuck Sq., near University Ave., Berkeley, tel. 510/649–0296.*

FOOD

REVISED BY SHARON SILVA

Waves of Asian and Mexican immigrants have made San Francisco a flavorful and festive hotbed of cheap taquerías, backstreet Chinese holes-in-the-wall, gracious Thai and Vietnamese establishments, reasonably priced sushi houses, and Korean barbecue joints. Oakland is known for Southern-style eats and its less touristy version of Chinatown; and Berkeley has its Gourmet Ghetto, with everything a foodie could want. Marin County and the South Bay, though generally more expensive, both have their share of worthwhile restaurants—Marin County's are known for their waterfront views.

For serious foodies, a trip to Alice Waters's legendary Chez Panisse (*see below*) is a must: It's the birthplace of the seasonal, food-as-art style of preparation now known as California cuisine. You can sample great renditions at hundreds of excellent sit-down restaurants throughout the Bay Area where entrées cost less than $10–$15. In addition, we've included a handful of the city's most cutting-edge restaurants, where entrées cost up to $20—but at any of these places you can get away with ordering appetizers for dinner or splitting a main course. Unless otherwise noted, the restaurants in this chapter accept one or more major credit cards.

SAN FRANCISCO

CASTRO/NOE VALLEY

The Castro District teems with lively restaurants, many with outdoor patios. Brunch is an institution here: Mimosas and espressos flow freely on weekend mornings, and the crowd is always jovial and loud. Follow the sunglasses-wearing masses to the two hottest brunch spots, **Café Flore** (*see* Chapter 5) and the **Patio Café** (*see below*) and brace yourself for a long afternoon of Bloody Marys. The after-hours eating scene around **Castro Street** is just as vibrant—you don't have to look too far for a casual dinner spot, even late into the night (*see box* Late-Night Grub, *below*). But if you really want to impress someone, the supertrendy **2223 Market** (2223 Market, at Noe St., tel. 415/431–0692) is considered the best restaurant in the neighborhood. The cuisine is all Californian, and entrées cost about $15 each.

LATE-NIGHT GRUB

Most of the city's restaurants close by 11 PM, even on weekends. But if you just danced up an appetite, you indeed can find a few places serving omelets and burgers, or even pot stickers, into the wee hours.

Bagdad Cafe. This 24-hour restaurant in the Castro—where people-watching is a high art—is as famous for its expansive street-level windows as for its home-style breakfasts. 2295 Market St., at 16th St., tel. 415/621–4434.

El Farolito. Stagger in here for a burrito as late as 2:45 AM (until 3:45 AM Friday and Saturday). At this hour you probably won't notice the grimy cafeteria-style atmosphere. 2777 Mission St., between 23rd and 24th Sts., tel. 415/824–7877.

Grubstake. Housed in a converted railroad car, this diner fits right in to the grungy late-night Polk Gulch scene. 1525 Pine St., between Polk St. and Van Ness Ave., tel. 415/673–8268.

Orphan Andy's. This all-hours Castro hangout has red-vinyl booths, a lunch counter, and a jukebox—bring a date. 3991A 17th St., at Market and Castro Sts., tel. 415/864–9795.

Pinecrest. A real, live retro diner—complete with a long Formica counter and old vinyl booths—Pinecrest serves juicy charbroiled half-pounders to late-night downtowners. 401 Geary St., at Mason St., tel. 415/885–6407.

Silver. Reputedly popular with Chinatown gangsters, Silver serves Chinese cuisine (including dim sum) around the clock in a glaring fluorescent setting. 737 Washington St., at Grant Ave., tel. 415/433–8888.

Sparky's. The menu might remind you of Denny's but—for what it's worth—Sparky's serves a much trendier post-club clientele. 242 Church St., near Market St., tel. 415/626–8666.

Just over the hill from the Castro, around 24th Street, **Noe Valley** is a placid oasis awash in young liberal professionals, including a sizable lesbian contingent. It's a popular destination on sunny weekend mornings for a lazy brunch and a bit of window-shopping with the dog or the stroller. At night Noe gets fairly quiet, as it's mostly residential.

UNDER $5

Hot 'n' Hunky. This pink, perky little restaurant with a preponderance of Marilyn Monroe posters on the walls is a Castro institution for thick, juicy burgers. With names like the Macho Man, I Wanna Hold Your Ham, and Ms. Piggy, the burgers here make ordering an exercise in goofiness. *4039 18th St., near Castro St., tel. 415/621–6365. Cash only.*

Marcello's. This place is right across the street from the Castro Theatre (*see* Movie Houses *in* Chapter 6)—very convenient when it's almost show time. They sell some of the best pizza in town—by the slice or the pie—and you can always find interesting combinations like ham and pineapple or spinach with black olives and feta. They're open late on weekends, and they deliver for free. *420 Castro St., near Market St., tel. 415/863–3900. Cash only.*

Tom Peasant Pies. Tom serves only one thing—pies. Not big, meaty pies, but butter-and-cholesterol-free, fresh-outta-the-oven pies for less than $3. One fits neatly into the palm of your hand, and two will easily satisfy your hunger. Start with ratatouille or potato-rosemary and finish with cherry–Anjou pear. Come early, as the doors close at 7 PM. *4108 24th St., at Castro St., tel. 415/642–1316; 4117 18th St., at Castro St., tel. 415/621–3632. Cash only.*

UNDER $10

Eric's Hunan and Mandarin. The airy space, hardwood floors, and scattered orchids that would normally adorn a more upscale eatery shelter a casual, neighborhood-y crowd at this Noe Valley favorite. If the reasonable prices don't shock you, the authentic and first-rate Chinese food will. Weekday lunch specials ($4) include an entrée and soup. *1500 Church St., at 27th St., tel. 415/282–0919.*

Josie's Cabaret and Juice Joint. By day it's a neighborhood hangout with a 100% vegetarian menu of fresh organic juices, fruit smoothies, salads, sandwiches, and breakfast items: Come on a sunny day and eat outside on the back patio. By night it's a well-known performance venue featuring gay comedy acts. There are cabaret performances Wednesday through Sunday; Monday is comedy night. Covers run $5–$20. *3583 16th St., at Market St., tel. 415/861–7933. Cash only.*

La Méditerranée. This small, personable restaurant on the edge of the Castro District serves great Mediterranean food, including dolmas, salads, hummus, *baba ghanoush,* and the like. If you can't decide, get the Middle Eastern combination plate (vegetarian or not): two phyllo pastries, a Levant sandwich, a kabob, and salad for $7.50. *288 Noe St., at Market St., tel. 415/431–7210; 2210 Fillmore St., at Sacramento St., tel. 415/921–2956; 2936 College Ave., at Ashby Ave., Berkeley, tel. 510/540–7773. Closed Mon.*

Waiters on Wheels (tel. 415/252–1470) and Dine-One-One (tel. 415/771–3463) deliver anything from burgers to Italian to Cajun to Japanese from San Francisco restaurants for a $6-per-stop fee. Pick up a free delivery guide at a newspaper stand.

Miss Millie's. The carved-wood booths, frilly curtains, and antique fixtures will get you in the mood for homemade jams, scones, and cinnamon rolls. Try the lemon-ricotta pancakes in blueberry syrup or a fluffy omelet filled with oven-roasted tomatoes, basil, and feta cheese and served with a scone and roasted root vegetables. *4123 24th St., at Castro St., tel. 415/285–5598. No dinner Sun.–Tues.*

No-Name (Nippon) Sushi. Everybody calls this small wood-paneled restaurant on Church Street No-Name Sushi, even though the proprietors did eventually put up a tiny sign in the window officially dubbing it NIPPON. Name or no name, locals know they'll get huge sushi combos at prices that are hard to believe—try $6–$10 on for size. (If you're a sushi snob, you'll know that such low prices do come at the price of freshness.) No alcohol is served, but most people bring theirs in a bag. *314 Church St., at 15th St., no phone. Cash only. Closed Sun.*

Pasta Pomodoro. At this bustling Castro hangout you can eat a supercheap plate of pasta and do a bit of cruising on the side. It's always full of people, but the waiting list moves fast. Try the polenta with fontina cheese and tomato sauce, or dig into a *caprese* sandwich, with fresh mozzarella, tomatoes, basil, and olive puree. *2304 Market St., at 16th St., tel. 415/558–8123; 2027 Chestnut St., at Fillmore St., tel. 415/474–3400; 655 Union St., near Columbus St., tel. 415/399–0300; 816 Irving St., at 9th Ave., tel. 415/566–0900.*

Patio Café. The Castro's premier brunch spot operates out of an enormous converted greenhouse, complete with fake parrots perched among the foliage. Feast on eggs or omelets with home fries or on sinful cheese blintzes with cherry sauce—and don't forget the requisite Bloody Mary (or two or three). Later in the day, come for sandwiches, burgers, and pastas or for a more formal dinner, like a grilled New York steak ($13). *531 Castro St., between 18th and 19th Sts., tel. 415/621–4640.*

UNDER $15

Thai House on Noe. The elegant dining room makes this Duboce Triangle restaurant a popular choice for an intimate dinner. Try the duck on a bed of spinach with hot chili sauce or seafood soup with or without coconut milk. If you get stuck waiting for a table, stroll down Henry and Noe streets—both are lined with some of the most colorful Victorians in the city. **Thai House II,** right around the corner on Market Street, has more room. *151 Noe St., at Henry St., tel. 415/863–0374. Thai House II: 2200 Market St., at Sanchez St., tel. 415/864–5006.*

A CANTONESE BREAKFAST

Dim sum, Chinese finger food, is traditionally served early in the day in large banquet halls, where servers push around carts full of savory pastries and dumplings you dip in a little soy sauce and pay for by the plate (the cart pushers stamp your bill every time you select a plate). Selections might include flaky taro cakes, sticky rice (steamed in bamboo leaves with meat and spices), shrimp and pork dumplings, steamed buns filled with barbecued pork or ginger chicken, and large rice noodles rolled around shrimp.

UNDER $20

Firefly. Firefly's homey atmosphere captures Noe Valley's small-town charm. The menu changes weekly and incorporates global influences in typical California fashion—you can order Mediterranean or Southeast Asian or American home cooking (or a variation on the above) on any given night. Innovative appetizers steal the show here: Try golden beet soup or shrimp and scallop pot stickers. Order carefully, though, as the bill can get pretty hefty. Reserve in advance. *4288 24th St., at Douglass St., tel. 415/821–7652.*

CHINATOWN

Finding something to eat in Chinatown is a cinch. Finding something *good* to eat is a little trickier. Your best bet is to wander through the heart of Chinatown—**Washington, Clay,** and **Sacramento streets** between Mason and Kearny streets—until you find a restaurant that has the four elements that spell success: small, spare, cheap, and packed with locals. **Stockton Street** is the main market street, where you can load up on chow fun noodles, gingerroot, and live turtles. If you're looking for dim sum, *see box, above.*

UNDER $5

Kowloon. This is the only place in the city with strictly vegetarian dim sum—hence its popularity with tree huggers and Buddhists. A cabbage-stuffed pot sticker or a crispy mushroom-potato cake sells for only about 60¢. If you'd rather go for a rice dish (brown rice optional), choose from a huge list that includes such exotica as vegetarian "duck gizzards" or vegetarian "eel." *909 Grant Ave., near Washington St., tel. 415/362–9888.*

Lucky Creation. This small restaurant in the heart of Chinatown serves fantastic meatless fare. From the green sign to the green menus, this place declares loud and clear its aim to please the vegetarian palate—and it's cheap. Try spicy bean cake over rice or braised eggplant in a clay pot. *854 Washington St., between Grant Ave. and Stockton St., tel. 415/989–0818. Cash only. Closed Wed.*

UNDER $10

Chef Jia's. A few doors down from the ever-popular House of Nanking, Chef Jia's manages to survive, indeed thrive, thanks to its top-notch Hunan and Mandarin cuisine. It's noisy and crowded, and the decor leaves a lot to be desired, but the onion cakes and the spicy string beans with yam are both to die for. *925 Kearny St., between Jackson and Columbus Sts., tel. 415/398–1626. Cash only.*

House of Nanking. This legendary Chinatown hole-in-the-wall serves excellent Shanghai home cooking at righteously low prices. You'll be crammed into tiny tables with total strangers, and the no-nonsense waiters will keep you on your toes, but all that only adds to the Nanking experience. Ask for the delicious shrimp cakes in peanut sauce—they're not on the menu—or try the Nanking chicken, a version of General Tso's chicken. *919 Kearny St., between Jackson and Columbus Sts., tel. 415/421–1429. Cash only.*

Meriwa. Enjoy a real Chinatown dim sum experience, chicken feet and all, at this wood-paneled, red-bannered banquet hall. Settle in among chatting Chinese-American families and gossiping old men sharing rounds of schnapps to feast on tasty dumplings and sticky rice. You can easily eat your fill here for around $6 or less. *728 Pacific Ave., at Stockton St., 2nd floor, tel. 415/989–8868.*

Yuet Lee. This ambience-free joint on the congested corner of Broadway and Stockton serves Cantonese cuisine with milder sauces and lots of exotic seafood. Share a huge platter of New Zealand mussels with black bean sauce, or try a nonfishy dish, like the home-style beef stew clay pot. It's open until 3 AM. *1300 Stockton St., at Broadway, tel. 415/982–6020. Cash only. Closed Tues.*

UNDER $15

R&G Lounge. No one is going to accuse this upscale, somewhat sterile restaurant of being too festive, but it's worth the minisplurge for superfresh Cantonese dishes such as clams with spicy black bean sauce or meaty shiitake mushrooms with tender greens. When money is no object, order the house special, salt-and-pepper crab; its price varies according to how hard the catch was for the fishermen. Lunch prices—around $5 a rice plate—are easier to swallow. *631B Kearny St., between Sacramento and Clay Sts., tel. 415/982–7877.*

THE CIVIC CENTER AREA

The Civic Center area comprises a few low-lying neighborhoods that aren't exactly what you'd call classy, except, of course, for the area immediately surrounding the Opera House and the Symphony Hall (*see* Chapter 6). **Hayes Valley,** to the west of the **Civic Center,** along Hayes and Grove streets between Franklin and Laguna streets, is a good example of gentrification in progress, with wine bars and chichi restaurants sprouting up beside fledgling art galleries and second-

If your wallet's feeling light, a number of bakery/cafés around Chinatown and the Richmond District sell dim sum to go at about $1 for three items.

hand stores. Running north of Civic Center on Polk Street, **Polk Gulch** gets some of the runoff from the drug and male-prostitution trade in the nearby Tenderloin. But a bunch of movie theaters, laid-back cafés, and terrific international and ethnic dives might convince you of the Gulch's seedy charm. Stretching northeast of the Civic Center toward downtown, the **Tenderloin** is definitely *not* where you want to take Grandma to dinner. Although there are a few authentic Vietnamese outposts in the area, the blocks surrounding Larkin, Market, O'Farrell, and Mason streets are sketchy after dark: Either stick to lunch or take a cab.

UNDER $5

Aladdin. At this casual Mediterranean restaurant in Polk Gulch you top off your meat- or falafel-filled pita with scrumptious Mediterranean salads, sauces, and grilled veggies from the buffet. The friendly guys behind the counter are always trying to force-feed you bonus falafel balls, but, sadly, the place is often empty. *1300 Polk St., at Bush St., tel. 415/441–2212.*

Café at the Main Library. After you've finished surfing the net on one of the Main Library's new glitzy color monitors, stop in at this sleek, light-wood café for a hearty sandwich of pesto and smoked turkey on five-grain bread. *Grove and Larkin Sts., tel. 415/557–4400.*

Main Squeeze. This space-age juice bar on Polk Street is full of industrial materials molded into postmodern pieces of fruit. Drink your fill of healthy juices and smoothies or try their vegetarian and vegan lunch and breakfast items. *1515 Polk St., at California St., tel. 415/567–1515. Cash only.*

Moishe's Pippic. This Hayes Valley Jewish deli will satisfy the corned beef pangs of relocated East Coasters. They've got it all: kosher salami, hot dogs, corned beef, chopped liver, tongue, bagels and lox, matzo ball soup, Polish sausage, knishes. . . it's a big Bronx cheer to obsessively healthy California cuisine. *425A Hayes St., at Gough St., tel. 415/431–2440. Cash only. Closed Sun. No dinner.*

UNDER $10

Ananda Fuara. Escape from grimy Market Street into this soothing vegetarian restaurant with sky blue walls and draped ivy plants. Servers sway by the tables in flowing saris, bringing sandwiches and entrées like curry with rice and chutney. The massive Brahma burrito will fill you up for the rest of the day. *1298 Market St., at 9th St., tel. 415/621–1994. Cash only. No dinner Wed., Sun.*

Cordon Bleu. If you're on your way to the Lumière Theater (*see* Chapter 6), stop right next door at this tiny Vietnamese counter for a satisfying meal prepared before your eyes. The two women who own the place only make a few things—kebabs, rice with a rich meat sauce, crispy imperial rolls, and five-spice roast chicken—but they're all dangerously addictive. Special Number 5 includes all of the above and can easily satisfy two carnivores. Lunch specials go for $3.50. *1574 California St., between Polk and Larkin Sts., tel. 415/673–5637. Cash only. Closed Mon.*

Mad Magda's Russian Tea Room & Mystic Cafe. Hand-painted floors and a tarot reader seated in the front window set the mood for this funky joint set amid the growing Hayes Valley glitter. Piroshkis (baked dough concealing savory fillings) have unusual fillings like roast beef and capers or smoked chicken and pears. The sandwiches have names like the Stalin (smoked turkey and cheddar) and the Khrushchev (ham and cheese). *579 Hayes St., between Octavia and Laguna Sts., tel. 415/864–7654. Cash only.*

Racha Café. Industrial meets tropical at this Thai outpost on the edge of the Tenderloin. Though the neighborhood is iffy (make sure you come via Polk Street at night), the wide range of vegetarian, seafood, and meat entrées is excellent, and the coconut milk–based soups (with chicken, seafood, or vegetables) are out of this world. *771 Ellis St., between Polk and Larkin Sts., tel. 415/885–0725.*

Swan Oyster Depot. Politicians from nearby city hall can open their mouths wider than this tiny fish-market eatery, which consists of nothing more than one long counter and some of the best seafood in town. Settle down to a bowl of clam chowder, thick sourdough bread, and an Anchor Steam beer. You might be lucky enough to spot Willie Brown downing a crab cocktail or a salad on the bar stool next to you. *1517 Polk St., between California and Sacramento Sts., tel. 415/673–1101. Cash only. Closed Sun.*

Tu Lan. This greasy little dive in a seedy section of downtown is famous for its fantastic Vietnamese grub. The imperial rolls with rice noodles and lemon beef salad are among the standout dishes on the expansive menu, which includes quite a few vegetarian choices. Bottles of imported beer are only $2—if you can get someone to bring you one. *8 6th St., at Market St., tel. 415/626–0927. Cash only. Closed Sun.*

UNDER $15

Nori Sushi. On Market Street in the no-man's-land between the Civic Center and the Castro, this joint consists of an L-shape bar, two booths, and one sushi master, Nori himself. Amazingly, most *nigiri* (finger-size pieces of fish on a roll of rice) and six-piece rolls are only $3, so two people can have a sushi fest for less than $25 (not including sake). Expect to find a crowd. *1815 Market St., No. 5, between Guerrero and Valencia Sts., tel. 415/621–1114. Cash only. Closed Mon.*

Suppenküche. In the Asian- and Mediterranean-oriented Bay Area dining scene, this Hayes Valley restaurant with a lively atmosphere and authentic but dignified German cuisine stands out as a novelty. Get ready to feast on venison sautéed in red wine sauce with red cabbage and noodles or farmers' sausage with sauerkraut and mashed potatoes. The weekend brunch packs a crowd. *601 Hayes St., at Laguna St., tel. 415/252–9289. No lunch weekdays.*

DOWNTOWN/EMBARCADERO

Downtown abounds with both old, classic restaurants that evoke San Francisco's golden years and trendy, new let's-do-lunch-and-expense-it bistros; both take advantage of the high-rolling Financial District's need to dispose of income. Except for a few options below, it's difficult to find a decent *and* inexpensive sit-down restaurant in this area—but it's usually worth it when you decide to go for it, especially in the "French Quarter," home to the almost identical Cafés **Claude** and **Bastille** (*see below*). On the other end of the fiscal spectrum, it's not so hard to find healthy soup-and-salad buffets catering to working stiffs on the go. Where downtown flows into the **Embarcadero,** stop by the bakery at **Il Fornaio** (1265 Battery St., at Greenwich St., tel. 415/986–0100) for a pizza or *panino* picnic on the pier.

UNDER $5

Specialty's. These five tiny take-out stands bake 14 kinds of bread, including potato-cheese and carrot-curry varieties, with which they make 40 different fresh sandwiches. They also have daily soup specials, pastries like zucchini bran muffins, and insanely rich sweets. If you don't feel like eating on the sidewalk, take your lunch over to the rooftop garden at Crocker Galleria, at the corner of Kearny and Post streets. *312 Kearny St., between Bush and Pine Sts.; 22 Battery St., between Market and Bush Sts.; 150 Spear St., between Mission and Howard Sts.; 1 Post St., at Market St.; 101 New Montgomery St., at Mission St.; tel. 415/896–2253 for daily specials or 415/512–9550 for phone orders. Cash only. No dinner weekends.*

UNDER $10

101 Restaurant. Just steps from the Powell Street station in the direction of the Tenderloin, this weary-looking but very reasonable restaurant serves Vietnamese favorites like barbecued beef with rice noodles, lettuce, mint, peanuts, and bean sprouts or chicken in coconut-milk curry with lemongrass. The lunch special ($4.75) includes soup, an imperial roll, and your choice of barbecued beef, chicken, or pork. *101 Eddy St., at Mason St., tel. 415/928–4490. Closed Sun.*

UNDER $15

Café Bastille. Nibble on neat little French appetizers like onion soup, pâté, or baked goat cheese on eggplant in a happening, Gallic atmosphere. For a more substantial meal, try a sandwich or real meat-and-potatoes fare like roast chicken or *steak frites.* Filled with Financial District workers and bohemians with a few bucks to blow, the café gets pretty fun and friendly, especially Wednesday through Saturday, when there's live jazz. *22 Belden Pl., between Pine and Bush Sts. and Kearny and Montgomery Sts., tel. 415/986–5673. Closed Sun.*

Café Claude. Live jazz accompanies your meal most nights at this youthful but bourgeois French bistro in an alley near Chinatown's gates. With a more relaxed atmosphere than Café Bastille (*see above*), it's a great place to while away a lazy afternoon or a late evening with a few glasses of wine and a plate of rich pâté. Specials are the way to go: When it's available, order the *coq au vin* (chicken in wine sauce) with potatoes au gratin. *7 Claude La., off Bush St. between Grant and Kearny Sts., tel. 415/392–3515. Closed Sun.*

Caffe Macaroni. This place is tiny and usually packed elbow to elbow, so to speak—though there's an additional room upstairs—but it's worth squeezing in for some of the city's most affordable, authentic southern Italian food, served with a Neapolitan flair. A "small" antipasti plate will warm up at least three people's appetites, and the pasta dishes are generous and delicious. Look for specials like squid-ink fettuccine heaped with fresh mussels, clams, calamari, and crab legs. *59 Columbus Ave., at Jackson St., tel. 415/956–9737. Cash only. Closed Sun.*

Yank Sing. With locations in the Financial District and South of Market, Yank Sing is a great place to feast on dim sum in a tasteful, modern setting. A meal should cost $10–$15, but watch out: Let your appetite run away with you, and next thing you know, stacks of plates are sliding off the table, and the waiter is handing you a bill the size of Beijing. *427 Battery St., at Clay St., tel. 415/362–1640; 49 Stevenson Pl., between 1st and 2nd Sts., tel. 415/541–4949. Closed Sat.*

FISHERMAN'S WHARF

Steer clear of the mediocre, high-priced seafood restaurants that crowd the wharf: The best dining experience you could have here would involve a loaf of sourdough, some cracked crab, a bottle of wine, and a seat on the pier. The corner of **Jefferson** and **Taylor streets** is jam-packed with street stands that hawk all sorts of seafood goodies, including shrimp or crab cups and thick clam chowder in a bread bowl. The only authentically rustic place to sit down and eat around here is **Eagle Café** (Pier 39, upper level, tel. 415/433–3689), where windows and patio tables offer a view of the waterfront and Alcatraz. Or grab an Irish coffee at the old-fashioned **Buena Vista Café** (2765 Hyde St., tel. 415/474–5044), purportedly the place where the drink was introduced in America. And, of course, there's always **Ben and Jerry's**—it's near the Red and White Fleet's ticket booth.

THE HAIGHT

The Haight (both its lower and upper sections) is renowned for its breakfast spots, including the **Pork Store Café,** the **Crescent City Café,** and **Kate's Kitchen** (*see below*). These places are frequented by ragged-looking youths who suck up coffee as if it's the primal life force. For dinner, the Haight has a few trendy hot spots and a preponderance of pizza, falafel, and burrito joints.

UNDER $5

Taqueria El Balazo. This isn't the Mission, but that's precisely Balazo's appeal: Its New Age Cal-Mex food is irresistible. Choose from three kinds of veggie burritos, all stuffed with saffron rice, beans, Mexican goat cheese, and vegetables sautéed on a vegetarian grill—or dig into the burrito Vallarta, with sautéed rock prawns and tender nopal cacti. Deadheads will find burritos named for their heroes, and the kitchen turns out huge dinner platters meant to be shared (about $5). Eat in the back room, and you will sometimes be treated to live flamenco guitar. *1654 Haight St., between Belvedere and Clayton Sts., tel. 415/864–8608. Cash only.*

UNDER $10

Crescent City Café. At this New Orleans–style café with six small tables and maybe a dozen counter seats, weekend brunch brings crowds in search of andouille sausage hash, or eggs creole (like eggs Benedict except with avocado and creole sauce). Thursday night there's a terrific barbecued ribs special ($9.50). *1418 Haight St., at Masonic St., tel. 415/863–1374.*

Kan Zaman. Patrons pack into this trendy Mediterranean restaurant to listen to hypnotic Middle Eastern music and indulge in hummus, *baba ghanoush,* and spinach pies. On Friday, Saturday, and Sunday nights the Fat Chance Belly Dancers strut their stuff. *1793 Haight St., at Shrader St., tel. 415/751–9656. Cash only.*

Kate's Kitchen. This wholesome breakfast spot is no secret: The line stretches out the door, especially on weekends. Chummy servers bring you specials like buttermilk-cornmeal pancakes, hush puppies with honey butter, and "fruit orgies"—fresh fruit with granola, yogurt, and honey. *471 Haight St., between Fillmore and Webster Sts., tel. 415/626–3984.*

Massawa. Come to this Ethiopian restaurant if you like trying unusual spices and eating with your hands. Dinner platters are filled with tender lamb or beef, along with side portions of lentils, greens, or yellow split-pea paste. There are also vegetarian plates. Everything comes with *injera,* a flat, spongy bread used instead of silverware to scoop up food. *1538 Haight St., between Ashbury and Clayton Sts., tel. 415/621–4129.*

Pork Store Café. Mounds of grits, big, fluffy omelets, and plate-size pancakes (try a chocolate short stack) are all slapped together on the same griddle. The café serves lunch, too, including comfort-food entrées like pork chops and applesauce with mashed potatoes, spinach, and biscuits. Check out the collection of posters from Haight-Ashbury street fairs past—they're almost as entertaining as the stream of locals strutting by. *1451 Haight St., between Ashbury St. and Masonic Ave., tel. 415/864–6981. No dinner.*

Spaghetti Western. The pierced-and-tattooed set hangs out at this chaotic Lower Haight spot, where Western-style breakfasts include corn bread, black beans, and assorted *huevos* (eggs). Gorge yourself on Spuds O'Rama, a huge mound of home-fried potatoes topped with cheese and sour cream, or the thick sourdough French toast blanketed with bananas and strawberries. *576 Haight St., near Steiner St., tel. 415/864–8461. No dinner.*

Squat and Gobble Café. Lower Haight types come to this sprawling café with the Sunday paper, a pack of Marlboro reds, and nothing to do all day (so it seems). Try the massive Lower Haight omelet, with fresh veggies, pesto, and cheese, or any number of inventive crêpes, including the Zorba the Greek, with feta, olives, artichokes, spinach, and cheddar. There's also a decent selection of salads and sandwiches. *237 Fillmore St., between Haight and Waller Sts., tel. 415/487–0551; 1428 Haight St., between Ashbury and Masonic Sts., tel. 415/864–8484.*

Thep Phanom. This comfortably stylish spot regularly turns up on critics' lists as the one of the city's best Thai restaurants. The authentically hot, colorful curries are undoubtedly one reason why, and the attentive but not hovering service is another. You can easily make a meal of the excellent appetizers and salads: fish cakes, minced duck salad, squid spiked with lime, and green papaya salad are standouts. *400 Waller St., at Fillmore St., tel. 415/431–2526. No lunch.*

Ya Halla. Though it's on a particularly grimy stretch of Haight Street, this Middle Eastern eatery has a loyal following. Everything is fresh and delicious—especially the eggplant moussaka, with roasted tomato, garlic, pine nuts, and rice pilaf; and the falafel, served with hummus and tabbouleh in a burrito-style *lavash* wrap. All meals come with a plate of feta and olives, but the *meze* (assorted appetizers) are too good to pass up. *494 Haight St., near Fillmore St., tel. 415/522–1509.*

UNDER $15

Cha Cha Cha. Though you may wait up to two hours for a table under the watchful eyes of the pseudo-Catholic icons that hang on the wall, you might not mind when you finally taste the tapas that make this place such a hit. Try fried plantains with black beans and sour cream or shrimp sautéed in Cajun spices; both are great with the house-made sangria. To avoid the crowds, come for a late lunch. *1801 Haight St., at Shrader St., tel. 415/386–7670.*

JAPANTOWN

In the **Japan Center** (1737 Post St., between Geary and Fillmore Sts.), the veritable essence of Japantown, a bunch of decent restaurants—spanning a wide range of price categories—display their edibles with shiny photos or shellacked plastic miniatures. If nothing piques your interest, explore the surrounding streets, especially **Buchanan** and **Webster streets** to the north of the center, for older, more divey places that occasionally turn out to be gems. The cheapest option of all is to visit the Japanese market **Maruwa,** on the corner of Post and Webster streets. Along with fruits and vegetables and all manner of Japanese products, the delicatessen has sushi, rice and noodle dishes, and individual cuts of meat. Afterward, catch a flick at the multiscreen AMC Kabuki 8 (*see* Movie Houses *in* Chapter 6), in the same complex as the center.

UNDER $10

Isobune. Patrons at this gimmicky but fun sushi restaurant pack in around a large table elbow to elbow and fish their sushi off little boats that bob about in the water in front of them. It may not be the best sushi you'll ever eat, but it's good enough for the price: $1.50–$3 for two pieces. *Japan Center, 1737 Post St., tel. 415/563–1030; 5897 College Ave., at Chabot St., Oakland, tel. 510/601–1424.*

Mifune. A steady stream of Asian and American patrons slurp up cheap, tasty *udon* (thick white noodles), *soba* (thin buckwheat noodles), and *donburi* (rice) dishes in the simple Mifune dining room. The house-made noodles come with various meats and vegetables; there's even one with jumbo shrimp. *Japan Center, 1737 Post St., tel. 415/922–0337.*

UNDER $15

Izumiya. Ignore the requisite plastic sushi prototypes in the window and the cheesy decor—this place is almost always packed with a young crowd, giving it a kind of Japanese Mel's Diner atmosphere. The house special, steamed orange roughy ($10.50, including salad, soup, and rice), is special for a reason, and the appetizers, such as clams steamed in sake, are equally fantastic. Sushi is on the menu, but raw fish is not the main draw here. *Japan Center, 1581 Webster St., tel. 415/441–6867. Closed Mon.*

Now and Zen. This friendly little vegan restaurant about a block from the Japan Center began as a wholesale vegan bakery—so, naturally, it has great cakes and pastries made without eggs, milk, or sugar. But now it also has a full range of delicious dinners and weekend brunches made from organic ingredients with a Japanese twist. Exotic mushrooms, interesting noodles, and Asian vegetables are tossed together in such intriguing plates as macro sukiyaki (a vegetable medley with tofu and Japanese mountain yam noodles in a savory soy broth with brown rice). Come with an open mind. *1826B Buchanan St., tel. 415/922–9696. Closed Mon. No lunch Tues.–Fri.*

MARINA DISTRICT/COW HOLLOW

Although not exactly a budget locale, the Marina has recently been flooded with scores of new culinary hot spots. A 10-minute walk west of Fisherman's Wharf will bring you to the corner of **Chestnut** and **Union streets,** the heart of this district, where grills, sushi spots, and California-cuisine eateries are a dime a dozen.

UNDER $10

Hahn's Hibachi. This tiny restaurant, little more than a take-out counter, dishes up healthy portions of Korean-barbecued chicken, beef, or pork with rice and kimchi. So many people order takeout that there's rarely a wait for the five or so tables. *3318 Steiner St., between Chestnut and Lombard Sts., tel. 415/931–6284; 1710 Polk St., at Clay St., tel. 415/776–1095; 1305 Castro St., at 24th St., tel. 415/642–8151. Cash only. Closed Sun.*

Pluto's. There's an entire wall covered with countless adjectives describing food—a fairly transparent attempt at making you hungry. But chances are you'll already be ravenous after waiting in line with the young Marina folks who come here in droves. The generous portions of American comfort food include herb-roasted Sonoma turkey with the smashed spuds of the day, as well as hefty salads and sandwiches. Breakfast is served on weekends. *3258 Scott St., at Chestnut St., tel. 415/775–8867.*

FARMERS' MARKETS

Stock up on seasonal and organic produce at the city's farmers' markets, held year-round. The market at the Ferry Building, at the downtown end of Market Street (Tuesday 11–3 and Saturday 8–1:30), has free samples of home-grown fruits and homemade cheeses and breads; it's also one of the best places in the city to get shellfish straight out of Tomales Bay. Other farmers' markets take place at the United Nations Plaza, Wednesday and Sunday 8–5, and at 100 Alemany Boulevard (tel. 415/647–9423), near Crescent Avenue in Bernal Heights, Saturday from dawn to dusk and Thursday in summer from 3 to 8.

Every Friday from 8 to 2 you can buy from East Bay farmers and bakers at the Old Oakland Certified Farmers' Market (Broadway and 9th St., tel. 510/452–3276). Oakland's other farmers' market is at Jack London Square (Broadway and Embarcadero) Sunday 10–2. You can also stock up on farm-fresh products at one of Berkeley's farmers' markets, sponsored by the Ecology Center (tel. 510/548–3333). Look for them every Saturday 10–2 on Center Street at Martin Luther King Jr. Way; Sunday 11–3 on Haste Street at Telegraph Avenue (from May through November); and Tuesday from 2 until 7 on Derby Street at Martin Luther King Jr. Way.

MISSION DISTRICT

Here you can wander from *taquería* to café to bookstore to taquería again in a salsa-and-*cerveza*-induced state of bliss. To add to the zillions of Mexican and Central American eateries that already crowd the neighborhood, a smattering of trendy restaurants has sprouted up in recent years, especially along **16th** and **Valencia streets**—this is without a doubt the favorite area in town for young hipsters to wine and dine. The Mission's restaurants are accessible from either the 16th Street/Mission or the 24th Street/Mission BART stations.

UNDER $5

Casa Sanchez. With a colorful outdoor patio, home-style cooking, and a friendly atmosphere, Casa Sanchez just might become your favorite taquería. Hefty combination platters and limitless chips and salsa (both homemade) will fill you to the bursting point. *2778 24th St., between York and Hampshire Sts., tel. 415/282–2400. Cash only.*

El Toro. This lively, gringo-frequented taquería presents you with many choices: Spanish or vegetarian rice, four kinds of salsa, four types of tortilla (white, wheat, red chili, or green chili), and no less than 10 types of protein, including *lengua* (beef tongue) and tofu *ranchero*. You'll have plenty of time to make up your mind, since the line often snakes out the door. *598 Valencia St., at 17th St., tel. 415/431–3351. Cash only.*

El Trébol. What El Trébol lacks in decor it quickly makes up for with incredibly cheap Central American fare and an animated, Spanish-speaking clientele. Specialties include *salpicón* (chopped beef), *chancho con yuca* (fried pork with cassava), and *pollo encebollado* (chicken with onions). Most entrées come with beans, rice, and tortillas. *3324 24th St., at Mission St., tel. 415/285–6298. Closed Sun.*

La Cumbre. Large, colorful Mexican paintings line the walls, and the requisite Virgin Mary statue guards the front door of this bustling taquería. If you like beef tongue, this is place to pack it into a taco or burrito. Or try *carne asada,* and throw your cholesterol cares to the wind. Meat and veggie dinner platters, which include beans and rice, will fuel you through the night and most of the next day. *515 Valencia St., between 16th and 17th Sts., tel. 415/863–8205.*

New Dawn. You'll find the most bizarre collection of kitsch you've ever seen in this slacker hangout, including a life-size Jesus wearing sunglasses. The food is as basic as it gets: Share an enormous plate of veggie home fries (vegetables topped with a load of potatoes) or go the familiar route with a three-egg breakfast. *3174 16th St., between Valencia and Guerrero Sts., no phone. Cash only. No dinner Mon., Tues.*

Pancho Villa. This always-packed taquería, a brother of El Toro (*see above*), is a step above the myriad others, with a full range of seafood dinners such as savory garlic prawns, as well as the requisite burrito selections. The eclectic, ever-changing artwork is fun to peruse, and mariachi bands often perform on weekends. *3071 16th St., between Mission and Valencia Sts., tel. 415/864–8840.*

Taquería Cancun. Surrounded by countless empty restaurants in the midst of Mission Street's mayhem, this taquería jams with locals and a cranked-up jukebox. They serve one of the best veggie burritos around—chock-full of beans, rice, and thick avocado slices—and a mean salsa *verde*. *2288 Mission St., between 18th and 19th Sts., tel. 415/252–9560. Cash only.*

Truly Mediterranean. This tiny take-out counter, tucked right next door to the popular Roxie movie house (*see* Chapter 6), serves all your basic Mediterranean salads and pita sandwiches; but their falafel deluxe (with eggplant and potatoes) and *shawerma* compete with neighboring taquerías when it comes to a cheap, filling, and tasty meal to go. *3109 16th St., between Valencia and Guerrero Sts., tel. 415/252–7482. Cash only.*

If you're looking to celebrate, head to one of the Mission's many Mediterranean or Spanish tapas restaurants, where live music keeps things lively, red wine flows freely, and plates are meant to be shared and lingered over.

UNDER $10

Boogaloos. Under the same ownership as Spaghetti Western (*see* The Haight, *above*), Boogaloos has sidewalk tables and a colorful interior full of pottery and abstract art. One of the better breakfast dishes is polenta and eggs with salsa, black beans, and sour cream. *3296 Valencia St., at 22nd St., 415/824–3211. Cash only. No dinner Mon., Tues.*

La Rondalla. A strolling mariachi band follows iron-haired waitresses in a room decorated with Christmas ornaments year-round; this has been going on since La Rondalla opened in 1951. The Mexican food is decent and reasonably priced, but the real draws here are the margaritas, the crazy atmosphere, and the late hours (until 3:30 AM). *901 Valencia St., at 20th St., tel. 415/647–7474. Cash only. Closed Mon.*

Nicaragua. The plate of fried plantains with *crema* (the Nicaraguan equivalent of French crème fraîche) and fried cheese is as flavorful (and fattening) as it gets; featherlight *yoltamál* (cornmeal) is another favorite. The restaurant is a classic dive, with plastic tablecloths and cheesy pictures of Nicaragua on the walls. The area is seedy, so be careful at night. *3015 Mission St., between 26th and César Chávez (Army) Sts., tel. 415/826–3672. Cash only.*

Panchita's. You could walk down 16th Street a hundred times without noticing this basic but fantastic El Salvadoran–Mexican restaurant where a jukebox plays mariachi tunes. For breakfast there's *huevos rancheros* (eggs with tortillas, cheese, and salsa), for dinner *carne desilachada* (shredded beef with egg, tomatoes, peppers, beans, and rice). Or order a pair of *pupusas* (a cornmeal round stuffed with cheese) with some *platanos con crema* (fried plantains with refried beans and cream) on the side. *3091 16th St., at Valencia St., tel. 415/431–4232.*

UNDER $15

Amira. This is the place to lie back on low couches with velveteen cushions, order *meze* (appetizers) and wine, and ogle belly dancers. It's also the place to indulge: Start off with the chef's intense walnut-garlic dip, then move on to Libyan chicken or Moroccan couscous. Belly dancers perform nightly, with live Near Eastern music on Wednesday, Friday, and Saturday, when reservations are advised and there's a $1 cover. *590 Valencia St., between 16th and 17th Sts., tel. 415/621–6213. Closed Mon. No lunch.*

Esperpento. Lines snake out the door at this great tapas joint—especially on weekends. Feast on clams with white beans, *calamares en su tinta* (squid in their own ink), or a huge paella (saffron rice cooked with chicken, sausage, and shellfish) dinner ($26 for two). The sangria is tastier and cheaper than at most tapas joints, and the room is lively and fun, with colorful Miró-esque touches. *3295 22nd St., between Valencia and Mission Sts., tel. 415/282–8867. Cash only.*

Scenic India. Tasty *shaag bhajee* (spinach with tomato and onion), chicken tandoori (half chicken baked in a clay oven), and other traditional Indian specialties are all served with delicious breads. Though service is slow there's never a wait for a table (a major plus in this neighborhood). *532 Valencia St., between 16th and 17th Sts., tel. 415/621–7226. Closed Mon.*

Slanted Door. Compared with all the party-oriented restaurants surrounding it, this place is decidedly subdued—but still wildly trendy. The vegetarian-friendly menu includes subtle dishes like vegetable curry with shiitake mushrooms, yams, and cauliflower or spicy stir-fried squid, delicately infused with red pepper, garlic, and other spices. Wash it down with a pot of exotic tea or a microbrew. *584 Valencia St., at 17th St., tel. 415/861–8032. Closed Mon.*

Ti Couz. An impatient crowd hangs around the bar sipping cider out of *bols,* waiting to get a taste of the succulent, piping-hot crêpes whipped up in the style of Breton crêperies in western France. Dinner crêpes come with savory fillings like ratatouille, smoked salmon, or mushrooms; dessert crêpes are filled with Nutella and banana or fragrant poached pears. *3108 16th St., at Valencia St., tel. 415/252–7373.*

Timo's. Visit this dimly lighted, cozy restaurant with a group of friends, and you can sample widely from its huge selection of South American-, Spanish-, and Mediterranean-style tapas. Feast your way through the delicate salads, roasted potatoes with garlic mayonnaise, grilled prawns, quail, and salt-cod potato cake with mint salsa, and more. *842 Valencia St., between 19th and 20th Sts., tel. 415/647–0558; Timo's Norte, 900 Northpoint (Ghirardelli Square), tel. 415/440–1200. No lunch.*

NORTH BEACH/RUSSIAN HILL

The old-time Italian neighborhood of North Beach has the highest concentration of restaurants (and lowest concentration of parking) in the city. **Columbus Avenue** and **Grant Avenue** north of Columbus are lined with reasonably priced restaurants with everything from old-fashioned "American-style" Italian food to trendy neo-Italian cuisine.

UNDER $5

Golden Boy Pizza. Young North Beach residents fill up the bar stools at this tiny dive to get fat, greasy slices. Check out what's available in the window—pesto vegetarian and clam garlic are good bets. The purple-coiffed people behind the bar might even smile at you as they warm up your square. *542 Green St., between Grant Ave. and Stockton St., tel. 415/982–9738. Cash only.*

San Francisco Art Institute Café. With the kind of view for which you normally have to pay through the nose, this unpretentious café inside an art school a couple of steep blocks up Russian Hill from North Beach has a reassuring sign that promises PSEUDO BOHEMIANS WELCOME—and the prices reflect that claim. There's a nice selection of burgers (some vegetarian), healthy salads, and irresistible baked goods. *800 Chestnut St., between Leavenworth and Jones Sts., tel. 415/749–4567. Cash only. Closed Sun.*

UNDER $10

Bocce Café. The choose-your-own-adventure menu might not blow you away, but Bocce continues to pack 'em in with its reasonable prices, jovial atmosphere, and cozy decor. Sit back on cushions and admire the high ceilings and ornate mirrors while you feast on one of five pastas with 15 different sauces—including clams, pesto, and sautéed eggplant. On warm Friday and Saturday evenings you can eat in the garden to the strains of live jazz. *478 Green St., at Grant Ave., tel. 415/981–2044. Closed Sun.*

Il Pollaio. This small Italian kitchen serves up tasty grilled chicken, and lots of it, in a homey atmosphere that attracts Italian old-timers year after year. Fill up on a fantastic half chicken with salad, crusty bread, and wine for less than $10. Desserts run from flan and cheesecake to chocolate mousse. *555 Columbus Ave., between Union and Green Sts., tel. 415/362–7727. Closed Sun.*

L'Osteria del Forno. Two Italian women have created an affordable menu and a chic-but-casual atmosphere for their tiny Italian restaurant. Focaccia sandwiches and thin-crust pizza are deliciously authentic, especially the pizza *bianca* with white cheese and wild mushrooms. There are usually one or two homemade pastas available daily—look for the spinach- or pumpkin-filled ravioli. *519 Columbus Ave., at Green St., tel. 415/982–1124. Cash only. Closed Tues.*

North Beach Pizza. On weekends you'll have to stand on the street and be tortured by the smell of garlic while you wait for a table. Once inside, you can sink your teeth into thick-crust pizzas heaped with pepperoni, spinach, pesto, feta, and mushrooms. Pizzas come by the pie only—sorry, no slices. *1499 Grant Ave., at Union St., tel. 415/433–2444; 1310 Grant Ave., at Vallejo St., tel. 415/433–2444; 800*

Stanyan St., at Beulah St., tel. 415/751–2300; 4787 Mission St., at Ocean Ave., tel. 415/586–1400; 1598 University Ave., at California St., Berkeley, tel. 510/849–9800.

UNDER $15

Ristorante Ideale. This is like a true Roman restaurant—the waiters are distracted but warmhearted, the antipasti are top-notch, and the atmosphere is refined but relaxed. You can stick to the antipasti menu and sample delectable *cozze con fagioli* (steamed mussels with garlic and fava beans), or you can go for a perfectly al dente pasta dish, like *pappardelle all'agnello* (homemade wide noodles with lamb-tomato sauce). In true Roman style, waiters here will let you linger for hours. *1309 Grant St., between Green and Vallejo Sts., tel. 415/391–4129. Closed Mon.*

Zarzuela. This warm, rustic Spanish restaurant suits its Russian Hill setting: Though it's always bustling, it doesn't have the "PAR-dee!" feel of tapas joints in the Mission—despite the efforts of the jolly waiters, who force you to clink glasses when they serve the wine. Sample small but satisfying plates of mushrooms in garlic sauce, tortilla *española,* or steamed mussels. There's also a heavenly saffron-rich paella for $28 (for two). *2000 Hyde St., at Union St., tel. 415/346–0800. Closed Sun.*

UNDER $20

Rose Pistola. With its big, open kitchen, nouveau light fixtures, and waitpeople rushing in and out of every aisle, this North Beach hot spot is the current rage—and well worth the hype. The menu, inspired by the food of Liguria, contains an assortment of small antipasti plates—like fava beans with pecorino cheese, pizzas from a wood-burning oven, and hearty main courses that can easily be shared. Reservations are hard to come by, but a number of tables are kept for walk-ins. *532 Columbus Ave., between Union and Green Sts., tel. 415/399–0499.*

Intimate restaurants, sidewalk cafés, and dimly lighted bars make North Beach a prime destination for a romantic tête-à-tête. If dinner and drinks don't do the trick, hike up to Coit Tower for a view that will leave your date swooning.

RICHMOND AND SUNSET DISTRICTS

From the way San Franciscans talk, you'd think the Richmond and Sunset districts were in another county. In fact, these districts flanking Golden Gate Park are only a few minutes from the Haight and Japantown by car or just three or four more stops on the MUNI. In the Richmond District, Vietnamese, Chinese, Burmese, and Japanese places line **Clement** and **Geary streets** between Arguello Boulevard and 9th Avenue and between 20th and 25th avenues, where you'll also find produce markets brimming with items strange to a Western eye. On the other side of the park, in the Sunset, **Irving Street** between 5th and 25th avenues yields numerous Chinese and Thai restaurants.

UNDER $10

Empress Garden. Although the Sunset teems with Chinese restaurants, this tastefully decorated establishment has muscled its way to the top. Every night of the week Asian locals pack in around the party-size tables to feast on the minced or deep-fried squab—the house specialty—and other delectable dishes. A fish tank filled with kicking crabs attests to the food's freshness. *1386 9th Ave., between Irving and Judah Sts., tel. 415/731–2388.*

Ton Kiang. Dim sum aficionados regularly head to this Richmond outpost for dumplings and rice-noodle rolls, stuffed bean curd sheets, and black bean spareribs. At dinner there are Hakka (southern Chinese) specialties: salt-baked chicken, wine-flavored meats and seafood, and braised, stuffed bean curd crowned with slivered vegetables. A second location serves lunch and dinner only. *5821 Geary Blvd., between 22nd and 23rd Aves., tel. 415/387–8273; 3148 Geary Blvd., at Spruce St., tel. 415/752–4440. No dim sum at Geary location.*

UNDER $15

Brother's Restaurant. Come to this minimalist Richmond joint for authentic Korean barbecue—lots of it. Each table comes with its own piping-hot wood-charcoal grill, which you use to sear your marinated short ribs, chicken, or shrimp. Once you've ordered your meat, servers will bring you never-ending bowls of kimchi, assorted pickled veggies, sushi seaweed wraps, and rice—until you cry for mercy. There are two locations only a block from each other; the one between 5th and 6th is more lively. *4128*

SWEET TREATS

Just Desserts. Since 1974 it's been a Bay Area favorite. Look for 10 branches throughout the Bay Area; the main location, on Church Street in San Francisco, has a secluded outdoor courtyard. 248 Church St., at Market St., tel. 415/626–5774.

Lovejoy's Antiques and Tea Room. This Noe Valley shop serves English high tea, with scones, finger sandwiches, and crumpets. 1195 Church St., at 24th St., tel. 415/648–5895.

Mitchell's Ice Cream. This family-owned shop in the Mission serves unusual homemade ice creams—try avocado or yam. 688 San Jose Ave., at 29th St., tel. 415/648–2300.

St. Francis Soda Fountain and Candy Store. In the Mission since 1918, St. Francis still makes its own ice cream, syrups, and candy. Order a phosphate and wax nostalgic. 2801 24th St., at York St., tel. 415/826–4200.

Swensen's. Climb to the top of Russian Hill, and you'll find the original Swensen's ice cream parlor. You might need a chocolate double dip (if not a respirator) to get going again. 1999 Hyde St., at Union St., tel. 415/775–6818.

Toy Boat. Come here for a scoop and marvel for hours at the hundreds of toys lining the walls. 401 Clement St., at 5th Ave., tel. 415/751–7505.

Geary Blvd., between 5th and 6th Aves., tel. 415/387–7991; 4014 Geary Blvd., near 4th Ave., tel. 415/668–2028.

Ebisu. This Inner Sunset sushi bar is one of the city's best—there's always a line out the door. The sushi specials, which include miso soup and tea, are a good way to sample a selection. Try the delicate *hirame* (halibut) or the slippery, pearly white *kaibashira* (scallops), and always ask the sushi masters which fish is on special. *1283 9th Ave., at Irving St., tel. 415/566–1770. Closed Sun.*

Khan Toke Thai House. In this dimly lighted Richmond District restaurant, you sit on the floor with your shoes off and are surrounded by delicately carved wood panels and a wild garden. The restaurant consistently wins awards in the "Best of the Bay Area" contest, despite most dishes costing only $5–$10. If you're feeling especially erudite, choose from a special section of the menu called "Thai curries mentioned in Thai literature." *5937 Geary Blvd., at 24th Ave., tel. 415/668–6654.*

P.J.'s Oyster Bed. Sharing a meal is the best policy at this happening Cajun restaurant; with an appetizer thrown in, most entrées will successfully fill two big eaters. The best dishes are superfresh oysters, gigantic bowls of gumbo, and the enormous shellfish roast, full of spicy crawdads and other bivalves. If there's a wait, put your name on the list and cross the street to Yancy's, a cavernous dive bar that's connected to the restaurant via an intercom. *737 Irving, at 9th Ave., tel. 415/566–7775.*

SOUTH OF MARKET

The SoMa warehouse wasteland yields surprisingly attractive and friendly restaurants on the unlikeliest, grimiest corners. Wander along **Folsom Street** between 7th and 12th streets or along **11th** and **9th streets** between Howard and Harrison streets, and you'll have the SoMa eating scene in the palm of your hand. Oddly, there are few late-night eating spots to satiate clubbers' cravings. Besides **Hamburger**

Mary's and **Club Za Pizza** (*see below*), you can try **20 Tank Brewery** (*see* Bars *in* Chapter 6), which serves sandwiches, nachos, and other munchies most nights until 1 AM and beer until 1:30 AM.

UNDER $5

Club Za Pizza. Next to the DNA Lounge (*see* Clubs *in* Chapter 6), Club Za is a convenient stop for a $3 slice (or "zlice" as they say). Fancifully named pies range from their Vegan Friendly (with cilantro pesto and lots of veggies) to Vegan Nightmare (with extra cheese and lots of meats); but the Potesto (with pesto, cheese, and potatoes) is king. Za is also popular with the lunchtime SoMa multimedia crowd, when you can get great "zalads" and "zoups." *371 11th St., between Folsom and Harrison Sts., tel. 415/552–5599; Little Za (takeout only), 2162 Polk St., between Vallejo St. and Broadway, tel. 415/563– 8515. Za Gourmet Pizza: 1919 Hyde St., between Green and Union Sts., tel. 415/771–3100.*

UNDER $10

Hamburger Mary's. The messy hamburgers and cluttered decor go together wonderfully. Come by at 1 AM to hang out with SoMa clubbers in various states of drunkenness. Vegetarians can feast on the tofu burger or the Meatless Meaty, a hot sandwich of mushrooms, cream cheese, and olives. *1582 Folsom St., at 12th St., tel. 415/626–5767.*

Manora's Thai Cuisine. Trendier than most Thai restaurants in the city, this place attracts big crowds— but the fresh, attractive dishes are worth the wait. Try garlic quail or spicy Japanese eggplant with prawns, chicken, and pork. *1600 Folsom St., at 12th St., tel. 415/861–6224. No lunch weekends.*

UNDER $15

South Park Café. Pretend you're Hemingway, Gertrude Stein, or Henry Miller in glorious Parisian exile while you gnaw on *boudin noir* (blood sausage) and *frites* (french fries). This French bistro opens at 7:30 AM weekdays with fresh croissants and coffee and stays open for country-cooked lunches and din- ners. *108 South Park Ave., between 2nd and 3rd and Bryant and Brannan Sts., tel. 415/495–7275. Closed Sun.*

UNDER $20

Lulu. A nouvelle French–Italian–Californian meal at Lulu's is worth the money. Besides, dishes are served family style, meaning you can try a little of everything and not spend too much. Roasted meat entrées and grilled vegetables are the specialty: Watch the "designated roasters" at the wood-fired oven with their offi- cial-looking walkie-talkies. Pastas, such as butternut squash gnocchi in sage and olive oil, are fantastically rustic, and thin-crust pizzas taste as amazing as they look. *816 Folsom St., at 4th St. tel. 415/495–5775.*

EAST BAY

Sure, San Francisco has enough restaurants to keep a gourmand feasting for years, but the East Bay outdoes San Francisco in some types of cuisine. Not only is it the home of "California Cuisine," it's also the best place to find an Ethiopian meal, or to pick up a barbecued rib dinner. Oakland's Chinatown rivals San Francisco's in authenticity, and Berkeley has a classier breakfast scene than the Haight for about the same price.

BERKELEY

California cuisine, that designer fuel for the yuppie generation, got its start in Berkeley, and locals take their food very seriously. The area around Shattuck Avenue at Vine Street has become known as the **Gourmet Ghetto** and is home to a number of high-quality restaurants, including the famed **Chez Panisse** (*see below*). On **Telegraph Avenue** between Dwight Way and the UC Berkeley campus, you'll find the city's cheapest restaurants, serving fast food with a Berkeley twist: Heaping green salads and gourmet sandwiches are far more common than burgers. West of campus along **University Avenue,** there's a string of mostly Asian and Indian restaurants. Both **College Avenue** (running south from cam- pus into Oakland) and **Solano Avenue** (just north of Berkeley in Albany) are lined with cafés, sandwich shops, and upscale restaurants that cater to the neighborhood's students and professors.

UNDER $5

Telegraph Avenue near the Berkeley campus is full of cheap eats. At Telegraph and Bancroft Way you'll find a cluster of food carts selling everything from burritos and smoothies to Japanese food, falafel sand-

A BIT OF BUDDHA IN EVERY BITE

Sunday between 10 and 2 (or later, depending on the crowd), families set up food stands in the courtyard behind the Thai Buddhist Temple and Cultural Center in Berkeley and serve up homemade specialties. In fair weather or foul, exchange your money for tokens and choose from among heaping plates of pad Thai, spicy soups, various seafood curries, and other exotic dishes. Almost everything costs less than $3; proceeds benefit the temple. 1911 Russell St., between Martin Luther King Jr. Way and Otis St., tel. 510/540–9734. 1 block west of Ashby BART.

wiches, and wonderfully stuffed potatoes—try the Berkeley's Best spud, with pesto and mozzarella. The ever-popular **Noah's Bagels** (2344 Telegraph Ave., tel. 510/849–9951; 3170 College Ave., Oakland, tel. 510/654–0941; 1883 Solano Ave., tel. 510/525–4447) spreads flavored cream-cheese schmears on chewy New York–style bagels. **Smart Alec's** (2355 Telegraph Ave., tel. 510/704–4000) is a vegan fast-food joint where you can get a veggie burger, air-baked fries, and soda for less than $4. For pizza along with an "eat-it-or-screw-you" attitude, stop by **Blondie's** (2340 Telegraph Ave., near Durant Ave., tel. 510/548–1129), popular with street freaks and bleary-eyed students in need of a pepperoni fix until 1 AM (2 AM Friday and Saturday); you'll even get a free slice on your birthday if you've got ID to prove it. **Bongo Burger** (2505 Dwight Way, at Telegraph Ave., tel. 510/540–9147; 1839 Euclid Ave., tel. 510/540–9573; 2154 Center St., tel. 510/540–9014) serves some of the cheapest meals in town—two eggs, home fries, and toast; a Polish dog; and a falafel sandwich each cost about $2. A few blocks south of campus at Dwight Way, **Ann's Soup Kitchen and Restaurant** (2498 Telegraph Ave., tel. 510/548–8885) dishes out exceptionally cheap breakfasts, homemade soups, and sandwiches.

Café Intermezzo. This Berkeley institution, with a harried, occasionally rude staff, indisputably serves the biggest and best salads around. The Veggie Delight is a family-size mound of greens topped with kidney and garbanzo beans, hard-boiled egg, sprouts, avocado pieces, and croutons. Salads are served with your choice of homemade dressings and include a bookend-size slab of homemade honey-wheat bread. *2442 Telegraph Ave., at Haste St., tel. 510/849–4592.*

Crêpes-a-Go-Go. Slimane Djili, the owner of this small café, used to sell crêpes on the streets of Paris. Now, bless him, he's settled on busy University Avenue, offering sweet and savory crêpes filled with Nutella and banana or spinach, green onions, and cheese. One is filling; with two you'll be staggering out the door. *2125 University Ave., at Shattuck Ave., tel. 510/841–7722. Cash only.*

Juice Bar Collective. Smack in the middle of the Gourmet Ghetto, the Juice Bar offers fresh and organic sandwiches and hot dishes like spinach lasagna in addition to their namesake smoothies. Try the Sunset, made with bananas, orange juice, and yogurt. *2114 Vine St., tel. 510/548–8473. Cash only. Closed Sun.*

UNDER $10

Berkeley Thai House. Locals and students in the know come to this restaurant near the Berkeley campus to wolf down pad Thai and other reasonably priced lunch specials. For dinner try the *mus-s-mun* (beef with red curry, peanuts, potatoes, carrots, and coconut milk) or the basil tofu. On a sunny day dine on the peaceful patio, sheltered from the street by tall bushes. *2511 Channing Way, at Telegraph Ave., tel. 510/843–7352.*

Bette's Oceanview Diner. This bright, crowded '50s-style diner, on the happening stretch of 4th Street near I–80, redefines American diner food: Instead of grilled American cheese and white bread, try jack and cheddar on sourdough. The wait can stretch to 45 minutes, so if you're in a hurry, grab a cup of strong coffee and a heavenly scone or get a take-out salad or sandwich from **Bette's To Go**, next door, and head for the Marina. *1807A 4th St., near University Ave., tel. 510/644–3230. No dinner.*

Blue Nile. This is one of Berkeley's best Ethiopian restaurants, serving everything from thick split-pea stew and pepper-cooked beef to *tej* (honey wine) and freshly blended fruit shakes. The food is served family style, and you use *injera* bread instead of silverware to scoop it up. *2525 Telegraph Ave., between Dwight Way and Parker St., tel. 510/540–6777. No lunch Sun.*

Brick Hut Café. This mom-and-mom café, a collective owned and operated by women, is one of the best breakfast joints around. It's also a hot lesbian pickup spot on an increasingly womanish stretch of San Pablo Avenue. The pesto eggs are a house favorite; there are also well-prepared salads, burgers, and sandwiches. The high ceilings, exposed-brick walls, polished wooden floors, and friendly waitstaff create an atmosphere conducive to postmeal lingering. *2512 San Pablo Ave., at Dwight Way, tel. 510/486–1124. No dinner.*

Cha Am. This place feels removed from Shattuck Avenue, even though its greenhouselike window seats overlook the street. Try the magical *Tom ka gai* (chicken and coconut soup) or the mixed seafood plate with chili, garlic, and vegetables. Although the food is usually more Berkeley than Thai, the steady clientele clearly doesn't mind. *1543 Shattuck Ave., at Cedar St., tel. 510/848–9664. No lunch Sun.*

Chester's Café. Looking out over the bay from Chester's sunny upstairs deck is one of the best ways to start a lazy weekend morning. The friendly staff will bring you mug after mug of hot coffee and weekend brunch specials like eggs Juneau (poached eggs and smoked salmon on an English muffin topped with Hollandaise sauce). *1508B Walnut Ave., at Vine St., tel. 510/849–9995. No dinner.*

Homemade Café. You'll probably have to wait for a table (at least on weekends), so grab a cup of coffee and a menu, park yourself on the sidewalk, and start deliberating. Will it be a whole-wheat buttermilk waffle with homemade blueberry sauce? Matzo *brei* (matzo with scrambled eggs and cheese)? Or their famous Home-Fry Heaven (home fries with cheese, salsa, sour cream, and guacamole or pesto)? *2454 Sacramento St., at Dwight Way, tel. 510/845–1940. No dinner.*

Juan's Place. Surrounded by steel factories and warehouses, this traditional Mexican restaurant has the feel of an old cantina, complete with piñatas, mirrored beer ads, and cheesy portraits of matadors—the perfect setting in which to indulge in large portions of tacos, burritos, and tamales. Try the crab enchilada with red sauce and cheese, and wash it down with a wine margarita from the adjoining bar. *941 Carleton St., at 9th St., tel. 510/845–6904.*

Kabana. Don't be deterred by the piecemeal decor, or you'll miss out on the deliciously spicy Pakistani food served by a friendly staff. Choose from vegetarian dishes made with eggplant, potatoes, chickpeas, or greens—or try a hefty portion of *biryani* or a curry made with tender clay-oven-baked lamb or chicken. *1106 University Ave., at San Pablo Ave., tel. 510/845–3355.*

Long Life Vegi House. Load up on healthy Chinese food at this longtime favorite just west of campus. If you're feeling adventurous, try vegetarian "pork" or "chicken," made with wheat gluten and soy protein. Otherwise, stick to standard vegetarian and seafood dishes like cold *tan tan* noodles with peanut sauce or prawns and string beans in black bean sauce. Lunch specials, at less than the cost of a bargain matinee, include soup, a spring roll, and an entrée over surprisingly tasty rice. *2129 University Ave., near Shattuck Ave., tel. 510/845–6072.*

Rick and Ann's. Join East Bay locals in bicycle shorts (babies and dogs in tow) as you wait for the best breakfast in town—and in Berkeley, that's really saying something. Try the Down South, a combination of two cornmeal pancakes, two spicy turkey sausages, and two fluffy scrambled eggs with cheese. The special omelets and scrambles are also delicious, as is the French toast, made with challah (egg bread). Breakfast is the draw here, but the dinner menu has the same straightforward appeal. *2922 Domingo St., near Ashby St., across from Claremont Resort, tel. 510/649–8538.*

Saul's. This Gourmet Ghetto nosherie is the closest thing to a New York deli in the East Bay. Shelves of Manischewitz products line the entryway, and a glass deli counter displays bowls of chopped liver, sauerkraut, and whole smoked fish. There are sandwiches stuffed with pastrami, corned beef, brisket, and tongue and Jewish specialties like knishes, potato latkes, and matzo ball soup. Saul's gets noisy and crowded during peak hours; avoid the lunch-hour wait by getting your food to go. *1475 Shattuck Ave., at Vine St., tel. 510/848–3354.*

UNDER $15

Pasand Madras Cuisine. If you feel like going for the gusto at this southern Indian restaurant, get a complete *thali* dinner, including lentil curry, lentil vegetable soup, spicy tamarind soup, yogurt with vegetables, a selection of Indian flat breads, rice pilaf, sweet mango chutney, and a dessert surprise—all for about $15. The all-you-can-eat lunch buffet (noon–2:30) is also a worthy $6.50 investment. A raised seating area lets you watch cross-legged sitar and tabla players who whip up a musical frenzy during dinner. *2286 Shattuck Ave., at Bancroft Way, tel. 510/549–2559.*

UNDER $20

Chez Panisse Café. Though the ground floor of Alice Waters's mecca for foodies is a big-deal affair (the multi-course dinner menu may cost $35–$65), you can sample the same artful presentations of local ingredients in the café upstairs for half the price. You can make same-day reservations for lunch, but for dinner go early and expect to wait an hour or more for a table. *1517 Shattuck Ave., at Cedar St., tel. 510/548–5049. Closed Sun.*

Kirala. In 1996 local papers voted this place the best East Bay Japanese restaurant. Justifiably so? Try the vegetable tempura, umpteen varieties of *robata* (grilled skewered meats or vegetables), or *soba* noodles—and decide for yourself. There's also a great selection of sushi, or opt for a full dinner served with good-for-the-soul miso soup, Japanese salad, and rice, all for about $16. Some nights the line for a table spills around the corner, but there's usually room at the sushi bar. *2100 Ward St., at Shattuck Ave., tel. 510/549–3486. No lunch Sat.–Mon.*

Venezia. Like a Venetian piazza, this place has colorfully painted walls and protruding wrought-iron balconies and flower boxes. There's even a clothesline strung overhead, complete with drying boxers. The food, too, has a Venetian twist: Start with a spinach salad with pears, pine nuts, and pecorino dressed with a balsamic vinaigrette. Check the board for daily pasta and fresh fish specials. *1799 University Ave., at Grant St., tel. 510/849–4681. No lunch weekends.*

MARKETS AND SPECIALTY STORES

Housed in a former bowling alley, **Berkeley Bowl Marketplace** (2777 Shattuck Ave., at Stuart St., tel. 510/843–6929) represents alternative and cooperative grocery shopping at its finest. Try **Trader Joe's** (5796 Christie Ave., at Powell St., tel. 510/658–8091) for inexpensive international gourmet food and reasonably priced wine and beer (the San Francisco branch is at 559 9th St.). **Seabreeze Market** (598 University Ave., tel. 510/486–8119) sells fresh shellfish, fruits, and vegetables, as well as sandwiches to go (the Berkeley Marina is close by). **Whole Foods** (3000 Telegraph Ave., at Ashby Ave., tel. 510/649–1333) is a health food supermarket with a deli, a bakery, an organic salad bar, and even a massage chair.

The collectively owned **Cheese Board** (1504 Shattuck Ave., between Cedar and Vine Sts., tel. 510/549–3183) has an incredible selection of cheeses and freshly baked breads. A few doors down, their offshoot **Cheese Board Pizza Collective** (1512 Shattuck Ave., tel. 510/549–3055) has ridiculously short open hours (Tuesday–Thursday 11:30–2, Monday and Friday 4:30–6:30, Saturday noon–3) but pizza that would wow the most finicky of pizza connoisseurs. They make just one kind of vegetarian pizza each day, with toppings like eggplant, red peppers, pesto, and feta cheese.

For freshly baked loaves—such as seeded baguettes or potato-rosemary bread—stop by the retail outlets of **Semifreddi's** (372 Colusa Ave., Kensington, tel. 510/596–9935) and **Acme** (1601 San Pablo Ave., Berkeley, tel. 510/524–1327; 2730 9th St., Berkeley, tel. 510/843–2978): Both supply many Bay Area markets with fresh bread daily.

OAKLAND

You'll find Southern-style barbecue shacks, El Salvadoran holes-in-the-wall, and plenty of other ethnic eateries in Oakland. **Chinatown,** though less colorful than its counterpart across the bay, has increasing numbers of Southeast Asian restaurants and markets, as well as the older and more established Chinese ones. You'll find them in the area bounded by 7th, 10th, Broadway, and Alice streets downtown. The **Fruitvale** district, encompassing the neighborhoods around the Fruitvale BART station, has dozens of cheap Mexican and Central American restaurants. It is safest, however, to restrict your visits here to main streets and daylight hours. Join the young professionals on **College Avenue** or **Piedmont Avenue,** where you'll find a wide selection of familiar delis, burger joints, gringo burrito shops, and upscale bistros. From downtown Oakland take Bus 59 or 59A to Piedmont Avenue; for College Avenue take BART to Rockridge.

UNDER $5

Taquería Morelia. Here are some of the best quesadillas around, complete with chopped tomatoes and cilantro. Locals of all ages flow between the restaurant and the adjacent dive bar, Talk of the Town, while carrying cheap beer and plastic baskets of tacos and burritos. *4491 E. 14th St., near High St., tel. 510/535–6030.*

Asmara Restaurant. Colorful baskets and rugs suspended from the ceiling cheer up the interior of this East African restaurant in north Oakland. Sample your choice of three meat or vegetarian items in the combination platter. In keeping with Ethiopian tradition, food is served family style with *injera* bread and a notable lack of utensils—use your fingers. *5020 Telegraph Ave., near 51st St., tel. 510/547-5100. No lunch Tues.*

Barney's Gourmet Hamburger. Sample one (or several) of 20 kinds of burgers, among them the Greek, Canadian, Russian, and Western—or load up on your spinach with the Popeye burger. For those who like their burgers meatless, there are tofu and garden burgers, too. *5819 College Ave., near Chabot Ave., tel. 510/601-0444; 4162 Piedmont Ave., Oakland, tel. 510/655-7180; 1591 Solano Ave., Albany, tel. 510/526-8185; 4138 24th St., San Francisco, tel. 415/282-7770; 3344 Steiner St., at Lombard St., tel. 415/563-0307.*

Cactus Taquería. This festive cafeteria-style Mexican restaurant in Rockridge has a dizzying array of fillings for burritos, tacos, *tortas*, and quesadillas. Try the excellently spiced vegetables, shrimp, *carne asada*, red or green chicken *mole*, or anything else; you can't go wrong here. *5525 College Ave., tel. 510/547-1305; 1881 Solano Ave., Berkeley, tel. 510/528-1881.*

Flint's. Regarded by some as the best barbecue shack in the world, Flint's caters to large appetites during the wee hours. Choose from pork or beef ribs, links, or chicken piled high on a sturdy paper plate, served with a couple slices of wheat bread (to soak up the grease) and potato salad. Both locations have takeout only; the neighborhoods are dicey, so be careful after dark. *3114 San Pablo Ave., at 31st St., tel. 510/658-9912; 6609 Shattuck Ave., at Alcatraz Ave., tel. 510/653-0593.*

Lois the Pie Queen. Despite the name most people come here for breakfast not dessert. A family-run diner with vinyl swivel chairs, checkered tablecloths, and root beer floats, Lois has all the breakfast favorites as well as excellent burgers and fries. For traditionalists there's the two-egg breakfast with homemade biscuits and grits, or try the Reggie Jackson Special (pork chops, eggs, hash browns or grits, and coffee or tea). Don't forget the pies that made Lois a monarch. *851 60th St., at Adeline St., tel. 510/658-5616. No dinner.*

Los Cocos. Fruitvale's best (and only) El Salvadoran restaurant is famous for its fried bananas and *pupusas* (stuffed tortillas). It may not look like much from the outside (or the inside), but the food is excellent and cheap. *1449 Fruitvale Ave., at 14th St., tel. 510/536-3079. Closed Mon.*

Lucy's Creole Kitchen. This sunny, friendly diner, trapped on a traffic island in downtown Oakland, has some of the best Southern seafood west of the Mississippi River delta. Daily hot lunch specials like jambalaya or smothered short ribs attract crowds from the neighborhood, as does straight-up Southern fare like black-eyed peas, yams, and greens. *1601 San Pablo Ave., at 16th St., tel. 510/763-6706. Cash only. Closed Sun.-Mon.*

Mama's Royal Café. Although you can get lunch here after 11:30, breakfast is the reason to come: It's served until closing. No fewer than 31 different omelets all come with home-style potatoes, fruit, and a muffin. Weekend mornings bring the Sunday paper and be prepared for a wait. *4012 Broadway, at 40th St., tel. 510/547-7600. Cash only. No dinner.*

Mexicali Rose. The massive portions at this lively place are served on sizzling hot platters (not plates— *platters*). The bilingual menu is heavy on meat dishes, though there are some vegetarian items. Two people could easily split the Mexicali Rose combo ($9.95): taco, stuffed chili pepper, green enchilada, guacamole salad, rice, beans, and a drink (whew!). Right across from the Oakland jail, Mexicali's regular clientele may include both recently released jailbirds and their arresting officers. *701 Clay St., at 7th St., tel. 510/451-2450. 6 blocks southwest of 12th St. BART.*

Nan Yang. Step into this airy restaurant in Rockridge for delicious Burmese food. Especially tasty dishes are the ginger salad, garlic noodles with spring or curry vegetables, and curried tofu with shrimp. Service is friendly, and there is an extensive vegetarian menu. *6048 College Ave., at Claremont Ave., tel. 510/655-3298. Closed Mon.*

Phó' Lâm Viên. This Vietnamese restaurant in Oakland's Chinatown is worth a trip for those with a sense of culinary adventure. Ignore the piped-in Muzak and focus on pork with fish sauce, spicy lemongrass gluten, and all sorts of *Phó* (noodle soups), *bún* (thin rice noodles), and rice dishes. This restaurant is the real McCoy. *930 Webster St., between 10th and 11th Sts., tel. 510/763-1484. Closed Tues.*

Spettro. A fine time should be had by all at this funky restaurant near Lake Merritt. The friendly staff creates interesting specials from around the globe nightly, in addition to main menu standards such as mussels, pastas, and pizzas with strange toppings such as peanut butter. On weekend nights sign your name on the list near the door and join the small crowds waiting happily (thanks to the complimentary house wine or beer) for a table. *3355 Lake Shore Ave., at Mandana Blvd., tel. 510/465–8320.*

Zachary's Chicago Pizza Inc. The stuffed pizza here comes surrounded by a wall of chewy crust and topped with a layer of oozing mozzarella and stewed tomatoes. Voted the number one East Bay pizzeria for 10 years running, Zachary's typically has a line snaking around the corner, so be prepared to wait. At lunchtime get a slice to go. *5801 College Ave., tel. 510/655–6385; 1853 Solano Ave., Berkeley, tel. 510/525–5950.*

UNDER $15

Le Cheval I. This gleaming restaurant in downtown Oakland serves delicious Vietnamese food with a French twist. Try the exotically named Firepot, with prawns, calamari, clams, fish balls, and vegetables. Singapore noodles, marinated beef, and a variety of fish dishes are generously proportioned and uniquely spiced. An appetizer not to be missed is the shrimp or tofu imperial rolls served with an addictive peanut sauce. *1007 Clay St., at 10th St., tel. 510/763–8957; Kaiser Center, 344 20th St., tel. 510/763–8953. No lunch Sun. at Clay St.; no dinner weekends at Kaiser.*

UNDER $20

Bay Wolf. At this elegant Oakland outpost you can sample Californian cuisine at its finest: grilled duck with ginger-peach chutney, for example, or smoked trout salad with arugula, pickled beets, and dill crème fraîche. The seasonal menu mixes Provençal, northern Italian, and Californian influences. When it's warm enough, you can dine on the outdoor patio. *3853 Piedmont Ave., between 40th St. and MacArthur Blvd.; tel. 510/655–6004. No lunch weekends.*

Kincaid's Bayhouse. On the waterfront at Jack London Square, this spiffy restaurant spit-roasts, sear-grills, and hardwood-broils steaks and seafood. Savor the renowned crab cakes or the Fireworks, prawns with a spicy tartar sauce. During happy hour (weekdays 4:30–6:30) you can hang out at the bar watching sailboats breeze into the harbor. *1 Franklin St., in Jack London Sq., tel. 510/835–8600.*

MARKETS AND SPECIALTY STORES

In Oakland's Rockridge District, **Market Hall** (5565 College Ave., at Shafer St.) is a one-stop gourmet haven. Sip a nonfat decaf mocha from **Peaberry's Coffee and Tea** between bites of delicious pastry from **Grace Bakery**. Sample free olives and cheese at the **Pasta Shop**. Pick up meat, poultry, fish, and fine wine from **Enzo's** and make your own feast.

Downtown Oakland has a huge variety of ethnic markets. Look for Chinese and Southeast Asian groceries in Chinatown. On the other side of Broadway, **Mi Rancho Tortilla Factory** (464 7th St., at Broadway, tel. 510/451–2393) sells the fixings for burritos and tacos. **Housewives Marketplace** (9th and Clay Sts., tel. 510/444–4396) is a warehouse full of specialty stands with a Southern flair. Here locals stock up on fresh produce and smoked meats such as ham hocks, as well as dry goods such as beans, roasted peanuts, and mix for Cajun jambalaya. **G. B. Ratto & Company** (821 Washington St., between 8th and 9th Sts., tel. 510/832–6503) is your source for delicacies like buffalo-milk mozzarella, many varieties of olive oil, and salted anchovies. They also prepare sandwiches (about $4) and have everything you need for a gourmet picnic.

MARIN COUNTY

In this land of the rich and established, you'll have to look hard for budget eats. If you're not in the mood to splurge, your best bet is to pack a picnic and dine in the open, far from the din of well-heeled civilization. For Marin County picnic supplies, and for restaurants on the Marin County coast, including Muir Woods and Mt. Tamalpais, Stinson Beach, Bolinas, and Point Reyes, *see* Marin County *in* Chapter 2.

SAUSALITO

Restaurants and cafés line **Bridgeway,** Sausalito's main street, but they're generally overpriced and crowded with sightseers. Expect to pay at least $15–$20 for seafood on the waterfront. If you head one block inland to **Caledonia Street,** you'll find much better bargains and a calmer atmosphere. Your cheapest bet is to picnic on one of the grassy areas between Bridgeway and the bay.

UNDER $10

Hamburgers. If you're lucky enough to see a few locals in Sausalito, it'll be in the line outside this hole-in-the-wall. As the name suggests, all they do here are a few variations on the hamburger-and-fries theme. Most people take their food to one of the benches in the park rather than eat in the steamy restaurant. If neither option appeals, head to Paterson's Bar next door, where they'll serve you the same burger for about a buck more. *737 Bridgeway, tel. 415/332–9471.*

Lighthouse Coffee Shop. Beginning at the crack of dawn, this no-frills eatery serves huge fruit pancakes and other breakfast and lunch specials. Hearty Danish food is the specialty: Try the meatballs with potato salad or the Copenhagen burger with horseradish, pickles, capers, onion, and egg yolk. *1311 Bridgeway, tel. 415/331–3034. No dinner.*

UNDER $15

Arawan. Once you've eaten at this unremarkable-looking place, you'll see why loyal Thai-food devotees patronize it regularly. Though the lunch specials are standard, they pull out all the stops at dinner, with savory entrées like *pla muk kra tiem* (sautéed calamari with garlic, pepper, and fresh mushrooms in oyster sauce). *47 Caledonia St., 1 block inland from Bridgeway, tel. 415/332–0882. No lunch weekends.*

TIBURON

With some exceptions, Tiburon's restaurants—found mostly on **Main Street**—are more notable for their views than for their food. Most have decks hanging out over the bay, but you'll pay for the privilege of gazing at the San Francisco skyline or at Angel Island. If you're short on cash, pack a picnic, take a ferry over from San Francisco (*see* Ferry Travel *in* Chapter 1), and eat on the grass at the tip of the peninsula.

After dark a rowdy over-30 crowd congregates at Sausalito's No Name Bar (757 Bridgeway, tel. 415/332–1392) to enjoy free live jazz, blues, or Dixieland music Wednesday–Sunday.

UNDER $10

Sweden House Café. The Swedish chef at this Tiburon café serves up fresh and unusual breakfast and lunch specials on a peaceful wooden deck jutting out over the water. Regulars order the Swedish pancakes with lingonberries and sour cream. For lunch there are salads and open-faced sandwiches—and decadent desserts. *35 Main St., tel. 415/435–9767. No dinner.*

UNDER $15

Sam's Anchor Café. One of the cheaper waterfront restaurants, Sam's is known across the Bay as *the* place to hang out on the deck sipping Famous Ramos gin fizzes and Bloody Marys. Even on wet and windy days, diehards and docked yachters take brunch (served on weekends until 2 PM) or dinner outside. Hearty breakfast dishes include the Hangtown Fry omelet, with oysters, bacon, scallions, and cheese. *27 Main St., tel. 415/435–4527.*

UNDER $20

Guaymas. Next to the Tiburon ferry landing you'll find some of the best, most innovative Mexican food in the Bay Area. After polishing off a basket of steaming, fresh corn tortillas and three salsas, you could easily make a meal of appetizers: Try *chalupas* (tortilla pockets with chicken breast, cheese, and jalapeños) and *cazuelitas* (potato and corn tortillas with baked zucchini and cheese). Entrées are equally tempting. Sit outside on the heated deck or enjoy the colorful adobe-style dining room. *5 Main St., tel. 415/435–6300.*

MILL VALLEY

You'll pass through Mill Valley on your way to Muir Woods, Mt. Tamalpais, Stinson Beach, or Point Reyes. If you're eager to push on to the coast, grab a quick slice at **Stefano's Pizza** (8 E. Blithedale Ave., at Throckmorton Ave., tel. 415/383–9666).

UNDER $10

Joe's Taco Lounge. The colorful walls lined with hot-sauce bottles and religious memorabilia from Mexico make for a festive dining atmosphere at Joe's. Settle in with the locals to enjoy excellent burritos, both meat and vegetarian. *382 Miller Ave., at La Goma Ave., tel. 415/383–8164.*

Mama's Royal Café. Full of thrift-store artifacts, board games, and psychedelic murals, this funky café serves unbeatable huevos rancheros and omelets, as well as various lunch and dinner items. Grab a board game and play a round of Battleship while you wait for your food to arrive. There's live rock and jazz Tuesday through Saturday 6 PM–10 PM. *393 Miller Ave., at La Goma Ave., tel. 415/388–3261.*

SAN RAFAEL

Compared to most of Marin County, San Rafael has a down-to-earth restaurant scene, with lots of cafés, Mexican joints, and other ethnic eateries lining **4th Street** downtown.

UNDER $10
Royal Thai. You'd hardly expect to find great Thai food in a leafy courtyard called the French Quarter in San Rafael. Nonetheless, Bay Area folks rave about this restaurant, started by a couple who defected from the kitchen at San Francisco's popular Khan Toke Thai House (*see above*). The friendly staff serves no-frills seafood and curry dishes in a restored Victorian house. *610 3rd St., between Hetherton and Irwin Sts., tel. 415/485–1074. No lunch weekends.*

San Rafael Station Café. This breakfast and lunch spot has a neighborhood feel—pictures of people's pooches line the mirror behind the counter, and locals hang out on weekends reading the paper and ingesting phenomenal amounts of cholesterol. There are omelets of every persuasion and a variety of sandwiches. *1013 B St., between 4th and 5th Sts., tel. 415/456–0191. No dinner.*

UNDER $15
Mayflower Pub and Grill. If you're sick of skimpy Californian cuisine, you'll appreciate dinners like the huge ploughman's platter or bangers 'n' mash (juicy pork sausages with mashed potatoes, vegetables, and gravy). Chummy locals congregate around the bar all day long, breaking into folk tunes on Friday and Saturday nights. Next door you'll find a store specializing in British foods. *1533 4th St., tel. 415/456–1011. From U.S. 101N, take Central San Rafael exit to 4th St. and turn left. No lunch weekends.*

SOUTH BAY

Once you've experienced the gastronomic bliss that awaits you in San Francisco, dining in the South Bay is bound to leave you nonplussed. You'll find a cluster of semi-intriguing restaurants around Palo Alto and the Stanford campus, but they're not as cheap as the eats in most student areas. You might do better to head to the coast—the food's no more exciting, but it's bound to taste better when you're gazing at the roaring Pacific.

PALO ALTO

Running west from U.S. 101 into the Stanford University campus is University Avenue, packed with California-casual restaurants, most with mediocre food. At **Mr. Chau** (3781 El Camino Real, at Curtner Ave., tel. 650/856–8938), open daily until 9, $3 goes a long way for buffet-style Chinese food. Another option is California Avenue, east of Stanford, where you'll find **Printer's Inc.** (310 California Ave., at Birch St., tel. 650/327–6500), a café-bookstore serving sandwiches and salads for less than $8.

UNDER $10
Jing Jing. This popular Chinese restaurant near the Stanford campus is *the* place to come for spicy food. Lunchtime brings a steady stream of students and professors who come for the $4–$5 lunch specials (11:30–2)—expect a wait. *443 Emerson St., off University Ave., tel. 650/328–6885.*

Mango Café. Come to this splashy neo-Jamaican outpost for Caribbean dishes such as hot curried goat with vegetables or jerk joints—a spicy chicken dish. Fruit-juice smoothies, served in glasses the size of fishbowls, come in a wide range of exotic flavors. *435 Hamilton Ave., at Fulton Ave., tel. 650/325–3229. From U.S. 101, take University Ave. exit west (toward Stanford), left on Fulton Ave.*

Miyake. Despite the din of sake-drinking college students and waiters yelling greetings to customers across the restaurant, you get surprisingly good sushi at a truly reasonable price—about $1–$2 per piece. For just a bit more you can order specialties like the *tazana* roll (yellowtail, wild carrots, sprouts, and flying fish roe). There's almost always a wait, so consider squeezing in at the sushi bar. *140 University Ave., tel. 650/323–9449.*

Oasis Beer Garden. This grubby but immensely popular college hangout near the Palo Alto–Menlo Park border serves tasty burgers and sandwiches; vegetarians will have to stick to pizza. You can play pinball, watch sports on TV, or soak up sun at one of the outdoor tables. *241 El Camino Real, Menlo Park, tel. 650/326–8896. Just north of Stanford campus at Cambridge St.*

UNDER $15

The Good Earth. Before wheat-grass blends and ginseng shots, there was the Good Earth, where generous portions of salads, sandwiches, and soups are served in a casual, down-to-earth atmosphere. Expect a wait on weekend mornings. *185 University Ave., tel. 650/321–9449.*

SAN JOSE

The Bay Area's biggest city has its fair share of good ethnic food—especially Vietnamese—though it's too far from San Francisco to warrant a special trip. (Chez Sovan is the one exception; *see below*). If you find yourself in San Jose and need a good, cheap meal, try **Taco Al Pastor** (400 S. Bascom Ave., at San Carlos St., tel. 408/275–1619), which has been serving excellent Mexican food for more than 15 years. You'll find the best grub in the downtown area between Santa Clara and San Salvador streets (which run east–west) and Almaden and 3rd streets (running north–south). The **Flying Pig Pub** (78. S. 1st St., between San Carlos and San Fernando Sts., tel. 408/298–6710) is recommended for its variety of finger foods (crab cakes and pig skins) and salads for under $7. Near Kelley Park **Phuong Nam** (2168 Story Rd., tel. 408/254–4823) has great South Vietnamese entrées for less than $10. From downtown go south on 1st Street, then turn left on Keyes Street, which turns into Story Road.

Chez Sovan. Carloads of Bay Area residents regularly make the 45-minute trek to San Jose for Chez Sovan's incredible Cambodian cuisine. The owners opened a second Chez Sovan just south of San Jose in Campbell, and now the original location serves lunch only. The food—including a selection of ginger-cooked meats and vegetables, coconut and leek soups, and other traditional Cambodian specials—is well worth the journey. *923 Oakland Rd., tel. 408/287–7619. 1 block north of Hedding, where 13th St. becomes Oakland Rd. Closed weekends. Other location: 2425 S. Bascom Ave., Campbell, tel. 408/ 371–7711.*

REFERENCE LISTINGS

BY CUISINE

AMERICAN

Under $5

Ann's Soup Kitchen and Restaurant *(Berkeley)*

Café at the Main Library *(Civic Center)*

Café Intermezzo *(Berkeley)*

Moishe's Pippic *(Civic Center)*

New Dawn *(Mission)*

San Francisco Art Institute Café *(North Beach/Russian Hill)*

Specialty's *(Downtown)*

Tom Peasant Pies *(Castro/Noe Valley)*

Under $10

Bagdad Cafe *(Castro/Noe Valley)*

Bette's Oceanview Diner *(Berkeley)*

Boogaloos *(Mission)*

Brick Hut Café *(Berkeley)*

Buena Vista Café *(Fisherman's Wharf)*

Chester's Café *(Berkeley)*

Crescent City Café *(The Haight)*

Eagle Café *(Fisherman's Wharf)*

Flint's *(Oakland)*

Flying Pig Pub *(San Jose)*

Grubstake *(Civic Center)*

Homemade Café *(Berkeley)*

Kate's Kitchen *(The Haight)*

Lois the Pie Queen *(Oakland)*

Lucy's Creole Kitchen *(Oakland)*

Mama's Royal Café *(Mill Valley)*

Mama's Royal Café *(Oakland)*

Miss Millie's *(Castro/Noe Valley)*

Orphan Andy's *(Castro/Noe Valley)*

Patio Café *(Castro/Noe Valley)*

Pinecrest *(Downtown)*

Pork Store Café *(The Haight)*

Rick and Ann's *(Berkeley)*

San Rafael Station Café *(San Rafael)*

Saul's *(Berkeley)*

Spaghetti Western *(The Haight)*

Sparky's *(Castro/Noe Valley)*

Squat and Gobble Café *(The Haight)*

Under $15

Sam's Anchor Café *(Tiburon)*

The Good Earth *(Palo Alto)*

BURGERS

Under $5

Hot 'n' Hunky *(Castro/Noe Valley)*

Under $10

Barney's Gourmet Hamburger *(Oakland)*

Hamburger Mary's *(SoMa)*

Hamburgers *(Sausalito)*

Oasis Beer Garden *(Palo Alto)*

CALIFORNIA

Under $5

Juice Bar Collective *(Berkeley)*

Main Squeeze *(Civic Center)*

Under $10

Pluto's *(Marina)*

Under $20

Bay Wolf *(Oakland)*

Chez Panisse *(Berkeley)*

Firefly *(Castro/Noe Valley)*

Lulu *(SoMa)*

CHINESE

Under $5

Kowloon *(Chinatown)*

Lucky Creation *(Chinatown)*

Under $10

Chef Jia's *(Chinatown)*

Eric's Hunan and Mandarin *(Castro/Noe Valley)*

Empress Garden *(Richmond/ Sunset)*

Jing Jing *(Palo Alto)*

House of Nanking *(Chinatown)*

Long Life Vegi House *(Berkeley)*

Meriwa *(Chinatown)*

Silver *(Chinatown)*

Ton Kiang *(Richmond)*

Yuet Lee *(Chinatown)*

Under $15

R&G Lounge *(Chinatown)*

Yank Sing *(Downtown)*

ETHIOPIAN

Under $10

Asmara *(Oakland)*

Blue Nile *(Berkeley)*

Massawa *(The Haight)*

FRENCH

Under $5

Crêpes-a-Go-Go *(Berkeley)*

Under $15

Café Bastille *(Downtown)*

Café Claude *(Downtown)*

South Park Café *(SoMa)*

Ti Couz *(Mission)*

Under $20

Bay Wolf *(Oakland)*

INDIAN

Under $10

Ananda Fuara *(Civic Center)*

Under $15

Pasand Madras Cuisine *(Berkeley)*

Scenic India *(Mission)*

ITALIAN

Under $10

Bocce Café *(North Beach/Russian Hill)*

Il Pollaio *(North Beach/ Russian Hill)*

L'Osteria del Forno *(North Beach/Russian Hill)*

Pasta Pomodoro *(Castro/Noe Valley)*

Under $15

Caffe Macaroni *(Downtown)*

Il Fornaio *(Downtown)*

Ristorante Ideale *(North Beach/Russian Hill)*

Spettro *(Oakland)*

Under $20

Rose Pistola *(North Beach/Russian Hill)*

Venezia *(Berkeley)*

JAPANESE

Under $10

Isobune *(Japantown)*

Mifune *(Japantown)*

Miyake *(Palo Alto)*

No-Name (Nippon) Sushi *(Castro/Noe Valley)*

Under $15

Ebisu *(Richmond/Sunset)*

Izumiya *(Japantown)*

Nori Sushi *(Civic Center)*

Now and Zen *(Japantown)*

Under $20

Kirala *(Berkeley)*

MEDITERRANEAN AND MIDDLE EASTERN

Under $5

Aladdin *(Civic Center)*

Bongo Burger *(Berkeley)*

Truly Mediterranean *(Mission)*

Under $10

Kan Zaman *(The Haight)*

La Méditerranée *(Castro/Noe Valley)*

Ya Halla *(The Haight)*

Under $15

Amira *(Mission)*

MEXICAN AND CENTRAL AMERICAN

Under $5

Casa Sanchez *(Mission)*

El Farolito *(Mission)*

Joe's Taco Lounge *(Mill Valley)*

El Toro *(Mission)*

El Trébol *(Mission)*

La Cumbre *(Mission)*

Pancho Villa *(Mission)*

Taquería Cancun *(Mission)*

Taqueria El Balazo (The Haight)

Taquería Morelia (Oakland)

Under $10

Cactus Taquería (Oakland)

Juan's Place (Berkeley)

La Rondalla (Mission)

Los Cocos (Oakland)

Mexicali Rose (Oakland)

Nicaragua (Mission)

Panchita's (Mission)

Taco Al Pastor (San Jose)

Under $20

Guaymas (Tiburon)

PIZZA

Under $5

Blondie's (Berkeley)

Club Za Pizza (SoMa)

Golden Boy Pizza (North Beach/Russian Hill)

Marcello's (Castro/Noe Valley)

Stefano's Pizza (Mill Valley)

Under $10

North Beach Pizza (North Beach/Russian Hill)

Spettro (Oakland)

Zachary's Chicago Pizza Inc. (Oakland)

SEAFOOD

Under $10

Lucy's Creole Kitchen (Oakland)

Swan Oyster Depot (Civic Center)

Under $15

P.J.'s Oyster Bed (Richmond/Sunset)

R&G Lounge (Chinatown)

Under $20

Kincaid's Bayhouse (Oakland)

SPANISH AND CARIBBEAN

Under $10

Mango Café (Palo Alto)

Under $15

Cha Cha Cha (The Haight)

Esperpento (Mission)

Timo's (Mission)

Zarzuela (North Beach/Russian Hill)

THAI

Under $10

Berkeley Thai House (Berkeley)

Cha Am (Berkeley)

Manora's Thai Cuisine (SoMa)

Racha Café (Civic Center)

Royal Thai (San Rafael)

Thep Phanom (The Haight)

Under $15

Arawan (Sausalito)

Khan Toke Thai House (Richmond/Sunset)

Thai House on Noe (Castro/Noe Valley)

VIETNAMESE AND CAMBODIAN

Under $10

101 Restaurant (Downtown)

Chez Sovan (San Jose)

Cordon Bleu (Civic Center)

Phó' Lâm Viên (Oakland)

Phuong Nam (San Jose)

Tu Lan (Downtown)

Under $15

Le Cheval I (Oakland)

Slanted Door (Mission)

OTHER

Under $10

Hahn's Hibachi (Korean; Marina)

Kabana (Pakistani; Berkeley)

Lighthouse Coffee Shop (Danish; Sausalito)

Mad Magda's Russian Tea Room & Mystic Cafe (Russian; Civic Center)

Nan Yang (Burmese; Oakland)

Sweden House Café (Swedish; Tiburon)

Under $15

Brother's Restaurant (Korean; Richmond/Sunset)

Mayflower Pub and Grill (British; San Rafael)

Suppenküche (German; Civic Center)

SPECIAL FEATURES

BREAKFAST/BRUNCH

Under $5

Ann's Soup Kitchen and Restaurant (Berkeley)

New Dawn (Mission)

Under $10

Bette's Oceanview Diner (Berkeley)

Boogaloos (Mission)

Brick Hut Café (Berkeley)

Chester's Café (Berkeley)

Crescent City Café (The Haight)

Homemade Café (Berkeley)

Kate's Kitchen (The Haight)

Lighthouse Coffee Shop (Sausalito)

Lois the Pie Queen (Oakland)

Mama's Royal Café (Mill Valley)

Mama's Royal Café (Oakland)

Miss Millie's (Castro/Noe Valley)

Patio Café (Castro/Noe Valley)

Pork Store Café (The Haight)

Rick and Ann's (Berkeley)

San Rafael Station Café (San Rafael)

Spaghetti Western (The Haight)

Squat and Gobble Café (The Haight)

Sweden House Café (Tiburon)

Under $15

Sam's Anchor Café (Tiburon)

The Good Earth (Palo Alto)

DINNER AND ENTERTAINMENT

Under $5

Taqueria El Balazo (The Haight)

Under $10

Bocce Café (North Beach/Russian Hill)

Josie's Cabaret and Juice Joint (Castro/Noe Valley)

Kan Zaman (The Haight)

La Rondalla (Mission)

Mama's Royal Café (Mill Valley)

Under $15

Amira (Mission)

Café Bastille (Downtown)

Café Claude (Downtown)

Pasand Madras Cuisine (Berkeley)

LATE-NIGHT EATS (AFTER 1 AM)

Under $5

Blondie's (Berkeley)

Club Za Pizza (SoMa)

El Farolito (Mission)

Hot 'n' Hunky (Castro/Noe Valley)

Marcello's (Castro/Noe Valley)

Taquería Cancun (Mission)

Under $10

Bagdad Cafe (Castro/Noe Valley)

Buena Vista Café (Fisherman's Wharf)

Grubstake (Civic Center)

Hamburger Mary's (SoMa)

Kan Zaman (The Haight)

Mexicali Rose (Oakland)

North Beach Pizza (North Beach/Russian Hill)

Oasis Beer Garden (Palo Alto)

Orphan Andy's (Castro/Noe Valley)

Panchita's (Mission)

Pinecrest (Downtown)

La Rondalla (Mission)

Silver (Chinatown)

Sparky's (Castro/Noe Valley)

OUTDOOR EATING

Under $5

Casa Sanchez (Mission)

Juice Bar Collective (Berkeley)

Under $10

Berkeley Thai House (Berkeley)

Bocce Café (North Beach/Russian Hill)

Boogaloos (Mission)

Chester's Café (Berkeley)

Josie's Cabaret and Juice Joint (Castro/Noe Valley)

Oasis Beer Garden (Palo Alto)

Sweden House Café (Tiburon)

Under $15

Café Bastille (Downtown)

Café Claude (Downtown)

Sam's Anchor Café (Tiburon)

Under $20

Guaymas (Tiburon)

Bay Wolf (Oakland)

VEGETARIAN

Under $5

Cheese Board Pizza Collective (Berkeley)

Juice Bar Collective (Berkeley)

Kowloon (Chinatown)

Lucky Creation (Chinatown)

Main Squeeze (Civic Center)

Under $10

Ananda Fuara (Civic Center)

Josie's Cabaret and Juice Joint (Castro/Noe Valley)

Long Life Vegi House (Berkeley)

Under $15

Now and Zen (Japantown)

CAFÉ CULTURE

REVISED BY JENNIFER BREWER

On Friday night Bay Area cafés are often as crowded as the local bars. No mere filling stations, they are where locals come to meet friends, gossip, discuss Descartes, read pulp fiction, pen poetry, or polish a dissertation. In particularly café-dependent societies like Berkeley and San Francisco, coffeehouses do more than just grind and brew coffee beans: Neighborhood artists display their works; bands ply their trade; and open-mike poetry readings can be found nightly. For up-to-date information on what's happening, check the "Calendar" section of the *Bay Guardian* or any free weekly.

Though you'll find a few slick megachains like Starbucks and Pasqua, most Bay Area coffeehouses are either family-run or local chains with no more than three or four branches. They come in every style imaginable, and sampling the range is part of the fun: You can drink your morning cappuccino in a cubbyhole with elegant sofas and classical music; savor your noon espresso in a postmodern warehouse space where Armani-clad admen mingle with mangled bike messengers; and linger over a late-night latte in a pillow-strewn, tapestried setting resembling an Ottoman sultan's chamber. If you're looking for the company of students, politicos, or New Age prophets, head to Berkeley. Otherwise, your scene awaits somewhere in San Francisco. Cafés are generally open from 6 AM or 7 AM to 11 PM on weekdays and until midnight (sometimes later) on weekends.

SAN FRANCISCO

San Franciscans have long been believers in the connection between coffee and the arts. Early acolytes of this philosophy included beat poets Jack Kerouac and Allen Ginsberg, who held all manner of performances at Caffè Trieste (*see below*), in North Beach. It's still a popular place to grab a demitasse on a rainy day, especially if you have someone with whom you can hold hands under the table. Postmodern hipsters will feel more comfortable in the cafés South of Market or in the Haight. The Mission, a hotbed for experimental art in San Francisco, has recently sprouted java dens attracting bohemians both new and old.

CASTRO DISTRICT

Café Flore. Flore is one of the Castro's premier gathering spots for pseudoartists, political activists, and trendy boys in black turtlenecks. If the outside tables are full, strike a pose until someone makes room—sharing tables is de rigueur. Expect plenty of noise, action, and in the midst of it all, an incredibly attrac-

WOULD YOU LIKE COFFEE WITH THAT?

Beyond the basic drinks like espresso, cappuccino, latte, and mocha, some café menus list a half-dozen or more caffeine concoctions. Figuring out how to order can be tough: Gone are the days of small, medium, and large. Instead, you must decide between a single or double (bonus points for ordering a doppio) in sizes short, tall, or grande and with wet or dry foam. Occasionally, cafés adopt an absurdist mix-and-match attitude. If you are asked, "Would you like the doppio in a grande cup with dry foam?" you have our permission to strangle the counterperson.

tive someone looking furtively your way. Preferred reading material: Jean Genet (just pretend to read). *2298 Market St., at Noe St., tel. 415/621–8579.*

Cup-a-Joe. This funky place with maroon walls has all the ingredients of a successful café: a mean cup o'joe, tasty pastries, and an art student clientele. They occasionally hold spoken-word performances; call for details. *3801 17th St., at Sanchez St., tel. 415/487–1661.*

Jumpin' Java. Escape the see-and-be-seen chaos of Castro cafés in the quiet, tree-lined neighborhood of Duboce Triangle. Although the *Bay Guardian* deems this "the best place to cruise nerdy gay guys," you'll also find a mix of students and couples. *139 Noe St., between Henry and 14th Sts., tel. 415/431–5282.*

Morning Due. On the border between the Castro and Mission districts is a refreshingly airy, well-lighted café with a good selection of light meals and snacks. The studious crowds and mellow world-beat music make it a good place to enjoy a novel; if you forgot to bring yours, they'll sell you a book from their shelves. Aspiring poets and folk musicians show up for an occasional open-mike Saturday night. *3698 17th St., at Church St., tel. 415/621–7156.*

Pasqua Coffee. The friendly crowd at the Castro branch of this normally impersonal local chain sets it apart from all the rest. Toned, tanned locals come for the excellent scones and coffee and stay for the stylish social scene. *4094 18th St., at Castro St., tel. 415/626–6263.*

CIVIC CENTER/HAYES VALLEY

Mad Magda's Russian Tea Room and Café. Magda's has an otherworldly feel, a bit like the Mad Hatter's tea party in *Alice in Wonderland*: There are deep blue ceilings, red walls, and a "magic" garden in back. For $13 you can get an expert palm, aura, or Tarot card reading Wednesday–Friday 1 PM–midnight and Saturday 11 AM–midnight. Preferred reading material: tea leaves. *579 Hayes St., between Octavia and Laguna Sts., tel. 415/864–7654.*

Momi Toby's Revolution Café. A Sunday-morning hangout for Hayes Valley locals, Momi Toby's encourages artistic expression by providing sketchbooks, crayons, and a working piano. Prefer to read quietly? You'll find quality literature shelved next to the counter. Beer, wine, and appealing snacks like tuna bagels and burritos are on the menu. There's live music on some weekends. *528 Laguna St., between Hayes and Fell Sts., tel. 415/626–1508.*

DOWNTOWN

Cafe de la Presse. This café, near the German and French cultural centers, has a French-speaking staff and stacks of *Le Monde* (among other European newspapers) at the counter. You can enjoy your espresso outdoors under sidewalk umbrellas, but the Parisian fantasy ends there: One look at the snarl of traffic from Bush Street to the Chinatown Gate will remind you this is a West Coast metropolis. *352 Grant St., at Bush St., tel. 415/398–2680.*

Yakety Yak. The bright facade of this mellow coffeehouse makes a rebellious contrast to its gray surroundings. Portfolio-toting artists from the nearby Academy of Arts come here for a caffeine fix, a huge selection of fresh pastries, and some on-line time with SF NET (*see box*, SF NET—A Café Connection, *below*). Open-mike poetry readings are held on Friday night 7–9. *679 Sutter St., at Taylor St., tel. 415/885–6908.*

HAIGHT-ASHBURY AND WESTERN ADDITION

Bean There. Set foot inside this airy, high-ceiling space, and you'll forget you're one block from grimy Lower Haight. Play a game of chess, have a snack, and sip your Caffè Duboce (latte with a dash of almond, caramel, or vanilla), the house specialty. On weekends neighbors laze at sidewalk tables with the Sunday crossword and the family dog. On weekday mornings locals line up for excellent organic coffees (sold by the pound). *201 Steiner St., at Waller St., tel. 415/255–8855.*

Café International. The sprawling sofas and cheerful backyard patio give this Lower Haight café a homey touch. Besides the usual snacks and coffee drinks, International serves up fresh fruit juices. Friday at 8 PM poets ply their verses at the open mike. *508 Haight St., at Fillmore St., tel. 415/552–7390.*

The Horse Shoe. For disaffected youths with tattoos, pierced body parts, and time on their hands, this is the place. Regulars come to play chess, to shout over cranked-up music, or to peruse the millions of posted flyers seeking band members or advertising obscure artistic events. *566 Haight St., between Steiner and Fillmore Sts., tel. 415/626–8852.*

Proper café etiquette includes busing your own table and tipping the counterperson.

Jammin' Java. This sunny, neighborly café one block south of frenetic Haight Street serves terrific, strong coffee drinks, decent snacks, and so-so desserts. The indoor and outdoor tables are populated day and night, and background music ranges from big band to hip-hop. *701 Cole St., at Waller St., tel. 415/668–5282; 1398 9th Ave., at Judah St., tel. 415/566–5282.*

MISSION DISTRICT

Café Istanbul. The Syrian owner of this unique café serves authentic and delicious Middle Eastern food and beverages in an exotic tapestried setting. The floor is festooned with pillows, and intricately scrolled gold-color trays function as tabletops. Take off your shoes and settle down with some dolmas (stuffed grape leaves), baklava (pastry with honey and nuts), or cardamom-spiked Turkish coffee. *525 Valencia St., between 16th and 17th Sts., tel. 415/863–8854.*

Cafe Macondo. The Macondo proves that even in the trendiest part of the Mission, the down-to-earth, neighborly coffeehouse lives on. The walls are plastered with revolutionary posters from all over Latin America, and a mix of students, intellectuals, and revolutionaries sits at the heavy wooden tables to read, study, or talk politics over steamy cups of *café*. *3159 16th St., between Valencia and Guerrero Sts., no phone.*

La Bohème. This Mission District institution draws a multiracial clientele that feasts on a variety of deli-style American, Greek, and Middle Eastern sandwiches. Weekend nights occasionally bring live guitar music. *3318 24th St., at Mission St., tel. 415/643–0481.*

Mission Grounds. Even though this place is near the popular Kilowatt club (*see* Live Music *in* Chapter 6) and other outposts of Mission nightlife, it isn't an evening café; come nightfall, it's just you and the dust bunnies. Crêpes and omelets are served all day. *3170 16th St., between Valencia and Guerrero Sts., tel. 415/621–1539.*

Radio Valencia. This friendly place is all about music, from the vintage instruments on the walls to the carefully chosen tunes playing over the speakers. Owner Don Allen used to work in radio in Wisconsin, and now he (and other staff members) draw up a fresh play list daily, displayed in a "menu" on each table. Come in for live jazz, blues, bluegrass, and swing Friday through Sunday nights. Besides coffee, there are a dozen or so microbrews on tap and excellent focaccia sandwiches and pizzas. *1199 Valencia St., at 23rd St., tel. 415/826–1199.*

Red Dora's Bearded Lady. A self-proclaimed "dyke café (everybody welcome)," this small coffeehouse is an outlet for San Francisco's young, energetic gay culture. Especially in the afternoon and on weekends the pierced-but-unpretentious come to lounge on mismatched furniture or in the lovely backyard garden. Dora's serves the usual café eats plus a tasty breakfast burrito and a tofu burger. Spoken-word and musical performances take place some Fridays and Saturdays at 8 PM after the café closes; call ahead to confirm. *485 14th St., at Guerrero St., tel. 415/626–2805.*

SF NET—A CAFÉ CONNECTION

If you're yearning to jump on the Internet bandwagon, try SF NET. As you drink your latte, you can dive into cyberspace and exchange messages with people at other cafés hooked up to the system. Just put in your quarter, log on with a nickname, and chat away, feeding the computer more money every so often. Your quarter also lets you connect with the Bay Guardian's on-line service and with Gay Net, Greenpeace, and the San Francisco Library's on-line catalog. You'll find SF NET in more than 13 cafés, including Brain Wash, Jammin' Java, and Yakety Yak.

NORTH BEACH

Caffè Greco. An international crowd fills this attractive café, whose windows overlook Columbus Avenue. Rich Italian espresso accompanies a variety of music—from Edith Piaf to Italian pop. You'll find a colorful selection of desserts; regulars worship the decadent tiramisu. *423 Columbus Ave., between Vallejo and Stockton Sts., tel. 415/397–6261.*

Caffè Trieste. This is the legendary home of the beat generation, where Kerouac and friends oozed cool from every pore. And it hasn't changed a bit since—including the '50s jukebox, which spouts opera. Saturday at 2 local Italian performers serenade guests with sentimental Italian tunes, accompanied by a live mini-orchestra. *601 Vallejo St., at Grant Ave., tel. 415/392–6739.*

The Gathering Café. Jazz aficionados should not miss this spot, where there's no cover charge for live music (except on weekends: $2–$3). The small marble tables and black-and-white-checked floor evoke a tiny jazz bar in Paris. It opens at 7 every night. *1326 Grant Ave., between Green and Vallejo Sts., tel. 415/433–4247.*

Mario's Bohemian Cigar Store and Café. For more than 50 years this old-fashioned Italian café has been serving espresso, beer, and of course a nice Chianti—the perfect accompaniment to homemade focaccia sandwiches and Neapolitan pizza. Views of Washington Square Park and the Church of Saints Peter and Paul enhance the Florentine mood. *566 Columbus Ave., at Union St., tel. 415/362–0536.*

North End Café. The young and the restless congregate here over massive bowl-size cups of strong coffee. Beware: One cup will render you giddy, two will leave you babbling incessantly. If that's not enough of a stimulant for you, the sheer number of beautiful people should give you a wake-up jolt. *1402 Grant Ave., at Green St., tel. 415/956–3350.*

Steps of Rome. Well-dressed—correction, make that *very* well dressed—young urbanites crowd this large, bright café. The music is loud, the conversation (ranging from intellectual banter to cheesy come-ons) louder, and the waiters might make a pass at your girlfriend or break into spontaneous song. *348 Columbus Ave., near Grant Ave., tel. 415/397–0435.*

SOUTH OF MARKET

Brain Wash Café and Laudromat. Where else can you drink beer, listen to live music, play pinball, and wash your clothes, all at the same time? The decor is hip and Jetsons-like, so even if you don't have your dirty socks with you, it's fun to come here for a two-egg breakfast, or just to sip coffee and stare through big windows at lonely warehouse-lined Folsom Street. There is live music (from acoustic to punk) Tuesday–Saturday at 10 PM, no cover. *1122 Folsom St., between 7th and 8th Sts., tel. 415/861–3663 or 415/431–9274.*

Café Natoma. In the shadow of the Museum of Modern Art and the impressive 1925 Pacific Telephone and Telegraph office tower, this place draws lunchtime museum goers and office workers (it closes daily at 4). Sandwiches are named after SoMa streets and alleys: Try the Natoma Street Original (smoked ham) or the Yerba Buena (veggie). *145 Natoma St., at New Montgomery St., tel. 415/495–3289.*

Caffè Centro. Young graphic artists, designers, computer programmers, and other denizens of "multi-media gulch" snag the sidewalk tables of this café overlooking South Park—a beautiful patch of green surrounded by trophy homes. It's most popular at lunchtime (closing time is 6:30 weekends, 4:30 weekdays). Preferred reading material: *Wired* magazine. *102 South Park Ave., between 2nd and 3rd and Bryant and Brannan Sts., tel. 415/882–1500. Open weekdays 7:30–6:30, Sat. 8:30–4:30.*

Mr. Ralph's. At this offbeat coffeehouse in a bright green tiled building you can unwind with a mellow, artsy professional crowd after cultural overload at the MOMA. Happy hour (weekdays 4:30–6:30) brings $2 pints; Friday evening there's free live jazz. *90 Natoma St., between 1st and 2nd Sts., tel. 415/243–9330.*

OUTLYING NEIGHBORHOODS

So you've ventured beyond the parts of the city where espresso bars run two to a block. Luckily, there are still places to get your caffeine fix in almost every neighborhood.

Blue Danube. Bring your purchases from nearby Green Apple Books (*see* Chapter 3) and enjoy an afternoon in the Richmond District with college students, resident youth, and thirty-somethings who still remember how to relax. On sunny days the wide-open windows are perfect for people-watching. *306 Clement St., between 4th and 5th Aves., tel. 415/221–9041.*

Cool Beans. Like the bar on *Cheers,* this brightly painted Inner Richmond café is a home away from home. Owners Sam and Henry—one of whom is usually behind the bar—will learn your name by your second visit, and it's easy to make the acquaintance of the locals who spend many of their daylight hours here. They also serve homemade soups and great sandwiches. *4342 California St., at 6th Ave., tel. 415/750–1955.*

In January 1995 San Francisco banned smoking in all cafés, though a liquor license provides a convenient loophole for those who want to light up with beer or cocktails.

Farley's. You'll find all the classic features of a good café at this Potrero Hill favorite: strong coffee, plenty of sidewalk tables, and paintings on the walls by neighborhood artists. And they offer a few bonuses, like a stack of board games, a magazine rack with more than 20 titles, regular storytelling events for kids, and occasional music and poetry nights. *1315 18th St., between Texas and Missouri Sts., tel. 415/648–1545.*

Java Beach. What do surfers at Ocean Beach do when the waves are blown out? They go to Java Beach, the only decent café in the Outer Sunset, to swap tales of conquered swells. Nonsurfers come to read, chat, study, or catch some of the occasional live music. *1396 La Playa St., at Judah St., tel. 415/665–5282.*

Royal Ground Coffee. Patrons here (mostly families and twenty-somethings) insist on calling this neighborhood Lower Pacific Heights to distinguish it from the seedy stretch of Fillmore south of Geary. Wherever it is, it's a terrific place to stop and refuel after exploring Japantown or Fillmore Street. *2060 Fillmore St., at California St., tel. 415/567–8822.*

Tart to Tart. The friendly owners of Tart to Tart whip up a mean cup of coffee and plenty of excellent desserts, salads, and sandwiches for Inner Sunset locals and UCSF medical students. *641 Irving St., between 7th and 8th Aves., tel. 415/753–0643.*

EAST BAY

The "People's Republic of Berkeley" would collapse without cafés. Students would have nowhere to be seen while "studying"; skate punks would have nowhere to hang while cutting class; artists and poets would have no place to share their angst. Around **Telegraph Avenue** south of campus and **Euclid Avenue** north of campus you'll find cafés crowded day and night with students; the crowds downtown and on **College Avenue** are more mixed. Oakland isn't exactly a latte town, but locals do gather at the cafés in the **Rockridge, Piedmont Avenue,** and **Grand Lake** areas, especially on sunny weekends. Smokers should take note: In 1994 Berkeley banned smoking in all indoor *and* outdoor cafés.

BERKELEY

Au Coquelet Café and Restaurant. There *is* life in Berkeley after midnight, and you'll find it here, a couple doors down from the UC Theatre (*see* Chapter 6). Au Coquelet stays packed late into the night with hungry, caffeine-craving movie goers and students. Sunday is also busy; brunch is served weekends until 3 PM. *2000 University Ave., at Milvia St., tel. 510/845–0433.*

Café Fanny. Opened by Alice Waters, the chef-owner of famed Chez Panisse (*see* Chapter 4), and named for her daughter Fanny, this west Berkeley café beckons yuppies of every generation to its trellised patio. The food is delicious though not cheap, and the portions are small—stick with buckwheat crêpes or cinnamon toast if money's tight. Come early: The café closes at 3 PM Sunday–Friday and Saturday at 4. *1603 San Pablo Ave., at Cedar St., tel. 510/524–5447.*

Caffè Strada. Strada's sprawling outdoor patio attracts a social mix of students and visiting foreigners (residents of International House, across the street). Relax in the sun with a newspaper or eavesdrop on your neighbors while sipping a Strada Bianca or a Strada Bianca Mocha—both are made with white chocolate, the house specialty. *2300 College Ave., at Bancroft Way, tel. 510/843–5282.*

Espresso Roma. Though it's in the sleepy Elmwood neighborhood, Roma is one of Berkeley's favorite late-night hangouts—the large café is always packed on weekends with locals from all walks of life. They serve a variety of beers and some overpriced salads and sandwiches. *2960 College Ave., at Ashby Ave., tel. 510/644–3773.*

Mediterraneum Caffè. The Med was featured in *The Graduate* and is a longtime hangout for Berkeley's resident thinkers, dreamers, and revolutionaries. These days it's one of the few places where lifelong Berkeleyans and open-minded students converge for conversation over a shot of caffeine (most students stick closer to campus). There are reasonably priced sandwiches and pastas as well as the usual coffee drinks. *2475 Telegraph Ave., between Haste St. and Dwight Way, tel. 510/549–1128.*

Nefeli Caffè. This Greek coffeehouse in north Berkeley is popular with students and professors for its "secret recipe" Italian-roast coffee and an innovative, reasonably priced menu. Sandwiches are made with eggplant, roasted peppers, feta, and Kalamata olive spread; they'll also pour you a glass of retsina (Greek wine). *1854 Euclid Ave., at Hearst St., tel. 510/841–6374.*

Peet's Coffee & Tea. What is now a coffee empire began in the '60s with this single unassuming café. Peet's now distributes its roasts worldwide and has more than a dozen cafés in the Bay Area, providing superstrong blends to experienced coffee swillers. *2124 Vine St., at Walnut St., tel. 510/841–0564.*

Red Café. Redbrick walls, exposed beam ceilings, and a massive skylight create a mellow setting for an older, artsy, postgrad crowd. The full kitchen serves vegetarian sandwiches, salads, and pastas, and the café has a fine selection of beers. Though there's frequent live jazz, it's not a late-night hangout: Be prepared to clear out at 7 PM on weekdays, 5 PM Saturday. *1941 University Ave., at Bonita St., tel. 510/843–8607.*

OAKLAND

The Edible Complex. This spacious Rockridge café doubles as an art gallery and is usually packed with students from the nearby California College of Arts and Crafts. As the name implies, there are tasty sandwiches and salads. *5600 College Ave., 1 block south of Rockridge BART, tel. 510/658–2172.*

Mama Bears. This friendly feminist café-bookstore carries new and used books in fiction and nonfiction. Readings, workshops, and lectures relating to women's issues take place frequently. There's also a lovely garden. *6536 Telegraph Ave., at 66th St., Oakland, tel. 510/428–9684.*

AFTER DARK

REVISED BY SHARRON WOOD AND JENNIFER BREWER

Though diehard night owls may find the Bay Area's nightlife a bit on the tame side, most admit that what the area lacks in high-intensity late-night energy, it makes up for with its sheer variety of options after dark. If you can't find your scene in one of the thousands of bars throughout the city and surroundings, you can see a movie classic in a funky theater, check out a live show at a local club, head to a performance space to watch some unbridled genius, or dance all night at an underground party.

In this chapter nightspots have been broken down into bars, live music, and clubs, but these distinctions are not hard and fast. More often than not, your favorite café will also serve beer, host a local band, and cater to groups of various inclinations depending on the night. The city's live-and-let-live attitude extends to its nightlife, which means you can always find your niche in the local club scene. Check *SF Weekly* or the *Bay Guardian* (both available at newsstands and cafés citywide), or the *SF Chronicle*'s Sunday "Datebook" section for listings of current happenings after dark. The free weeklies *Bay Times* and *Bay Area Reporter* are good sources for gay and lesbian listings.

SAN FRANCISCO

BARS

CASTRO DISTRICT

This safe, very gay quarter of San Francisco hosts some of the wildest festivals in the city. You're far more likely to kindle a romance here if you're enamored of the same sex, but open-minded straight folks frequent a few of the less intense pickup bars after an evening at the grand old Castro Theatre (*see* Movie Houses, *below*). Bars in this neighborhood tend to get busy early: By 2 PM on Saturday many bars are already full of an intensely social crowd whiling away the afternoon.

The Café. Formerly known as Café San Marco, this large, lively bar with mirrored walls and neon lights used to cater mainly to lesbians, but these days you'll find plenty of men here as well. If there's no room on the dance floor, you can hang out on the balcony and watch the Castro strut by. *2367 Market St., near Castro St., tel. 415/861–3846.*

IMBIBING OUTSIDE

Never mind that most evenings in San Francisco are so cold and damp they'll leave you running for a fireplace and a hot toddy—there are those rare balmy days just begging for a bar with a patio. For an alfresco beer or cocktail, try the following spots.

In the otherwise sedate Noe Valley, the Rat and Raven (4054 24th St., tel. 415/285–0674) attracts a mostly postcollegiate crowd to its patio, which is open from noon to about 6. Zeitgeist (199 Valencia St., tel. 415/255–7505), probably the city's friendliest biker bar, has an outdoor patio where you can hear the traffic whizzing by. In Cole Valley try Finnegan's Wake (937 Cole St., tel. 415/731–6119), where loyal locals toss back several pints. And if the young, black-clad crowd at Café du Nord is too trendy for you, head a few doors down to Lucky 13 (2140 Market St., tel. 415/487–1313), where a laid-back tattooed-and-pierced set drinks the many beers available on tap. For the ultimate outdoor drink, try Mission Rock Resort (817 China Basin, tel. 415/621–5338), where two decks look out over the San Francisco Bay and a mellow crowd drinks Buds from the bottle. Live music plays most weekends; call to find out if it's scheduled for the afternoon or evening.

The Detour. Minimally decorated with a chain-link fence and pool table, this bar attracts a young, good-looking crowd on the prowl. Urgent techno music and Saturday-night go-go dancers set the racy mood. If you forget the address, listen for the music, since the black-on-black sign is impossible to see at night. *2348 Market St., between Castro and Noe Sts., tel. 415/861–6053.*

Midnight Sun. Two large video screens help alleviate the need for conversation in this crowded, colorful bar that shows a mix of campy TV shows and current music videos. The thirty-something crowd tends toward the clean-cut and upscale. *4067 18th St., near Castro St., tel. 415/861–4186.*

Orbit Room. The Orbit has a smart-looking high-ceiling drinking area where you can enjoy a cocktail or espresso with a mostly straight crowd that doesn't mind the artsy, slightly uncomfortable bar stools. The subdued lighting, stucco walls, and innovative design scheme make you feel as if you're on display at some swank art gallery. *1900 Market St., at Laguna St., tel. 415/252–9525.*

The Phoenix. For high-energy dance action outside SoMa, the Phoenix is a convenient standby. Great lighting and industrial decor go a long way toward spicing up the tiny dance floor. Admission is only $1 on Friday and Saturday. *482 Castro St., between 17th and 18th Sts., tel. 415/552–6827.*

Twin Peaks. David Lynch has nothing to do with this casual, loungelike gay bar; in fact, the Peaks has been around for more than 15 years and proudly claims to have been the first gay bar in the city with clear—as in, not tinted—floor-to-ceiling windows. Twin Peaks enjoys its high visibility on the corner of Market and Castro; on weekends expect big crowds of both newcomers and an older, established clientele. *401 Castro St., at Market St., tel. 415/864–9470.*

CHINATOWN

By day a maelstrom of gaudy souvenir shops, pungent markets, and overcrowded sidewalks, Chinatown transforms into a quieter neighborhood at night, when most people on the streets are en route to or from one of the neighborhood's many Chinese restaurants. Step into one of the local bars for a reminder of whose part of town this is.

Li Po's. The dark, cavernous setting and incense-burning altar lend an oddly mystical feel to Li Po's. By 1 AM the coveted back booths are filled with boisterous escapees from the North Beach scene, who are almost daring enough to join in the occasional karaoke. *916 Grant St., between Jackson and Washington Sts., tel. 415/982–0072.*

Mr. Bing's. A heterogeneous mix of drinkers lines the narrow V-shape bar at this hangout on the edge of Chinatown. The scenery includes ubiquitous video poker machines and a jukebox that plays scratchy Sinatra tunes. *201 Columbus Ave., at Pacific St., tel. 415/362–1545.*

DOWNTOWN AND CIVIC CENTER AREA

Beware of this area after sundown: Prostitution and drug dealing are common on many corners—especially in the Tenderloin, which is loosely bordered by Larkin, O'Farrell, Mason, and Market streets. Nevertheless, there are a few bars worth braving if you have door-to-door transportation (when in doubt, call a cab).

Edinburgh Castle. This diamond in the rough was established before the Tenderloin earned its reputation for squalor. A British pub with a beautiful bar, it's a great place to play darts, make friends with thick-accented U.K. types, eat fish-and-chips, and down pints of Guinness or Bass—it also has the best single-malt collection in the Bay Area. Local bands make occasional appearances; if you're lucky, you might catch a Scottish bagpipe troupe. *950 Geary St., between Polk and Larkin Sts., tel. 415/885–4074.*

Jacks. Posters of blues legends hang on the wall, John Lee Hooker has been known to stop by on occasion, and quality live blues bands play on Friday and Saturday nights. Weeknights you'll have to make do with a wide selection of draft beer (as well as 70 different bottled kinds). This lower Fillmore club is not in the best of San Francisco's neighborhoods. *1601 Fillmore St., at Geary Blvd., tel. 415/567–3227.*

Motherlode. This Tenderloin landmark is the city's most popular transvestite haven, although there's no "dress" code posted at the door. The area is often dangerous and the crowd occasionally seedy, but the flamboyant patrons provide an energetic, entertaining night of thrills. Come for the free drag shows on Friday and Saturday nights—but please refrain from gawking. *1002 Post St., at Larkin St., tel. 415/928–6006.*

Place Pigalle. The vibes are hip and European (but definitely not pretentious) at this sleek, low-key, French-owned Hayes Valley wine bar and gallery space. Stop in for a glass of wine after work and stay for the evening; there's live jazz from Thursday through Saturday nights and occasional spoken-word performances during the week. *520 Hayes St., between Octavia and Laguna Sts., tel. 415/552–2671. Cover: up to $5.*

HAIGHT AND THE WESTERN ADDITION

Always hot on the heels of the latest trend, the Haight has some good bars that capitalize on the city's recent passion for retro cocktail emporiums. The neighborhood is especially popular with cocktail-quaffing consumers who have just loaded up on pricey flower-child togs—as well as a sprinkling of middle-aged hippies and slacker kids. When you want a watering hole that's slightly rougher around the edges, head for the Lower Haight, where you're likely to be find local barflies in their twenties.

The Deluxe. The year is perpetually 1945 at this slick retro bar in the Upper Haight. Patrons enjoy donning their finest '40s duds (hairdos and shoes included), sipping martinis, and acting *very* cool. You'll usually find a crooner, complete with backup swing band, or at least owner Jay Johnson doing Sinatra his way. *1511 Haight St., between Ashbury and Clayton Sts., tel. 415/552–6949. Cover: $3–$5 weekends.*

Mad Dog in the Fog. This British-style pub in the heart of the Lower Haight is frequented by neighborhood folk in search of cold beer and televised rugby. For lukewarm rugby fans there are other diversions: a dartboard inside, a beer garden outside, and trivia competitions for beer and cash prizes on Monday and Thursday. Mornings there are greasy breakfasts like the Greedy Bastard (bacon, sausage, baked beans, scrambled eggs, and tomato; $6)—and all dishes more than $6 include a free pint until 2:30 PM. *530 Haight St., between Fillmore and Steiner Sts., tel. 415/626–7279.*

Midtown. Watch Lower Haight Street have a beer. The clientele is young, tattooed, perpetually smoking, and good at pool. Arrive early on weekends to snag the lone table, as the crowd can be fierce in the standing room. *582 Haight St., between Fillmore and Steiner Sts., tel. 415/558–8019.*

Murio's Trophy Room. Murio's, in the Upper Haight, is often overcrowded with bikers and Haight Street slackers, but it can be fun and low-key on weekdays. When the conversation lags, amuse yourself with the pool table, jukebox, and TV. *1811 Haight St., between Shrader and Stanyan Sts., tel. 415/752–2971.*

RACK 'EM

Forget bars; for an hourly fee you can practice your bank shot at one of San Francisco's pool halls. At Hollywood Billiards (61 Golden Gate Ave., near Market St., tel. 415/252–9643), every Monday students play for up to five hours for only $5 ($10 Tuesday and Thursday). It's open 24 hours, but beware—it's not in the best neighborhood. At South Beach Billiards (270 Brannan St., near 2nd St., tel. 415/495–5939)—a sleek SoMa pool hall open nightly until 2— tables are a steep $12 an hour, $15 an hour weekend nights, but only $10 all-night Monday. Chalkers (101 Spear St., at Mission St., tel. 415/512–0450) has 30 tables, a full bar, and a grill menu. Its rates are $10 an hour for two on weeknights, $12 on weekends.

Noc Noc. Step inside this Lower Haight institution and you'll find yourself in a postmodern cave complete with chunky Flintstones-style furniture and a very eclectic music repertoire. Expect a healthy variety of beers and a couple kinds of wine including sake—but no hard liquor. *557 Haight St., between Fillmore and Steiner Sts., tel. 415/861–5811.*

The Toronado. A narrow, dark Lower Haight dive, the Toronado attracts a leather-clad set with one of the widest selections of microbrews in the city. The jukebox blares a refreshing mix of kitschy country and western in addition to the standard grunge anthems. *547 Haight St., between Fillmore and Steiner Sts., tel. 415/863–2276.*

MARINA DISTRICT

The nightlife in this affluent, homogenous neighborhood is typified by the bevy of bars in the Triangle, the intersection of Fillmore and Greenwich streets, which attract hordes of sporty young professionals. The crowds are clean-cut, and the neighborhood is one of the safest in the city.

Pierce Street Annex Drinking Establishment. Packed with the young and beautiful, this festive bar has a dance floor, pool tables, and nightly drink specials. Tuesday is karaoke night, and Thursday is devoted to live acts, including San Francisco's popular Bud E. Luv. *3138 Fillmore St., near Greenwich St., tel. 415/567–1400.*

MISSION DISTRICT

A young bohemian crowd dressed in fashionable black clothes and chunky platform shoes frequents the many bars, cafés, restaurants, and clubs in this hip neighborhood. Not so long ago the neighborhood had a shady reputation, and the poorly lighted side streets are still dicey: If possible, stay on 16th or Valencia streets, where dense clusters of bars and restaurants make for heavy foot traffic.

The Albion. Elbow your way into this cramped bar and fight for a seat under the glow of pink neon lights. If you're left standing, you can always shoot some stick or edge your way closer to the occasional live music. *3139 16th St., between Valencia and Guerrero Sts., tel. 415/552–8558.*

Dylan's. Welsh memorabilia decorate the walls of this Potrero Hill pub named after Wales's most famous poet. You may not understand the bartender's thick accent, but he'll understand you when you order a pint. Jazz music on Wednesday night draws a big crowd. *2301 Folsom St., at 19th St., tel. 415/641–1416.*

500 Club. Here's a little slice of Americana—complete with a huge neon martini sign, two cramped pool tables, and three comfy vinyl booths. The hard-drinking regulars are joined by younger patrons on weekends, when it's difficult to find a place to stand. *500 Guerrero St., at 17th St., tel. 415/861–2500.*

Lone Palm. Push open the huge black door, and you will enter an oasis of class. Dimly lighted tables, a retro '40s atmosphere, and skilled cocktail shakers behind the bar combine to make this an intimate setting in which to sip martinis with that certain someone. *3394 22nd St., at Guerrero St., tel. 415/ 648–0109.*

Make Out Room. The dark, quiet street and beckoning marquee may have you convinced this is some shady strip joint. In fact, it's a perfectly reputable, popular bar with a spacious floor, which means you won't get jostled too unmercifully on crowded weekend nights. Expect to pay a cover for occasional live band performances. *3225 22nd Ave., between Mission and Valencia Sts., tel. 415/647–2888. Cover: $3–$6.*

The Rite Spot. The piano in the corner, candlelighted tables, and understated decor all lend a sense of timelessness to this outer Mission bar that's a favorite among locals. They also serve light meals, so you won't have to leave if you get the munchies. *2099 Folsom St., at 17th St., tel. 415/552–6066.*

The Uptown. Sit at the long oak bar and get rowdy with friendly barflies, grab a game of pool with neighborhood hipsters, or stand outside watching the sometimes sordid street life. Several well-worn couches in back make you feel right at home. *200 Capp St., at 17th St., tel. 415/861–8231.*

Zeitgeist. This is the original no-frills biker bar—albeit a bit trendier and friendlier—for every kind of biker. In the afternoon it fills with bike messengers relating the day's near encounters with the Big Grille in the Sky; by night the BMW motorbike crowd clogs the outdoor deck, waiting its turn at the lone pool table. *199 Valencia St., at Duboce Ave., tel. 415/255–7505.*

NOB HILL AND RUSSIAN HILL

Nob Hill's bars are largely limited to lounges in the luxury hotels that make this neighborhood famous. Prepare to dress up and pay a lot to enjoy the ambience. Russian Hill, on the other hand, is largely populated by the city's young, upwardly mobile professionals. Don't look for casual dives here, but you just might be able to find a financially solvent date in one of Russian Hill's singles bars.

If you prefer cocktails to coffee with your sunrise, head to Vesuvio (see below), the Motherlode (see above), or the Peaks (1316 Castro St., near 24th St., tel. 415/826–0100), all of which open at 6 AM for your drinking pleasure.

Johnny Love's. This Russian Hill lounge is much touted by the press as *the* singles bar for postcollege types who have managed to find a steady job; in other words, it's the most upscale meat market in town. The entertainment varies widely but often consists of a rock or acoustic band followed by DJ'ed dancing. *1500 Broadway, at Polk St., tel. 415/931–8021.*

Red Room. A trendy clubbing crowd frequents this lounge-y cocktail bar attached to the Commodore Hotel. Its impressive entrance opens to a curved wall of red bottles stacked to the ceiling and a shockingly red interior. Prepare to match wits against the top 10% of the social food chain. *827 Sutter St., at Jones St., tel. 415/346–7666.*

Tonga Room. Nostalgic for 1950s-style kitsch? Come to the Fairmont Hotel to sip on tropical drinks that are filled with paper umbrellas and Polynesian paraphernalia. Every 30 minutes or so, a simulated rainstorm blows through the bamboo-and-palm-filled room, and at 8 most nights an almost comically bad soft-rock band performs from a thatched hut in the middle of a lagoon. Even during happy hour (5–7) drinks cost $2.50–$4.50, and the greasy all-you-can-eat buffet is an additional $5—but where else will you find such Tiki treats? Enter the hotel on California Street between Mason and Powell streets and turn right down the first hall. *Fairmont Hotel, California and Mason Sts., tel. 415/772–5278.*

NORTH BEACH

North Beach is famous for its Italian restaurants, cafés, and tiny cobblestone alleys. Although it does have a small red-light district on Broadway, the generally civil crowd, which usually includes a number of out-of-towners, is more attracted to the bars, cafés, and jazz clubs that line Columbus and Grant avenues.

Hi-Ball Lounge. Found near the Wall-to-Wall Sex Parlor, this swank bar features some of its own red-light-district furnishings—leopard-skin drapery and red-velvet booths—but none of the sleazy clientele. Before the Hi-Ball days, this spot was a hangout for jazz greats such as John Coltrane and Miles Davis, and the bar tries to maintain that legendary atmosphere with live swing bands. Unfortunately, the tiny dance floor is too cramped for dancing; instead, slip into your favorite cocktail attire and swill smooth martinis. *473 Broadway St., near Columbus Ave., tel. 415/397–9464. Cover: Thurs. and Sun. $5, Fri.–Sat. $7.*

San Francisco Brewing Company. A thirty-something crowd that is equal parts jazz lovers and beer connoisseurs frequents this popular brewery. The daily brews on tap are always good, and the frequent mel-

WHERE TO WHISPER SWEET NOTHINGS

Tired of elbowing your way into a crowded club just so you can shout to your date over the blare of speakers? This most romantic of cities also has the most romantic of bars. To enjoy the following places, put on your classiest duds and prepare to nurse an expensive drink while gazing longingly into your date's eyes.

Act IV Lounge (333 Fulton St., at Franklin St., tel. 415/553–8100), in the Inn at the Opera, has plush Victorian decor, low lighting, and a crackling fireplace, which make up for high drink prices and slightly snooty service. Forget about trying to get in before or after an opera or symphony performance. Quiet jazz music is performed at the Art Deco Redwood Room (Taylor and Geary Sts., tel. 415/775–4700), in the Clift Hotel. The older crowd tends to be stuffy, but with any luck you'll be so engrossed with your date you won't notice. The newly renovated Harry Denton's Starlight Room (450 Powell St., tel. 415/395–8595), on the 21st floor of the Sir Francis Drake Hotel, is the most romantic of the city's skyline bars. Plush velvet booths and dim lighting set the mood for live or recorded jazz, with a heavy emphasis on Sinatra tunes.

low jazz ensures they go down smoothly. The improv comedy performed on some weeknights is a mixed bag—take your chances. *155 Columbus Ave., tel. 415/434–3344.*

Savoy-Tivoli. This cavernous North Beach institution caters to an amorous set recuperating from a hard day in the Financial District. The large, covered front patio opens when the weather's nice, making the Savoy prime territory to drink wine, watch the world go by, and make believe you're in Italy. If it's raining, shoot pool in the back. *1434 Grant Ave., between Union and Green Sts., tel. 415/362–7023.*

Specs'. Its given name is Specs' Twelve Adler Museum Café, but this classic North Beach hangout for the perennially half-sloshed is popularly known as Specs'. It's a jovial, divey, no-attitude sort of place where you can gaze for hours at the quirky memorabilia papering the walls. *12 Adler Pl., tel. 415/421–4112. Off Columbus Ave., next to Tosca (see below), between Broadway and Pacific Sts.*

Tosca. A mostly opera jukebox and a beautiful old espresso machine create a worldly environment—no wonder celebrity patrons (including Francis Ford Coppola and Mikhail Baryshnikov) are occasionally spotted in the enormous red booths. Try one of the excellent liqueur-laced coffee drinks. *242 Columbus Ave., near Broadway, tel. 415/391–1244.*

Vesuvio. A bohemian hangout during the beat era, Vesuvio is the ideal place to sip a glass of red and peruse the copy of *Howl* you just bought next door at the City Lights bookstore. The best seats are upstairs and all the way back, where large windows look out on Columbus Avenue. *255 Columbus Ave., near Broadway, tel. 415/362–3370.*

SOUTH OF MARKET

A once-roughshod but increasingly upscale area of warehouses, outlet stores, and artists' studios, South of Market has plenty of dance clubs and upscale supper clubs (*see box,* Music to the Mouth, *below*), plus several standout drinking holes you should go out of your way to check out–come early and toss back a few before the sweaty postclub crowds invade.

Café Mars. Although it's situated in a somewhat removed area of SoMa, Mars is a happening bar and frequently fills to the gills with an increasingly upmarket crowd—patrons are likely to have come from the Marina or Russian Hill. On Wednesday the bar becomes the Cosmic Lounge as DJs spin the latest spacey jazz. Other nights shoot pool in the back and enjoy Martian Martinis, made with Finlandia cranberry vodka with a dried cranberry twist, and delicious tapas from the kitchen. *798 Brannan St., near 7th St., tel. 415/621–6277.*

Hotel Utah. All manner of local rock, jazz, and acoustic sounds reverberate off the woody interior of this casual SoMa bar. If you don't want to hang in the tiny music room, take a seat at the long mahogany bar (shipped from Belgium during the Civil War) and avail yourself of the fine assortment of beer and liquor. The friendly crowd ranges from lawyers to bikers to dogs (yes, dogs); the wooden floor occasionally creaks; and a fine view of a U.S. 101 off-ramp is yours through the front windows. *500 4th St., at Bryant St., tel. 415/421–8308.*

Julie's Supper Club. Past music greats (captured in black-and-white photos) gaze down at professionals and clubsters nibbling interesting appetizers and sipping cocktails. As the name implies, Julie's is a place to dine, but the art-deco-style interior and innovative munchies, including calamari and quesadillas, make this a good place for an after-work or pre-club cocktail as well. There's live music on Friday and Saturday. *1123 Folsom St., near 7th St., tel. 415/861–0707. Cover: $5–$8.*

20 Tank Brewery. With a large selection of microbrews and some hearty appetizers and pizzas, this former warehouse is a good place to fuel up before heading across the street to DNA or Slim's. On weekends it can feel like a frat party, with cheesy '80s tunes. *316 11th St., near Folsom St., tel. 415/255–9455.*

The message is in the music at St. John Coltrane's African Orthodox Church (351 Divisadero St., near Oak St., tel. 415/621–4054), where Sunday 11:45 AM services consist of a rousing three hours of the jazz great's sounds of salvation.

LIVE MUSIC

Although not at the forefront of any musical revolution, San Francisco has an eclectic and energetic music scene. Bars and clubs feature live music on any given night of the week, usually for a modest cover, and sometimes you can see talented bands for free in parks, music stores, bars, and cultural centers. For a price, you can also see the kinds of national and international acts that you'd find in any world-class metropolis. Your best bets for up-to-the-minute music listings are the *SF Weekly* and the *Bay Guardian*.

The **Great American Music Hall** (859 O'Farrell St., between Polk and Larkin Sts., tel. 415/885–0750), a gorgeous old theater that serves as a midsize concert venue, books an innovative blend of rock and world music. Tickets cost around $9–$16. Boz Scagg's club, **Slim's** (333 11th St., tel. 415/522–0333), specializes in bluesy rock icons, roots music, and the occasional indie band; tickets are $10–$20. MTV-friendly bands often play at the **Warfield** (982 Market St., between 5th and 6th Sts., tel. 415/775–7722) or at the historic **Fillmore** (1805 Geary Blvd., at Fillmore St., tel. 415/346–6000), where tickets run about $15–$25. To avoid paying steep service charges for events at the Fillmore, stop by their box office on Sunday 10–4. **Bimbo's 365 Club** (1025 Columbus, at Chestnut St., tel. 415/474–0365), a stylish concert venue swathed in red draperies, books a lot of big names in jazz, swing, and world music; tickets are $10–$20, usually with a two-drink minimum.

ROCK

Bottom of the Hill. Squeeze into this classic dive bar at the bottom of Potrero Hill to hear promising local talent and touring bands. On Sunday afternoon, $3 will gain you admission not only to the live music but also to the all-you-can-eat barbecue (served at 4). *1233 17th St., at Texas St., tel. 415/626–4455. Cover: $3–$6.*

The Chameleon. This cheap, cramped bar in the Mission is a haven for indie bands and local experimental music. When your eardrums start to hurt, head downstairs for Ping-Pong and video games. On Sunday at 8 PM, the Chameleon hosts wacky viewings of the Simpsons—during commercials they turn the sound off and give you the opportunity to win prizes for guessing the names of obscure '70s hits. *853 Valencia St., between 19th and 20th Sts., tel. 415/821–1891. Cover: up to $5.*

MUSIC TO THE MOUTH

Want more than a mariachi band with your meal? Supper clubs—an old concept combining live music, classy duds, and fancy food—are sprouting up all over. In the classic vein, the plush Eleven (374 11th St., at Harrison St., tel. 415/431-3337) serves a moderately priced Italian menu ($10-$15) while jazz, funk, and Latin ensembles play from atop a 15-ft loft. 330 Ritch Street (330 Ritch St., off Townsend St. between 3rd and 4th Sts., tel. 415/522-9558), with its jazz, salsa, and swing, attracts a classy crowd; tapas and dinner are served until 3:30 AM Friday and Saturday. At Sol y Luna (475 Sacramento St., at Battery St., tel. 415/296-8191), a well-dressed crowd dances to salsa or watches flamenco shows after dinner.

Also check out Julie's Supper Club (see Bars, above), which serves California cuisine in a 1950s-style setting; Bruno's (see Live Music, above), where meals are expensive but the setting refined; and Coconut Grove (1415 Van Ness Ave., tel. 415/776-1616), the most upscale joint in town—Tom Jones was featured on opening night. In Marin's Mill Valley, the new Panache Supper Club (639 E. Blithedale, tel. 415/388-3493) is wildly popular, especially when the $19.95 three-course lobster dinner is being served.

Kilowatt. Weekends this Mission bar hosts local alternative-rock bands reaching maximum noise levels. The dark, smoky bar is usually filled with a mix of neighborhood locals. *3160 16th St., between Guerrero and Valencia Sts., tel. 415/861-2595. Cover: $5-$7.*

Paradise Lounge. The Paradise is like a carnival fun house with something unexpected around every corner: three different musical stages from which to choose, Sunday-night poetry slams, Tuesday-night open mikes, pool tables, free-flowing booze, and a constant flow of people. Although the quality of music varies widely (to put it kindly), it's almost always a reliable weekend destination. *1501 Folsom St., at 11th St., tel. 415/861-6906. Cover: about $5.*

Purple Onion. Indulge in pints of Pabst Blue Ribbon, kick back in one of the oversize red-vinyl booths, and enjoy garage-style punk and surf music at this once-famous underground North Beach lounge, a popular hangout for what's left of the overdressed mod scene. The Onion is open Friday and Saturday only. *140 Columbus Ave., between Pacific Ave. and Jackson St., tel. 415/398-8415. Cover: $5.*

JAZZ

San Francisco's jazz scene has exploded of late, with a rash of local bands who have taken it upon themselves to fuse the edges of funk, hip-hop, and jazz to create a distinctive new sound. Venues like the Elbo Room (*see below*), Café du Nord (*see below*), and Eleven (*see box, above*) devote much space to these new acts: Look for the **Broun Fellinis** (freestyle jazz with a funky bass line), **Alphabet Soup** (upbeat, reggae-influenced jazz along with a pair of rappers), the **Supernaturals** (a loungey new direction taken by former members of the band the Loved Ones), and the **Charlie Hunter Trio** (traditional jazz). Oakland has more mainstream big-name acts.

Bruno's. Divided into a full-scale restaurant and a lounge-y bar, Bruno's has been wildly popular since it reopened in 1995. Nightly the intimate club showcases local jazz and swing acts, many of them up-and-coming stars of the San Francisco scene—though sometimes the patrons here are too busy being fashionable to pay much attention to the band. Relax in the red-vinyl booths with a martini or squeeze up closer (if that's possible) to the band. *2389 Mission St., at 20th St., tel. 415/550–7455. Cover: $3–$5.*

Café du Nord. The specialty at this large, crowded Castro club is jazz you can afford. Saturday night usually features the sultry crooning of local faves LaVay Smith & her Red Hot Skillet Lickers. Wednesday brings the Downhear Experimental Series, showcasing some of the finest local talent, and other nights feature lounge, salsa, swing, and big-band music. Those more interested in playing pool or socializing can do so in the front of the bar, while music lovers groove uninterrupted in the back. Dinner is served Wednesday–Saturday. *2170 Market St., at Sanchez St., tel. 415/861–5016. Cover: $3–$5.*

CoCo Club. A variety of acts comes through this small woman-owned restaurant and performance space South of Market—everything from acoustic rock to avant-garde jazz and blues. The tiny, comfortable interior also hosts a few lesbian events each week, as well as Planet Fox, a monthly "cabaret lounge and drop-in drag clinic." The entrance is on Minna Street. *139 8th St., between Mission and Howard Sts., tel. 415/626–7668. Cover: $3–$5.*

Elbo Room. This stylish Mission watering hole becomes unmanageably popular as the night progresses. Head upstairs for some of the best local live jazz and hip-hop acts, as well as occasional DJs. Forgot your dancing shoes? Join the locals packed around the pool table—the drinks are cheap enough to keep you around until closing. Happy hour stretches from 3 to 9, and you can often win tickets to shows at their Web site, www.elbo.com. *647 Valencia St., near 17th St., tel. 415/552–7788. Upstairs cover: about $5.*

The city's best margaritas are mixed at Puerto Alegre (546 Valencia St., near 16th St., tel. 415/626–2922), about a block from the Elbo Room.

Jazz at Pearl's. This sedately romantic North Beach joint generally showcases mainstream, traditional jazz in a dimly lighted setting. However, if you stick around late, you just might catch some smokin' improvisational jams. During shows there's a two-drink minimum. *256 Columbus Ave., at Broadway, tel. 415/291–8255. No cover.*

Noe Valley Ministry. An adventurous booking policy draws some serious talent—from experimental jazz and blues artists to well-known world-music acts—into this no-smoking church in Noe Valley that moonlights as a performance space. Call ahead for tickets ($10–$15) if you don't want to be disappointed at the door. *1021 Sanchez St., between 23rd and Elizabeth Sts., tel. 415/282–2317.*

Up and Down Club. Sleek deco digs give this multilevel SoMa supper club the feel of a New York lounge. Upstairs you'll find a DJ laying down tracks but little room in which to dance. Downstairs, jazz, including Latin and acid varieties, heats up the room. The club is closed on Sunday. *1151 Folsom St., between 7th and 8th Sts., tel. 415/626–2388. Cover: $5, free Wed.*

BLUES

Although Oakland's blues scene is more renowned, San Francisco's devoted blues followers are pros at supporting local acts. Several venues, most notably **Slim's** (*see above*) and the **Great American Music Hall** (*see above*), are often stops for traveling blues legends.

Blue Lamp. This friendly downtown bar books a variety of blues, jazz, folk, and rock bands nightly and attracts an equally diverse mix of patrons. Arrive early to stake your spot near the fireplace. *561 Geary St., between Taylor and Jones Sts., tel. 415/885–1464. Cover: $2 Thurs., $4 Fri.–Sat.*

Grant and Green Blues Club. This dark, smoky bar hosts some raucous blues shows—a welcome contrast to the very civilized cafés and coffeehouses that dominate North Beach. *1731 Grant Ave., at Green St., tel. 415/693–9565. Cover: free–$4.*

CLUBS

In San Francisco hard-core club hoppers often take their nightlife more seriously than their jobs. Spaces large and small play music for every age, style, and level of rhythmic ability. There's a huge variety of quite cheap and casual dance venues, as well as some that ooze pretension. Dance purists can even find spaces that allow no alcohol or smoking. On the other end of the spectrum are raves and dance parties—still going strong in warehouses and fields—where substance abuse is by no means limited to alcohol and smoking.

SHALL WE DANCE?

If you find yourself stumbling over two left feet instead of cutting a rug, get theeself to the dance club. At Café du Nord (see Live Music, above) samba, mambo, and cha-cha lessons are included in the $3 cover Tuesday at 9 PM, while Sunday means free swing lessons at 8 PM ($3 after 9 PM). Head to 330 Ritch Street (330 Ritch St., off Townsend St. between 3rd and 4th Sts., tel. 415/522–9558) for free swing instruction (included in the $5 cover) Wednesday at 8:30 PM and lessons in Latin dance steps Saturday at 8:30 PM ($5). Ten dollars buys you salsa lessons and dancing Thursday through Saturday at 8 PM at Kimball's Carnival (see Live Music, above). Barring the above, a coy glance and a polite inquiry might enlist the company of a willing and—you hope—capable partner.

For flyers on the club scene, check smaller, more alternative retail and record shops. Many spaces host various clubs on different nights of the week; the *Bay Guardian* and *SF Weekly* have complete listings of the Bay Area's rotating club nights (call ahead because the hot spots change quickly.) For current listings of gay and lesbian clubs (as well as the latest gossip), flip through the free monthlies *Odyssey* and *Oblivion,* available in cafés and bookstores around the Castro District.

STRAIGHT

Bahia Cabana. A multigenerational international crowd comes to samba at this tropical downtown supper club with mural-covered walls. Thursday and Friday are salsa nights; other evenings expect Brazilian and various Latino bands and on Monday techno trance. *1600 Market St., at Franklin St., tel. 415/626–3306. Cover: $5–$10.*

Cat's Grill and Alley Club. The small back room of this mostly after-hours club in SoMa features everything from jazz to jungle to ambient house. Saturday the club hosts "So What," featuring hard-core industrial music and the occasional mosh pit. *1190 Folsom St., near 8th St., tel. 415/431–3332. Cover: about $5.*

Cesar's Latin Palace. Cesar's Latin All-Stars play fiery salsa most nights, with occasional guest artists from all over Latin America. Early on you'll find older folks and even families here; things heat up later in the evening when it's mostly young, well-dressed Latinos. Open Friday–Sunday only, the club keeps going until 5 AM. *3140 Mission St., near César Chávez (Army) St., tel. 415/648–6611. Cover: about $10.*

Club 181. Open Friday and Saturday only, this dance club with a mix of live and DJ'ed music has a room dedicated to—gasp—album rock, in case you haven't caught on to trip-hop or deep house yet. Three separate rooms mean you ought to be able to find your scene here somewhere. *181 Eddy St., at Taylor St., tel. 415/673–8181. Cover: $8.*

Deco. If it weren't for the strains of funk, hip-hop, and acid jazz spilling out the front entrance of this low-rent downtown club, it might be mistaken for a neighborhood bar with an impressive selection of beers. Three floors, each with its own spin jockey and unique ambience, will amuse you till the wee hours of the morning. Women usually enter for free before 11 PM. *510 Larkin St., between Turk and Eddy Sts., tel. 415/441–4007. Cover: free–$6.*

DNA Lounge. This dependable choice for after-hours dancing (weekends until 4 AM) has eclectic acts that range from rockabilly nights to tattoo and piercing shows. The crowd isn't afraid to break a sweat on the dance floor, but many come just to kick back in dimly lighted corners downstairs. On Friday dance to the '70s retro band Grooveline. DJs usually come on after the live music. Wednesday's "Afrosheen" features reggae, soul, and R&B. *375 11th St., at Harrison St., tel. 415/626–1409. Cover: $5–$15.*

Nickie's BBQ. Red-vinyl booths and Christmas lights decorate this urban Lower Haight hole-in-the-wall that's entirely lacking in pretension. Nightly you can listen to '70s funk, soul, hip-hop, reggae, Latin, and world-beat booms. This is the cool venue pictured on the album cover of the sizzling, modern dance-floor jazz compilation *Home Cookin'* (Ubiquity Records). *460 Haight St., between Webster and Fillmore Sts., tel. 415/621–6508. Cover: $3–$5.*

Oz. Far from the industrial warehouses South of Market, Oz has one of the city's swankiest locations, on the top floor of the Westin St. Francis Hotel. The cover is outrageous, and the music—mostly funk, pop, house, and hip-hop—is hardly cutting edge, but it might be worth a trip just to enjoy the spectacle of out-of-towners desperately trying to keep the beat. Marble floors and a fantastic view of the city are perks you won't find at any other dance club in the city. Cushy sofas are the perfect setting for flirtation. *335 Powell St., at Geary St., tel. 415/774–0116. Cover: $15 Fri.– Sat., $8 Mon.–Thurs., $5 Sun.*

MIXED

The Box. This Thursday-only artsy-industrial SoMa club plays hard-core hip-hop, funk, soul, and house without attitude. For an extra treat, go-go platforms mounted on the walls showcase dancers who gyrate at full throttle. The city's most accomplished DJs—including "Mixtress" Page Hodel, San Francisco's most famous gay DJ—and club dance troupes appear here. Although the club is lesbian-run, the multicultural crowd includes straights, too. *715 Harrison St., between 3rd and 4th Sts. Cover: $6 ($5 for members).*

El Río. This casual neighborhood hangout in the Mission attracts a healthy mix of men and women, straight and gay and all those in between, with different dance parties every night. On sunny afternoons nothing is more relaxing than a cold brew under the palm tree in El Río's back patio, and if you come on a Sunday, you can work off the beer with some fiery salsa dancing during "Latin Spin." The neighborhood isn't the best; women especially should avoid walking alone on Mission Street at night. *3158 Mission St., near César Chávez (Army) St., tel. 415/282–3325. Cover: up to $7.*

All aboard for some serious salsa. Friday and Saturday nights the Mexican Bus winds its way through the city depositing dancers at various Latin Clubs. Join the fun for $30 (cover charges included). Call 415/546-3747 for details.

Sound Factory. This club is tame and mainstream by city standards, but Friday night's deep-house dance extravaganza has been embraced by all-nighters as a favorite after-hours hangout. Modeled after the clubs in New York and Los Angeles, the large SoMa space has a literal maze of pulsating rooms. Call for upcoming clubs and events. *525 Harrison St., at 1st St., tel. 415/243–9646. Cover: about $10.*

1015 Folsom. There's a different scene at "Club 1015" every night. Look for disco, techno, and house—and themed parties with names like "Eurotrash." Every Saturday the ever-popular Release (tel. 415/337–7457) keeps you up all night with '70s funk and disco, deep house, and hip-hop. Though the club has a dress code on weekends, it's more casual weeknights after hours. Its events consistently showcase quality turntable talent, and there's a cozy lounge upstairs, conveniently shielded from the blare of the speakers. Call for a complete listing of events. *1015 Folsom St., at 6th, tel. 415/431–1200. Cover: $10 weekends, $5 weeknights.*

The Trocadero. On Wednesday only the Trocadero hosts the oldest fetish dance party in California: "Bondage A Go-Go." It's a light introduction to the real S&M subculture, where you may engage in acts of light bondage, get whipped by a professional dominatrix, or just stand to the side and gawk. Other nights this SoMa club features industrial dancing and live hard-core music. The Trocadero is all ages when the music is live, but only those 18 and over are allowed for "Bondage A Go-Go" and DJ events. *520 4th St., between Bryant and Brannan Sts., tel. 415/995–4600. Cover: $4–$7.*

GAY AND LESBIAN

Club Townsend. This vast SoMa disco hosts the high-energy Sunday "Pleasuredome," with local DJs churning out sounds for a largely male crowd followed by a where-do-they-get-the-energy Sunday tea dance until 6 AM. "Club Universe," on Saturday, is less gender-specific, and the artsy decor changes to create a stunning new illusion each week. *177 Townsend St., between 2nd and 3rd Sts., tel. 415/974–1156. Cover: $10.*

Covered Wagon. Black light illuminates the Western decor on the walls as well as the lint on your shirt at this dark SoMa bar. Afternoons the CW sees a lot of bike messengers taking a breather, but at night it caters primarily to gay women, with live funk, soul, and ska some nights, DJs and dancing on others.

SOUNDS FOR SILENT SCREENINGS

Defying classification in any musical category, the Club Foot Orchestra consists of nine musical adventurers with backgrounds in orchestral, popular, and world music. Though they started off playing in clubs South of Market, today they're best known for writing scores to classic silent films and performing during the screenings. If at all possible, see them when they're accompanying a film at the Castro Theatre, when tickets are usually $10; they also play at Bruno's (see Live Music, above). Check the papers for their schedule.

The bar serves as a preclub watering hole to a mixed crowd early on weekend nights but grows increasingly female by the end of the night. *911 Folsom St., at 5th St., tel. 415/974–1585. Cover: $3–$6.*

The EndUp. Home of the "misplaced weekend," this primarily gay bar has an outdoor patio (threatened by closure due to neighborhood complaints about noise), a pool table, a gazebo, and a waterfall, all surrealistically situated almost directly beneath U.S. 101. The elevated dance floor couldn't possibly accommodate everyone, so the sweaty crowd gets down wherever it suits them. Come at 9 AM for the "Sunday T*Dance," a tradition for nearly a quarter of a century. On Monday night the EndUp hosts "Club Dread" ($5), a DJ'ed reggae dance party, and "Fag Fridays" feature go-go dancers and some of the best-looking boys you'll see all week. *995 Harrison St., at 6th St., tel. 415/357–0827. Cover: $5–$10.*

Esta Noche. Tucked away in the Mission, Esta Noche plays a good mix of hard-pumping Latin, house music, and '70s disco. The crowd consists mostly of young Latino men, and Anglo patrons are respectfully requested to refrain from doing the cha-cha. Women, though few, will not feel unwelcome. *3079 16th St., at Valencia St., tel. 415/861–5757. Cover: $3–$4.*

The Stud. This SoMa club is a San Francisco legend and a good watering hole any night of the week. Dress up or come as you are and have fun flirting with innocent out-of-towners. Thursday night is often set aside for lesbian events; on Wednesday the club draws in a postcollegiate crowd for dancing to '70s and early '80s classics. The Tuesday-night club, "Trannyshack," is especially popular, when cross-dressers enjoy "makeup tips and cheap cocktails." *399 9th St., at Harrison St., tel. 415/252–7883. Cover: $3–$6.*

MOVIE HOUSES

Although most cities rely on multiscreen megatheaters to satisfy its film goers, the Bay Area is fortunate to have more than a handful of tiny independent theaters, where fervent buffs insist on viewing "films" and not "movies." San Francisco also happens to be one of the nation's most prolific cities for independent filmmaking—in particular, documentaries, shorts, and experimental and avant-garde films. The **Artists' Television Access** (992 Valencia St., at 21st St., tel. 415/824–3890), a nonprofit media arts center in the Mission, screens offbeat films for $5.

During spring and summer five big film festivals roll through town, starting in early March with the 16-year-old **San Francisco International Asian-American Film Festival** (tel. 415/863–0814), during which most films are shown at the Kabuki (*see below*). In mid-April look for the **San Francisco International Film Festival** (tel. 415/931–3456), which features quality films from all over the world. During the last two weeks in June the much-loved **International Lesbian and Gay Film Festival** (tel. 415/703–8650) coincides with Gay Pride Week and is the largest such event in the world. The **Jewish Film Festival** (tel. 510/548–0556) breezes into town—one week at the Castro Theatre in San Francisco and one week at the UC Theatre in Berkeley—at the end of July and beginning of August. Finally, September brings the relatively small but increasingly popular **Festival Cine Latino** (tel. 415/553–8135).

For new releases everyone goes to the **AMC Kabuki 8** (1881 Post St., at Fillmore St., tel. 415/931–9800), even though some of the multiplex's eight screens are tiny and seating is limited. Tickets run

$7.50. Take advantage of the validated parking in Japan Center, since this isn't the safest place to leave your car. **Landmark Theaters** (tel. 415/352–0810 for show-time information) runs a number of artsy and foreign film houses in the city, including the Embarcadero Center Cinema (One Embarcadero Center), Clay Theatre (2261 Fillmore St., at Clay St.), Lumière Theatre (1572 California St., at Polk St.), Opera Plaza Cinema (601 Van Ness Ave., at Golden Gate Ave.), and Bridge Theatre (3010 Geary Blvd., at Blake St.). The Landmark Theater card, which can be used at any of their numerous locations throughout the Bay Area, gives you five admissions for $25, weekend nights excluded. Other theaters you might want to visit: The **Alhambra** (2330 Polk St., at Union St., tel. 415/775–2137) wins points for its Art Deco style but unfortunately seems to screen a single movie for ages. If you've just *got* to see a loud action flick, the **United Artists Coronet** (3575 Geary Blvd., at Arguello St., tel. 415/752–4400) impresses with its huge capacity, large screen, and Sony Dynamic Digital Sound. The *Bay Guardian* and *SF Weekly* have complete listings and reviews for both first-run theaters and rep houses.

Casting Couch Micro Cinema. Come to this deluxe 46-person screening room for an intimate and unique viewing experience. Sink into one of the sofas and let the waitstaff bring you cookies while you check out their roster of all-independent films. Arrive 15 minutes before show time to secure a seat. *950 Battery St., between Green and Vallejo Sts., tel. 415/986–7001. Admission: $8.50.*

Castro Theatre. Built in 1922 and still the most beautiful place to see a film in San Francisco, the Castro shows a wide selection of rare, foreign, and unusual films, which play anywhere from a night to a week or two. The specialties here are camp, classics of all genres, and new releases of interest to lesbian and gay viewers. The man who rises out of the floor playing a Wurlitzer organ is guaranteed to make you giggle. *429 Castro St., between Market and 18th Sts., tel. 415/621–6120. Admission: $6.50.*

Red Vic. Films at this co-op range from the artsy to the cultish to the rare, and you can have your herbal tea in a real mug to accompany your popcorn sprinkled with nutritional yeast. If you get here early, snag one of the couches before lovebirds beat you to it. *1727 Haight St., between Cole and Shrader Sts., tel. 415/668–3994. Admission: $6.*

The Roxie. This slightly run-down Mission theater shows political, cult, and otherwise bent films of widely varying quality. Though some fabulous films pass through here, they also play a lot of silly old flicks that might just as well be forgotten. *3117 16th St., at Valencia St., tel. 415/863–1087. Admission: $6.*

San Francisco Cinemateque. Dedicated to the perpetuation of experimental filmmaking, the San Francisco Art Institute's nonprofit theater screens rare avant-garde films, documentaries, and independent films. Screenings usually take place Thursday at the Center for the Arts at Yerba Buena Gardens (*see* Multimedia Performance Spaces, *below*) and Sunday at the Institute. *San Francisco Art Institute, 800 Chestnut St., between Jones and Leavenworth Sts., tel. 415/558–8129. Admission: $6.*

THEATER

Some of San Francisco's best theater talents can be found in its smaller multicultural and experimental ensembles. Local troupes worth watching include the **Sick and Twisted Players,** a mostly gay group that specializes in campy staged interpretations of films like *The Rocky Horror Picture Show.*

For more mainstream tastes, **ACT** (American Conservatory Theater), the city's major theater company, presents about eight plays annually, from October through late spring, in the newly renovated Geary Theater (415 Geary St., at Mason St., tel. 415/749–2228). Broadway-type shows usually appear at the downtown **Curran Theater** (445 Geary St., at Mason St., tel. 415/474–3800). The 2,500-seat **Orpheum** (1192 Market St., near the Civic Center, tel. 415/474–3800) is used for the biggest touring shows. For discounts try TIX Bay Area (251 Stockton St., between Post and Geary Sts., tel. 415/433–7827), a same-day half-price ticket booth on Union Square. Most venues also provide discounts for students with ID.

Sometimes a night of theater involves more conflict, climax, and denouement than you're prepared to commit to, and you just feel like a little no-brainer entertainment. The productions ($10–$12) at **Josie's Cabaret & Juice Joint** (*see* Castro/Noe Valley *in* Chapter 4), an established gay cultural center, lean toward campy cabaret and riotous stand-up, though you'll see the occasional serious piece as well. At **Climate Theater** (285 9th St., at Tehama St., tel. 415/978–2345), you can catch small ensembles and solo performers doing original work. Tickets are $7–$10.

If you're interested in modern theater, don't miss the **San Francisco Fringe Festival** (tel. 415/931–1094), which brings local, national, and international experimental theater to venues throughout the city just after Labor Day. Another event to watch for is the **San Francisco Shakespeare Festival** (tel.

415/422–2222), which brings the Bard's work to parks throughout the Bay Area from August to October. San Francisco performances are held in Golden Gate Park, usually in September.

Asian American Theater Company. Recently relocated to New Langton Arts (*see* Multimedia Performance Spaces, *below*), this company presents the works of Asian and Asian-American playwrights. Tickets go for $8–$21. *Administrative office: 1840 Sutter St., Suite 207, at Webster St., tel. 415/440–5545.*

Beach Blanket Babylon. This zany San Francisco revue has been selling out most nights for the past three decades, with talented musicians, polished performers, impeccable timing, extralarge headgear, and a zesty, zany script that changes to incorporate topical references and characters (not to mention an ongoing love affair with the British royal family). A significant chunk of your $18–$45 ticket cost goes to local charities. Those under 21 may attend Sunday matinee performances only. *Club Fugazi, 678 Green St., at Powell St., tel. 415/421–4222.*

BRAVA! Brava! For Women in the Arts is the official name of this resident theater company, a stronghold of women's stage work. The mostly experimental programming includes works by local playwrights and performance artists and frequently showcases the work of the Latina community. Tickets cost up to $16. *2789 24th St., at York, tel. 415/826–5773.*

Exit Theatre. One of the best venues downtown is this two-stage café-theater, where small but imaginative productions sometimes draw on video, music, or other media. Political satire is a favored topic of many productions, and no one is safe from their far-reaching comedic jabs. Tickets range from $6 to $12. *156 Eddy St., at Mason St., tel. 415/673–3847.*

Lorraine Hansberry Theatre. A consistently high-quality locus of African-American theater, the Lorraine Hansberry performs experimental, musical, and classical works by African-Americans and other writers of color. The work of talented young playwrights is often premiered at the theater. Tickets cost $15–$22. *620 Sutter St., at Mason St., tel. 415/474–8800.*

Magic Theatre. The Magic is San Francisco's standby for the modern and mildly experimental. Sam Shepherd wrote a lot of his plays for this venue in the late '70s and early '80s; the theater continues to premiere innovative American works, and Sam himself returns from time to time. In 1997 they staged the West Coast premiere of David Mamet's *The Cryptogram* to much acclaim. Tickets for performances run $17–$24. *Fort Mason Center, Bldg. D, tel. 415/441–8822.*

The Marsh. This self-described "breeding ground for new performances"—get it?—hosts primarily new works by local artists. Though the shows are not consistently excellent, they are almost always intriguing. The 99 house seats include a cozy corner of sofas. The "Monday Night Marsh New Works Series" ($6) presents works in progress, and the "Growing Stage" program presents performances and workshops for children. Most performances cost $6–$10, though children's programs are usually less. *1062 Valencia St., near 22nd St., tel. 415/826–5750.*

San Francisco Mime Troupe. Since 1961 this provocative ensemble has been staging free scathing political comedies and musicals in Golden Gate and other Bay Area parks on weekends at 2 PM from July 4 through Labor Day. Call for its current whereabouts. *Tel. 415/285–1717.*

Theater of Yugen. This theater's mission is to bring the Japanese aesthetic to Western audiences. Of the four East-West fusion works staged each year, three are primarily in English and deal with Japanese stories or themes, while the fourth is *kyogen,* traditional Japanese comedy, performed in Japanese on a simple black-draped stage. Tickets cost $10–$15, with reduced rates for previews. Performances take place both at the Noh Theatre (2840 Mariposa St., at Alabama St., tel. 415/621–7978) and the Cowell Theater, at Fort Mason (Pier 2, Laguna St. at Marina Blvd., tel. 415/441–5706).

Theatre Rhinoceros. The only strictly gay and lesbian theater company in San Francisco stages reliable plays in its tiny Mission District hall. Though you can catch dramas here, you're more likely to see a comedy with a wry twist: Witness *The Big Drag,* advertised as "a hard-boiled yarn of girls, guns, and genre dysphoria." Ticket prices are $12–$18. *2926 16th St., tel. 415/861–5079.*

MULTIMEDIA PERFORMANCE SPACES

As technology has increasingly affected theater, video, dance, and music, it has also become a powerful medium in itself. The following venues are committed to exploring the evolving relationships among performance media.

Audium. This theater of sound-sculpted space explores the relationship between music and space. You sit in pitch darkness, surrounded by 169 speakers that saturate you with sounds; the effect of the 72-minute performance is both intense and unsettling. The show's affable composer, Stan Shaff, who handles the controls during the shows, is happy to discuss his art afterwards. This small theater—only 49 seats—is open Friday and Saturday only; shows start promptly at 8:30 PM. *1616 Bush St., at Franklin St., tel. 415/771–1616. Admission: $10.*

Center for the Arts at Yerba Buena Gardens. The bright yellow and red of this modern theater's lobby give way to the more metallic luster of the interior space. Though budget problems have threatened the center's ambitious mission, it still draws top dancers, musicians, and dramatists and sometimes combines them in large-scale ways. The theater itself has superb acoustics and souped-up technological gadgets. Despite the 750 seats it feels like an intimate space. Tickets start at $9. *701 Mission St., at 3rd St., tel. 415/978–2787.*

George Coates Performance Works. Technological wizard George Coates mixes the latest computer technology with the stage. Performances, held under the soaring vaulted ceiling of a former church, involve music, video, and motion and use only a scrim and special lighting to create "virtual" sets. Tickets cost $14, $24, and $34, though tickets to previews are only $10. *110 McAllister St., at Leavenworth St., tel. 415/863–8520.*

Intersection for the Arts. This stark stone-walled space in the Mission seats 65 for viewing performance art, performative readings, the competitive "Poetry Slam Finals," workshops, chamber operas, and lectures. The gallery space upstairs features intriguing sound and visual installations. The 30-year-old Intersection is San Francisco's oldest alternative art space, and its shows are consistently good. Ticket prices vary widely but are usually around $10–$20. There's free evening parking at 670 Valencia Street. *446 Valencia St., between 15th and 16th Sts., tel. 415/626–2787.*

Luna Sea (2940 16th St., Room 216C, tel. 415/863–2989) is a women's group upstairs from Theatre Rhinoceros, in the Mission; they sponsor readings, music, and other events, often as benefits.

New Langton Arts. This far-reaching organization has been around for a couple decades, providing local performance and installation artists with grants to complete their work and an audience to appreciate it. New Langton's work is similar to that of Theater Artaud (*see below*) but on a smaller scale. Upstairs is a bright, continually changing gallery; downstairs is a 75-seat well-equipped multimedia theater. Admission is $5–$8. *1246 Folsom St., at 8th St., tel. 415/626–5416.*

Theater Artaud. Artaud has one of the most interesting performance halls in town: a cavernous converted cannery. The 300-seat space creates eerie echoes that generally add to the effect. The excellent local and traveling shows—often dance, drama, and music all at once—provide insight into the experimental scene both in San Francisco and internationally. Tickets run $10–$25 and are cheaper weeknights. The neighborhood is seedy, but the experience is worth it. *450 Florida St., between 17th and Mariposa Sts., tel. 415/621–7797.*

Venue 9. Energetic performers stage a variety of events at this South of Market venue run by the Foot-Loose Dance Company. In 1997 their "Women's Work" series featured musical, theater, dance, and comedy performances, as well as provocative films made by women. Admission varies from $5 to $12, with many shows charging from $6 to $10 on a sliding scale. *252 9th St., at Folsom St., tel. 415/626–2169.*

CLASSICAL MUSIC

Herbst Theater. World-class soloists and occasional groups play at the elegant Herbst, in the Veterans Building downtown, usually charging $20 and up per seat. Though the theater is plush, the acoustics are mediocre. *401 Van Ness Ave., tel. 415/392–4400.*

San Francisco Conservatory of Music. The city's major music school has something going on almost nightly, whether it's performed by students, faculty, or the Conservatory Orchestra. Quality is unpredictable, but with the school's fine reputation, odds are you'll see something worthwhile. General admission is $10; most student recitals are free. *1201 Ortega St., at 19th Ave., tel. 415/759–3477.*

San Francisco Contemporary Music Players. The biggest name of any contemporary company in the area hosts only about six performances a year at the Center for the Arts (*see* Multimedia Performance Spaces, *above*) in both the main theater and the intimate 300-seat Forum Theater. Concerts generally feature brand-new works by contemporary composers, with some by "oldies" like John Cage. Tickets are $14 for general admission, and prices include a preconcert discussion with composers and other guests. *701 Mission St., at 3rd St., tel. 415/978–2787 or 415/252–6235 for programming information.*

San Francisco Opera. The opera's grand-scale performances each season usually include one exorbitantly lavish production each year: 1997's program included a 4½-hour program of Wagner's *Lohengrin*. Prices are equally exorbitant, ranging from $20 to $100. Flash a student or senior ID (or anything that looks like one) two hours before curtain time and you may score tickets for $15–$20; call ahead to make sure discount tickets are available. At press time the War Memorial Opera House (301 Van Ness Ave.) was closed for earthquake retrofitting, but you should be able to see it in all its renovated splendor during the 1997–1998 opera season. *Box office: 199 Grove St., at Van Ness Ave., tel. 415/864–3330.*

San Francisco Symphony. Under the baton of American-born conductor Michael Tilson Thomas, the symphony performs at Davies Symphony Hall, where the interior architecture looks odd but creates good acoustics for even the cheapest balcony seats ($25). The best deals, though, available for most but not all performances, are the $10–$12 center terrace seats: A limited number are available in advance but sell out quickly; 40 more go on sale two hours before the show. The seats hover directly over the orchestra, yielding an off-balance sound but a fantastic face-on view of the conductor and an intimate look at the musicians' work. *Davies Symphony Hall, 201 Van Ness Ave., at Grove St., tel. 415/864–6000.*

San Francisco Women's Philharmonic. After a nearly two-year hiatus, this talented group of performers resumed advancing the work of women composers, conductors, and performers in 1997. The first of their three 1997 performances was received warmly by critics, boding well for their future success. Their performances, held at Herbst Theater, are often preceded by a discussion with the artists. Tickets cost $25–$30. *44 Page St., Suite 604D, tel. 415/437–0123 or 415/392–4400 for reservations.*

DANCE

The world's very best dance troupes pass through the Bay Area, many stopping at **Zellerbach Hall** (*see* Classical Music *in* East Bay, *below*) or at the neoclassical **Palace of Fine Arts** (3301 Lyon St., San Francisco, tel. 415/567–6642). Modern dance has been embraced locally with a fervor, and the Bay Area has quite a few progressive and experimental companies. Probably the most important entry on the Bay Area's dance calendar is the **San Francisco Ethnic Dance Festival** (tel. 415/474–3914), held for several days in June. The auditions, held in mid-January, are the best dance bargain of the year: $5 for a full day of entertainment. Call ahead for the exact dates and times. Check the *Bay Guardian* for schedules and dependable recommendations.

Dancer's Group Studio Theater. This small, informal space is packed to capacity most Friday and Saturday nights, with avid audiences enjoying the vibrant creativity of local choreographers. Many performances incorporate text with music and movement to examine a variety of personal and political themes. Intermediate and advanced dance lessons are offered at $9 a session. *3221 22nd St., at Mission St., tel. 415/824–5044.*

San Francisco Ballet. Though this company has never been known for cutting-edge performances, they have recently started attracting more notice for their staging of modern works: In 1997, for example, the traditional charmer *La Sylphide* was paired with *Drink to Me Only with Thine Eyes,* set to 13 piano etudes by Virgil Thompson. Ticket prices can be steep, ranging from $18 to $85. *Box office: 455 Franklin St., at Fulton St., tel. 415/703–9400.*

Third Wave Dance House. The spirit of Third Wave is African-driven. Performances, which cost $10–$15, are often experimental and almost always feature live percussionists. Dance classes for all abilities, at $10 a pop, delve into Brazilian, Haitian, hip-hop, and West African dance traditions, among others. *3316 24th St., at Mission St., tel. 415/282–4020.*

EAST BAY

East of the Bay Bridge you'll find plenty of bars and a handful of live music venues: Come to Oakland to sample world-class blues and jazz and a burgeoning improv scene or to Berkeley to drink with a predominantly collegiate crowd. Pore through the free weekly *East Bay Express* for a complete events calendar, including films, lectures, readings, and music.

BARS

BERKELEY

Berkeley has very few high-concept bars, but you'll find plenty of casual places to have a beer. The bars along Telegraph Avenue can't help but appeal to student tastes and budgets. To peer more deeply into Berkeley's psyche, head to one of the watering holes scattered along San Pablo Avenue, which tend to be seedier but more genuine despite the diminished collegiate contingent.

The Albatross. This no-nonsense watering-hole attracts students and working folk. The cheap draft beer (starting at $1.50) tastes even better with the free popcorn, and there are a cozy fireplace and a whole row of dartboards occupying a good-size portion of the bar. This is the sort of place where grad students borrow the bar's Scrabble game and settle in for a quiet evening. *1822 San Pablo Ave., between Hearst Ave. and Delaware St., tel. 510/849–4714. From Berkeley BART, Bus 51 west to San Pablo Ave., walk 1½ blocks north.*

Le Bateau Ivre. Beautifully decorated in French provincial style, this elegant establishment nevertheless felt compelled to install a neon sign with the decidedly unalluring English translation of its name (from an Arthur Rimbaud poem): THE DRUNKEN BOAT. Still, it remains a place both romantic and subdued, complete with fireplace and candlelighted tables—the perfect setting for one of the creamiest pints of Guinness this side of Dublin. On summer evenings the outdoor patio feels like a Parisian sidewalk. *2629 Telegraph Ave., at Carleton St., tel. 510/849–1100. 6 blocks south of UC campus.*

Bison Brewing Company. Homemade stout, cider, ale, and snakebites bring in a mixed crowd of Berkeley frat boys and tattooed types—especially during happy hour (4–6 weekdays, 3–8 during daylight savings time). Live bands ranging from blues to Irish folk entertain from Thursday through Saturday: Shout over the music or steal away to the upstairs patio or one of the new sidewalk tables if you need a quiet moment. There is often free live jazz on Sunday afternoon. *2598 Telegraph Ave., at Parker St., tel. 510/841–7734. 5 blocks south of UC campus. Cover: $1–$2.*

Ivy Room. This self-styled dive bar attracts a congenial mix of students, working-class folks, and retired bikers with its live, mostly bluesy music and $2 Buds. The welcoming bar staff and colorful cast of regulars make for excellent company when you're out to pull a few pints, even on a weeknight. *858 San Pablo Ave., at Solano Ave., tel. 510/524–9299. From Berkeley BART, Bus 43 west to Solano Ave.*

Jupiter. This spacious wine-and-beer bar across from the Berkeley BART station is popular for its outdoor beer garden, 20 microbrews on tap, and free live jazz on weekends. The end of the week draws large down-to-earth crowds, but it's almost always mellow enough to allow for conversation. *2181 Shattuck Ave., near Center St., tel. 510/843–8277.*

The Pub. Officially titled Schmidt's Tobacco & Trading Co., the Pub is a cozy gathering spot for cheap pints and thick coffee. Overstuffed sofas, oak tables, and a pipe-tobacco aroma complement a game of chess or a good novel: If you forgot your book, borrow one of theirs. Weekend nights are busy and loud, but during the week you'll find studious types drinking hot chocolate and poring over their books. *1492 Solano Ave., tel. 510/525–1900. From Berkeley BART, Bus 43 north to Santa Fe Ave.*

Pyramid Brewery and Alehouse. A huge, block-long facility just opened in 1997, Pyramid pumps out 80,000 barrels of beer a year to be shipped to California stores and imbibed on the premises. From the spacious bar, filled with copper-top tables and dark-wood decor, you can watch the brewers through the windows—and smell the works in progress. *901 Gilman St., tel. 510/527–9090.*

Spats. The inventive drink selection here rivals anyone's anywhere: Choose from concoctions like the Borneo Fogcutter (rum, brandy, fruit juices, and liqueurs) or the Nutty Buddy (Frangelico, cream, and crème de cacao)—then settle into a cushy old Victorian sofa in the parlorlike bar. Messy nachos and other appetizers keep people here through happy hour and into the dinner hour. *1974 Shattuck Ave., tel. 510/841–7225. 2 blocks north of Berkeley BART.*

Triple Rock Brewery. The 1950s reign supreme at this popular microbrewery, where vintage posters and nostalgic knickknacks line the walls. The crowd is noisy in a collegiate sort of way, but folks are friendly. The outdoor patio area is the best place to enjoy one of their home brews and the excellent munchies. *1920 Shattuck Ave., at Hearst Ave., tel. 510/843–2739. 3 blocks north of Berkeley BART.*

OAKLAND

Oakland's bars are generally cheaper and rougher around the edges. Rockridge bars, however, often fill with students—from UC Berkeley and the nearby California College of Arts and Crafts—and are barely distinguishable from those in Berkeley. Downtown bars, near Jack London Square and off Broadway between 10th and 20th streets, appeal mostly to the gainfully employed and get hopelessly crowded on weekends. The farther you venture from central Oakland, the seedier the bars become; be careful when walking around at night.

The Alley. This is the only bar in Oakland where you can sit at a piano and sing along with your drunken *compadres.* It's been in business since the late 1940s and has the clientele and bar staff to prove it. It's dark, musty, and unassuming—a great place to hang out with low-key locals. Live piano music usually begins at 9 PM. *3325 Grand Ave., 3 blocks east of Lake Merritt, tel. 510/444–8505. From 19th St. BART, Bus 12 east to Santa Clara Ave.*

George and Walt's. G&W's celebrated its 50th anniversary in 1996, and its regular clientele remains loyal (though whether to its dim, smoky, but comfortable bar or to its big screen TV remains undecided). Students and sports fans swear by their beers on tap. *5445 College Ave., tel. 510/653–7441. 1 block north of McNally's (see below).*

McNally's Irish Pub. This place has the smell and feel (not to mention the whiskey selection) of a real Dublin pub. Grab a pint of Guinness, Bass, or Harp and warm yourself by the stone fireplace or groove to the jukebox while playing bumper pool in back. *5352 College Ave., tel. 510/654–9463. 4 blocks south of Rockridge BART.*

Pacific Coast Brewing Company. In old downtown Oakland, this brew pub serves four home brews and has 15 other beers on tap. Its polished appearance attracts a clean-cut thirsty-something crowd. The beers are top drawer. *906 Washington St., near 10th St., tel. 510/836–2739. From 12th St. BART, 3 blocks southwest on Broadway, 1 block west to Washington St.*

Stork Club. It would seem that only hard-core boozers would be drawn to the tinsel-and-Christmas-light decor, but this bar has recently gained a reputation for booking innovative local bands. The crowd neatly divides itself in half by the bar, which runs down the middle: The younger, hipper music-loving crowd is on the left, and the barflies who arrived for the 6 AM opening are on the right. *380 12th St., tel. 510/444–6174. 1½ blocks east of Broadway. Cover: $4–$5.*

LIVE MUSIC

The quality of the East Bay's music scene is sporadic: Some nights the great number of events taking place in the area make it difficult to choose; others will leave you hunting for something to do. Berkeley is better known for its student bars and cafés than for its music venues. Though rock, folk, jazz, and world music are prevalent in the East Bay, it's the soulful blues that lure people into the depths of Oakland, home of the West Coast blues.

ROCK

924 Gilman Street. This all-ages alcohol-free cooperative features local hard-core garage and punk bands. Green Day got its start here (and has brought the place a fair amount of fame), but now that they're famous, you're not likely to find them playing here. Most shows cost $5, but you have to buy a $2 membership (valid for one year) to get in the first time. *924 Gilman St., at 8th St., Berkeley, tel. 510/525–9926. From Berkeley BART, Bus 9 north to 8th St.*

Berkeley Square. Once the finest venue in Berkeley for live alternative music, this 18-and-over club still occasionally attracts big names. The current booking policy—which caters primarily to teenage skate punks—won't ensure its continued success, but they have recently added dinner service in an effort to revitalize the club. Call for a current schedule. *1333 University Ave., Berkeley, tel. 510/841–6555. From Berkeley BART, Bus 51 west. Cover: $5–$10.*

JAZZ

Jazz greats come through Oakland on a regular basis, making appearances at established venues and putting on special shows. **Koncepts Cultural Gallery** (tel. 510/763–0682) stages a variety of musical events, including the annual Improvised Music Duet Series, during which musicians are thrown into pairs to make beautiful music together.

Kimball's East. In Emeryville, a small community tucked between Berkeley and Oakland, look for this excellent jazz and supper club, which books well-known jazz musicians from Wednesday through Sunday. Downstairs, **Kimball's Carnival** draws big names in Latin jazz and Caribbean music, with an audience of mostly older professionals. *5800 Shellmound St., Emeryville, tel. 510/658–2555. From MacArthur BART, Bus 6 or 57 west on 40th St. to Pacific Park Plaza. Cover: $10–$25.*

Yoshi's. A well-respected club and restaurant near Jack London Square, Yoshi's serves up sushi and jazz in sophisticated style. The clientele knows its music, and past acts have included Cecil Taylor, Anthony Braxton, and Ornette Coleman. *510 Embarcadero, Oakland, tel. 510/238–9200. Cover: $5–$35.*

BLUES

In the years following World War II, Oakland gave birth to the gritty, hurts-so-bad-I'm-gonna-die music known as the West Coast blues. Even after 50 years it still flourishes in clubs and bars all over town. Dedicated to the preservation of blues, jazz, and gospel, the **Bay Area Blues Society** (tel. 510/836–2227) sponsors shows and festivals year-round and is a wellspring of information about West Coast blues. These folks are also the ones to call for information on the famed **Oakland Blues and Heritage Festival,** which takes place every September.

Blake's. This restaurant and jazz joint has been a Berkeley institution since it opened in the late 1940s. The ground-floor dining room serves decent food, and the upstairs bar (Leona's) provides brews and free popcorn to a sedate postcollegiate crowd. The real reason to come, though, is the cramped basement downstairs—a no-frills bar with a sawdust-covered floor: Here you'll find some of the best blues and funk acts in the area plus the occasional alternative rock band. If you venture downstairs to use the bathroom, you'll get an earful of the band, and you can decide if they're worth the cover charge. *2367 Telegraph Ave., near Durant Ave., Berkeley, tel. 510/848–0886. 1 block from UC campus. Cover: $2–$7.*

Eli's Mile High Club. The reputed birthplace of West Coast blues remains a consistently good bet, continuing to highlight promising local acts plus more renowned performers. It's a small club with a pool table, soul food, and music from Thursday through Saturday. The club opens at 8 PM, and the music usually starts around 9:30. *3629 Martin Luther King Jr. Way, Oakland, tel. 510/655–6661. From Berkeley, Bus 15 south on Martin Luther King Jr. Way. Cover: $4–$8.*

Fifth Amendment. High-quality blues and jazz acts play to a largely African-American crowd of professionals, students, and local old-timers. Dress up a bit for some absolutely searing music. *3255 Lakeshore Ave., Oakland, tel. 510/832–3242. From MacArthur BART, Bus 57 to corner of Lakeshore Ave. and Lake Park Way. No cover.*

FOLK

Freight and Salvage. At this smoke- and alcohol-free coffeehouse you'll find Berkeley's thriving (and aging) folk music community enjoying a wide variety of entertainment—everything from world-class accordionists to spoken-word performers to lefty singer–songwriters. Certain Tuesdays are open-mike nights ($2.50). *1111 Addison St., near San Pablo Ave., Berkeley, tel. 510/548–1761. From Berkeley BART, Bus 51 west to San Pablo Ave., 1 block south to Addison St. Cover: $7–$15.*

Starry Plough. This popular Irish pub near the Berkeley–Oakland border has an eclectic mix of folk music and not-too-extreme rock bands. Join the older, politically left crowd for a pint or two of Guinness, Bass, or Anchor Steam and a game of darts. On Monday at 7 PM pros and amateurs take part in free Irish dance lessons. *3101 Shattuck Ave., at Prince St., Berkeley, tel. 510/841–2082. From Ashby BART, walk 3 blocks south. Cover: up to $6.*

WORLD MUSIC

Ashkenaz. In December 1996, owner David Nadel was shot and killed outside this beloved Berkeley club—an event that shocked the East Bay community all the more because this world-music emporium has been a fixture here since the early '70s. At press time, a series of fundraising events were being staged to help fund the club's reopening. Once fully reopened, Ashkenaz will continue on as before, with a different live beat every night, from African to zydeco to Bulgarian folk. *1317 San Pablo Ave., Berkeley, tel. 510/525–5054. From Berkeley BART, Bus 9 west to San Pablo Ave. Cover: $5–$10.*

CLASSICS ON THE CHEAP

On summer Sundays, the Stern Grove Midsummer Music Festival (tel. 415/252–6252) brings various performing artists to Stern Grove in San Francisco for 2 PM performances. The Brown Bag Opera series (tel. 415/565–6434) pitches divas against traffic noise: Performances are held at 12:15 at 1 Bush Street, among other Bay Area locations. You can also find free, or nearly free, concerts at local universities: Berkeley's free Wednesday Noon Concerts (Hertz Hall, tel. 510/642–4864 or 510/642–2678) showcase talented professors and students; Oakland's Mills College (see below) is well known for its sometimes-free contemporary music program; and the San Francisco Conservatory of Music (see above) hosts free amateur performances.

La Peña. This Latin American cultural center offers a wide selection of live music, political lectures, performance pieces, and workshops on Central and South American issues. Many shows are benefits, so covers often masquerade as donations, ranging from a few bucks to $15. *3105 Shattuck Ave., Berkeley, tel. 510/849–2568. Next to Starry Plough (see above).*

CLUBS

With San Francisco just across the bay, there was never a need for the East Bay to develop a dance club scene of its own. You can check the *East Bay Express* under "Dance Clubs" for a thorough listing, but you're likely to discover that East Bay clubbers make the trek to the city when they want serious after-hours dancing. And there is **Blake's** (*see* Live Music, *above*), a sweaty basement ruled by funk, soul, hip-hop, and rare grooves, which may not be the pinnacle of cool, but it should serve your dance needs just fine.

Caribee Dance Center. Occasional live music is supplemented six nights a week (closed Thursday) with dancing to reggae, salsa, and African music. Drinks cost $2–$5. *1408 Webster St., Oakland, tel. 510/835–4006. From 12th St. BART, 2 blocks east on 14th St. Cover: $5–$10.*

White Horse Inn. Get down under a gleaming disco ball at this easygoing place on the Oakland–Berkeley border. Most patrons are gay or lesbian, but other fun seekers are welcome. A DJ is in the house Thursday–Saturday after 9 PM, and the bar's open daily 3 PM–2 AM. *6551 Telegraph Ave., at 66th St., Oakland, tel. 510/652–3820. From MacArthur BART, Bus 40 south on Telegraph to 66th St. No cover.*

MOVIE HOUSES

Of the several big cinema complexes that show first-run releases in the East Bay, the **Grand Lake Theatre** (3200 Grand Ave., near I–580, tel. 510/452–3556), just east of Oakland's Lake Merritt, is by far the most stylish, and no wonder—it dates from 1926. In Berkeley, Landmark's **UC Theatre** (2036 University Ave., between Milvia St. and Shattuck Ave., tel. 510/843–6267), in operation since 1917, shows foreign films and classics; double features are juxtaposed with great creativity, and billings change daily. The theater is cavernous, the seats lumpy, and you get to see John Waters ask you not to light up. *The Rocky Horror Picture Show* plays at midnight on Saturday: Come armed with toilet paper and a garter belt, if you dare.

Pacific Film Archive. Housed in the UC Berkeley Art Museum, the PFA caters to hard-core film enthusiasts with its impressive collection of rare and foreign titles. Films change nightly and often center around a certain theme—past offerings have included "Space, Time, and Memory" and "an Evening with Ingmar Bergman." Filmmakers often show up to discuss their work before the show. *2625 Durant Ave., tel. 510/642–1412. Admission: $6–$7.*

Paramount Theatre. An Art Deco landmark in downtown Oakland, the Paramount Theatre is a beautifully restored motion picture palace that now houses both the Oakland Symphony and the Oakland Ballet (*see below*). Classic and silent films are featured intermittently on Friday and Saturday evenings, complete with preshow organ music and old newsreel clips; live rock and jazz performances also take place here. Seating is reserved; buy tickets early since the seats toward the back are in the stratosphere. Tours of the theater are available for $1 on the first and third Saturdays of the month at 10 AM. *2025 Broadway, near 19th St., tel. 510/465-6400.*

THEATER

Berkeley Repertory Theatre. Berkeley is currently cultivating an arts movement downtown, with the Berkeley Repertory Theater as its keystone. The company stages performances every night except Monday; they also have some matinees in the smaller theater. The works are rarely experimental, but they are meticulously produced and well worth the $25–$39 ticket price. A limited number of half-price tickets are available at the box office on the day of performance starting at noon. *2025 Addison St., tel. 510/845-4700.*

Black Repertory Group. Founded in 1965, this Oakland company continues to be committed to the production of works by black authors and the celebration of black culture in the United States. The words of the likes of Langston Hughes and James Weldon Johnson are frequently represented in amateur but heartfelt musical and dramatic productions. Admission is $10, but the Saturday matinee is only $5. Some of the most interesting works are the one-act plays, shown for $3 on Sunday. *3201 Adeline St., tel. 510/652-2120.*

For $25 the PFA will set you up in a private screening room with a film of your choice: Choose from their vast library—particularly strong in Soviet and Japanese films—of 16-millimeter films. Call their reference line (tel. 510/642-1437) for details.

CLASSICAL MUSIC

Although the East Bay puts on fewer major productions, you can easily find an inexpensive venue for a concert. For chamber music, jazz, or world music in a beautiful, intimate setting, try the **Maybeck Recital Hall** (1537 Euclid Ave., at Buena Vista, Berkeley, tel. 510/848-3228), designed by revered Berkeley architect Bernard Maybeck. UC Berkeley's **Zellerbach Hall** (Lower Sproul Plaza, tel. 510/642-9988) presents solo recitals, as well as chamber, orchestra, and contemporary renderings of classical works by some of the finest names in the world.

Berkeley Opera. If you think opera is a stuffy affair, this 18-year-old company may change your mind. For example, in 1997 they performed a new translation of Rossini's *The Italian Girl in Algiers,* retitled *The Riot Grrrl on Mars.* Many of its lead singers come from the San Francisco Opera Chorus; a few have reportedly gone on to the Met. The opera performs about three operas each season in the intimate Julia Morgan Theater (2640 College Ave.); tickets cost up to $26—a reasonable investment for opera lovers who have experienced only large houses. Tickets can be purchased by phone or at the opera venue. *Tel. 510/798-1300.*

Berkeley Symphony Orchestra. By an unbelievable stroke of luck, the Berkeley Symphony Orchestra has managed to hang onto Kent Nagano, a world-famous conductor who spends part of the year with Berkeley, part with the renowned Lyon Opera in France. His inspired performances—often featuring music by 20th-century composers—are well worth the $25–$30 ticket price. *Tel. 510/841-2800.*

Mills College. One of the hottest places around for contemporary composition and performance, Mills College hosts an extensive season of classical and experimental concerts during the academic year. Their whimsical and outlandish hall is in the Oakland hills; if you're coming by car, call ahead for directions. Many shows are free; some run $5–$10. *5000 MacArthur Blvd., Oakland, tel. 510/430-2296. From Coliseum BART, Bus 56 west.*

DANCE

One Oakland-based troupe to watch for is the **Dance Brigade** (tel. 510/652-0752), a casually feminist troupe that delights in subverting the classics. Also in Oakland, look for **Dimensions Dance Theater** (1428 Alice St., Studio C, tel. 510/465-3363), a young, vibrant company that produces "choreodramas" teeming with African influences.

Oakland Ballet. Thirty-two years in the business hasn't corrupted this company. Though it's a classical troupe, company productions often bear a heavy thematic weight, exploring the outer boundaries of classicism. Seasons often feature revivals of early 20th-century classics as well as new works set to contemporary music. Performances are held in the grand old Paramount Theatre downtown (*see* Movie Houses, *above*); tickets run $12–$38. *1428 Alice St., tel. 510/452–9288.*

MARIN COUNTY

Quiet, residential Marin is not the place for night owls. If you do find yourself in Marin after sundown, head to the Sweetwater in funky Mill Valley (*see below*) or to any of the many fine bars and clubs in San Rafael.

LIVE MUSIC

Fourth Street Tavern. A fireplace contributes to the mellow atmosphere at this no cover, no attitude bar that books mainly R&B and rock. *711 4th St., near Lincoln St., San Rafael, tel. 415/454–4044. No cover.*

New George's. New George's routinely wins Bay Area polls for "Best Nightlife in Marin." Check out the live jazz, R&B, and acoustic entertainment, heavy on local talent and touring old favorites. *824 4th St., at Cijos St., San Rafael, tel. 415/457–1515. Cover: none–$12.*

Sweetwater. This tiny Mill Valley club is a favorite hangout of famous locals like bluesman Roy Rogers who often stop by to jam. It's been called the "best little roadhouse west of Texas," and it attracts some of the finest jazz and R&B talents in the country. There's a two-drink minimum in addition to the cover. *153 Throckmorton Ave., at Miller Ave., Mill Valley, tel. 415/388–2820. Cover: $5–$20.*

THEATER

Marin Theatre Company. Drawing on the North Bay's formidable talent pool, this award-winning theater company is entering its 31st season, which runs from September through June, with a compelling mix of contemporary comedies, musicals, and dramas. *397 Miller Ave., at Evergreen St., Mill Valley, tel. 415/388–5208. Tickets: $10–$32.*

SOUTH BAY

Like any big city, San Jose has a big nighttime scene and a busy cultural calendar. Look for nightclubs and dance floors within the larger hotels, as well as a burgeoning cluster of small clubs in an area called SoFA—the South of First Area—along 1st and 2nd streets south of San Carlos Avenue.

Palo Alto is a different story. As any Stanford student will lament, the town is seriously hurting in the nightlife department. Still, Stanford University is surrounded by a few lively bars and clubs that draw an affluent student crowd.

BARS

In Palo Alto, you can shoot pool, down suds, and meet locals at the **Blue Chalk Café** (630 Ramona Ave., tel. 650/326–1020), where a twenty-something group comes for espresso and beer. More trendy and with a notably impressive beer selection is **Gordon Biersch Brewery** (640 Emerson St., tel. 650/323–7723), where the young and beautiful mix and mingle. In San Jose, join the hip young crowd at **Café Matisse** (371 S. 1st St., at San Carlos St., tel. 408/298–7788), open daily until midnight.

Antonio's Nut House. At deliciously divey Antonio's, you can get Guinness on tap, free peanuts dispensed by a mechanical gorilla, and drinks until 2 AM nightly—a rarity around here. *321 California Ave., at Birch St., Palo Alto, tel. 650/321–2550. 2 blocks north of El Camino Real.*

Rose and Crown. Suburban Anglophiles, Stanford graduate students, and young professionals flock to this clubby British pub in Palo Alto. They serve everything from creamy pints to 20-year-old port, but the back room's dartboards are what really bring in the crowds. *547 Emerson St., at University Ave., Palo Alto, tel. 650/327–7673.*

LIVE MUSIC

Agenda. You have two options at this sizzling nightspot in downtown San Jose's trendy SoFA (South of First Area) district: The Speakeasy Cellar spins dance music from the '70s, '80s, and '90s, Wednesday–Saturday. Upstairs, a swank Parisian-style lounge grooves to nightly live jazz, R&B, and swing. *399 S. 1st St., at E. San Salvador St., San Jose, tel. 408/287–4087. Cover: $3 Fri.–Sat.*

Cactus Club. The Cactus Club isn't fancy, but for years it's been the best spot in San Jose for indie rock, particularly up-and-coming local bands. As if that weren't enough, there's DJ'ed dancing on Tuesday (house music), Thursday (Gothic/industrial), and Saturday (hip-hop); live music on other nights; and darts, video games, and snacks whenever your dancin' feet need a break. *417 S. 1st St., at E. San Salvador St., San Jose, tel. 408/491–9300. Cover: $3–$10.*

Café Borrone. Students come here in droves to listen to free Dixieland jazz on Friday nights. Hang out inside or out back on the brick patio. *1010 El Camino Real, near Ravenswood Ave., Menlo Park, tel. 650/327–0830.*

The Edge. No wonder it wins "Best Club" in the *Metro* year after year: The South Bay's hottest venue for live music has three huge floors and a great sound system. National rock acts play here, and some of the burbs' best DJs spin funk, techno, new wave, and disco on Tuesday, Friday, and Saturday. The Edge even lures hipsters out of San Francisco. *260 California Ave., at El Camino Real, Palo Alto, tel. 650/324–3343. Cover: $2–$15.*

JJ's Blues. This tiny family-run joint can't be beat when you're hankering for good ole Chicago-style blues (they also book jazz and Latin rock). Open 15 years, it's drawn legends like Albert Collins and John Lee Hooker. There are free popcorn and live music nightly, with a jam at 6 and a band at 9. *3439 Stevens Creek Blvd., between Winchester and Cypress Sts., Santa Clara, tel. 408/243–6441. From downtown San Jose, take W. San Carlos St. (which becomes Stevens Creek Blvd.) 1 mi west. Cover: $7–$12 Fri.–Sat.*

MOVIE HOUSES

Stanford Theatre. Founded and financed by Hewlett Packard, Jr., this 1920s-style movie palace has all the trappings of the grand old days, right down to the velvet seats. It screens exclusively Hollywood classics, including silent films accompanied by the theater's mighty Wurlitzer organ. *221 University Ave., Palo Alto, tel. 650/324–3700. Admission: $6. Closed Mon.–Thurs.*

THEATER AND CLASSICAL MUSIC

San Jose Center for the Performing Arts. Designed by the Frank Lloyd Wright Foundation, this 2,700-seat venue is home to the acclaimed **San Jose Symphony** (tel. 408/288–2828), the **San Jose Cleveland Ballet** (tel. 408/288–2800), and the **American Musical Theatre of San Jose** (tel. 408/453–7108). All perform from September through May. Summer months are devoted to traveling productions such as *Les Miserables. 255 Almaden Blvd., at W. San Carlos St., San Jose, tel. 408/277–3900.*

San Jose Repertory Theatre. The only professional resident theater company in Silicon Valley is considered one of the Bay Area's best. Each season (September through June) it stages six major contemporary and classical works in its brand-new 517-seat facility. *101 Paseo de San Antonio, near Santa Clara St., San Jose, tel. 408/291–2255. Tickets: $12–$27.*

WHERE TO SLEEP

REVISED BY SUZANNE STEIN AND KATHLEEN DODGE

S an Francisco's lodgings are as varied as its neighborhoods. If mainstream isn't your style, you can opt instead for an artist's bed-and-breakfast complete with easels and plenty of light, a Haight District landmark whose nightly accommodations include the Summer of Love Room, a gay B&B in the Castro, or a mansion with a nightly magic show. Those in search of scenic open space outside the city will find it in Marin County's woodsy hostels and campgrounds, where beach campsites often cost less than $12. The San Mateo County coast has plenty of hostels and campgrounds that are as beautifully situated as those in Marin—and much less populated. To add to your choices, there are scores of motels in the East Bay, bed-and-breakfasts in Marin, and business-oriented chain hotels in the South Bay: Take your pick.

SAN FRANCISCO

The city proper has a surprisingly large assortment of reasonably priced accommodations, even if the 14% hotel tax does take an extra bite out of your wallet. For a great no-frills deal, stay in one of nine hostels, where a bed costs a mere $12 or so, or in one of the residential hotels that populate downtown and North Beach. For a bit more ($40–$60 a night), many small downtown hotels have charming European-style rooms (translation: the toilet's down the hall)—an option worth considering, since downtown is also the public transportation hub.

If you don't reserve one to two weeks in advance in summer, you may be exiled to the strip of generic motels along Lombard Street in the Marina District. These motels are about a 20-minute bus ride from downtown (on Bus 76) but are quite close to Fisherman's Wharf, the Marina Green, and the Golden Gate Bridge. On Lombard you'll pay $60–$80 for a double—stay here only if you're desperate. The area South of Market has its share of similar last-resort places on 6th Street, but the neighborhood can be unsafe; if you do want to stay in SoMa, try a hostel.

All prices listed are for a standard double room in high season (although you'll find that "low season" in San Francisco hardly means much difference in room rates), excluding tax. Virtually all hotels in the Bay Area have rooms or entire floors where smoking is prohibited.

HOTELS AND MOTELS

Directions below are given from the downtown BART/Muni stations along Market Street. To reach the stations from San Francisco International Airport, take SamTrans (see Bus Travel in Chapter 1): The 7F is an express bus with luggage limits, and the 7B is a local bus that allows heavy bags. Either will drop you on Mission Street one block south of Market Street; just ask the driver for the stop nearest your station.

THE CASTRO

Not surprisingly, the most prominent gay neighborhood in the United States offers a wide variety of accommodations tailored to gay and lesbian travelers, though all are welcome. The hotels nearest Castro Street are pricey, but those on upper Market are more affordable; the entire neighborhood is generally safe at night. **Beck's Motor Lodge** (2222 Market St., 94114, tel. 415/621–8212) is a passable, gay-cruising-type budget option, with doubles for $95. Those in search of a women-only atmosphere should call the **House O' Chicks** (tel. 415/861–9849; call for address), where the proprietors like to speak with potential guests before accepting reservations for their two rooms ($75). To stay in the Castro in June, reserve way in advance, as thousands of visitors arrive in the area for the San Francisco Lesbian, Gay, Bisexual, Transgender Pride Celebration—San Francisco Pride, for short (formerly known as the Gay and Lesbian Freedom Day Parade). For a map of Castro lodging, see the Haight and Castro Lodging map, below.

UNDER $55

Twin Peaks. Transportation lines to downtown, the Marina, Golden Gate Park, and just about every other part of the city are within a block or two. The tiny but tidy rooms are nondescript, and there are no in-room phones, but the price is right: Doubles range from $35 to $41 ($45–$51 with bath). Weekly rates are $140–$190, depending on room size. 2160 Market St., between Church and Sanchez Sts., 94114, tel. 415/621–9467, fax 415/863–1545. From Montgomery St. BART/Muni, Muni F, K, L, or M streetcar to Church St.; walk 1 block southwest on Market St. 60 rooms, 3 with bath. In-room safes.

UNDER $85

24 Henry. Rian and Walter, the friendly proprietors, cater to a mostly gay and lesbian clientele. The rooms are colorful and cozy, the showers are big enough for two, and a complimentary breakfast is served in the Victorian-style parlor. Singles are $55–$80 per night, doubles $75–$90, suites for three people with kitchens $95–$120. 24 Henry St., between 14th and 15th Sts., 94114, tel. 415/864–5686 or 800/900–5686, fax 415/864–0406. From Montgomery St. BART/Muni, Muni N Judah streetcar to Noe St.; walk 4 blocks south to Henry St. 6 rooms, 2 with bath.

UNDER $130

Dolores Park Inn. Consistently rated one of San Francisco's 10 best by the San Francisco Chronicle, this 1874 Victorian is on a sedate street between the Mission and the Castro, one block south of Mission Dolores Park. Singles are $69, doubles $99–$165, including breakfast and access to the garden and parlor. There's a two-night minimum stay. 3641 17th St., near Dolores St., 94114, tel. 415/621–0482. From any downtown BART/Muni station, Muni J streetcar to 16th and Church Sts.; walk 1 block south on Church St. to 17th St. 4 rooms, 1 with bath. Kitchenettes.

Inn on Castro. Hyper '70s pop-art decor brings a cheery look to this immaculate B&B in a restored Edwardian. The low-slung couches around the fireplace are a cozy place to sip your complimentary brandy. Prices range from $95 for a double with shared bath to $160 for a suite with private bath and sundeck—all include a full breakfast of fruit, muffins, and pancakes or omelets. 321 Castro St., near Market St., 94114, tel. 415/861–0321. From Montgomery St. BART/Muni, Muni F, K, L, or M streetcar to Castro St.; walk 1 block north. 8 rooms, 7 with bath.

CHINATOWN

Its narrow sidewalks lined with storefront meat and produce markets, Chinatown is almost as quiet at night as it is busy during the day. Bounded by North Beach, the Financial District, and Union Square, it's in the heart of the city, and it's chock-full of inexpensive restaurants. The **YMCA** (855 Sacramento St., near Grant St., 94133, tel. 415/982–4412) has 33 beds for men only, with free access to a swimming pool, the gym, and a basketball court. Rooms are $29 for a single, $38 for a double, all with shared

ZEN AND THE ART OF SLEEPING

The San Francisco Zen Center, between the Civic Center and the Lower Haight, has a few rooms for visitors with an honest interest in enlightenment. For $40–$45 (single) or $56–$62 (double with shared bath) you get a spotless, nicely furnished room overlooking a courtyard, plus a hearty breakfast. This working temple also has a longer-term guest-student program. Reserve in advance, especially during summer. 300 Page St., at Laguna St., 94102, tel. 415/863–3136. From Market St. downtown, take Bus 7 or 71 west to Page and Laguna Sts.

bath. It's women only at the **Gum Moon Women's Residence** (940 Washington St., at Stockton St., 94108, tel. 415/421–6937), where doubles run $21.50 per night or $86 per week; guests have access to a full kitchen and laundry facilities, as well as two spacious common rooms, each with TV. For a map of Chinatown hotels, *see* Downtown San Francisco Lodging map, *below.*

UNDER $45

Hotel Astoria. Steps from the Chinatown Gate, this hotel can be a real bargain—provided you're willing to share a bathroom. Singles with TV cost $36 a night, doubles with two twin beds are also $36, or $56 with bath. Rooms are decent and clean, and the neighborhood is prime. *510 Bush St., at Grant Ave., 94104, tel. 415/434–8889 or 800/666–6696, fax 415/434–8919. From Montgomery St. BART/Muni, walk 2 blocks west on Post St., 2 blocks north on Grant Ave. 70 rooms, 50 with bath. In-room safes.*

UNDER $60

Grant Plaza. This large hotel on a lively Chinatown thoroughfare offers a bargain for groups of four—two double beds for $79. All rooms (singles $49, doubles $59) have private bath, color TV, phone, free toothbrushes, and use of irons, sewing kits, and hot pots at the front desk. It's a favorite with families and older travelers. *465 Grant Ave., between Bush and Pine Sts., 94108, tel. 415/434–3883 or 800/472–6899, fax 415/434–3886. From Montgomery St. BART/Muni, walk 2 blocks west on Post St., 2½ blocks north on Grant Ave. 72 rooms with bath.*

CIVIC CENTER

The area around the Civic Center *should* be a great place to stay: Davies Symphony Hall, the Opera House, and a slew of theaters, museums, and galleries are all within easy walking distance, and many of the city's public transport lines converge here. Unfortunately, the Civic Center can be quite dangerous, especially at night, due to an active drug and prostitution scene in the Tenderloin. After dark solo travelers—particularly women—should steer clear of the triangle formed by Market, Polk, and Geary streets; the section of Jones Street that runs through here is especially nasty and should be avoided even during the day. For a map of Civic Center hotels, *see* Downtown San Francisco Lodging map, *below.*

UNDER $40

YMCA. Although it's in one of the shadiest parts of the Tenderloin, the Y is probably your best bet here for clean, safe accommodations, and the amenities might make you forget the sketchy surroundings. Guests have free access to a full-size swimming pool, sauna, fully equipped weight room, aerobics classes, and morning muffins and coffee. Tired-looking singles with shared bath and clean sheets start at $28. Singles with private bath go for $40, and three triples start at $65. The cheapest sleeps are the 12 dorm-style bunk beds that cost a mere $17 each. *220 Golden Gate Ave., at Leavenworth St., 94102, tel. 415/885–0460, fax 415/885–5439. From Civic Center BART/Muni, walk 1 block east on Market St., 1 block north on Leavenworth St. 106 rooms, 6 with bath. Laundry.*

UNDER $55

Aida Hotel. Tourists from all over the world sleep at this centrally located hotel one block from the Civic Center BART station. Doubles with TV and phone cost $39; rooms with private bath cost $10 more. Show this book to the desk staff, and you'll get a $5–$10 discount. The low-grade motel decor won't satisfy a true diva, but the rooms are surprisingly large, and those on the top floor are full of sunlight. And since there are 174 rooms, you can probably get something at the last minute, even during high season. *1087 Market St., at 7th St., 94103, tel. 415/863–4141 or 800/863–2432, fax 415/863–5151. From Civic Center BART/Muni, walk 1 block northeast on Market St. 174 rooms, 100 with bath.*

UNDER $100

Albion House. Opened as a saloon in 1906, this charming B&B is conveniently close to Market Street, city hall, and the Hayes Valley shopping and dining strip; the area is also relatively safe at night. Afternoon tea and evening wine and brandy are served in the old-fashioned drawing room, where a marble-columned fireplace and a baby grand piano complete the nostalgic mood. The smallish, well-appointed doubles start at $95, including full gourmet breakfast; ask about off-season discounts. *135 Gough St., between Oak and Page Sts., 94102, tel. 415/621–0896, or 800/625–2466, fax 415/621–3811. From Civic Center BART/Muni, walk 3 blocks southwest on Market St., right on Gough St. 10 rooms with bath. Restaurant, laundry.*

UNDER $100

Phoenix Hotel. This lively hotel is a tropical paradise on the edge of the Tenderloin, with bamboo furniture and the piped-in poolside sounds of squawking macaws, croaking frogs, and jungle music—all sufficient enticements for illustrious guests such as R.E.M, the Red Hot Chili Peppers, and Pearl Jam. In keeping with their swinging motif, the front desk provides complimentary condoms *and* dental floss. In high season you'll pay $90 for a single or double (Continental breakfast included), but rates go down as much as $20 in winter. *601 Larkin St., at Eddy St., 94109, tel. 415/776–1380 or 800/248–9466, fax 415/885–3109. From Powell St. BART/Muni, Bus 31 west on Eddy St. 44 rooms with bath.*

A special legal exemption was obtained for the Phoenix's swirling black-tile swimming pool floor, since an obscure state law requires pool bottoms to be a certain shade of blue.

DOWNTOWN

This fog-shrouded neighborhood is home to San Francisco's Theater District, some shady local bars, and a handful of snazzy restaurants. Its many turn-of-the-century and Victorian buildings lend the area an old-world charm, and its central location affords easy access to North Beach, the Financial District, and Chinatown. Downtown, however, also adjoins the Tenderloin: Be cautious of the suspect characters who come out at night. The safest area is west of Mason Street and north of Sutter Street.

UNDER $50

Adelaide Inn. On a short, dead-end street just minutes from Union Square, this sunny place attracts Europeans with its off-kilter, mismatched decor. Rates include Continental breakfast; some kitchen facilities are also available. Singles start at $42, doubles at $48. *5 Isadora Duncan La., near Taylor St., 94102, tel. 415/441–2261, fax 415/441–0161. From Montgomery St. BART/Muni, Bus 38 northwest to Geary and Taylor Sts.; walk ¾ block north on Taylor St. and turn left. 18 rooms without bath. Kitchenettes.*

Nob Hill Pensione. This European-style inn offers basic furnishings in spacious, sunny rooms, most with shared baths. Doubles start at $40 ($50 with private bath). The hotel's friendly staff and perks including phones with voice mail and satellite TVs attract a few live-in residents. *835 Hyde St., near Sutter St., 94109, tel. 415/885–2987, fax 415/921–1648. From Powell St. BART/Muni, walk 5 blocks north to Sutter St., then 10 blocks west; or take Bus 2, 3, or 4 to Hyde St. 50 rooms, 8 with bath. Restaurant, bar, in-room safes, laundry.*

Stratford Inn. Nestled smack between the Powell Street cable car turnaround and Union Square, this tidy little bargain inn is ideal for those who spend their time out and about. The halls are brightly lighted, if a bit run-down, and the multilingual staff is friendly. Doubles with shared bath ($40–$60) are dark and spartan but are often large and always clean, and you have free access to an indoor pool and fitness center at the nearby Sheehan Hotel. *242 Powell St., between O'Farrell and Geary Sts., 94102, tel. 415/397–7080, fax 415/397–7087. From Powell St. BART/Muni, walk 2½ blocks north on Powell St. 98 rooms, 70 with bath. Laundry.*

MARINA

Chestnut St.

Lombard St.

Octavia St.

Gough St.

Franklin St.

Van Ness Ave.

Polk St.

Larkin St.

Hyde St.

Leavenworth St.

Greenwi

Filbert S

Union St

RUSSIAN
HILL

Green St.

Vallejo St.

Broadway Tunnel

Pacific Ave.

Broadway

Jackson St.

PACIFIC
HEIGHTS

Taylor St.

Alta
Plaza

Lafayette
Park

Washington St.

Clay St.

Sacramento St.

California St.

N
HI

Pierce St.

Steiner St.

Fillmore St.

Webster St.

Buchanan St.

Laguna St.

Gough St.

Franklin St.

Van Ness Ave.

Polk St.

Larkin St.

Leavenworth St.

Jones St.

Pine St.

Bush St.

Sutter St.

Post St.

Geary St.

O'Farrell St.

Ellis St.

Eddy St.

Turk St.

Hyde St.

JAPANTOWN

Geary Expressway

POLK
GULCH

Golden Gate Ave.

McAllister St.

Market St.

Alamo
Square

Fulton St.

City Hall

CIVIC
CENTER

Hayes St.

Grove St.

Civic Center
BART Station

7th St.

8th St.

Adelaide Inn, **25**

Aida Hotel, **22**

Albion House, **8**

Amsterdam, **13**

The Andrews, **26**

Art Center Bed and
Breakfast, **2**

AYH Hostel at
Union Square, **34**

Biltmore Hotel, **14**

Brady Acres, **15**

Cornell, **27**

European Guest
House, **19**

Ft. Mason
International
Hostel, **3**

Globetrotter's
Inn, **35**

Grand Central
Hostel, **17**

Grant Plaza, **31**

Green Tortoise
Guest House, **12**

Gum Moon Women's
Residence, **11**

Hotel Astoria, **32**

Hotel Bohème, **10**

Hotel David, **24**

Interclub Globe
Hostel, **20**

The Mansions
Hotel, **6**

Marina Motel, **1**

New Central Hotel
and Hostel, **18**

Nob Hill
Pensione, **9**

Pacific
Tradewinds, **30**

Phoenix Hotel, **16**

San Francisco
International
Student Center, **21**

San Francisco
Residence Club, **28**

San Francisco Zen
Center, **7**

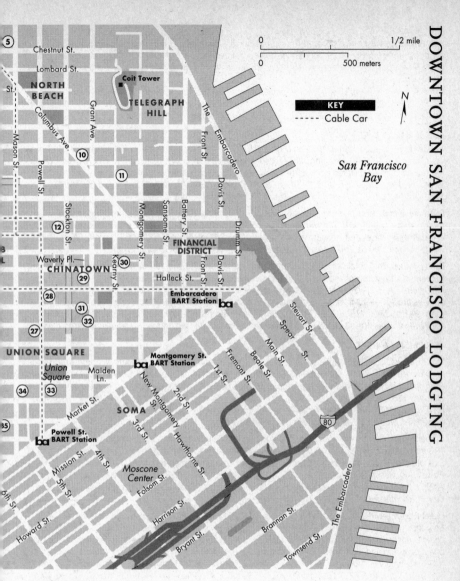

San Remo Hotel, **5**
Stratford Inn, **33**
Travelodge, **4**
YMCA
Chinatown, **29**
YMCA
Downtown, **23**

UNDER $65

San Francisco Residence Club. At the top of Nob Hill, this friendly family-owned pension built in 1910 offers a great deal: Breakfast and dinner (except Sunday) are included with a night's stay. Clean, spacious rooms have Victorian furnishings, and some see out to Angel Island. Even if your room doesn't come with a view, you can still enjoy the sunny garden or dabble on the lobby's Steinway. Singles are $42–$95 nightly, $255–$500 weekly; doubles are $60–$95 nightly, $400–$600 weekly. *851 California St., at Powell St., 94108, tel. 415/421–2220, fax 415/421–2335. From Powell St. BART/Muni, walk 8 blocks north or take cable car to California St. 84 rooms, 6 with bath. Laundry.*

UNDER $85

Amsterdam. This comfortable, clean Victorian B&B is two blocks from Nob Hill. Singles with queen beds are $79–$89; doubles start at $89; deluxe doubles with private Jacuzzi and outdoor patio go for $129. The sunny, cloistered deck garden is a great spot to enjoy the complimentary breakfast. *749 Taylor St., between Sutter and Bush Sts., 94108, tel. 415/673–3277 or 800/637–3444. From Montgomery St. BART/Muni, Bus 2, 3, or 4 west to Sutter St. 34 rooms with bath.*

Biltmore Hotel. Run by the same folks who run the Amsterdam next door, the Biltmore has sunny rooms, some with great downtown views, for $55 (singles), $65 (doubles), and $75 (deluxe suites with wet bar, microwave, and refrigerator). *735 Taylor St., 94108, tel. 415/775–0630, fax 415/673–0453. From Montgomery St. BART/Muni, Bus 2, 3, or 4 west to Sutter St. 60 rooms with bath.*

Brady Acres. This small, comfortable hotel near the Theater District is fully decked out, with in-room microwaves, toasters, coffeemakers, and mini-refrigerators filled with chocolates and jam—plus answering machines, TVs, radio/cassette players, and apricot and papaya shampoos in the bathrooms. Singles and doubles are $60–$90; if you pay for six nights, the seventh is free. *649 Jones St., between Post and Geary Sts., 94102, tel. 415/929–8033 or 800/627–2396, fax 415/441–8033. From Montgomery St. BART/Muni, Bus 38 west to Geary and Jones Sts. 25 rooms with bath. In-room safes, kitchenettes, laundry.*

UNDER $100

The Andrews. This 1905 Queen Anne–style Victorian has small, charming rooms with iron bedsteads, flowered curtains, and gracious service. A buffet-style Continental breakfast is served in the hallway of every floor each morning, and complimentary wine is served in the hotel restaurant in the evening. Doubles run $86–$92; there is also one suite for $119. *624 Post St., at Taylor St., 94109, tel. 415/563–6877 or 800/926–3739, fax 415/928–6919. From Powell St. BART/Muni, walk 4 blocks north on Powell, left on Post St. 48 rooms with bath. Restaurant.*

Cornell. This small French country–style hotel on Nob Hill has flower- and lace-filled singles for $75–$90 and doubles for $85–$100. The French owners also operate a small restaurant in the cellar with a $19 prix fixe menu, stained glass, and medieval accoutrements on the walls. *715 Bush St., between Powell and Mason Sts., 94108, tel. 415/421–3154 or 800/232–9698, fax 415/399–1442. From Powell St. BART/Muni, walk 5½ blocks north on Powell St., left on Bush St. 58 rooms, 48 with bath. Restaurant, in-room safes.*

Hotel David. David's deli, the main act at this hotel and restaurant, has been serving knishes on Theater Row for more than 40 years, and the omnipresent David is as entertaining and gracious a host as you could wish for. A night in an immaculate single or double ($79–$119) includes breakfast and a 15% discount on lunch and dinner. The hotel also provides free pickup from San Francisco International Airport for guests who stay two nights or more. Two floors are reserved for nonsmokers. *480 Geary St., at Taylor St., 94102, tel. 415/771–1600 or 800/524–1888, fax 415/931–5442. From Powell St. BART/Muni, walk 2½ blocks north on Powell St., 2 blocks west on Geary St. 54 rooms with bath. Restaurant.*

HAIGHT AND WESTERN ADDITION

During its heyday in the '60s and '70s, the Haight saw rock bands (the Grateful Dead, Janis Joplin), poets (Allen Ginsberg), and runaway hippie children all settle in at various times. Staying here will give you a sense of the Haight's history and transformation; it will also put you close to other fine neighborhoods like the Castro and the Mission District. Northeast of the Haight, the once-seedy Western Addition is now undergoing something of a revival as artists and musicians discover its (relatively) cheap rents. Still, both areas can be dicey at night; be especially careful in the Western Addition near the subsidized housing west of Webster Street as well as all along Haight Street—particularly between Laguna and Pierce streets.

HAIGHT AND CASTRO LODGING

Golden Gate Park

HAIGHT ASHBURY

COLE VALLEY

Buena Vista Park

Corona Heights Park

CASTRO

MISSION

Harvey Milk Plaza

Castro St. MUNI Station

Church St. MUNI Station

Mission Dolores

Mission Dolores Park

16th St./Mission BART Station

101

157

UNDER $55

Metro Hotel. The first thing you'll notice about the Metro is its neon sign lighting up Divisadero Street, a major thoroughfare in the Western Addition. This is a good middle-range option popular with gay and lesbian travelers, Europeans, and the occasional rock band. The high-ceiling rooms (doubles $50–$94) are large, clean, and comfortable, and the café downstairs serves breakfast and lunch on a sunny out-door patio behind the hotel. *319 Divisadero St., between Oak and Page Sts., 94117, tel. 415/861–5364, fax 415/863–1970. From Market St. downtown, Bus 7 or 71 west to Divisadero and Haight Sts.; walk 1½ blocks north on Divisadero. 24 rooms with bath. Restaurant.*

UNDER $70

Auberge des Artistes. This elegant Edwardian structure is nestled on a shady stretch of Fillmore Street, on the outskirts of Alamo Square Park. Though the neighborhood is a bit shady, you need not set foot outside, so satisfied will you be to study the extensive collection of art books or relax in the sunny gar-den. A full gourmet breakfast is served in the dining room, where you can gaze at a full-scale replica of a Gustav Klimt mural. If you're feeling the urge to create, ask about accessing the darkroom or arrang-ing live-drawing sessions. Luxurious doubles (some with fireplace, one with a whirlpool tub) run $65 to $100. *829 Fillmore St., between Grove and Fulton Sts., 94117, tel. 415/776–2530, fax 415/441–8242. From Montgomery St. BART/Muni, Muni F, K, L, or M streetcar to Church St., then Bus 22 Fillmore north to Grove St. 5 rooms, 2 with bath.*

UNDER $90

The Red Victorian. An immensely popular Haight Street landmark, the Red Vic has rooms with various themes: Try the Japanese Tea Garden Room (single $77, double $96) or the Summer of Love Room (single $69, double $86), complete with a tie-dye canopy and authentic '60s concert posters. New double-glass windows ensure that even street-side rooms are tranquil, and proprietress Sami Sunchild takes good care of her guests. Stays of three days or longer garner substantial discounts. *1665 Haight St., between Belvedere and Cole Sts., 94117, tel. 415/864–1978, fax 415/863–3293. From Market St. downtown, Bus 7 or 71 west to Haight and Cole Sts. 18 rooms, 4 with bath.*

Stanyan Park Hotel. This somewhat sterile hotel nevertheless offers a respite from the Haight's hippy-dippy hoopla of incense and tie-dye and is an excellent starting point for forays into Golden Gate Park. Wide, characterless hallways lead to immaculate doubles (from $85, including breakfast). The $185 suites, which can easily sleep six, are bigger and better-furnished than most San Francisco apartments, with full kitchens. *750 Stanyan St., between Waller and Beulah Sts., 94117, tel. 415/751–1000, fax 415/668–5454. From Market St. downtown, Bus 71 west to Haight and Stanyan Sts.; walk 2 blocks south on Stanyan St. 36 rooms with bath.*

THE MARINA AND PACIFIC HEIGHTS

The Marina District is a quiet, safe residential neighborhood popular with young folks climbing the corpo-rate ladder. It's a long walk from North Beach, Chinatown, and downtown, but the views of the bay and the Golden Gate Bridge from the nearby waterfront are tremendous. Posh Pacific Heights sits above the Marina and shares its spectacular views; this neighborhood, too, is safe, quiet, and very dull at night, though a star-studded cast slumbers within its confines (Meg Ryan, Danielle Steele, and Nicolas Cage, to name a few). Union and Fillmore streets have a good selection of yuppified restaurants and singles bars. Unfortunately, most cheap lodgings in this area lie along busy Lombard Street (not on the "world's crookedest" part), a major thoroughfare leading to the Golden Gate Bridge. The **Travelodge** (1450 Lombard St., at Van Ness Ave., 94123, tel. 415/673–0691) isn't too bad—in a last resort kind of way—with clean singles ($99) and doubles ($105), which are as much as $30 less during low season. Some of the smaller motels closer to Van Ness Avenue attract drug dealers, prostitutes, and other shady types, so look carefully before check-ing in. For a map of Marina and Pacific Heights hotels, *see* Downtown San Francisco Lodging map, *above.*

UNDER $80

Marina Motel. This quiet, family-owned motel is an excellent alternative along the generally bland Lom-bard strip. Built as little apartments in 1939, most rooms ($65–$75) include fully equipped kitchens, garage parking, and views of a courtyard garden resplendent with pink bougainvillea and colorful murals by local artists. Off-season you can rent by the week for $375–$400. The multilingual staff will give you breakfast discount coupons for nearby Judy's Cafe. *2576 Lombard St., at Divisadero St., 94123, tel. 415/921–9406, fax 415/921–0364. From Embarcadero BART/Muni, Bus 30 northwest to Chestnut and Divisadero Sts.; walk 1 block north. 38 rooms with bath. Kitchenettes.*

UNDER $130

Art Center Bed and Breakfast. The owners like to call this place a country inn with a city built around it; when you see it, you'll understand why. The inn, near the Presidio and the singles bars of Union Street, is cluttered with paintings of the big-eyed-animal-and-children type. If you want to take brush to canvas, the proprietors will be glad to set up an easel for you, and you can go to the garden in back for inspiration. Three studios and a pair of two-room suites ($105 per day) have double beds, TV, radio, and access to a small community kitchen. A three-room apartment with the same amenities runs $145 for two people. *1902 Filbert St., at Laguna St., 94123, tel. 415/567–1526. From Embarcadero BART/Muni, Bus 41 northwest to Laguna St.; walk 1 block north and turn left. 5 rooms with bath. Laundry.*

The Mansions Hotel. Barbra Streisand, Paul Simon, and Joe Montana have all stayed at this historic 1887 landmark in Pacific Heights. It's a strange blend of kitsch—there's a pig museum full of the owner's "porkabilia"—and old-world charm: Witness the quaint sitting rooms with Victorian antiques and the tiny, overgrown flower garden. The cost of a comfortable room includes breakfast and entrance to the nightly magic show featuring Claudia the Hauntress. Doubles start at $129; guest suites range $189–$350. On weekends rates go up by $20. *2220 Sacramento St., at Laguna St., 94115, tel. 415/929–9444 or 800/826–9398, fax 415/567–9391. From Embarcadero BART/Muni, Bus 1 west to Laguna St. 21 rooms with bath. Restaurant.*

NORTH BEACH

North Beach—where Italian immigrants and beat poets once converged on narrow sidewalks—is a uniquely San Francisco experience and a great place to stay. Near downtown, Chinatown, and Fisherman's Wharf, this is also where most tourists congregate—hotel rates are accordingly high. Although North Beach is close to many of the city's most popular restaurants, bars, and cafés, you should also be aware of a row of tacky strip joints along Broadway. An appealing, low-cost lodging option is the **Green Tortoise Guest House** (*see* Hostels, *below*). For a map of North Beach hotels, *see* Downtown San Francisco Lodging, *above*.

UNDER $75

San Remo Hotel. A short walk from Fisherman's Wharf and North Beach, the friendly San Remo is an incredible bargain in a pricey area. Quiet, spotless doubles with shared bath, redwood furnishings, and stained-glass windows cost $60–$80; the more you spend, the better your view. *2237 Mason St., between Francisco and Chestnut Sts., 94133, tel. 415/776–8688 or 800/352–7366, fax 415/776–2811. From Montgomery St. BART/Muni, Bus 15 north to Chestnut St.; walk 1 block west to Mason St. 64 rooms, 1 with bath. Restaurant, bar.*

UNDER $125

Hotel Bohème. Near the outdoor cafés that sidle up to Columbus Avenue, Bohème was once a hangout for beatnik poets such as Allen Ginsberg. Plush striped carpeting and black-and-white snapshots on the hallway walls will make you feel as if you've just stepped into a smoky, suspenseful scene from an old private-eye show—minus the smoke (all rooms are nonsmoking). Doubles cost $120; there's also one suite that goes for $125 (for three) or $130 (for four). *444 Columbus Ave., at Vallejo St., 94133, tel. 415/433–9111, fax 415/362–6292. From Montgomery St. BART/Muni, Bus 41 north to Vallejo St. 15 rooms with bath. Restaurant.*

HOSTELS

Hostels affiliated with American Youth Hostels (AYH), the American branch of Hostelling International (HI), promise a certain welcomed predictability (for example, all have guest kitchens), but private hostels are often cheaper and filled with a more diverse crowd. Most hostels have no age restrictions, and both families and seniors can often be found among the backpacking college types. Due perhaps to the dearth of budget lodging in the area, hostels are extremely popular; make reservations before you arrive. In a pinch you can also try to get one of 12 dorm beds at the YMCA (*see* Civic Center, *above*).•

AYH Hostel at Union Square. This huge hostel one block from Union Square sleeps 230 people in rooms with one to four beds (in summer, $16 for members, $19 for nonmembers). The interior is bright and pleasant; amenities include a TV room, a smoking room, a library, and a kitchen (with microwaves, toasters, and refrigerators). Bulletin boards are covered with information on San Francisco nightlife and other attractions. About 40% of the rooms are set aside for reservations, which must be made at least 48 hours in advance ($14 deposit). The crowd is made up mostly of international students. *312 Mason St., between O'Farrell and Geary Sts., 94102, tel. 415/788–5604 or 800/909–4776, ext. 02. From Powell St. BART/Muni, walk 1½ blocks north on Powell St., 1 block west on O'Farrell St., turn right. 230 beds. Reception and check-in daily 24 hrs. Kitchen.*

European Guest House. A good choice for fans of SoMa nightlife, this midsize hostel has decent bunk-bed lodgings in four-person dorms ($13 per person) and doubles ($15 per person). A sundeck, a common room, a kitchen, and laundry facilities make up for the less-than-savory showers: Bring your flip-flops and close your eyes. *761 Minna St., near Mission St. between 8th and 9th Sts., 94103, tel. 415/861–6634, fax 415/621–4428. From Civic Center BART/Muni, walk 2 blocks south on 8th St., turn right on Minna St. 24 beds. Reception and check-in 24 hrs. Kitchen, laundry.*

Fort Mason International Hostel. Perched high above the waterfront, this AYH hostel will dazzle you with its views of the bay and the Golden Gate Bridge. Reservations must be made at least 24 hours ahead with a credit card or at least two weeks prior to arrival with a one-night deposit. Get here early if you don't have a reservation, as available space often sells out by 8 AM. Beds are $16 a night, and everyone is required to perform a chore each day. *Mailing address: Fort Mason, Bldg. 240, Box A, 94123, tel. 415/771–7277 or 800/444–6111, fax 415/771–1468. From Transbay Terminal, Bus 42 to Van Ness Ave. and Bay St.; turn right on Bay St. and follow signs. 160 beds. Lockout 11 AM–1 PM. Reception and check-in 24 hrs. Kitchen, laundry.*

Globetrotter's Inn. The lack of restrictions and small size (it sleeps only 48 people) are among the strengths of this independent hostel on the edge of the down-and-out Tenderloin District. It's not as new or as sunny as some others, but the staff has done its best, putting artwork on the walls and creating a comfortable common space with a TV, plants, and a 24-hour kitchen. A space in a double or in a four- or six-person dorm costs $12; singles are $24. Children are not allowed. *225 Ellis St., between Mason and Taylor Sts., 94102, tel. 415/346–5786. From Powell St. BART/Muni, walk ½ block north on Powell St., 1½ blocks west on Ellis St. 48 Beds. Reception and check-in daily 8 AM–midnight. Kitchen, laundry. Cash only.*

Green Tortoise Guest House. From the popular people who have brought you budget bus travel for the past 20 years comes one of the best hostels in San Francisco. Green Tortoise is just steps from North Beach on the neon Broadway strip, a few blocks from downtown and Chinatown. European student backpackers book most of the rooms, which are clean, spacious, and rarely vacant—call ahead. There's no curfew or lockout, and the managers are friendly and mellow. Single bunks cost $15 per night; private singles are $25–$30 and private doubles $35–$39. Rates include breakfast, and guests also have access to a sauna. *494 Broadway, between Montgomery and Kearny Sts., 94133, tel. 415/834–1000, fax 956–4900. From Montgomery St. BART/Muni, Bus 15 or 9X north. 40 rooms (110 beds). Reception and check-in 24 hrs. Kitchen, laundry. Cash only.*

Interclub Globe Hostel. Intended for international travelers (though passport-carrying Americans are not turned away), this SoMa hostel has few rules and a warm, relaxed atmosphere—not to mention a pool table and a sundeck with a grand view of the city. Dorms sleep four or five, and each has a bathroom; two floors are reserved for nonsmokers. A dorm bed is $13 per night. During nonsummer months there are seven private rooms (doubles $36) that also rent by the week for $220. At the lively adjoining canteen, you can get dinner for less than $5. Older travelers and families will feel comfortable here. *10 Hallam Pl., near Folsom St. between 7th and 8th Sts., 94103, tel. 415/431–0540, fax 415/431–3286. From Civic Center BART/Muni, walk 3 blocks south on 8th St., turn left on Folsom St. 120 beds. Reception and check-in 24 hrs. Laundry. Cash only.*

New Central Hotel and Hostel. This former flophouse, in a central but seedy location, has been transformed into a decent hostel. Dorm space costs $15 per night ($95 per week); singles are $25 per night, doubles $35. Other perks include an exercise room, free coffee, breakfast, social events, a pool table, a jukebox, table tennis, and TV rooms. All visitors, even Americans traveling within the United States, must show travel documents to stay here. *1412 Market St., at 10th and Fell Sts., 94102, tel. 415/703–9988, fax 415/703–9986. From Van Ness Ave. Muni, walk 1 block northeast on Market St. 250 beds. Reception and check-in 24 hrs. Kitchen, laundry.*

Pacific Tradewinds. This extremely friendly, homey place in Chinatown has 28 dorm-style beds with kitchen access and a TV-less common room that's great for meeting fellow travelers. If you want to come in after midnight, the proprietors will give you a key (with a $20 deposit). They'll also let you know about cheap restaurants and other attractions in the area. Beds are usually $16 per night, but ask about off-season discounts. If you stay seven nights, you pay for only six; in summer they ask that you pay for the week in advance. *680 Sacramento St., near Kearny St., 94111, tel. 415/433−7970, fax 415/291−8801. From Montgomery St. BART/Muni, walk 1 block west on Post St., then Bus 15 north on Kearny St. 28 beds. Reception and check-in daily 8 AM–midnight. Kitchen.*

San Francisco International Guest House. Tucked away on the outskirts of the Mission District in a 100-year-old building, this nicely maintained hostel has a five-day minimum-stay requirement that's known to breed—how shall we say it—intimacy; although there are no age restrictions, seniors and families may feel more comfortable elsewhere. There are two full kitchens, a TV room, and a funky, orange-color reading room. Rooms of two to four people go for $13 per person ($11 if you stay more than 28 days and pay in advance). International travel documents are required. *2976 23rd St., at Harrison St. (next to the laundromat), 94110, tel. 415/641−1411. From 24th St. BART/Muni, walk 1 block north on Mission St. to 23rd St., then 6½ blocks east. 28 beds. Reception and check-in 24 hrs. Kitchen.*

San Francisco International Student Center. Right in the middle of SoMa, the student center has 16 dorm rooms, a small kitchen, a common room, and an owner who doesn't believe in television. There are no age restrictions, but the atmosphere is decidedly young and funky. Beds cost $13 a night, $84 a week. *1188 Folsom St., near 8th St., 94103, tel. 415/255−8800, fax 415/487−1463. From Civic Center BART/Muni, walk 3 blocks south on 8th St. to Folsom St. 38 beds. Reception and check-in 9 AM–11 PM. Kitchen. Cash only.*

EAST BAY

BERKELEY

Lodging in Berkeley is often either shabby or downright expensive—sometimes both. If that isn't enough, it's also often hard to come by: In mid-May, when thousands of graduating Berkeley students don caps and gowns, reservations become absolutely essential, since most of the nicer hotels sell out four to five months in advance. To add insult to injury, all Berkeley lodgings add 12% tax to the prices listed below.

Most of the city's motels are on **University Avenue** west of campus, and most of these are not recommended. Your life isn't necessarily in danger here, but expect a general air of seediness (i.e., velvet curtains, the reek of cheap perfume . . .). It's best to stick to the campus end of University Avenue; the farther west you go, the shoddier the surroundings become. To reach all the motels in the vicinity from Berkeley BART, walk two blocks north to University Avenue and head west, or take Bus 51.

Berkeley has no youth hostels, but the **YMCA** (2185 Milvia St., 94704, tel. 510/848−6800, fax 510/848−6835)—open to both men and women—is cheap and within easy reach of Berkeley's sights. Clean dorm-style singles with shared bath cost $25; there are also a few doubles ($33) and triples ($40). After 14 days you're eligible to stay longer (in single rooms only) for around $100 per week. Guests have access to a kitchen and to a basketball court, weight room, and Olympic-size swimming pool at the fitness center next door.

UNDER $60

Campus Motel. The bright blue South Pacific–style sign out front is the best thing about this hotel on noisy University Avenue. Still, it's close to campus (six blocks west), and the rooms are tidy, plain, and cheap, with cable TV and coffeemakers. Singles are $50, doubles $55 and up. *1619 University Ave., between McGee Ave. and California Sts., 94703, tel. 510/841−3844, fax 510/841−8134. 23 rooms with bath.*

Flamingo Motel. True to its name, this plain but functional motel on University Avenue is painted pink. Four-person, two-bed rooms cost $60. *1761 University Ave., at Grant St., 94703, tel. 510/841−4242, fax 510/841−4449. 25 rooms with bath.*

Golden Bear Motel. One of the nicer budget lodgings in town, the Golden Bear has clean doubles for $49. The surrounding neighborhood is a little shady, so be careful walking around at night. Bus 52, across the street, will whisk you to the Berkeley campus. *1620 San Pablo Ave., 94702, tel. 510/525−6770, fax 510/525−6999. From North Berkeley BART, walk 3 blocks west to San Pablo Ave. and turn right. 42 rooms with bath. Restaurant.*

Travel Inn. Another pink motel on University, this place is cheap, clean, and far enough from the street to escape traffic noise. Though the rooms are generic, they have new TVs and phones. Singles cost $40, doubles $50. *1461 University Ave., between Sacramento and Acton Sts., 94702, tel. 510/848–3840, fax 510/848–3846. 3 blocks south of North Berkeley BART. 42 rooms with bath. In-room safes, laundry.*

UNDER $80

Travelodge. If you're not concerned about price or atmosphere, you can always settle for the generic blue-and-white Travelodge, three blocks from campus, where basic, very clean doubles start at $78. *1820 University Ave., near Grant St., 94703, tel. 510/843–4262, fax 510/848–1480. 30 rooms with bath.*

UNDER $100

Beau Sky Hotel. This small hotel on the southern edge of campus has a porch overlooking colorful Durant Avenue. The large rooms (singles from $80, doubles from $90) are functional and clean, even if the decor is secondhand hodgepodge. Some rooms have balconies, all have TV and telephone, and the newly opened restaurant downstairs serves Californian-Italian cuisine for lunch and dinner. Continental breakfast is included. *2520 Durant Ave., 94704, tel. 510/540–7688, fax 510/540–8089. From Berkeley BART, walk 3 blocks south on Shattuck Ave., turn left on Durant Ave., continue 4 blocks. 20 rooms with bath. Restaurant.*

Berkeley City Club. This landmark building with gorgeous high ceilings and Moorish-Gothic architecture was designed in 1927 by famed northern California architect Julia Morgan. It is now a private social club and hotel with rather spartan singles and doubles for $95 (Continental breakfast included). Many rooms have bay views, and guests have access to the club's fitness center and pool. *2315 Durant Ave., 94704, tel. 510/848–7800, fax 510/848–5900. From Berkeley BART, walk 3 blocks south on Shattuck Ave., turn left on Durant Ave. 42 rooms with bath. Restaurant, bar, laundry.*

French Hotel. This little hotel in north Berkeley is close to boutique shopping and several of Berkeley's best gourmet restaurants, including Alice Waters's world-famous Chez Panisse. Doubles with a minuscule patio cost $85–$95 (there's one room available for $68); those without patio include a complimentary breakfast. Guests can take breakfast in the cozy brick-walled café downstairs. *1538 Shattuck Ave., between Cedar and Vine Sts., 94709, tel. and fax 510/548–9930. From Berkeley BART, walk 6 blocks north on Shattuck Ave. 18 rooms with bath. Restaurant.*

Gramma's Rose Garden Inn. Though this stretch of Telegraph Avenue is heavily trafficked and short on trees, Gramma's rambling Victorian hideaway does its best to make everything look rosy. Open the gates, and you'll enter a wonderland of flower beds, cute stone paths, and chintz. Doubles in the main house are $89–$99, garden-house rooms are $110–$130, and the surrounding, more spacious cottages run $135–$165. Many rooms have fireplaces and balconies, two have bay views, and all include a hearty breakfast. *2740 Telegraph Ave., at Stuart St., 94705, tel. 510/549–2145, fax 510/549–1085. From Ashby BART, walk 5 blocks east on Ashby Ave., turn left on Telegraph Ave. 40 rooms with bath.*

UNDER $120

Hotel Durant. An elegant lobby, friendly staff, and convenient location one block from campus make this hotel a popular choice with visiting parents and Cal Bears fans (book ahead for graduation and big football games). The rather small rooms all have big beds, mahogany writing tables, and forest green thick-pile carpet. Singles cost $99, doubles $109–$119; Continental breakfast is included. Ask about student discounts. *2600 Durant Ave., at Bowditch St., 94704, tel. 510/845–8981 or 800/238–7268, fax 510/486–8336. From Berkeley BART, walk 3 blocks south on Shattuck Ave., turn left on Durant Ave., continue 5 blocks. 103 rooms with bath. Restaurant, bar.*

UNIVERSITY HOUSING

University Summer Visitor Housing (2601 Warring St., 94709, tel. 510/642–5925, fax 510/642–9701) has summer dorm accommodations at 2424 Channing Way for $38–$50 per night. Rooms have the bare basics: bed, desk, chair, and phone. For an additional $3 per day you'll get linens, soap, and parking. There are lots of young people around, and the dorms are a very safe place to stay.

OAKLAND

Travelers concerned about price and safety should consider staying in San Francisco since Oakland's budget lodging scene is pretty bleak. Hotels are either geared toward executives with expense accounts, or they're in the middle of dicey neighborhoods. And, sad to say, Oakland has no youth hostel. If you're desperate, there are faceless chain motels in downtown Oakland and near the airport with rooms for $50–$75 per night.

UNDER $110

Best Western Inn at the Square. Traveling theater companies appearing at the nearby Paramount Theater often stay at this squeaky clean hotel just a block from the waterfront shopping and dining of Jack London Square and a short walk from the ferry pier. All rooms (singles $85, doubles $105) have cable TV, coffeemakers, and phones; some have balconies. Especially nice is the sweeping, sunny courtyard with a pool and brand-new deck furniture, perfect for sunbathing. *23 Broadway, at 3rd St., 94607, tel. 510/452–4565 or 800/633–5973, fax 510/452–4634. From 12th St. BART, walk west on Broadway 9 blocks. 102 rooms with bath.*

CAMPING

Anthony Chabot Regional Campground. Perched above Lake Chabot southeast of downtown Oakland, this is one of the East Bay's most scenic sleeping options. Tent sites in a pleasant wooded area are $14 per night, plus a $5 reservation charge. The campground is close to hiking and biking trails (*see* Hiking and Biking *in* Chapter 8), and the lake is great for fishing. Reserve ahead in summer. The nearest bus stop is 1½ mi from the park entrance; from there you'll have to hike. *Tel. 510/562–2267. From I-880, I-580 east to Redwood Road exit; turn left and follow Redwood Rd. 4½ mi to park gate (it's another 2½–3 mi to campground). 63 sites. Drinking water, fire grates, flush toilets, picnic tables, showers.*

MARIN COUNTY

Across the Golden Gate Bridge from San Francisco, Marin County is home to a couple of idyllic hostels and to plenty of breathtaking campgrounds. In addition, the **Bed and Breakfast Exchange of Marin** (tel. 415/485–1971) books brief or extended stays in private homes and B&Bs; expect to pay $65–$150 per night. They can also arrange a quintessential Marinite experience for you: lodging for four to six people in a houseboat (about $225 per night).

ALONG U.S. 101

SAUSALITO

Though tourists crowd Sausalito's streets during the day, all but the deepest of pocket have to find somewhere else to spend the night. Luckily, an excellent hostel and free camping are only a 10-minute drive away.

UNDER $85

Alta Mira Continental Hotel. This Spanish-style hotel in the Sausalito hills is well worth the price for the extraordinary bay and city views and is within walking distance of central Sausalito (albeit up a steep hill). Doubles start at $80; rooms with a view (some with private deck) are $105–$125. Even if you stay in one of the cheaper rooms, you can still enjoy the view of the bay from the hotel terrace. Every guest room has a TV and a telephone. *125 Bulkley Ave., 94965, tel. 415/332–1350, fax 415/331–3862. From U.S. 101, Sausalito exit, follow signs onto Bridgeway, turn right at Princess Ave. (the 9th stoplight), continue 3 blocks. 29 rooms with bath. Restaurant.*

HOSTEL

Golden Gate AYH-Hostel. Built in 1907, this friendly hostel is in the historic Fort Barry section of the Marin Headlands, just up the hill from the visitor center. In addition to endless hiking trails and breathtaking scenery, guests enjoy a communal kitchen, a laundry room, a tennis court, a Ping-Pong table, a pool table, and a common room with a fireplace. Dorm beds cost $12 per night; in another building private rooms are available for couples and families, starting at $36. Getting to the hostel by public transit is tricky: From San Francisco catch Golden Gate Transit Bus 10 or 50 from the Transbay Terminal and ask to be let off at the bottom of the Alexander Avenue off-ramp; from here it's a stiff 5-mi hike. On Sunday only Bus 76 goes from the Transbay Terminal all the way to the Marin Headlands Visitor Center, one block from the hostel. *Fort Barry, Bldg. 941, 94965, tel. 415/331–2777. From U.S. 101, Alexander Ave. exit, cross under freeway, make first right after* MARIN HEADLANDS *sign; continue 1 mi, turn right on McCullough Rd., left on Bunker Rd.; follow signs to visitor center. 103 beds. Lockout 9:30–3:30, reception open daily 7:30 AM–11:30 PM. Kitchen, laundry.*

CAMPING

Marin Headlands. There are three areas for tent camping, all available at no charge, in this beautiful section of the Golden Gate National Recreational Area, just a few miles north of San Francisco. Hawk Camp (three sites) is the most primitive; to get there requires a 3½-mi hike. Campers can drive within 100 yards of the sites at Bicentennial (three sites). At Haypress (five sites) you'll have a comfortable ¾-mi walk in. None of these campgrounds has water, fires are not allowed, and backcountry permits are required. To reserve a site, call between 9:30 and noon no more than 90 days in advance. *Tel. 415/331–1540. 11 sites. Pit toilets, food lockers, picnic tables (Haypress only).*

TIBURON AND ANGEL ISLAND

Tiburon has no cheap lodging. If you don't want to head to the Golden Gate Hostel a few miles south (*see above*), consider a ferry trip to Angel Island for a night of camping.

CAMPING

Angel Island State Park. Here you can get away from it all without losing sight of the city. Nine shower-less, primitive sites ($10 Sunday and Monday, $11 Friday and Saturday) are scattered around the island. Sites 3 and 4, with views of the Golden Gate Bridge, are the most popular; Sites 1 and 2, surrounded by pine trees and with a view of the East Bay, offer more privacy and shelter from the wind. Wherever you camp, prepare for a 2-mi hike. Reserve a few weeks ahead for a weekend stay; on weekdays you can almost always get a site on the same day. For directions, *see* Tiburon and Angel Island *in* Chapter 2. *Tel. 415/435–1915 for information or 800/444–7275 for reservations. 9 sites. Barbecues, drinking water, pit toilets, food lockers, picnic tables.*

SAN RAFAEL

Although the hotels in this very down-to-earth town could hardly be called budget, they're more affordable than the rest of Marin County. Smokers, be forewarned that San Rafael is an adamant no-smoking town—even lighting up in the privacy of your hotel room is an infraction subject to fine.

UNDER $55

Panama Hotel. In this rambling, circa-1920s Spanish ranch–style hotel you'll find individually furnished rooms—the Bordello Room has a bidet; the Roy Rogers Room is cowboy kitsch—some with canopy beds and claw-foot tubs. Rooms without bath start at $50 ($79–$129 with bath), including breakfast. The hotel restaurant has a trellised outdoor seating area that's perfect for enjoying your lattes and scones. *4 Bayview St., 94901, tel. 415/457–3993 or 800/899–3993, fax 415/457–6240. From U.S. 101, Central San Rafael exit, left on 3rd St., left on B St., continue 4 blocks to where B St. becomes Bayview St. 15 rooms, 9 with bath. Kitchenettes.*

UNDER $100

425 Mission. The homey rooms in this wood-shingled cottage come complete with antiques, rosewood and wicker furniture, and the occasional claw-foot tub. You can hang out on the redwood deck or in the backyard porch swing when the weather is nice or lounge in the comfortable downstairs living room. Rooms run $85–$105, including a gourmet breakfast; Dutch baby pancakes are the specialty. Guests have access to the hot tub, and if you stay awhile, the innkeeper will do your laundry for free. *425 Mission Ave., 94901, tel. 415/453–1365. From U.S. 101, Central San Rafael exit, continue 5 blocks to Mission Ave., turn right. 4 rooms, 2 with bath.*

CAMPING

China Camp State Park. The trappings of civilization fade as you enter the 1,600-acre China Camp State Park, 4 mi northeast of San Rafael near San Pablo Bay. The 30 walk-in sites aren't far from the parking lot or from each other, but they're well sheltered by oak trees. And you get hot water to boot. Sites are $15 per night ($12 off-season), and parking costs an additional $3. Call Destinet (tel.

800/444–7275) to reserve. *Tel. 415/456–0766. From U.S. 101, N. San Pedro Rd. exit, follow signs. 30 sites. Drinking water, fire grates, flush toilets, food lockers, picnic tables, showers.*

COASTAL HIGHWAY I

MT. TAMALPAIS

Hard-core hikers will be happy with the Pantoll campsites (*see below*), which are near the Mt. Tamalpais ranger station and many trailheads. The Steep Ravine cabins, perched along the rocky coast, are better suited for those who want to escape civilization and its trappings—including roads and flush toilets. Both are supremely worthwhile.

CAMPING

Pantoll. Fifteen campsites, relatively close together but well sheltered by trees, are about a 100-yard walk from the parking lot of the Pantoll ranger station in Mt. Tamalpais State Park. The fee is $15 ($16 on weekends) per night. A 16th site ($3 per person) is reserved for those without a car. All sites are available on a first-come, first-served basis. *Tel. 415/388–2070. From Hwy. 1, follow signs to Mt. Tamalpais State Park, then Panoramic Hwy. to Pantoll ranger station. 16 sites. Barbecues, drinking water, flush toilets, food lockers.*

Steep Ravine Campground and Cabins. Off Highway 1 in Mt. Tamalpais State Park, Steep Ravine has six walk-in campsites for $9 per night, $7 off-season. Cabins with two double beds (read: wooden platforms—bring a sleeping bag) and two small bunk beds, as well as an indoor wood stove and outdoor barbecue, cost $30 per night. If you can deal with a pit toilet, this place is unbeatable—just you and a few other guests with an endless view of the dramatic coastline. Unfortunately, Steep Ravine is not an unknown gem, so cabins are fully booked well in advance, except in winter. *Tel. 800/444–7252 for reservations. From U.S. 101, Stinson Beach/Hwy. 1 exit, follow Hwy. 1 until you see signs. Drinking water.*

STINSON BEACH

Stinson Beach is full of B&Bs that are quaint in every detail except price. Expect to pay upwards of $90 a night.

UNDER $75

Stinson Beach Motel. One of Stinson's only affordable lodging options consists of six endearing 1912 cottages (all without phone) surrounding a gravel courtyard abundant with star jasmine, climbing geranium, and lilac. Doubles are $60, and two four-person apartments with kitchens go for $80. If you can't get a room here, try the Redwoods (tel. 415/868–1034) just next door, where a double room including breakfast will cost you about $60. *3416 Hwy. 1, 94970, tel. 415/868–1712. 6 cottages.*

POINT REYES

In addition to its excellent hostel, Point Reyes National Seashore has four free campgrounds, open to backpackers only, in isolated wilderness areas. You may have to hike in as far as 6 mi to reach one—but in these surroundings that's hardly a chore.

HOSTEL

Point Reyes AYH-Hostel. Eight miles west of the Point Reyes Visitor Center and surrounded by hiking trails, this place makes a great base camp—which is why it's so popular with both foreign travelers and weekenders from San Francisco. The two common rooms have wood-burning stoves and plenty of reading material. Beds cost $12; there is one private room for families with small children. *Mailing address: Box 247, Point Reyes Station, CA 94956, tel. 415/663–8811. From Hwy. 1, head left (west) on Bear Valley Rd. (1 block beyond stop sign in Olema), continue 1½ mi, turn left at LIGHTHOUSE/BEACHES/HOSTEL sign, left after 6 mi onto Crossroads Rd. 44 beds. Lockout 9:30–4:30, reception open daily 7:30 AM–9:30 AM and 4:30 PM–9:30 PM. Kitchen.*

CAMPING

To reserve a campsite up to two months in advance in Point Reyes ($10 per site), call the **Bear Valley Visitor Center** (tel. 415/663–8054) weekdays between 9 and 2. Trails to the campgrounds leave from the visitor center, which is on the entrance road (turn left off Highway 1 just past Olema on Bear Valley Road). All sites have barbecues, food lockers, picnic tables, and pit toilets.

Coast Camp is a 2-mi hike from the youth hostel parking lot (*see above*) or an 8-mi trek from the visitor center, but you'll sleep within a stone's throw (100 yards) of the ocean at any of the 14 sites. People tend to avoid the 12 sites at **Glenn Camp** because it's 5 mi from the nearest road, but it's in a quiet valley surrounded by trees, perfect for those who want to get away from civilization. The two group and 12 individual sites at **Sky Camp** are the most popular; they're a 2½-mi walk from the visitor center and 2 mi from the nearest parking area. The campground is perched on a small mountain ridge with an outstanding view. For the true misanthrope, **Wildcat Camp,** a stiff 6½ mi from the nearest road, has seven sites on a bluff, just a short walk from the beach. Privacy is never a problem.

Samuel P. Taylor State Park. This is a good choice if all the campgrounds in Point Reyes are full—or if you need creature comforts such as hot showers, flush toilets, and easy access to the road. Six miles east of Point Reyes on Sir Francis Drake Boulevard, 60 campsites are available for $12–$16 per night (hike-in and bike-in sites cost $3 per person). Reservations can be made through Destinet (tel. 800/444–7275); during summer even weeknights are booked in advance. Golden Gate Transit Bus 65 stops at the park on weekends and holidays (*see Bus Travel in* Chapter 1). *Tel. 415/488–9897. From U.S. 101, take Sir Francis Drake Blvd. about 15 mi west. 60 sites. Barbecues, fire grates, flush toilets, food lockers, picnic tables, showers.*

SOUTH BAY

Though the area along U.S. 101 is crowded with strip malls, fast-food restaurants, and chain motels where double rooms invariably cost $50–$70 per night, there are a few decent lodgings in Palo Alto. For a cheap weekend getaway, the San Mateo County Coast has two excellent hostels and several secluded campgrounds.

PALO ALTO

Although Palo Alto isn't exactly a mecca of budget accommodations, it's the most happening place to stay in the South Bay—a healthy number of upscale restaurants, bars, and cafés cater to the Stanford University community. Most of Palo Alto's budget motels are along **El Camino Real.**

UNDER $65

Coronet Motel. Traffic on El Camino Real makes it noisy, but the Coronet wins points for location and value (there's even a tiny pool). It's only a few blocks from Stanford University, and the Stanford Shopping Center is a short drive away. Doubles are $55–$60, and the rooms—many with kitchenettes—are comfortable, if not exactly modern. *2455 El Camino Real, between California Ave. and Page Mill Rd., 94306, tel. 650/326–1081. From U.S. 101, take Embarcadero Rd. exit west, turn left on El Camino Real. 21 rooms with bath.*

UNDER $100

Cowper Inn. The spacious, airy rooms in this Victorian B&B are filled with antiques, and all have phone and cable TV. Doubles start at $65 with shared bath, $110 with private bath, and $120 with a kitchenette (breakfast included). Sip sherry and munch on almonds in the parlor after spending the day exploring the nearby San Mateo Coast. *705 Cowper St., at Forest Ave., 94301, tel. 650/327–4475, fax 415/329–1703. From U.S. 101, take University Ave. west 2–3 mi, turn left on Cowper St., continue 2 blocks. 14 rooms, 12 with bath. Kitchenettes, laundry.*

HOSTELS

Hidden Villa Hostel. This is an actual working farm—complete with animals and organic gardens. Set in a 1,500-acre canyon in the Los Altos Hills between Palo Alto and San Jose, it's surrounded by hiking trails and peaceful dirt roads. Large, rustic dorm-style cabins dot the canyon, and each cabin has communal bathroom facilities. HI members pay $10 per night, nonmembers $13. You can also reserve a private room for $23. There's no curfew, but lockout is 9:30–4:30. *26870 Moody Rd., Los Altos 94022, tel. 650/949–8648. From San Francisco, I–280 south past Palo Alto to El Monte/Moody Rd. exit, turn right on El Monte Ave., left on Moody Rd. (at stop sign), continue 1¾ mi. Or from San Francisco, take SamTrans Bus 7F from Transbay Terminal (see Bus Travel in Chapter 1) to Palo Alto, then SamTrans Bus 35 to Foothill College; walk 2 mi to hostel. 35 beds. Reception open daily 8–9:30 and 4:30–9:30. Closed June–Aug.*

Sanborn Park Hostel. This is one of the most attractive hostels in California, perfectly situated for avid hikers and bicyclists and easily reached by public transit. The main cottage, a log cabin that dates from 1908, is surrounded by the dense 300-acre redwood forest of Sanborn Park, also home to a nearby nature museum. Hostelers stay in a large hall and have access to a rec room, a volleyball court, a grill, laundry facilities, and the standard HI kitchen—all for $9 per night ($11 for nonmembers). Bring your own food, since the only restaurants and grocery stores are 4 mi away in downtown Saratoga. Sheet rental costs 50¢. *15808 Sanborn Rd., Saratoga 95070, tel. 408/741–0166. From San Francisco, I–280 south to Saratoga/Sunnyvale exit, turn right, go 5½ mi to Hwy. 9, turn right (toward Big Basin), go 2½ mi, turn left at* SANBORN SKYLINE COUNTY PARK *sign, go 1 mi, and turn right. Or from Sunnyvale CalTrain station, take Santa Clara County Transit Bus 54 or 27 to Saratoga post office; call hostel for ride. 39 beds. Curfew 11* PM, *lockout 9–5, reception open daily 5* PM–11 PM. *Kitchen, laundry. Cash only.*

SAN MATEO COUNTY COAST

The desolate coastline south of San Francisco has some of the area's most striking scenery. **Half Moon Bay,** the largest and most centrally located town, is not the best choice for budget accommodations. Instead, head for Montara or Pescadero, where the Bay Area's two best lodging deals await you.

PACIFICA AND MONTARA

The hostels here are far more memorable than the generic budget motels. Of the latter, the **Sea View Motor Lodge** (2160 Francisco Blvd., 94044, tel. 650/359–9494) is a step above the others: Airy, comfortable doubles, many with an ocean view, go for $50 ($70 for a quad with a kitchenette). Highway 1 is distressingly close, but you're within walking distance of the beach and old town.

HOSTEL

Point Montara Lighthouse AYH-Hostel. This functioning lighthouse and its adjoining hostel are perched on a cliff a half mile south of Montara State Beach. Best of all, you get incredible views of the coastline and access to a beach and tide pools. Inside, there's a fireplace in the comfortable living room, a communal kitchen, a dining area, and an outdoor redwood hot tub ($5 per person per hour, two-person minimum). Beds go for $12 per night ($14 for nonmembers), and everyone must perform a small chore. Reservations can be made up to six months in advance with a night's deposit. *Hwy. 1 at 16th St., Montara 94037, tel. 650/728–7177. From Daly City BART, SamTrans Bus 1L or 1C southbound; ask driver to let you off at 14th St. 45 beds. Curfew 11* PM, *lockout 9:30–4:30, reception open daily 7:30–9:30 and 4:30–9:30. Kitchen, laundry.*

HALF MOON BAY

On the southern outskirts of town, the distinctly European **Cameron's Inn** (1410 S. Cabrillo Hwy., 94019, tel. 650/726–5705) has three clean, simple doubles with shared bath ($60–$70) that are as cheap as you'll find in the area. Big beds and fine-art prints lend some style to the rooms, but that doesn't diminish the noise of big rigs downshifting on the highway. The **San Benito House** (356 Main St., 94019, tel. 650/726–3425), built at the turn of the century, has 12 rooms with a beautiful backyard garden and a pricey restaurant overlooking Main Street. Nightly rates are $60 (shared bath), $75–$95 (private bath), with a 20% weekday discount. If all else fails, a 20-room **Ramada Inn** (3020 Hwy. 1, 94019, tel. 650/726–9700 or 800/272–6232), at the north end of town, has doubles starting at $85 weekdays, $95 weekends, including breakfast.

UNDER $100

Old Thyme Inn. If you're going to splurge on coastal accommodations, head to this romantic 1899 Victorian inn. The Laura Ashley–clad rooms, each named after a different herb, are all decked out with fresh-cut flowers, a bedside stuffed animal, and charming antiques. All this for $90–$125 ($125 and up for a fireplace and a whirlpool bath). A bountiful English breakfast is served in the parlor, where sherry and candy await you every evening. *779 Main St., 94019, tel. 650/726–1616, fax 650/726–6394. 7 rooms with bath.*

CAMPING

Half Moon Bay State Beach. Because of its proximity to downtown Half Moon Bay, this place attracts teenage partyers and weekend warriors, especially during summer. You'll fall asleep to the sound of waves and arise to the smell of the sea, but it's hardly the great outdoors. At the base of a small sand dune, the 55 characterless sites cost $14 per night ($12 off-season); all sites are doled out on a first-come, first-served basis. *95 Kelly Ave., 94019, tel. 650/726–8820. From Hwy. 1, Kelly Ave. west. 55 sites. Barbecues, drinking water, fire grates, flush toilets, food lockers, picnic tables, showers.*

LA HONDA

Outdoorsy types have four excellent choices of lodging in La Honda. There's a hostel that caters to backpackers, and three of the area's parks have campgrounds.

HOSTEL

Hiker's Hut. This A-frame cabin in Sam McDonald County Park sits atop a ridge 1½ steep mi above the parking lot—from the deck you can see the ocean on a clear day. There's sleeping space for 14 people; the fee is $10 per night per person ($8 for Sierra Club members). Reservations require a 50% check deposit and must be made well in advance, especially for summer weekends. Reserve through the Loma Prieta chapter of the Sierra Club (3921 E. Bayshore Rd., Palo Alto 94303, tel. 650/390–8411). *Take Hwy. 84 ½ mi west of La Honda, turn left on Pescadero Rd., drive 2 mi to Sam McDonald parking lot (follow signs). Kitchen, pit toilets.*

CAMPING

Memorial County Park has 135 quiet sites ($14), with picnic tables, fire pits, and hot showers, in a thick old-growth forest. Although popular with car campers on summer weekends, the campground is sparsely visited at other times. Sites are allotted on a first-come, first-served basis. In **Portola Redwood State Park,** the 53 family sites and seven hike-in sites ($15–$16) see little light in their cool berth beneath the redwoods. The family sites have running water, showers, fire pits, and picnic tables. Reserve through Destinet (tel. 800/444–7275). **Pescadero Creek County Park** has 15 hike-in sites ($7) in the midst of a dense second-growth forest along the river. Contact the rangers at Portola Redwood State Park (tel. 650/948–9098) to secure a spot. For directions to these parks and information on exploring them, *see* South Bay *in* Chapter 2.

PESCADERO

This pristine town overlooks miles of unblemished coastline; an enchanting hostel and peaceful campgrounds are situated among the redwoods.

HOSTEL

Pigeon Point Lighthouse Youth Hostel. Perched on a small bluff 5 mi south of Pescadero State Beach are four bungalow-style dorms, plus an outdoor, bluff-side hot tub ($3 per person per half hour). Free tours of the historic lighthouse on the grounds are also available. One night in any of the 54 comfortable beds costs $11 ($14 for nonmembers); another $10 secures a private room for two. All guests must do a chore each day of their stay. The maximum stay is three nights. *Pigeon Point Rd. and Hwy. 1, 94060, tel. 650/879–0633. From Daly City BART, take SamTrans Bus 1L to Half Moon Bay, then SamTrans Bus 96C. Curfew 11 PM, lockout 9:30–4:30, reception open daily 7:30–9:30 and 4:30–9:30. Kitchen.*

CAMPING

Surprisingly few visitors venture out to the 27 campsites ($17) and 18 hike-in sites ($7) in quiet **Butano State Park** (tel. 650/879–2040). The drive-in sites have fire rings, picnic tables, and food lockers. Reservations can be made through Destinet (tel. 800/444–7275) up to eight weeks in advance but are usually not necessary. None of the sites has showers. For directions to Butano and information on the park, *see* The San Mateo County Coast *in* Chapter 2.

THE GREAT OUTDOORS

REVISED BY SHARRON WOOD

I t's no surprise that Bay Area residents have a discriminating palate for the outdoors—many people choose to live here precisely because it's so easy to drive 15 minutes from the city to enjoy some of the country's most spectacular natural attractions. The cool, moist woodlands of Marin County are prime territory for hikers, bikers, horseback riders, and bird-watchers. Afternoon breezes make San Francisco Bay ideal for windsurfing. And when the summer winds die down, you can put away your sail and dust off the surfboard for the winter waves. Rock climbers, in-line skaters, mountain bikers, and sea kayakers will have no trouble finding new challenges in the Bay Area. This is California, after all, where even Silicon Valley professionals surf more than the Internet.

A great place to get the inside scoop on the outdoors is at **Outdoors Unlimited** (OU; 550 Parnassus Ave., at 3rd Ave., tel. 415/476–2078), where volunteers teach everything from fly-fishing to CPR, organize backpacking and cycling outings, lead moonlight kayak trips, and rent out top-notch equipment. The office is open Monday and Friday 11:30 AM–1:30 AM, Tuesday–Thursday 5 PM–8 PM. Berkeley's **Cal Adventures** (2301 Bancroft Way, tel. 510/642–4000 or 510/643–8029), on the UC campus, offers a wide variety of affordable outings and lessons in such sports as sailing, kayaking, wind surfing, backpacking, and rock climbing. They also rent equipment at low prices. The office is open weekdays 10–6.

The nonprofit **Environmental Traveling Companions** (ETC; Fort Mason Center, Bldg. C, tel. 415/474–7662) leads sea kayaking, river rafting, and cross-country skiing expeditions in and around the Bay Area for people with special needs—physical as well as financial—as well as for the population at large (*see* Disabilities & Accessibility *in* Chapter 1).

The best places to stock up on pamphlets, books, and maps are San Francisco's **Rand McNally** (595 Market St., at 2nd St., tel. 415/777–3131), Oakland's **Sierra Club Bookstore** (6014 College Ave., tel. 510/658–7470), and Berkeley's **REI** (1338 San Pablo Ave., tel. 510/527–4140), which also hosts free wilderness lectures, book signings, and slide presentations. **Transit Outdoors,** published by the Bay Area Open Space Council, is a free guide to accessing Bay Area parks and trailheads via public transportation; it's available at public libraries and park districts. Also check out www.transitinfo.org/outdoors.

FITNESS CENTERS AND POOLS

In this city of beautiful bodies, you'll have only to walk a block or two to pump iron, swim laps, or aerobicize. Although some clubs are members-only, most facilities sell day passes for an average charge of

$10 to $20. The **Embarcadero YMCA** (169 Steuart St., tel. 415/957–9622) has racquetball, a 25-meter swimming pool, and aerobics classes. The $12 drop-in fee includes use of the sauna, steam room, and whirlpool, plus a magnificent view of the bay. The various branches of **24-Hour Fitness** (960 Potrero Ave., tel. 415/437–4188; 1200 Van Ness Ave., tel. 415/776–2200; 350 Bay St., tel. 415/395–9595; 100 California St., tel. 415/434–5080; 2nd St. at Folsom St., tel. 415/543–7808) are open to the public for a $15 drop-in fee. Most branches have saunas, Jacuzzis, and steam rooms, plus aerobics classes and a complete line of fitness equipment. The **World Gym** (260 De Haro St., at 16th St., tel. 415/703–9650), though a bit off the beaten track, is a must-see for bodybuilding enthusiasts; a lack of extensive spa facilities is a fair trade-off for the extensive weight-training and aerobic equipment. The day rate of $10 ($20 between 4 PM and 8 PM weekdays) includes aerobics classes. If you prefer working out in a women-only atmosphere, try the **Women's Training Center** (2164 Market St., tel. 415/864–6835), where a $10 day fee includes use of the sauna.

The facilities at some hotels are open to nonguests for a fee: Try the swanky clubs at the **Hotel Nikko** (222 Mason St., tel. 415/394–1153) or the **Fairmont** (950 Mason St., tel. 415/772–5000), where the fees are $20 and $15, respectively, or save a buck and work out at the **San Francisco Hilton** (333 O'Farrell St., tel. 415/771–1400) or the **Marriott** (55 Fourth St., tel. 415/896–1600 or 800/228–9290); both charge $10.

If you're more inclined to work out in water, the San Francisco Recreation and Park Department (tel. 415/666–7201) manages one outdoor swimming pool and eight indoor pools throughout the city. Fees are $3 for adults over 18. The **Sava Pool** (19th Ave. and Wawona St., tel. 415/753–7000) is one of the more popular (and crowded) pools. **Hamilton Pool** (Geary Blvd. and Steiner St., tel. 415/292–2001) is a favorite among serious lap swimmers. The **Embarcadero YMCA** (*see above*) has a 25-meter pool, gym, and spa facilities for a $12 day fee. The University of San Francisco's **Koret Health and Recreation Center** (Parker Ave. at Turk St., tel. 415/666–6820), a few blocks from the Golden Gate Park panhandle, has an especially well maintained Olympic-size pool and a fitness center. Visitors have access to both facilities before 2 PM daily for an $8 fee. The Potrero Avenue branch of **24-Hour Fitness** (*see above*) has a 25-meter pool with three lanes; the $15 fee covers the pool as well as the fitness center. Some hotels allow nonguests to use their swimming pools for a fee. Try the **Sheehan Hotel** (620 Sutter St., tel. 415/776–6500), a few blocks from Union Square: Its four-lane lap pool is open to the public for a $4 fee.

HIKING AND BIKING

If you want to hit the trail with just your feet, contact the **Golden Gate Hikers,** sponsored by Hostelling International. You don't have to be an HI member to hike—just bring a buck for each event, a bag lunch, and a $3–$5 carpool fee. For free information on upcoming hikes, write to 1717 Cabrillo St., San Francisco 94121 or call the **Hikers' Hotline** (tel. 415/550–6321). At **Outdoors Unlimited** (*see* chapter introduction), in a truly cooperative spirit, all the hiking trips are free—save the cost of transportation. Anyone may sign up on the trip sheet posted at the OU office on the UCSF campus (550 Parnassus Ave., tel. 415/476–2078) up to 11 days prior to a scheduled jaunt. The **Sierra Club** also sponsors hikes all over the Bay Area. They're free, though a donation may be requested, and carpoolers are expected to share gas, parking, and bridge tolls. Pick up a schedule at the Sierra Club Bookstore (*see* chapter introduction).

Northern Californians have the dubious distinction of having literally reinvented the wheel with the creation of the mountain bike. If you want to rub spokes with other cyclists on a planned recreational ride, check out the calendar of events in the free monthly *Northern California Bicyclist,* available at bike shops. The **Sierra Club** organizes group rides on terrain that ranges from farmland to challenging hills. You need at least a 10-speed bike for all but the most level routes, and you must wear a helmet. Pick up their activities schedule at the Sierra Club Bookstore (*see* chapter introduction) for a list of planned rides. The best in-depth guides to biking in the Bay Area include *Bay Area Bike Rides,* by Ray Hosler (Chronicle Books, $10.95), *Cycling the San Francisco Bay Area,* by Carole O'Hare (Bicycle Books, $12.95), and *Marin County Bike Trails* (Penngrove Publications, $11.95).

SAN FRANCISCO

HIKING

The **Coastal Trail** follows 9 mi of San Francisco's shoreline, from the cliffs near Golden Gate Bridge over dirt roads, onto residential sidewalks, around craggy headlands, and along the beach all the way down to Fort Funston. Begin at the **Golden Gate Bridge** toll plaza parking lot. Walk west underneath the toll plaza, turn left onto Merchant Road, and continue west to find the trailhead. After about 10 minutes you get your first hint of why this hike is not to be missed: The view takes in 200-ft cliffs, the Golden Gate Bridge, and the Marin Headlands all at once. The trail then heads inland; when the path ends on Lincoln Boulevard, take the dirt road to the right that leads to **Baker Beach.** Enjoy the sandy dunes and salty air as you forge ahead in a westerly direction; cross the parking lot and head into the forest (keep to the right every time the trail forks). About five minutes later, the trail spits you out onto **El Camino del Mar,** which travels through the extravagant **Seacliff** neighborhood. The dirt trail begins again on the right just where the houses end. The next 1.7 mi of the trail passes through **Lands End,** San Francisco's wildest little corner, full of rocky cliffs, grassy fields, crashing surf, and magnificent views. Wise hikers will heed the warning signs and stay off the unstable cliffs. The dirt trail ends in a parking lot overlooking the **Sutro Baths**; head downhill past the aptly named **Cliff House** to **Ocean Beach.** From here to **Fort Funston** (4.7 mi south) you'll pass **Golden Gate Park** and the **San Francisco Zoo** on your left. If you make it all the way to Fort Funston, you'll find picnicking areas with great views of the ocean and local hang gliders practicing their craft. Once you hit Ocean Beach, you can catch a bus back to downtown at almost any cross street. For a map, call or visit the **Golden Gate National Recreation Area Visitor Center.** *West end of Point Lobos Ave. at the Great Highway, under the Cliff House, tel. 415/556–8642. From Montgomery BART, Bus 38, 38L, or 38AX to Cliff House. Open daily 10–5.*

On the third Sunday in May crowds of costumed carousers and competitive runners race across the city, from the bay to the ocean, in the annual Examiner *Bay-to-Breakers (tel. 415/512–5000, ext. 2222).*

For a less strenuous and time-consuming urban stroll, try the **Golden Gate Promenade.** Starting from the same parking lot as the Coastal Trail, head east down the stairs that lead to **Fort Point National Historic Site.** From here follow the 3.5-mi mostly asphalt path, which traces the bay from Fort Point to the **Hyde Street Pier.** The popular jogging route takes you by the windsurfers at Crissy Field, around the yacht harbor, past Marina Green, and over the hill of Fort Mason to Aquatic Park, near Fisherman's Wharf.

For another intimate encounter with the native flora and fauna of San Francisco, try **the Presidio** (*see* Neighborhoods *in* Chapter 2). Check out the 2-mi **Ecology Trail** that starts at the southeastern corner (Presidio Blvd. and Pacific Ave.) of the Presidio. The trail travels through cool, springy forest beds and provides an intimate introduction to some of San Francisco's most distinctive plant life. For information on this and other Presidio trails, as well as a schedule of guided tours offered by the National Park Service, stop at the **Presidio Visitor Information Center.** Ask about the sporadic "Pedaling the Presidio" tour, a 6-mi ride that includes stops at several historic and scenic spots. *Montgomery St., Bldg. 102, tel. 415/561–4323. Open daily 9–4.*

BIKING

If you plan to do a lot of riding, pick up a of the *San Francisco Biking/Walking Guide* ($3) at the Berkeley TRiP Commute Store (*see* Transportation *in* Chapter 1); the comprehensive map shows street grades and bike-friendly routes. **Park Cyclery** (1749 Waller St., at Stanyan St., tel. 415/751–7368) rents mountain bikes for $5 an hour or $25 a day.

One of best rides in San Francisco takes you through Golden Gate Park, into the Presidio, across the Golden Gate Bridge, and along the coast, for a total distance of 21 mi. Start at the west end of Golden Gate Park, where **John F. Kennedy Drive** hits the Great Highway. Follow JFK Drive along a slight incline to the east end of the park, turn left on **Conservatory Road,** left again on **Arguello Boulevard,** exit the park, and head through residential neighborhoods and onto the curvy, downhill roads of the **Presidio.** Hang a right on Moraga Avenue, then take another right onto **Presidio Boulevard** for a quick tour of the historic former military base. Make a hard left onto **Lincoln Boulevard** almost immediately; it leads to the windy view area and toll plaza of the Golden Gate Bridge, where signs tell you how to cross according to the time and day of the week. When you return, follow Lincoln Boulevard west; it turns into **El Camino del Mar** and runs through the beautiful, grand **Seacliff** neighborhood. At the Palace of Legion of Honor, the road veers right and becomes **Legion of Honor Drive** before dumping you back onto **Clement Street.** Turn right on Clement, and when it dead-ends, take **Point Lobos Avenue** past the **Cliff House** back to the Great Highway, where you can either collapse on the beach for some well-earned rest, continue down the coast, or head back into Golden Gate Park.

EAST BAY

The extensive **East Bay Regional Park District** (tel. 510/562–7275) spans two counties, includes 80,000 acres of parkland, operates 54 regional parks, and provides a varied terrain of dark redwood forests, blustery hills with ocean views, lakes, and grassy fields. At any one of six visitor centers you can get free maps and the useful "Regional Parks" brochure ($1), which includes information on all the parks and attractions. Parking and admission to all East Bay parks is free unless otherwise noted. For rentals, try **Missing Link Bicycle Co-op** (1988 Shattuck Ave., Berkeley, tel. 510/843–7471), where a mountain bike goes for $25–$35 a day.

The 31-mi **Skyline Trail** connects the six East Bay Regional Parks running through the Berkeley-Oakland hills. From the north trailhead in **Wildcat Canyon Park,** the trail snakes south through **Tilden Regional Park** (*see below*); **Sibley Volcanic National Reserve,** with its volcanic dikes and peaks made of lava and volcanic debris; **Huckleberry Botanic Regional Reserve,** known for its endangered and rare plant life; and **Redwood Regional Park** (*see below*); the southern trail terminus is at **Anthony Chabot Regional Park** (*see below*).

TILDEN REGIONAL PARK

Named after Major Charles Lee Tilden, first president of the park district board, Tilden Park contains 2,078 acres of eucalyptus trees and rolling hills, filled with hikers, cyclists, picnickers, and poison oak. As in most Bay Area parks, mountain bikes are limited to the fire trails. To reach Tilden Park, take University Avenue east from I–80 to Oxford Street; go left on Oxford, right on Rose, and left on Spruce Street to the top of the hill. Cross Grizzly Peak Boulevard, make an immediate left on Canon Drive, and follow the signs. From the Berkeley BART, AC Transit Bus 67 gets you as far as Spruce and Grizzly Peak on weekdays and directly to **Lake Anza** on weekends. In summer AC Transit Bus 65 will transport both you and your bike from the Berkeley BART station to Grizzly Peak at the top of Spruce Street. To reach **Inspiration Point** by car from University Avenue, turn left on Oxford Street, right on Rose Street, and left on Spruce Street. Follow Spruce to the top of the hill, then turn right on Wildcat Canyon Road; the Inspiration Point parking lot is on your left after about 15 minutes. Stop by the **Environmental Education Center** (tel. 510/525–2233), at the north end of the park, for maps and information.

HIKING • Tilden contains two of the highest points in the East Bay: **Volmer Peak** (1,913 ft) to the south, and **Wildcat Peak** (1,250 ft) to the north. You can hike to Wildcat Peak from **Inspiration Point** along **Nimitz Way,** a 4½-mi road with views of the bay and of the San Pablo and Briones reservoirs.

To avoid poison oak and brambles, head to the central part of the park. Starting at the Lake Anza parking lot, walk northeast on the **Lake Anza Trail,** which encircles the lake. When you reach the far northeast corner of the lake, look for the **Wildcat Gorge Trail,** which will be on your left. The initial steep descent past a century-old springhouse is no indication of things to come: The trail tunnels through a wide, rocky gorge but eventually rises to 80 ft above the creek that carved it. Continue for a half mile until the trail forks. To the right, the **Curran Trail** rises sharply for .7 mi to Inspiration Point. Otherwise, the Wildcat Gorge Trail, one of the nicest in Tilden, continues on through groves of California bay laurels. About a third of a mile up the trail on your right, you'll pass a hill with a practically vertical path upward (this isn't on the official Tilden map). At the top of the hill you'll have a 360-degree view of the park. Return to the Wildcat Gorge Trail and backtrack to Lake Anza for an easy to moderate 1½-hour hike.

The moderate 1½-mi, 800-ft climb through woods and fields to the top of Wildcat Peak begins at the Environmental Education Center: Head east on the **Laurel Canyon Trail,** cross the fire road, continue uphill, and turn left onto the **Wildcat Peak Trail.** A turnoff to the right leads all the way to the top, where you can look out over Oakland, San Francisco, and Marin. Head back down the way you came, turn right onto Wildcat Peak Trail, and go left on the **Sylvan Trail,** which leads back to the nature center.

BIKING • To escape the asphalt obstacle course of Berkeley's streets, take this strenuous 7-mi loop along the ridge of the Berkeley Hills and into Tilden Park. From the intersection of **Grizzly Peak Boulevard** and **Spruce Street** in north Berkeley, head south up Grizzly Peak Boulevard. This is the hardest part of the ride; at times this winding, steep street has only a narrow shoulder, and riding on it can be hairy. Not far beyond the two lookouts, make a left on **South Park Drive,** which takes you down through Tilden Park and past several picnic grounds. The street dead-ends at **Wildcat Canyon Road;** go left and ride over rolling hills past Lake Anza and back to the intersection with Grizzly Peak Boulevard. Taking this loop in the opposite direction involves potentially dangerous sharp curves and limited visibility. Spruce Street is the main access road to Grizzly Peak Boulevard north of town; **Tunnel Road,** which goes up into the hills past the Caldecott Tunnel, is the main access road to the south.

A beautiful, moderately strenuous 13½-mi loop through both Tilden and Wildcat Canyon Park begins just west of the Inspiration Point parking lot (*see above*). Head down the rocky **Meadows Canyon Trail,** which starts to the left of the paved Nimitz Trail; when you come to **Loop Road,** hang a left, which will lead you to the **Environmental Education Center.** On the west side of the EEC, pick up the **Wildcat Creek Trail,** and 6 mi farther head right on the **Belgum Trail** for a steep and often muddy ascent of just less than a mile. Make another right onto the **San Pablo Ridge Trail,** a steep uphill grade that affords spectacular views of the bay. From here you can pick up the paved **Nimitz Way Trail,** which leads back to Inspiration Point. For a shorter ride that avoids the most challenging stretch of the Belgum Trail, turn right off Wildcat Creek Trail onto the **Conlon Trail.**

WILDCAT CANYON REGIONAL PARK

Not nearly as developed or crowded as Tilden, Wildcat Canyon has the feel of a forgotten country back road; here you'll share the grassy hills and stunning views of San Pablo Bay with grazing cattle. The main entrance is on Park Avenue, at the north end of the canyon; this is also the site of the park visitor center (tel. 510/236–1262). To get here, take I–80 to the Solano/Amador exit. Turn left on Amador and at the second stop sign, turn right on McBryde Street and follow signs to the park office. From the El Cerrito del Norte BART station, take AC Transit Bus 68, which stops a few hundred feet from the park entrance.

HIKING • The best trail loop is a moderate 4-mi hike: From the **Wildcat Creek Trail**—which starts at the EEC in Tilden Park (*see above*) and is different from the Wildcat *Peak* Trail—go 1½ mi up through the tall grass on the **Mezue Trail** for an excellent view; then turn right and continue for ¾ mi along the paved **Nimitz Way.** Turning right onto the **Havey Canyon Trail** will return you to the Wildcat Creek Trail on a winding 1½-mi path.

REDWOOD REGIONAL PARK

More than a hundred years ago sailors entering San Francisco Bay used the giant redwood trees growing on the hills east of Oakland as a landmark. Unfortunately, most of those trees were mowed down at the start of the California gold rush. Only a few virgin redwoods remain in Redwood Regional Park, but the second-growth forest is still impressive.

Since Huckleberry Botanical Preserve is outside the fog belt, it's a good place to see the first blossoms of the season. Hike the nature trail there in early spring. To reach Huckleberry, follow the directions for Redwood Regional Park.

Free trail maps are available at the **Skyline Gate entrance.** To get there, take I–580 to Highway 24, then head east to Highway 13S. Exit north on Joaquin Miller Road and turn left on Skyline Boulevard; the Skyline Gate entrance is about 4 mi farther on the right. From the Coliseum BART station, AC Transit Bus 46 takes you to Skyline Boulevard; from there head up the hill a third of a mile to the park. To get to **Redwood Gate,** take I–580 east toward Hayward and exit at 35th Avenue/MacArthur Boulevard. Take 35th Avenue, which becomes Redwood Road, east past Skyline Boulevard. The park entrance is about 3 mi farther down the road. Parking inside costs $3 on weekends, but you can park along the road for free. There is no public transit to Redwood Gate.

HIKING • Connecting the north and south entrances are two main trails, the **East Ridge Trail** and the **West Ridge Trail.** Both, along with the **Stream Trail,** start at the Skyline Gate parking lot. The West Ridge Trail is the main thoroughfare through the park, and too much time on its broad path may get you flattened by a charging mountain biker (most other trails are limited to hikers). From the Skyline Gate entrance, take the 3-mi Stream Trail, which after a steep (and often hot and dry) descent to the valley floor, meanders through the redwoods. If you'd rather have shade and the company of redwood groves on your way down, follow the West Ridge Trail a little farther, to the strenuous **French Trail.** To return to the Skyline Gate entrance from the valley floor, simply follow any trail heading up and to the right; you'll soon connect with the West Ridge Trail, which will lead you back to the park entrance.

BIKING • The 9-mi bike loop through the redwood forest is moderately difficult, with some strenuous areas. From **Redwood Gate** follow the road past the picnic areas to the trailhead. **Canyon Trail** begins with a steep climb (which gets nice and muddy in the rainy season). After a half mile bear left on the **East Ridge Trail** for a gentle 3½-mi ascent to the **West Ridge Trail.** The road levels for a bit, but the downhill stretch has plenty of danger zones, so watch your speed. After about 5 mi, the West Ridge Trail becomes the **Bridle Trail,** which runs into the Fern Dell picnic area. From here turn right and take the **Stream Trail** all the way back.

ANTHONY CHABOT REGIONAL PARK

South of Redwood Regional Park and only 20 minutes from downtown Oakland, Chabot covers almost 5,000 acres. This is one of the few East Bay parks with a campground (*see* Chapter 7), and the blue waters of Lake Chabot are a refreshing sight after a long haul. The flat 9-mi walk around the lake's perimeter gives you a close-up view of the wildflowers and waterfowl that abound in this habitat. There's no swimming allowed, but you can rent a rowboat, a canoe, or a pedal boat ($10 per hour, $30 per day, plus a $30 deposit). For hiking, biking, and camping information, call 510/635–0135, ext. 2570; for lake information dial 510/582–2198. To get to the park from I–580E, exit at 150th Avenue/Fairmont Drive East, which merges with Lake Chabot Road; then follow the signs. Avoid the $3 parking fee by stationing your car somewhere along the road.

The hilly 14-mi loop around Chabot Park passes over all sorts of great biking terrain. From the parking area at the marina, take the **East Shore Trail.** Cross the bridge and turn right on the **Live Oak Trail** for a steep, rutted ascent of just under a mile that will deter any 10-speeder and even a few mountain bikers. Then turn right on the **Towhee Trail** to the **Red Tail Trail.** Follow Red Tail—where you will be serenaded by the sounds of gunshots from the local rifle range—until you meet the **Grass Valley Trail.** Follow the **Brandon Trail**—a U-turn after the gate at the end of the Grass Valley Trail—to the **Goldenrod Trail**; if you make it this far, your reward is a drinking fountain for cows and humans to share. Next is the **Bass Cove Trail,** another rain-rutted trail that ends up on the **West Shore Trail,** which takes you back to the lake.

MARIN COUNTY

Just over the Golden Gate Bridge you'll find virgin redwoods, grassy mountain fields, and beaches where the roaring Pacific crashes against the cliffs. Many of Marin's best hiking and biking areas—Muir Woods, Mt. Tamalpais, and Point Reyes National Seashore—lie along Highway 1, which winds its way up the coast.

In a bit of California irony, the birthplace of the mountain bike is now a battleground, with bikers squaring off against hikers who want to keep the two-wheelers off the trails. Marin County has been particularly zealous about curtailing the use of mountain bikes: Trails that haven't been closed to bikers have a 15 mph speed limit (5 mph around turns), and rangers aren't shy about giving out hefty tickets ($180–$200) for violations.

There are bike shops all over Marin, and those offering rentals are strategically placed near favorite routes. One good option is **Start to Finish Bicycles** in San Rafael (1820 4th St., at H St., San Rafael, tel. 415/459–3990), where mountain bike rentals run $15 for four hours, $20 for eight hours, and $30 for 24 hours.

MARIN HEADLANDS

Part of the **Golden Gate National Recreation Area,** the headlands are home to rolling hills covered with coyote bush, low-lying grasses, precipitous bluffs, hardy wildflowers, and sandy beaches—dress in layers, as wind and fog are always present. You can easily get here by bike—just hop on the Golden Gate Bridge and take the first exit (Alexander Avenue). If you're driving, pass under the freeway at Alexander Avenue, turn right before the entrance to U.S. 101S, and follow the signs to the **visitor center** (tel. 415/331–1540); it's open daily 9:30–4:30. Here you can see natural history exhibits, pick up a free trail map, purchase more detailed guides, and get trail suggestions from the staff. Most trails start here, and parking is free. On Sunday and holidays only, Bus 76 travels from the Transbay Terminal to the visitor center.

HIKING • For an easy stroll you can skirt the 1½-mi perimeter of **Rodeo Lagoon.** For something more substantial, head north up the **Coastal Trail.** From the visitor center parking lot head up the closed-off road (*not* the left stairway). Persevere for about 2 mi, turn right onto the **Wolf Ridge Trail,** and head up the grassy hill (alias Wolf Ridge) for 1½ mi to the top, where you can look down on Tennessee Valley. Then continue less than a mile down the verdant leeward side of the hill until it hooks up with the **Miwok Trail,** which you follow south. The trail wanders above the edge of grassy Gerbode Valley, where you may spot a black-tailed deer or a bobcat basking in the chaparral. Two miles later you'll be back at the visitor center.

The **Tennessee Valley Trail,** at the end of Tennessee Valley Road (from U.S. 101N take the Highway 1 exit west and make the first left), is a broad path that meanders next to a small creek and through grassy fields for an easy 2 mi. In no time you'll be on **Tennessee Beach,** in the company of many families. Here, during very low tide, you may be able to glimpse the namesake of the valley—the shipwreck of the S.S. *Tennessee.* For a more strenuous, 8-mi round-trip hike, follow the Tennessee Valley Trail about a mile from the parking lot and veer right onto the **Coastal Trail.** After ¾ mi, the trail wildly snakes above the secluded **Pirates Cove** for about 2 mi, with stunning views of the jagged coast, and eventually leads you down to **Muir Beach.** Before you head back, relax a while at the pub of the **Pelican Inn** (*see* Muir Beach *in* Chapter 2). On your return see the less dramatic side of the Tennessee Valley by turning left off the Coastal Trail at **Coyote Ridge Trail** after a mile. Keep your eyes peeled here for deer, bobcats, hawks, and great horned owls. Continue for 1½ mi and take the **Fox Trail** back to the Tennessee Valley Trail. You complete the 8-mi round trip with a short walk north back to the parking lot.

BIKING • A popular series of fire trails gives you intermittent views of the Golden Gate and the Pacific. Take the **Miwok Trail** (from the parking area near the visitor center) to the **Bobcat Trail** and continue 3½ mi uphill to the **Marincello Trail.** This gravelly downhill run drops you on **Tennessee Valley Road,** which leads to the beach. To return, go back up Tennessee Valley Road and pick up the **Old Springs Trail,** which picks up on the road leading into Miwok Stables. Once you get back to the Miwok Trail, hang a right and head back down to the trailhead. The entire trip is 11½ mi and is mostly moderate, with a few steep sections. Rangers sometimes lead mountain-biking tours along this route; call for details.

ANGEL ISLAND

Almost all 750 acres of this island in San Francisco Bay are covered with forest or sweeping grasses. In June 1996 Angel Island began a controversial campaign to eradicate all non-native flora—eucalyptus trees were hit the hardest—but you can still gaze in awe at sweeping ocean views. **Perimeter Road,** which circles the island, is very steep and gravelly in some places. For information on ferry travel to the island, *see* Tiburon and Angel Island *in* Chapter 2. For recorded information call 415/435–1915; dial 415/435–5390 to speak to a ranger.

In the annual 7-mi Dipsea Race, usually held the second Sunday in June, runners sprint from Mill Valley over Mt. Tamalpais, ending up at Stinson Beach. The race originated in 1905 and now has almost a cult following; there was even a movie about it.

HIKING • All trails lead in from Perimeter Road. On the **Sunset Trail,** immediately southeast of park headquarters (behind the picnic area, west of the ferry landing), 2 mi of ascending switchbacks afford stunning views of San Francisco to the west. As you circle the 781-ft summit, called **Mt. Caroline Livermore,** you'll reach a crossroads; take a left up the paved road to the top for a 360-degree view of the Bay Area. After you backtrack to the crossroads, return to the ferry via the **North Ridge Trail** to view the east side of the island. The entire loop takes 2½–3 hours.

BIKING • The few areas not closed to cyclists are great for scenic, easy spins. **Perimeter Road** is a 5½-mi twirl around the island; the **Fire Road** is a 3½-mi elevated loop. You can bring your bike over on the ferry; otherwise, rent a mountain bike by the ferry landing for $12 an hour or $25 a day (including helmet); here you can also pick up a free trail map.

MUIR WOODS

The good news: This is one of the few places in the world where you'll find ancient, towering redwoods (the oldest has been around more than 1,200 years). The bad news: Droves of tourists are aware of this. An estimated 1.5-million sightseers shuffle past the redwoods annually (8,000–10,000 daily in summer), but happily, fewer than 10% venture onto the network of hiking trails that start here. You can make a quick escape by following any of the trails that head up from the valley floor and connect with the 60 mi of trail in Mount Tamalpais State Park. The trail guide for sale at the park entrance ($1) provides great explanations of various flora and fauna. Cyclists are prohibited on everything but fire roads; you'll find free bike maps at the Muir Woods Visitor Center/Kiosk detailing where you can and cannot go. For recorded information call 415/388–2595.

For a spectacular view and workout, head up the **Ben Johnson Trail** after crossing the fourth bridge from the park entrance. You'll climb up through the forest for 2 mi (the last half mile is quite steep despite the switchbacks) until you reach the top of a hill with postcard views of several canyons and the Pacific. You can either head east on the **Dipsea Trail** to complete a 4½-mi hike or follow it 2 mi west down a steep gulch to **Stinson Beach.** The 9-mi round-trip hike is one of the best around. Weekends and holidays only you can shorten the hike back by hopping on the hourly Golden Gate Transit Bus 63 (*see* Stinson Beach *in* Chapter 2) at the Stinson Beach park entrance. This will take you to the Mountain Home Inn. From there you can pick up the **Panoramic/Ocean View Trail,** which leads 2 mi downhill to the parking lot. *Tel. 415/388–2596. From U.S. 101, follow signs from Stinson Beach/Hwy. 1 exit.*

MT. TAMALPAIS

Home to Miwok Native Americans for thousand of years before the first European explorers arrived, Mt. Tamalpais (or Mt. Tam, as it's known) is now a playground for hikers and bikers. About 50 mi of trails crisscross the park, and more than 750 species of plant life provide endless scenery. The 2,571-ft summit dominates the Marin skyline; on a clear day you can spot the Sierra Nevada from the top.

HIKING • Of all Mt. Tam's well-worn trails, the 3-mi trip to the top is the most popular. Park at the Bootjack day-use area (5 mi from Panoramic Highway, *see below*) and head north on the **Bootjack Trail** (which also connects Mt. Tam to Muir Woods). At the Mountain Theater turn right onto Ridgecrest Boulevard, following the well-marked paths to the summit. If you want to drive up most of the way, park at the free East Peak parking lot. From there an easy mile on a paved road gets you to the top for a humbling view. Those traveling by bus may take Golden Gate Transit Bus 10, 20, or 50 from the Transbay Terminal and transfer at the Marin City Transfer Center to Golden Gate Transit Bus 63. This deposits you at the Pantoll ranger station.

The 2-mi **Steep Ravine Trail** follows a redwood-lined creek down to the ocean, with waterfalls all along the way. The trail begins at the west end of the parking lot at the **Pantoll ranger station** (tel. 415/388–2070), where you can pick up an excellent trail map ($1). It's all downhill to **Stinson Beach**; take the brutal but scenic 1½-mi **Dipsea Trail** or stick to the trail that leads to **Rocky Point** and the **Steep Ravine Environmental Camp** (1 mi south of Stinson Beach on Highway 1), where you can view seals, sea lions, star fish, and beach crabs. The less strenuous **Rock Spring Trail** starts at the Mountain Theater—an amphitheater with stone seats cut into the hillside—and climbs gently up to the West Point Inn, where you can relax and enjoy a lemonade before returning to the theater or charging uphill another 2 mi to the Middle Peak. To get to the Pantoll ranger station from U.S. 101, take the Stinson Beach/Highway 1 exit, turn left at the first traffic light onto Highway 1, and then turn right onto Panoramic Highway. Parking at the station is $5, but parking is free at roadside pullouts.

BIKING • Before you embark on two wheels, get a map from the **Pantoll ranger station** to find out which trails are legal. From there you can set out for Mt. Tam's **East Peak**; the long but gradual uphill climb pays off at the top, where you get an exhilarating view. If you continue past the East Peak, you're in for an all-day journey. From the ranger station take the **Old Stage Road** uphill a half mile to West Point Inn, where you can grab a glass of lemonade. From the inn go left on the **Old Railroad Grade**, which runs for 2 mi almost to the top of Mt. Tam. It's one of the most popular riding paths on the mountain and gets quite crowded on weekends.

From the top you can either head back the way you came or turn your ride into a 20-mi loop that takes you back down Mt. Tam and halfway up again. If you've got the stamina, go down **East Ridgecrest Drive** and pick up the **Lagunitas–Rock Springs Trail,** which begins on the other side of the dirt parking lot. After a short climb, the trail descends to Lake Lagunitas, where you'll turn right to circle the lake. Turn right again on **Lakeview,** and eventually you'll meet the **Eldridge Grade,** where you start another ascent. Go left at **Indian** and enjoy a steep and bumpy downhill ride. Turn right on **Blithedale Ridge** (past the Hoo Koo E Koo Trail) and take either of two spurs that drop down to the right toward the **Old Railroad Grade.** When you hit West Point Inn—now are you ready for that lemonade?—go left on **Old Stage Road** and head back to the ranger station.

BOLINAS

The 45-mi **Coast Trail** stretches from the Palo Marin trailhead in Bolinas (*see* Marin County *in* Chapter 2) into the middle of the Point Reyes National Seashore. The trailhead is at the end of Mesa Road, just past the bird observatory. For a healthy day hike follow the trail to **Bass Lake** (5½ mi round-trip) or **Pelican Lake** (7 mi round-trip). Either way you'll walk through eucalyptus groves and untamed wetlands and along the edge of the cliffs that overlook the Pacific Ocean. Camping along the trail is allowed only within the boundaries of the national seashore and in designated campgrounds; permits are required.

POINT REYES

Though it's close to the city, Point Reyes seems a world away. Gazing at the rest of Marin County from this national seashore, you'll feel as if you're on a separate island—which is almost true, except that the Tomales Valley joins the little peninsula to the mainland. The San Andreas Fault runs right through the valley, putting Point Reyes on a different tectonic plate than the rest of the continent. Within the peninsula the geography varies greatly; in just a few miles you can see meadows, forests, peaks with panoramic vistas, craggy cliffs overlooking the ocean, and isolated coves. The area erupts with wildflowers from mid-February through July; and though winter sees a lot of rain, that's when the rivers and ponds teem with life and the whales migrate south.

The **Bear Valley Visitor Center** (tel. 415/663–1092) has trail maps, exhibits, and an informative slide show about the park; from there a 1½-mi path leads to **Kule Loklo,** a reconstructed Miwok village that sheds light on the daily lives of the region's first inhabitants. To get to the visitor center, take Bear Valley Road off Route 1, just west of the village of Olema. On weekends only Golden Gate Bus 50, 70, or 80 from the Transbay Terminal connects with Bus 65, which takes you as far as the visitor center. Call ahead for bus schedules—Bus 65 runs only once a day in each direction. Its schedule gives you six hours at Point Reyes, but the round-trip takes four or five hours, so consider reserving a campsite and spending a night under the stars (*see* Marin County *in* Chapter 7).

HIKING • For a hike along a narrow peninsula, with the Pacific crashing on one side and Tomales Bay gently lapping the other, head all the way north to **Tomales Point.** From the visitor center take Bear Valley Road, go left at the stop sign on Sir Francis Drake Boulevard, and bear right at Pierce Point Road, which ends at the historic Pierce Point Ranch. The **Tomales Point Trail** picks up here and heads right through the Tule Elk Range; keep your eyes peeled for these graceful animals. Three miles down the road, the official trail ends, and the sandy footpaths to the cliffs (1½ mi) begin.

For a steep, strenuous hike head to the highest point in the park, Mt. Wittenberg (1,407 ft). Beginning just off the Bear Valley Trailhead, at the south end of the park, the **Mt. Wittenberg Trail** rises 1,250 ft; the final push follows an unmaintained offshoot up to the peak, where you'll be rewarded with a panorama of land and sea. To get down, head back to the Mt. Wittenberg Trail, turn right, and take the **Horse Trail** to the Bear Valley Trail, where another right completes your 6-mi loop.

BIKING • Most of the pristine trails in Point Reyes National Seashore are closed to bikers, but a few open paths and the park's paved roads make for scenic riding. For an easy, beautiful ride, take the **Bear Valley Trail** from the south end of the parking lot. About 3 mi into the ride you'll reach a rack where you can lock your bike while you hike about a mile out to the coast.

A more strenuous, 13-mi ride leaves from Five Brooks, a well-marked parking area off Highway 1, about 3 mi south of Olema. Pick up the **Olema Valley Trail,** which leads to the **Randall Trail** (on the left); cross Highway 1, ascend to Bolinas Ridge, and go right on the **Bolinas Ridge Trail.** About 1⅓ mi down the road, pick up the **McCurdy Trail,** cross Highway 1 again, and take the Olema Valley Trail all the way back.

SOUTH BAY

The gently rolling hills that shelter the San Mateo County Coast provide excellent opportunities for hiking and biking. The area is much less crowded than Marin County, and its small towns and farms give it a sleepy country feel. Plan on driving to these parks since most are inaccessible by public transit. The inland town of **La Honda,** on Highway 84 (*see* The San Mateo County Coast *in* Chapter 2), is a good place to stop for picnic supplies before you head into one of the nearby state or county parks.

PACIFICA

Biking is prohibited on most trails around here, but hiking opportunities abound. The hike along **Sweeney Ridge** is mediocre, but its proximity to the city and an amazing view of the coastline make it a worthwhile getaway. To reach the peak, hike 2 mi up a moderate grade through coastal scrub and grasslands that bloom with wildflowers in spring; the trailhead is at the end of Sneath Lane. A monument to the Spanish captain, Gaspar de Portola, who supposedly discovered San Francisco Bay from this point in 1769, stands atop the peak. Most people are content to contemplate the view from here, but if you want to keep going, you can hike the **Baquiano Trail** about 2 more mi down to Pacifica (be prepared for wind and zero visibility on foggy summer afternoons). To get here, take I–280 or Skyline Boulevard (Highway 35) to the Sneath Lane exit in San Bruno. Follow Sneath Lane west to the Sweeney Ridge Gate, about a 10-minute drive.

San Pedro Valley County Park has several mellow hiking trails that take you through shady woods and meadows exploding with wildflowers. In winter and spring the half-mile **Brooks Falls Overlook Trail** affords great views of a three-tiered 275-ft waterfall. The even-shorter **Plaskon Nature Trail** abounds with plants and wildlife. For more trail tips or a detailed guide to the nature trail, stop by the **visitor center** (600 Oddstead Blvd., tel. 650/355–8289), open weekends 10–4 only. The park entrance fee is $3, though it's usually not collected on weekdays. To reach the park, take Highway 1 into Pacifica and turn east on Linda Mar Boulevard. When it dead-ends, make a right onto Oddstead Boulevard; the entrance is 50 yards up on the left.

SADDLE SORES?
BUM'S THE WORD

Golden Gate Park Stables (JFK Blvd. at 36th Ave., in Golden Gate Park, tel. 415/668–7360) has daily one-hour guided rides for $25. For $35 the East Bay's Chabot Riding Stables (14600 Skyline Blvd., tel. 510/638–0610) will guide you on horseback along a large, two-hour loop through the hills and valleys surrounding Anthony Chabot Regional Park. South of San Francisco on Highway 1 lies Sea Horse Ranch (tel. 415/726–9903); rent a horse ($25 an hour or $40 for two hours) for an unguided ride through 10 mi of verdant trails, ending in a stretch of sandy beach.

LA HONDA

Eleven miles east of Highway 1 along Highway 84 lies the beautiful and secluded **Portola Redwood State Park.** Stop by the **visitor center** (tel. 650/948–9098) at the entrance, where you must pay a $6 per-car day-use fee (walk-ins are free). Here you can also purchase a trail map for $1 or get information on guided nature walks and other activities.

HIKING • For a moderately difficult 4½-mi hike through towering redwood groves, catch the steep **Coyote Ridge Trail,** just north of the visitor center. Follow it to Upper Escape Road, where you'll turn left; then turn left again onto the **Slate Creek Trail,** shoot downhill on the steep **Summit Trail,** and follow the service road back to the visitor center. To reach Portola, take I-280 to Highway 84W to Skyline Boulevard (Highway 35). Go south 7 mi, then turn west on Alpine Road.

BIKING • Some of the best mountain biking in the area is found in **Pescadero Creek County Park,** near La Honda. You can access the trails from nearby **San Mateo County Memorial Park** (9500 Pescadero Rd., Loma Mar, tel. 650/879–0212): From Memorial's visitor center take Pescadero Road back toward La Honda, turn right on Wurr Road, cross the bridge, and you'll come to the well-maintained dirt-and-gravel **Old Haul Road,** where you can ride to your heart's content.

BUTANO STATE PARK

This little-known state park in the Santa Cruz Mountains occupies a small canyon heavily forested with redwoods and ferns. Even when its campsites are full, you can still find solitude in Butano. Be sure to buy the 50¢ map available at the entrance station: In addition to marking the trails, it has information on the park's wildlife communities.

HIKING • A great hike that will introduce you to the park's beautiful terrain starts at the **Año Nuevo Trail,** to the right of the entrance station (watch out here for stinging nettles and poison oak). Less than a half mile up the steep ascent, you'll come to the **Año Overlook**—on a clear day you can see south to Año Nuevo Island. Continuing on, you'll run into **Olmo Fire Road.** Turn left and then left again on the **Goat Hill Trail** for a 2-mi walk through the quiet forests. When the trail hits the main road, follow it to the right for the highlight of the hike: **Little Butano Creek Trail,** where the trail meanders along Little Butano Creek, which is crisscrossed by fallen redwoods. At the end of the trail turn right onto the main road, right again onto **Mill Ox Trail,** then left onto **Jackson Flat Trail,** which takes you through forests and fields of wildflowers while the creek rushes along far below. Jackson Flat will deposit you back at the entrance station—for a total hike of about 7 mi. For a gentler introduction to Butano, join one of the ranger-led 1½-hour nature walks, which leave from the park entrance every Saturday and Sunday at 2.

To get to Butano, take Highway 1 about 15 mi south from Half Moon Bay to Pescadero; turn left on Pescadero Road, right on Cloverdale Road, and go about 5 mi to the park entrance. It costs $6 to park within the grounds, but you can usually ditch your car for free at the turnoff just south of the Cloverdale Road entrance.

BIKING • You can ride on any of the 10 mi of fire roads, though mountain bikes are forbidden on trails. Your best bet is to park at the entrance gate near the corner of Cloverdale and Canyon roads, about a mile north of the main park entrance, and ride **Butano Fire Road.** If you're in good shape, you can take it all the way to **Olmo Fire Road,** which leads back to the park's main road, and pedal back to your car.

IN-LINE SKATING

On Sunday, **Golden Gate Park** closes to motor vehicles to make way for a confluence of skaters and cyclists that glide through the park. The **Marina District** is another hotbed for bladed youths on weekday afternoons and weekends. The numerous parks around the Bay Area are agreeable for sport blading (skating on unpaved surfaces), and devotees highly recommend **Angel Island**—but it's bumpy going for novices. Experienced (and fearless) East Bay skaters head to **Tilden Park** (*see* Hiking and Biking, *above*). Nimitz Way provides almost 9 mi (round-trip) of paved path, some of it with distant views of San Francisco Bay.

Skates on Haight (1818 Haight St., tel. 415/752–8375) rents in-line skates ($6 per hour, $24 per day) right outside the entrance to Golden Gate Park. **Skate Pro Sports** (2549 Irving St., at 27th Ave., in the Sunset District, tel. 415/752–8776) charges $5 an hour, $20 a day. If you want to skate along the Marina Green boardwalk, rent skates from **Marina Skate and Snowboards** (2271 Chestnut St., near Scott St., tel. 415/567–8400), where the rate is $5.50 an hour, $19 a day. All rental stores give free lessons; Marina Skate and Snowboards and Skate Pro Sports even throw in a free rental for the duration of the lesson.

Friday nights you can watch nearly 500 in-line skaters flying through San Francisco on a 13-mi figure eight. The Midnight Rollers meet at the Ferry Building at 8 PM. Join them, or just observe. Contact David Miles (tel. 415/752–1967) for information.

PICKUP GAMES

BASKETBALL

The following San Francisco courts usually get going weekday afternoons as well as weekend mornings between 8 and 11. **Grattan Playground** (Grattan and Stanyan Sts.), near Golden Gate Park, sees casual play weekday afternoons around 3:30; weekends draw larger crowds and more ferocious competition. In the Marina, the popular **Moscone Recreation Center** (Chestnut and Laguna Sts.) has courts with night lighting and unforgiving double rims. Games at the **Potrero Hill Recreation Center** (Arkansas and 22nd Sts.) get highly competitive, especially Monday and Thursday nights. Relatively low-key four-on-four games begin early on weekends at the two full-length courts of Noe Valley's **James Lick Middle School** (Clipper and Castro Sts.). The small courts in the Panhandle of Golden Gate Park, between Oak and Fell streets, have competitive games going all the time.

In north Berkeley the short court at **Live Oak Park** (Shattuck Ave. and Berryman St.) hosts weekend three-on-three games, but the number of people waiting to play can be considerable. A more intimidating game goes on at **Ohlone Park** (Hearst Ave. near California St.). In south Berkeley the court at **People's Park** (Haste St. between Telegraph Ave. and Bowditch St.) is always hopping, usually with UC students cutting class. If you *really* want to get serious, you'll find competitive players on the courts at the **Recreational Sports Facility** on the UC Berkeley campus (2301 Bancroft Way, tel. 510/643–8038), but you'll have to shell out $8 for a gym day pass to play.

SOCCER

Sunday mornings year-round a crowd gathers at Golden Gate Park's **Polo Field** (Middle Dr. W near Martin Luther King Jr. Dr.) for impromptu soccer games, where the players—almost exclusively male—represent a wide range of skill levels. League teams square off at the three fields behind the **Beach Chalet**, at the westernmost edge of the park. You'll find women's teams there on Saturday and men's on Sunday. Wednesday after work postcollege footsters play at the **Marina Green** (Marina Blvd. and Fillmore St.), where lack of night lighting means less play on shorter winter days.

In Berkeley the field at the top of **Clark Kerr Campus,** also known as **Dwight/Derby** (off Dwight Way east of Warring St.), has coed pickup games weekday evenings, women's (usually) Tuesday or Thursday evening, and mostly men's on weekend mornings; the courts quiet down when the university is not in session. Down the hill, **Willard Park** (Derby St. between Hillegass Ave. and Regent St.) usually has Friday-afternoon pickup games from 2 or 3 until 6. In winter a casual mixed game can often be found between

Russell and Oregon streets, just off Martin Luther King Jr. Way, at 10 AM Sunday. Serious, testosterone-charged pickup games take place weekdays at 5 and weekends at 4 on **Kleeberger Field's** AstroTurf (Piedmont Ave. at Stadium Rim Way).

ULTIMATE FRISBEE

The rules of ultimate Frisbee combine those of football and soccer, except that ultimate is a noncontact sport with no referees, and players call their own fouls. For the latest on pickup games in Berkeley and Oakland, call the **East Bay Ultimate Hotline** (tel. 510/464–4494).

Sharon Meadow, off Kezar Drive in Golden Gate Park, sometimes sees coed pickup games of up to 40 people. Frisbee fanatics gather here every Tuesday and Thursday evening while it's still light out and on late mornings every weekend. **Julius Kahn Playground** (W. Pacific Ave. between Spruce and Locust Sts.), near the southeast corner of the Presidio, hosts pickup games Wednesday evening and Saturday morning. Other popular places to play in the East Bay are **Cedar Rose Park** (Oxford St., between Cedar and Rose Sts.), which hosts games Sunday morning at 11 and, in summer, Thursday at 6 PM, and **Oakland Tech High School** (4351 Broadway, at 43rd St.), where games take place weekends at 1 PM.

VOLLEYBALL

On weekends in San Francisco people set up their own nets at the **Marina Green** (*see* Soccer, *above*) and nearby at the **Moscone Recreation Center** (*see* Basketball, *above*). At both locations you'll usually find high-skill two-on-two games. Also intimidating are the six-on-six weekend games at several spots along JFK Drive in **Golden Gate Park.** You can rent nets for $13 for the weekend at **Outdoors Unlimited** (*see* chapter introduction).

The **San Francisco Recreation and Parks Department** hosts friendly open play, usually on Monday night at 7 ($2); call ahead since times and locations vary. You'll also find games at the **South of Market Rec Center** (270 6th St., at Folsom St., tel. 415/554–9532), the **Glen Park Rec Center** (Bosworth St. and O'Shaughnessy Blvd., tel. 415/337–4705), and for women-only play, **St. Mary's Rec Center** (Murray St. and Justin Dr., tel. 415/695–5006).

In the East Bay, **People's Park** (*see* Basketball, *above*) has two outdoor sand courts, but you may have to fight for your right to play. Pickup games take place Tuesday night at the asphalt court in **Live Oak Park** (*see* Basketball, *above*). Players also set up on the grass in **Ohlone Park** (Hearst Ave. between Sacramento Ave. and Milvia St.) on Saturday morning. For $5 you can take part in open play on either indoor sand or hard courts in Emeryville, at **City Beach Sports and Recreation Center** (4701 Doyle St., at 47th St., tel. 510/428–1221).

ROCK CLIMBING

Although the proper rigging can be expensive, it's a death wish to buy used climbing gear, and nobody rents ropes in the Bay Area for liability reasons. **REI** (*see* chapter introduction) is a good place to go for the essentials; they also rent climbing shoes for $8 the first day, $5 for each subsequent day. **Marmot Mountain Works,** in Berkeley (3049 Adeline St., tel. 510/849–0735), has a knowledgeable staff that can outfit you with the climbing basics.

Indoor climbing gyms have become popular places for newcomers to learn the sport and meet climbing buddies. **Cal Adventures** (*see* chapter introduction) offers all sorts of classes, from one-day rock-wall introductions ($40) to weekend climbing classes that include camping at Pinnacles National Monument ($90). Cal Adventures also has an outdoor climbing wall available to all those who can pass a belay proficiency test. You can rent equipment (shoes, harness, belay device, and a helmet) for $2; a day's access to the wall costs $8. **CityRock Gym,** in Emeryville (1250 45th St., tel. 510/654–2510), is in a 6,000-sq-ft warehouse with sculpted walls up to 40 ft high and a separate area for bouldering (free climbing). A day spent climbing the walls will cost you $14, $20 if you need shoe and harness rentals. They also have a full-service climbing school, where two-hour introductory and intermediate lessons taught by some of the nation's top climbers cost $35. **Class 5 Fitness,** in San Rafael (25B Dodie St., tel. 415/485–6931), has 35-ft walls ($12 day fee) and rents shoes and harness ($6) for in-house use; they also conduct climbing classes. The relatively new **Mission Cliffs Rock Climbing Center** (2295 Harrison St., tel. 415/550–0515), site of the National Indoor Championships, sells day passes for $14 and rents equipment for $6. And, finally, if you already know what you're doing, you can hoist yourself up the climbing wall at **REI** (*see* chapter introduction) Thursday 5 PM–8 PM and Saturday 10–noon.

One of the best places for new climbers to practice and meet seasoned veterans is **Indian Rock Park,** in north Berkeley, where Shattuck Avenue dead-ends (*see* East Bay *in* Chapter 2). When Indian Rock gets too crowded, more experienced climbers head to Morter Rock, a few hundred feet uphill. Arid **Mt. Diablo State Park** has excellent climbing areas up to 120 ft high in some areas. The sandstone rock varies in hardness, with new routes simply waiting to be discovered. The two main climbing areas are the more charted Boy Scout Rocks, in the southeast corner of the park, and Pine Canyon, just past the North Gate fee station, which is closed from early February to late June for the raptor nesting season. Head east on Highway 24 toward Walnut Creek, then south on I-680. Exit at Diablo Road, follow it to the park entrance ($5 day-use fee), and look for the Rock City parking lot to the right.

In a beautiful wooded area of the Santa Cruz Mountains, **Castle Rock State Park** is sandstone rock, with some routes recommended for novices. To get here, take I-280 south past Palo Alto, continue south on Route 85, west on Big Basin Road, and then left on Skyline Boulevard. After 2 mi look for the parking lot to the right. Directly south of Stinson Beach along Highway 1—look for the dirt pullout about a mile south of Stinson—**Mickey's Beach** is popular with nude bathers as well as serious rock climbers. The greenstone rock edges its way toward the ocean, making 30–65 ft of spectacular climbing on well-established routes with names like Endless Bummer. The rocky outcropping to the north is suitable for bouldering. For information on other locations, including route maps and difficulty levels, look for *Bay Area Rock,* a guide-book by local expert Jim Thornburg, available at CityRock and other stores ($9.95).

Don't surf at Mavericks in Half Moon Bay unless you know what you're doing. Its 35- to 40-ft waves are some of the biggest in the world and can be lethal—even for Hawaiian expert surfer Mark Foo.

WATER SPORTS

SAILING

The San Francisco Bay is one of the most challenging places in the country to sail, with a remarkably consistent westerly wind. If you're up for testing the winds, you can rent a 15-ft Coronado from **Cal Adventures** (*see* chapter introduction). Another option is to sign up for a one-day excursion with one of the local sailing clubs; most start from the Berkeley Marina, at the west end of University Avenue. AC Transit Bus 51M heads to the marina from downtown Berkeley. The **Olympic Circle Sailing Club** (1 Spinnaker Way, near the Berkeley Marina, tel. 800/223–2984) conducts a variety of afternoon sails for about $65. **Spinnaker Sailing/Rendezvous Charter** (Pier 40, South Beach Harbor, San Francisco, tel. 415/543–7333) has a two-hour sunset sail ($22.50) on Wednesday, Friday, and Saturday, as well as Sunday-afternoon excursions.

SEA KAYAKING

The Bay Area's many lagoons, estuaries, inlets, and of course ocean waters allow both novices and experts to roll their kayaks gleefully year-round. Check the quarterly bulletin published by **Outdoors Unlimited** (*see* chapter introduction) for listings of free kayak and canoe workshops and volunteer-led trips. OU's day trips and moonlight paddles are some of the cheapest around—some are free, and others cost $60. Berkeley's **Cal Adventures** (*see* chapter introduction) has sea-kayaking day trips, instruction, and rentals at cut-rate prices, including comprehensive five-day classes for a bargain $120–$150. **California Canoe and Kayak** (409 Water St., Jack London Sq., Oakland, tel. 510/893–7833 or 800/366–9804) offers the widest range of classes and trips, including lessons and outings for women only. Two-day introductory classes run $90, and outings cost $80–$600, depending on destination and length of the trip. **Sea Trek** (Schoonmaker Point Marina, Sausalito, tel. 415/488–1000 or 415/332–4465) also has classes and rentals, and they offer special kayak trips with naturalist guides. Sea Trek rents equipment for about $7–$10 an hour, and a seven-hour introductory class costs $95. Other outings include a full-day trip to Angel Island for $95–$100.

A good place for beginners is **Richardson Bay,** between Tiburon and Sausalito in Marin County. With its calm waters, gorgeous locale, and bird-watching opportunities, Richardson makes a good launching point for an intermediate-level trip to Angel Island or an advanced trip through the rough and dangerous currents under the Golden Gate Bridge. For even calmer waters head farther north to **Bolinas Lagoon,** a protected estuary where you'll paddle past egret nesting sites. **Drake's Estuary,** another bird-infested spot, is a beautiful bay on the Point Reyes peninsula with calm waters for beginners. The placid waters of **Tomales Bay,** also off the coast of Point Reyes National Seashore, claim a resident flock of white pelicans as well as jellyfish and starfish. Beginners and intermediates will feel comfortable in the western part of the bay, with its stunning views of coves and beaches on shore.

EXTREME SWIMMING

Who needs to jump out of an airplane or ski down a sheer cliff face when you can swim in San Francisco Bay? Not as thrilling, you think? We'll see what you say when you hit the 55°F water. To minimize the dangers of boat traffic and strong tides, hook up with the members of the Dolphin Swimming and Boating Club (502 Jefferson St., tel. 415/441–9329) or the South End Rowing Club (500 Jefferson St., tel. 415/776–7372), both at Aquatic Park; they'll give you pointers and maybe even convince you to join in the biannual swims to Alcatraz Island—yikes!

SURFING

Throughout the Bay Area, swells are best during fall and winter, when storms far out at sea send ripples across the Pacific. Call **Wise Surfboards** (tel. 415/665–9473) for a recorded message on conditions in the city. For conditions at Stinson Beach call the **Livewater** surf shop (*see below*); for Santa Cruz conditions call the **O'Neil Surf Shop** hot line (tel. 408/475–2275); for Pacifica conditions call the **Nor-Cal** surf shop (*see below*).

Two world-class surfing instructors offer lessons near Santa Cruz. Champion surfer Richard Schmidt (tel. 408/423–0928) teaches classes through the **Santa Cruz Parks and Recreation Department** (tel. 408/429–3663): A two-day group lesson, two hours each day, costs $68. You can also sign up for private lessons with Schmidt; for $60 an hour (equipment included), he guarantees first-timers will ride their boards. Or head to Cowell Beach, where instructor Ed Guzman conducts **CLUB ED Surf School** (tel. 800/287–7873) in front of the Dream Inn. A two-hour group lesson ($70) starts you off on an oversize board, perfect for beginners who don't yet have their balance. If you don't get the hang of it the first time, you can come back for another two-hour lesson for only $45. Ed also rents a variety of boards for about $25 a day, wet suits for $10, and booties for $3.

At **Outdoors Unlimited** (*see* chapter introduction), weekend wet-suit rentals run $17–$21. **Livewater** (3450 Hwy. 1, Stinson Beach, tel. 415/868–0333) rents surfboards for $20–$30 a day, wet suits for $10. To the south, local surfers staff the **Nor-Cal Surfshop** (5460 Cabrillo Hwy., Pacifica, tel. 415/738–9283), where you can rent a soft board for $10 a day. In Santa Cruz, the **O'Neil Surf Shop** (1149 41st Ave., tel. 408/475–4151) rents boards for $10 a day and wet suits for $8 a day.

Surf's up at **Ocean Beach,** west of Golden Gate Park, but you may wish it would go back down. Winter waves get as big here as anywhere in the world (20–25 ft), but experienced surfers complain about their shape. Even when the swells are manageable, the current is strong. You don't have to be an expert to surf Ocean Beach, but it's not a place to learn unless you're into self-abuse. Waves are cleaner at **Fort Point,** beneath the Golden Gate Bridge on the southeast side, though the current and rocks may deter beginners.

Beginners will have better luck outside the city. Drive north along Highway 1 to **Stinson Beach,** where shallow beach break is not demanding, and the waves are neither fast nor big. This is a popular beach for sunbathing, but the water is rarely crowded. Or drive 45 minutes south of San Francisco along Highway 1 to **Pacifica State Beach,** also known as **Linda Mar Beach.** Pacifica breaks best at high tide, with smaller waves for beginners at the south end of the beach. Just north of the rocky promontory, **Rockaway Beach** has bigger waves, but it's more crowded and competitive. Adventurous types go to the isolated state beaches between Pacifica and Santa Cruz.

WINDSURFING

The San Francisco Bay ranks as the third-best spot for windsurfing in the United States, after Oregon's Royal Gorge and Maui. Summer is the season to tack across the bay: From April to August westerly winds provide optimal conditions for windsurfing almost anywhere in the Bay Area. Winds are sporadic during the rest of the year, blowing either north or south. During winter the air can be as cold as the water, and you'll need a full wetsuit. Some summer days are hot enough to go bottomless (in regard to wet suits, that is).

Berkeley Boardsports (2936 Lyon St., tel. 415/929–7873) rents high-performance Windsurfers for $45 a day, not including wet suit. Beginners will find more basic boards at the store's other branches: on Gilman Street in Berkeley (tel. 510/527–7873), Crown Beach in Alameda (tel. 415/925–0543), and Larkspur Landing in San Rafael (tel. 415/925–8585). Rates are generally $20 for two hours or $30 per day, including wet suit.

Cal Adventures (*see* chapter introduction) has cheap windsurfing lessons: Seven hours of instruction on the bay with an added hour of recreational windsurfing, board included, costs $60. Since conditions on the bay are harsh for a beginning windsurfer, however, you may want to consider learning on a lake. **Spinnaker Sailing** (3160 N. Shoreline Blvd., Mountain View, tel. 415/965–7474) offers beginner and advanced classes ($130 for two days) on an artificial lake. To learn on a real lake, make the half-hour drive east from Oakland to **Windsurf Del Valle** (Lake Del Valle, Livermore, tel. 510/455–4008), the country's largest windsurfing school. The $95 six-hour beginners' course usually lasts two days, but the instructors will give you additional days of instruction for free if you need more help.

The **San Francisco School of Windsurfing** (3Com Park or Lake Merced, tel. 415/753–3235) specializes in increasing your skill level quickly. Beginners start at Lake Merced, but you soon learn to tackle the more popular bay. The two-day beginning course costs $130 (equipment included). Rentals cost $16 an hour, including wet suit, booties, and harness; all-day rentals are $40.

If you and your Windsurfer are swept out to San Quentin, just east of Larkspur Landing, you will be escorted off the property by some distinctly unamused prison guards. Don't laugh—it's happened before.

Alameda's **Crown Beach,** with easy access to shallow waters, has the best conditions in the East Bay for learning the sport. The wind is usually light and blows toward the shore, so if you zig when you should have zagged, you won't be lost at sea. The beach is 10 minutes from downtown Oakland: Drive south on Broadway, go through the Webster Street tube to Alameda, continue on Highway 61, turn right on 8th Street, and look for the sign. Or take Bus 51 south on Broadway from downtown to Webster and Santa Clara streets, then walk a quarter mile west to the water.

In Marin County, **Larkspur Landing** is good for mixed windsurfing abilities. The light wind close to shore accommodates beginners, while the more advanced windsurfer will be challenged farther out in the bay. Mornings are calmest and best for beginners; the wind picks up in the afternoon. The drawback: When the wind is light, you have to paddle out from the rocky shore while keeping a wary eye out for ferries. From U.S. 101 take the San Rafael/Richmond exit east and continue a quarter mile past the Larkspur Ferry terminal.

The **Berkeley Marina,** at the west end of University Avenue, requires intermediate to advanced skills. Access to the water is problematic because you must launch off either the dock or the rocks—and big weekend crowds mean you may have to wait for even one of these spots. The windy and choppy conditions provide plenty of wave-jumping opportunities for experienced windsurfers who like to spend time in the air. From I–80 take the University Avenue exit west to the end.

Crissy Field, in San Francisco's Presidio, challenges even advanced windsurfers. Beach access makes getting into the water easy, but with the strong tides and currents, getting out is a task. The current could easily sweep an unprepared windsurfer under the Golden Gate Bridge and into the Pacific or take you across the bay to Treasure Island. In addition, boat and ship traffic makes the water tough to navigate. Proceed with caution: More rescues are required here than in all other Bay Area sites combined.

Flat water, strong winds, and easy bay access make **3Com Park** (formerly known as Candlestick) a favorite with windsurfers who want speed. Winds average 19–25 mph, but they can get as high as 55 mph. You have to be an expert to handle the offshore winds, which carry you right into the bay—if the wind dies, you'll be stranded there. Parking costs $8 on game days during baseball season and $20 during football. For directions to the park, *see* Spectator Sports, *below*.

Waves are choppy at **Coyote Point,** south of San Francisco International Airport. The wind is moderate close to the shore, but farther out the surf will challenge even the most experienced. The entrance fee for **Coyote Point Park** (tel. 650/573–2592) is $4, well worth it for the use of hot showers. Follow U.S. 101 south past the airport to the Poplar Avenue exit, take Humboldt Street, turn right on Peninsula Avenue, go right across the overpass, and bear left onto Coyote Point Drive.

SPECTATOR SPORTS

BASEBALL

The baseball rivalry between San Francisco and the East Bay is as intense as ever. The National League's **San Francisco Giants** (tel. 415/467–8000) hope to have a new downtown ballpark completed by 2000. In the meantime they continue to play at **3Com Park,** in the far-southeast corner of the city. Tickets are $6 for bleacher seats, $7–$21 for those on the plaza level. Bus 9x ($5 round-trip) heads for 3Com Park from Montgomery BART on game days, or take U.S. 101 south to the 3Com Park exit. The American League's **Oakland A's** (tel. 510/638–0500) play at the newly renovated **Oakland Coliseum.** Bleacher seats cost $4, those on the plaza level are $5–$25. The stadium is connected via an elevated walkway with the Coliseum BART station.

BASKETBALL

Since the **Golden State Warriors** secured first pick in the 1995 NBA draft, many people feel they are now a team worth watching. Tickets ($19.50–$60) go on sale in late September or early October and sell out fast; call BASS. The Warriors play at the Oakland Coliseum Arena.

FOOTBALL

The **San Francisco '49ers** have built a huge fan base from all over northern California, and tickets for home games at 3Com Park are nearly impossible to get. Season-ticket holders have a lock on most seats, and when the rest go on sale in July, they usually sell out within the hour, despite the $40 and up price tag. Call the ticket office (tel. 415/468–2249) to find out what date tickets go on sale (usually in mid-July); then call BASS (tel. 415/776–1999 or 510/762–2277) at 9 AM that day.

The big news is the return of the **Oakland Raiders** from Los Angeles, a move that is bringing Raiders fans all over the Bay Area out of hiding. The city of Oakland is also thrilled, no doubt, by the revenue and publicity to be raked in by that the popular team, which left Oakland for Los Angeles in 1982 ("L.A. Traitors," newspaper headlines blared at the time). The Raiders play at the Oakland Coliseum. For ticket information, call 800/949–2626.

HOCKEY

The **San Jose Sharks** (tel. 408/287–4275) has a loyal following, and tickets to games in the new San Jose Arena ($15–$73) sell quickly. The season runs October–April. From San Francisco CalTrain will get you to the San Jose Arena. There's also a shuttle to and from parking lots in downtown San Jose.

SOCCER

On April 6, 1996, the **San Jose Clash** (tel. 408/985–4625) kicked off major-league soccer at **Spartan Stadium** with an exciting win over D.C. United. Whether San Jose embraces the Clash as it did the Sharks remains to be seen, but ticket sales are already brisk. The season runs April–September; tickets are $12–$35. Take CalTrain to the San Jose station, then take Bus 25 in the direction of East San Jose.

COLLEGE SPORTS

The Bay Area's two big universities, UC Berkeley (known as Cal) and Stanford University, in Palo Alto, have been arch rivals for close to a century—especially when it comes to football. The **Cal Bears** football team, which plays in Memorial Stadium on the east side of campus, has improved a bit in recent years, and you'll find that even the most blasé Berkeley bohemian may work up a sweat over their more important games. Tickets cost $14 for general admission and about $22 for reserved seating. The Cal men's and women's **basketball** teams are not exactly championship teams, but they have a loyal fan base. Games are usually played at Harmon Gym on campus, and men's tickets (about $18) are usually snatched up the day they go on sale. (Games also occasionally take place at the Oakland Coliseum; for these, last-minute tickets are usually available.) Women's basketball tickets cost $5 general admission, $7 reserved. **Baseball,** played at Evans Diamond on the corner of Bancroft Way and Oxford Street, costs $5. To buy tickets for Cal sports, call 800/462–3277.

Stanford's spectator sports revolve mainly around their football team, the **Cardinal** (named for the color, not the bird), which plays at Stanford Stadium. The other strong team on campus is women's **basketball,** a consistent NCAA championship contender. For information on tickets for all Stanford sports, call 800/232–8225 weekdays 9–4. Football tickets cost $10 general admission, $25 reserved, and about $50 for the Big Game, and they go on sale at the beginning of June. Tickets to **men's basketball** games, played at Maples Pavilion, go on sale in September and cost $15 for reserved seats, $6 general admission. **Women's basketball** costs $13 reserved, $6 general admission. **Baseball games** are played at Stanford's Sunken Diamond. Tickets cost $5 and are available at the game.

9 DAY AND WEEKEND TRIPS

REVISED BY DEKE CASTLEMAN, KATHLEEN DODGE, JONATHAN LEFF,

AND JENNIFER WEDEL

hether you're looking for a day at the beach or a weekend in the mountains, a New Age healing session or an isolated cross-country ski trail, odds are good you'll find what you want somewhere in the diverse and gorgeous country surrounding San Francisco. Perhaps more than any other major American city, San Francisco is distinguished by its proximity to dramatic natural terrain and interesting small towns. North of the city lies California's world-famous **Wine Country;** to the south, **Santa Cruz** is a gathering point for surfers, New Agers, and neohippies. Continuing south, **Monterey** brims with tourists, harbor seals, and an incredible aquarium, while **Big Sur** rewards hardy campers and hikers with its rugged beauty. An afternoon's drive east at the right time of year will bring you to that most un-Californian phenomenon: snow—in the mountains surrounding **Lake Tahoe** or in **Yosemite,** California's favorite national park. Tahoe is home to some of the country's best skiing, while Yosemite provides northern Californians with a place to rock climb, hike, and hang out with the bears and other wildlife of the Sierra Nevada. You can escape to any one of these world-class spots in no more than four hours if you've got access to a car, and with patience and a little pretrip planning, public transit will get you into the great wide open as well.

THE WINE COUNTRY

Believe it or not, California's Wine Country lives up to its reputation. It's that beautiful, that elegant, occasionally that snooty, and definitely worth the 50-mi northeast trek from San Francisco. Wine novices shouldn't feel intimidated—just drink away and ask questions later. Many wineries will pour you glass after glass of free samples. Choose carefully, though: A number of Napa Valley wineries charge a $3–$6 tasting fee, which can add up if you're making the rounds.

Most vineyards are concentrated in the Napa and Sonoma valleys, but the Wine Country actually stretches north through Healdsburg and all the way into Lake and Mendocino counties. Vintners have been making wine here for well over 100 years, but it was only in 1976, when a cabernet sauvignon from

Bartholomew Park Winery, **21**
Beaulieu Vineyards, **9**
Benziger, **18**
Beringer Winery, **6**
Buena Vista, **22**
Château St. Jean, **15**
Clos Pegase, **2**
Field Stone, **1**
Freemark Abbey, **5**
Gundlach-Bundschu, **23**
Hakusan Sake Gardens, **25**
Kunde, **16**
Mumm Napa Valley, **8**
Nichelini, **14**
Niebaum - Copolla Estate, **7**
Ravenswood, **20**
Robert Mondavi, **10**
RustRidge, **13**
S. Anderson, **11**
Schug, **24**
Sterling Vineyards, **3**
Trefethen Vineyards, **12**
Valley of the Moon, **19**
Wellington, **17**
Wermuth, **4**

Stag's Leap won a blind taste test in Paris, that Californians began boasting and people all over the world began buying. Since then production has skyrocketed. Twenty-five years ago there were only about 25 wineries; now there are nearly 300.

Napa Valley has the greatest number of wineries, but many are expensive and pretentious. Once upon a time visitors were greeted with open arms—and flowing bottles—by jolly vintners thankful for even a trickle of business. These days you'll have to search out Napa Valley's back-road wineries to get this kind of reception. Alternatively, head to Sonoma, home to a greater number of small, family-run wineries. In both counties the farther you stray from the main drag, the better off you'll be. Remember to call ahead though, since many smaller wineries have tours by appointment only.

If you need a break from the wineries, you can luxuriate in the hot springs, mud baths, and bubbling mineral baths of Calistoga; loiter in the lovely Spanish mission and old adobes of Sonoma; or browse through the small museums devoted to former residents Jack London and Robert Louis Stevenson, both of whom wrote about the area. Be forewarned, though: An overnight stay in the Wine Country can take a monster-size bite out of your budget. Lodging tends to be even more expensive than in San Francisco, and food is pricey as well. Consider making the Wine Country a day trip from San Francisco. Otherwise, you can economize by eating at roadside produce stands and sleeping in the state parks. You might not even notice the difference after a couple samples of wine.

BASICS

VISITOR INFORMATION

The **Napa Valley Visitors' Bureau** (1310 Napa Town Center, 94559, tel. 707/226–7459), open daily 9–5, provides information and maps. (Note: They don't answer the phone on weekends.) The **Sonoma Valley Visitors' Bureau** (10 East Spain St., Sonoma 95476, tel. 707/996–1090), open daily 9–5 (until 7 in summer), gives advice on what to see and do in the "other" valley. Additionally, most wineries carry *Spotlight's Wine Country Guide,* a free monthly with maps, coupons, and winery information.

WHEN TO GO

During the autumn harvest season you'll see some real action in the wine cellars. In both spring and fall wildflowers and mustard plants bloom amid the endless rows of manicured vines. Try to avoid the Wine Country in summer: The dry, dusty valleys become even drier and dustier, and the crowds can be suffocating.

COMING AND GOING

BY CAR

Traffic can be heavy, especially on weekends and during rush hours (7–9 and 4–6). From San Francisco take **U.S. 101** north over the Golden Gate Bridge and connect with **Highway 37E,** near Ignacio. From here take **Highway 121** north to **Highway 12N** for Sonoma, or follow Highway 121 as it curves east toward **Highway 29** for Napa. If you're only visiting the Napa Valley or are coming from the East Bay, take **I–80** north and exit at Highway 37W, in Vallejo. Highway 37 joins up with Highway 29 north to Napa. Even when traffic is heavy, it shouldn't take more than two hours; on good days you'll be there in less than an hour.

BY BUS

Golden Gate Transit (tel. 415/455–2000 or 707/541–2000) provides bus service from San Francisco and Marin County to towns throughout Sonoma County. Bus 90 makes the two-hour trek from San Francisco to Sonoma ($4.50) twice every weekday. On weekends you'll have to take the bus to Petaluma and transfer to **Sonoma County Transit** (*see* Getting Around, *below*). **Greyhound** has service from San Francisco's Transbay Terminal (*see* Bus Travel *in* Chapter 1) once a day to Napa—2½ hours, $15 one-way—and Middletown, 4¼ hours, $19 one-way; twice daily to Sonoma, lasting three or four hours depending on whether you change in Vallejo or Santa Rosa ($17 one-way). Tickets are cheaper midweek.

GETTING AROUND

Unless you've hit one winery too many, orienting yourself in the Wine Country shouldn't be too difficult: Both the Napa and Sonoma valleys have main north–south arteries (Highways 29 and 12, respectively) that connect towns and vineyards alike. **Highway 29** begins in the medium-size town of Napa and stretches north through Yountville, Oakville, Rutherford, St. Helena, and Calistoga, continuing north to Middletown and Clear Lake. A parallel route, **Silverado Trail,** avoids most of Highway 29's traffic lights (and jams), making for a more scenic and speedy ride. In the Sonoma Valley **Highway 12** runs north from Sonoma's main plaza, zigzagging east and then north through the towns of Glen Ellen and Kenwood before reaching Santa Rosa. East–west crossroads between the two valleys are **Highway 121** from Napa, the scenic **Oakville Grade/Trinity Road** from Oakville, and the **Petrified Forest Trail** from Calistoga.

BY CAR

In summer much of Napa's traffic can be avoided by staying off Highway 29 and exploring the less crowded and more scenic Silverado Trail, which parallels the highway a mile to the east. Exit Highway 29 at any point between Napa and Calistoga and follow the Silverado Trail signs.

BY BUS

Seeing the Wine Country by public transit requires creativity, but hey—that's half the fun. In particular, **Sonoma County Transit** (tel. 707/576–7433 or 800/345–7433) connects all cities in Sonoma County, with buses running weekdays 6 AM–6:30 PM (some until 10 PM), weekends 8–6. Fares are less than $2 to most places, and the routes get you within walking distance of a few wineries: Kunde, Château St. Jean, and Valley of the Moon, to name a few. **Napa Valley Transit** (1151 Pearl St., at Main St., tel. 707/255–7631) offers frequent service between Napa and Yountville ($1), St. Helena ($2), and Calistoga ($2) Monday–Saturday. In between you can be dropped off at Beaulieu, Beringer, Prager Port Works, and Sutter Home wineries.

BY BIKE

For the ultimate California experience, rent a bike and pedal from winery to winery along the scenic, flat roads of Napa and Sonoma. The latter is less congested, but Napa is better for hard-core wine tasters since the wineries there are closer together. Cyclists on Highway 29 must contend with traffic, especially on summer weekends—stick to Silverado Trail or Solano Avenue (an access road that parallels Highway 29 from Napa to Yountville). In the town of Sonoma the best cycling route is along Arnold Drive, which splits off from Highway 12 about 4 mi south of town and rejoins the highway just south of Glen Ellen. **Napa Valley Bike Tours and Rentals** (4080 Byway E, at Salvador Ave., tel. 707/255–3380 or 800/707–2453), at the north end of Napa, rents bikes for $6 per hour or $20 per day. Farther north, **St. Helena Cyclery** (1156 Main St., at Spring St., tel. 707/963–7736) charges $7 per hour, $25 per day, or $110 per week. **Sonoma Valley Cyclery** (20093 Broadway, Sonoma, tel. 707/935–3377), on Highway 12, can set you up with a mountain bike for $6 per hour or $20 per day. All these shops offer biking maps and tour suggestions.

For an easy ride through Sonoma's fields and vineyards, take East Napa Street east from Sonoma's downtown plaza; turn left at the **Sebastiani** Winery (4th St. E), then right on Lovall Valley Road. From here follow signs to any of several wineries in the foothills, including **Bartholomew Park, Ravenswood**, and **Buena Vista** (see Wineries, below). For a longer ride, continue on Lovall Valley Road and turn right on Thornsberry Road, which leads to the **Gundlach-Bundschu** Winery (see Wineries, below). After you've tasted your fill, take Denmark Street back toward town. The entire trip is about 7 mi.

SONOMA VALLEY

Although Napa Valley receives most of the hype, Sonoma Valley is the birthplace of California's wine industry, and it's a better bet for budget travelers. Unlike Napa, almost all Sonoma's wineries offer free tastings, meaning you can imbibe to your heart's content without spending a dime. In addition, most of its wineries are small, family-owned concerns, more relaxed and less crowded than those in Napa. In summer the **Sonoma Valley Jazz Society** holds free concerts around town; call 707/996–7423 for details.

> Before stocking up on vino at a winery, check the local supermarket—they often have lower prices.

The town of **Sonoma** may have recently grown into an upscale bedroom community for San Francisco commuters, but behind the trendy restaurants and clothing boutiques lies some rich California history. It was here that Father José Altimira built the last and northernmost of the California missions, **Mission San Francisco Solano** (1st and Spain Sts., tel. 707/938–1519). The missionaries planted the region's first vines here in 1823 to make sacramental wine. For a $2 fee (also good for entrance to Lachryma Montis and the army barracks) you can see the reconstructed priests' quarters and a collection of 19th-century watercolors by Chris Jorgenson. Catercorner to the mission lies grassy **Sonoma Plaza,** the largest such plaza in California and the epicenter of Sonoma life. Around the plaza many adobe buildings remain from the days of Spanish and Mexican rule, including old army barracks and the restored **Toscana Hotel** (20 E. Spain St., tel. 707/938–5889). From Friday through Sunday between 1 and 4, kindly gray-haired docents will recount the hotel's colorful past as a general store, a library, and a home to Italian stonemasons. Behind the hotel is Depot Park and the free **Sonoma Depot Museum** (270 1st St. W, tel. 707/938–1762), which chronicles Sonoma Valley history on and off the rails. It's worth a quick peek inside to see a pair of grizzly bear's feet worn by Ulysses S. Grant to a San Francisco masquerade ball in the 1860s. Three blocks west of the plaza lies **Lachryma Montis** (3rd St. W, off W. Spain St., tel. 707/938–1519), the ornate home of the last Mexican governor, General Vallejo. Vallejo named the home Mountain Tears after the area's many natural hot and cold springs. Admission to the grounds is $2.

WHERE TO SLEEP

Beds don't come cheap in the Sonoma Valley: Even at Sonoma's least expensive motel, **El Pueblo Inn** (896 W. Napa St., on Hwy. 12, 95476, tel. 707/996–3651 or 800/900–8844), a clean and generic double will run you $80 weekdays, $94 weekends ($65 in winter). The good news is there are plenty of appealing campgrounds. Alternatives are to make the half-hour drive north on Highway 12 to Santa Rosa, which has much more affordable lodgings, or consider staying at one of Sonoma's reasonably priced bed-and-breakfasts. **Hollyhock House** (1541 Denmark St., off 8th St. E, 95476, tel. 707/938–1809) is an old two-story farmhouse on a quiet country road, with geese, a friendly gray cat, and a comfy back porch. The two doubles cost $65–$90 on summer weekends ($60 in winter), but you can lower the price of the cheaper room to $60–$65 by staying more than one weekend night or coming on a weekday. In Glen Ellen, the **Jack London Lodge** (13740 Arnold Dr., at London Ranch Rd., 95442, tel. 707/938–8510) has comfortable doubles for $75; off-season specials can lower rates to $55–$60.

THE BEAR FLAG REPUBLIC

For a short period in 1846, Sonoma belonged not to Mexico, Spain, or the United States, but to the lesser-known Bear Flag Republic—the brainchild of Captain John C. Frémont and a ragtag group of Yankee trappers who decided to resolve tensions between the Mexican government and non-Mexican immigrants by throwing the Mexican general Mariano Vallejo in prison and creating their own country. The republic was broken up a month later when the U.S. Navy arrived, but the bear remains on the California state flag.

CAMPING • Sugarloaf Ridge State Park. Only 8 mi north of Sonoma on Highway 12, Sugarloaf has 50 campsites scattered around a large meadow. There are 25 mi of trails for hiking, biking, and horseback riding (*see* Outdoor Activities, *below*), and plenty of deer to be seen. Campsites cost $16 ($12 in winter). Reserve ahead through Destinet (tel. 800/444–7275), especially in summer and on weekends. *2605 Adobe Canyon Rd., Kenwood 95452, tel. 707/833–5712. From Sonoma, Hwy. 12 north, right on Adobe Canyon Rd., which dead-ends at park. 50 sites. Barbecues, drinking water, flush toilets.*

FOOD

Sonoma is *the* place to get your fill of pesto this and roasted-goat-cheese that. Fortunately, there are some options for those long on gourmet taste but short on cash: Put together a picnic at the **Sonoma Farmers' Market** Friday from 9 to noon in Depot Park or visit the market in the plaza Tuesday evening from 4:30 until dusk. Both markets take place summer only. At other times you can taste free samples at the **Sonoma Cheese Factory** (2 Spain St., Sonoma, tel. 707/996–1931), where Sonoma Jack cheese is made. At the mellower family-owned **Vella Cheese Company** (315 2nd St. E, Sonoma, tel. 800/848–0505), watch cheese being rolled by hand Monday–Wednesday from 12:30 to 2:30. Or visit **Viansa** (25200 Arnold Dr., on Hwy. 121, tel. 707/935–4700), a slick commercial winery equipped with an Italian-style marketplace that puts out a spread of samples—chocolate sauces, preserves, mustards, oils, and, of course, wine.

For breakfast try the **Basque Boulangerie Café** (460 1st St. E, tel. 707/935–7687), where you can dunk award-winning, made-from-scratch Basque pastries into freshly brewed espresso. Come dinnertime, dive into delicious pasta dishes in the $10 range on the patio at **Pasta Nostra** (139 E. Napa St., tel. 707/938–4166). Or head down the alley east of the plaza to spirited **Murphy's Irish Pub** (464 1st St. E, tel. 707/935–0660) for homemade lamb stew and vegetables ($6.50), a pint of stout, and live Irish tunes (most weekends). For a Mexican-food fix, the roadside **Cocina Cha Cha** (897 W. Napa St., tel. 707/996–1735) serves crisp tacos with ground beef for only 99¢ and enormous burritos that easily feed two.

For an excellent sit-down meal, trek out to the one-street town of Glen Ellen, where you'll find the **Sonoma Mountain Grill** (13690 Arnold Dr., tel. 707/938–2370). The fresh fish special—with a heaping salad, vegetables, and rice—costs less than $15. The grill is closed Wednesday, and there's no dinner Tuesday.

WINERIES

It was in the Sonoma Valley that California began its upstart drive to compete with old-world wineries: In 1857 Count Agoston Haraszthy, the "father of California wine," brought thousands of European grapevine cuttings to the United States and started the **Buena Vista** Winery (18000 Old Winery Rd., Sonoma, tel. 800/926–1266). You can easily spend a leisurely day driving south along Highway 12 through the 17-mi-long valley, stopping to sip wine, learn local history, have a picnic, and nap in the sun (the wineries below are listed north to south). Unless otherwise noted, wineries offer free wine samples all day long in their tasting rooms. If you're interested in touring a particular winery, call ahead to schedule an appointment.

Château St. Jean. The palatial grounds here include a fishpond, a fountain, and an observation tower with a spectacular view of the vineyard and surrounding area. Though tasting is free, the room is crowded, and the staff may be too busy to be very helpful. For a more relaxed time, kick back on the lawn with a picnic and a bottle of their excellent gewürztraminer. *8555 Hwy. 12, Kenwood, tel. 707/833–4134 or 800/543–7572. From Sonoma, Hwy. 12 north past Glen Ellen and look for sign on right. Open daily 10–4:30.*

Kunde. The folks at Kunde claim it's the friendliest winery in the valley, which may well be true. Enjoy free tastings in their airy tasting room or take the half-hour tour through the vast cave cellars. If things are slow, you may even get a tour of the property, including the owner's duck sanctuary and the ruined stone winery where Geena Davis was married. *10155 Hwy. 12, Kenwood, tel. 707/833–5501. From Sonoma, Hwy. 12 north 7 mi; winery is on right, just past Glen Ellen. Open daily 11–5.*

Wellington. Run by a father-son team, this tiny winery opened its doors in 1994, and it's still obscure enough to escape the tourist hordes. Plant yourself in the tasting room—where a terrace looks out on the Sonoma Mountains—and sample unlimited wines. Be sure to try the Estate chardonnay, a combination of fruit and clove flavors that tastes like liquid Christmas. *11600 Dunbar Rd., Glen Ellen, tel. 707/939–0708. From Sonoma, Hwy. 12 north 7 mi, exit left at Dunbar Rd. Open daily 11–5.*

Benziger. If all this wine tasting leaves you with a powerful thirst, visit this trendsetting winery, where some merlot vines are currently being torn out to make room for hops. Take a free tram tour of the winery before heading 2 mi east to their brand-new spin-off, the **Sonoma Mountain Brewing Company.** *1883 London Ranch Rd., Glen Ellen, tel. 707/935–3000. From Hwy. 12, take Glen Ellen (Arnold Dr.) turnoff and follow signs for Jack London State Park. Open daily 10–5.*

Valley of the Moon. This intimate winery off the main drag is a breath of fresh air compared to the more crowded vineyards in the upper valley. Be sure to sample their port, a brandy-fortified wine that packs a punch. *777 Madrone Rd., Glen Ellen, tel. 707/996–6941. From Sonoma, Hwy. 12 north 6 mi to Madrone Rd. Open Apr.–Oct., daily 10–5; Nov.–Mar., daily 10–4:30.*

Ravenswood. The motto here is *Nulla Vinum Flaccidum* (No Wimpy Wines), and their merlots and zinfandels are definitely worth writing home about. If you didn't bring a picnic to eat on the terrace, try their barbecued chicken or ribs with bread, coleslaw, and potato salad, available weekends in summer and early fall. *18701 Gehricke Rd., Sonoma, tel. 707/938–1960. From plaza, Spain St. east, turn left on 4th St. E, right onto Lovall Valley Rd., left on Gehricke Rd. Open daily 10–4:30.*

Bartholomew Park Winery. Oak-shaded picnic tables, 3 mi of marked hiking trails, and a thick blanket of spring wildflowers will make you wonder whether you came for the vino or the view. All the grapes here are hand-harvested, and you can sample the wares while wandering the adjoined viticulture museum. *1000 Vineyard La., Sonoma, tel. 707/935–9511. From plaza, Napa St. E, turn left on 7th St. E, turn left on Castle Rd., follow to winery entrance. Open daily 10–4:30.*

Gundlach-Bundschu. The motto of this 137-year-old family-owned winery is "We make serious wines, but we don't take our wine too seriously." Indeed, in the main building (surrounded by trellised wisteria), old photographs of the family sit alongside a picture of Bacchus in shades. Then there are the corks, inscribed: LEAVE THE KIDS THE LAND AND MONEY—DRINK THE WINE YOURSELF. Call ahead for tickets to their summertime outdoor Shakespeare performances ($17). *2000 Denmark St., Sonoma, tel. 707/938–5277. From plaza, take E. Napa St. east, turn right on 8th St. E, left on Denmark St., and look for sign on left. Open daily 11–4:30.*

Schug. Walter Schug will personally pour you free tastes of his European-style wines at this mellow family-run winery. Afterward, explore the rooms where the wines are aged and bottled. *602 Bonneau Rd., Sonoma, tel. 707/939–9363, or 800/966–9365. From plaza, Hwy. 12 south, then Hwy. 121 west until it hits Hwy. 116 at stop sign; Bonneau Rd. is straight ahead. Open daily 10–5.*

OUTDOOR ACTIVITIES

Throughout Sonoma you'll find gentle hills covered with live oak and wildflowers. Spring and autumn are the best times for hiking and mountain biking in area parks. One of the more popular routes, either on foot or two wheels, is the Bald Mountain Trail, in **Sugarloaf Ridge State Park** (*see* Camping, *above*); you face a steep 3½-mi trek to the summit, but you'll be rewarded by a view that on a clear day stretches all the way to the Sierra Nevada. When the summer heat makes the backs of your legs stick to the car seat, head to **Morton's Warm Springs** (1651 Warm Springs Rd., off Hwy. 12 in Kenwood, tel. 707/833–5511), a low-key resort full of picnicking families and splashing kids. An entrance fee ($4.25, $5.75 weekends) gets you access to two spring-water pools, a small creek, a grassy picnic area, a snack bar, and a game room. Morton's is open daily from mid-May through August (weekends only in early May and September).

NAPA VALLEY

Although Sonoma is cheaper and more welcoming, it's Napa Valley, about a 20-minute drive east of Sonoma on Highway 121, that lures most visitors to the Wine Country. When the traffic backs up for miles on Highway 29, it's clear that Napa Valley has become one of the Bay Area's biggest attractions north of Fisherman's Wharf. Though the crowds can be distressing, the scenery is still beautiful, the wine (in some cases) still free, and the town of **Napa** still lined with the attractive Victorian houses and California bungalows that make it all worthwhile. In summer the chamber of commerce sponsors free concerts in downtown Napa's **Veterans Memorial Park,** at the corner of 3rd and Main streets. One of the most popular is the **Napa Valley Jazz Festival,** held annually in mid-July.

Wine may take center stage in the Napa Valley, but a fair share of hedonists come here solely for a peaceful soak in the valley's hot springs and mud baths, most in or near Calistoga. Though you'd perhaps hesitate to throw yourself in a roadside ditch and roll around in the muck, folks in the Wine Country believe that mud baths and sulfur springs heal all manner of ills. Poverty is not one of them: You'll pay a pretty penny for a day of pampering. On the bright side, you can spend the night at any of several resorts for a decent price, and gain free access to mineral pools and Jacuzzis.

WHERE TO SLEEP

Although some of the most expensive lodging in the Wine Country is here in the posh Napa Valley, you'll also find campgrounds and inexpensive motels. In summer reserve at least three weeks ahead.

NAPA • One of Napa's cheapest options is the **Silverado Motel** (500 Silverado Trail, 94559, tel. 707/253–0892), where a tacky but fairly clean room is $45 weekdays, $65–$75 weekends ($45 in winter). The **Napa Valley Budget Inn** (3380 Solano Ave., off Hwy. 29, 94558, tel. 707/257–6111) has clean but spartan doubles starting at $60 ($86 Friday or Saturday). The swimming pool is perfect after a long day at the wineries, many of which are within biking distance. At the **Wine Valley Lodge** (200 S. Coombs St., 94558, tel. 707/224–7911), where Elvis once slept, comfortable rooms cost $60 weekdays ($50 if you pick up a flyer at the visitor center), $90 weekends. Amenities include a pool and a barbecue in the courtyard.

Campers, take note: There isn't any public transportation to the campgrounds, so prepare to walk or bike back to civilization. If all else fails, head 20 mi east from Rutherford on Highway 128 to Lake Berryessa. The lake is divided into seven campgrounds, including **Pleasure Cove** (tel. 707/966–2172) and **Spanish Flat** (tel. 707/966–7700), for a total of 225 campsites (about $16 per site) near the water. Although you get direct access to swimming, fishing, picnicking, and waterskiing facilities, the area around the lake is barren, dusty, and very hot during summer. Reserve ahead on summer weekends.

Bothe-Napa State Park. This is the Wine Country's most attractive campground, in the Napa foothills amid redwoods, madronas, and tan oaks, only 5 mi north of St. Helena and its wineries. The sites are reasonably private, and the park is one of the few with a swimming pool (an additional $3 fee), much used on hot summer days. The campsite fee is $15–$16 from April through October or $12 off-season. Reserve through Destinet (tel. 800/444–7275). *3801 St. Helena Hwy. N, Calistoga 94515, tel. 707/ 942–4575. From St. Helena, north on Hwy. 29. 48 sites. Drinking water, fire grates, flush toilets, picnic tables, showers.*

CALISTOGA • Pleasure seekers planning to hit both the wineries and the hot springs should consider staying in Calistoga. If you want to stay on the main drag, the **Calistoga Inn** (1250 Lincoln Ave., 94515, tel. 707/942–4101) has clean, simple bed-and-breakfast rooms with shared baths and full-size beds for $55 ($68 Friday and Saturday); downstairs there's a restaurant and pub with fine home brews. For $54 (second night $5 off) you can get a cabin for two at the **Triple S Ranch** (4600 Mount Home Ranch Rd., 94515, tel. 707/942–6730). There's no phone or TV, but the complex does have a swimming pool and a steak house. The ranch is north of Calistoga off Highway 128; take Petrified Forest Road west for 2½ mi until you reach Mount Home Ranch Road. Or try the **Holiday House** (3514 Hwy. 128, 94515, tel. 707/942–6174), 3 mi north of Calistoga; watch for the white picket fence. The three rooms here ($60 one night, $50 per night if you stay two) are a (slight) step above Motel 6.

Calistoga Ranch Club. A mere two minutes north of the Silverado Trail, the Ranch Club scores points for convenience and accessibility—not to mention its pool and laundry facilities. Although it's no isolated retreat, it *is* set off the main road with a fair amount of shade and greenery. Tent sites for four people run $19. You can also rent a rustic cabin (sleeps four) for $49—or for a slice of Americana, an Airstream trailer (sleeps five) with kitchen for $89. And you thought mobile homes were passé. . . . *580 Lommel Rd., Calistoga 94515, tel. 707/942–6565. From St. Helena, head north on the Silverado Trail. 58 camp-sites, 4 cabins, 2 Airstream trailers. Barbecue pits, drinking water, flush toilets, picnic tables, showers.*

FOOD

If wine tasting is Napa Valley's main attraction, eating is a close second. The best way to eat well without breaking the bank is to stock up at one of the area's makeshift farmers' markets. One of the biggest is the **Napa Valley Farmers' Market,** held May through October on Tuesday mornings in Napa (West St., between 1st and Pearl Sts., tel. 707/252–2105) and Friday mornings in St. Helena (Old Railroad Depot, tel. 707/252–2105).

If you're spending the day in Calistoga, cruise down to the **Calistoga Roastery** (1631 Lincoln Ave., tel. 707/942–5757), great for bottomless cups of coffee and decadent ice cream lattes. For cheap Mexican food, head to the west end of Lincoln Avenue, where it dead-ends at the **Calistoga Drive-In Taquería** (1207 Foothill Blvd., tel. 707/942–0543).

Calistoga Inn. The California cuisine at this casual restaurant is excellent, and the portions fair for the price. Try the Moroc-can lamb stew with yams, apples, and raisins ($8.50), or cool off in the trellised garden with one of their award-winning home-brew ales or lagers—only $2 during happy hour (week-days 4–6). Dinner often brings live music in the front room. *1250 Lincoln Ave., tel. 707/942–4101.*

If you've gone sour on the grapes, head to Hakusan Sake Gardens (intersection of Hwys. 12 and 29, tel. 707/258–6160), where $1 buys you samples of warm and cold sakes plus a view of a Buddhist sand-and-sculpture garden.

The Diner. Although several good restaurants line Washington Street in Yountville, this 22-year-old diner is the best for the price. You can get huge plates of American or Mexican food for lunch and dinner or specialty eggs and pancakes for breakfast. *6476 Washington St., Yountville, tel. 707/9442626. Closed Mon.*

Pometta's Deli. This place is famous for its barbecued chicken platters ($7), but you can also get box lunches to go ($9.50–$12.50). Stick around after lunch to try your skills at the tournament horseshoe pits on the grounds. *Hwy. 29 at Oakville Grade, Oakville, tel. 707/944–2365.*

Red Hen Cantina. Enjoy a fajita ($25 for two people) or a hefty side dish (tamales, burritos, chili *relleños*) on the outdoor patio. You'll be hard pressed to escape without indulging in one of the margar-itas, which range in size from normal ($5) to *muy grande* ($40). *5091 St. Helena Hwy. (Hwy. 29), 5 mi north of Napa off Oak Knoll Rd., tel. 707/255–8125.*

WINERIES

If you're having trouble deciding which of the Napa Valley's hundreds of wineries to visit, first determine whether you prefer the more sophisticated tours at big-name wineries such as **Robert Mondavi** (1708 St. Helena Hwy., Oakville, tel. 707/259–9463) or the more intimate format at smaller, lower-profile wineries such as **Trefethen Vineyards** (1160 Oak Knoll Ave., Napa, tel. 707/255–7700). Some wineries have additional selling points: **Clos Pegase** (1060 Dunaweal La., tel. 707/942–4981) is worth seeing for its architecture and art collection alone; at **Sterling Vineyards** (1111 Dunaweal La., tel. 707/942–3300), you get the added bonus of a gondola ride and a dazzling view. Consider whether you mind pay-ing the $3–$5 tasting fee that many wineries charge; if so, you might seek out the freebies at some smaller wineries, where the extra attention paid to the product often means better wine. Unless other-wise noted, the wineries listed below offer free wine samples and tours by appointment only (though their tasting rooms are open all day). Wineries are listed from north to south.

Field Stone. The friendly staff may have to turn down the stereo blasting Bob Dylan when you arrive, but they will quickly set you up with free glasses of their award-winning wines. Don't be fooled by the casual, rural setting; their product is strictly top-notch. Bring some cheese and fruit, and picnic on one of the many wine-barrel tables scattered throughout the grounds. *10075 Hwy. 128, Healdsburg, tel. 707/433–7266. From Calistoga, 15 mi north on Hwy. 128. Open daily 10–5.*

Wermuth. Ralph Wermuth—equal parts vintner, philosopher, mad scientist, and stand-up comedian—will make your trip to Wermuth worthwhile. He proudly presents tastings of gamay accompanied by

TASTING NOTES

If you want to pass yourself off as a wine aficionado, you'll need to know some rules of tasting. First, move from light wines to dark, so you don't "clutter your palate." Begin by vigorously swirling an ounce of wine in your glass. Raise the glass to your nose and inhale deeply. Take a sip—you're encouraged to slurp— and swish the wine around in your mouth to pick up the more subtle flavors. Notice the finish (or aftertaste) and then sum it up with some astute comment—"It's a cheeky little wine, reminiscent of running naked through verdant pastures" will do just fine.

chocolate chips to "bring out the flavor," and colombard paired with that gourmet standby Cheez-Its. Wife and partner Smitty Wermuth designs the winery logos, which depict the old Italian basket presses still used here in the crush. *3942 Silverado Trail, Calistoga, tel. 707/942–5924. From Hwy. 29 north, Hwy. 128 east to Silverado Trail; continue north past Bale La. and look for sign on right. Tasting fee $1. Open Wed.–Sun. 11–5.*

Freemark Abbey Winery. In 1886 Josephine Tychson made history as the first woman to establish a winery in California. Today Freemark cabernets and estate-grown wines are still going strong. *3022 St. Helena Hwy. N, tel. 707/963–9694. Tasting fee $3. Open Mar.–Dec., daily 10–4:30; Jan.–Feb., Thurs.–Sun. 10–4:30; tours daily at 2.*

Beringer Winery. Thanks to a government license to make sacramental wine during Prohibition, Beringer has remained in continuous operation since 1876. A half-hour tour takes you through the winery's 100-year-old caves and beautiful grounds. *2000 Hwy. 29, St. Helena, tel. 707/963–7115. Open Apr.–Oct., daily 9:30–5; Nov.–May, daily 9:30–4; tours daily every half hr on the half hr.*

Niebaum-Coppola Estate. Francis Ford Coppola fans won't want to miss this dramatic château where Dracula's own private label is produced. Occupying vineyards once part of the old Inglenook estate, these wines are strictly first class. After you've tasted and toured, check out Don Corleone's desk and chair from *The Godfather* at the on-site film-history museum. *1991 St. Helena Hwy. (Hwy. 29), tel. 707/963–9099. Tasting fee $5. Open daily 10–5.*

Mumm Napa Valley. A joint venture of Mumm—the French champagne house—and Seagram, this is considered one of California's premier sparkling-wine producers, and its tour is particularly educational. An art gallery has a permanent exhibit of photographs by Ansel Adams that record the wine-making process. *8445 Silverado Trail, tel. 707/942–3434. Tasting fees $3.50–$6. Open daily 10:30–6, tours 11–3.*

Beaulieu Vineyards. Affectionately known as BV, Beaulieu has supplied wine to President Eisenhower and Queen Elizabeth, among other notables—and yet the staff is far from snooty. If you like dessert wine, be sure to taste their lovely brandy-fortified muscat. Free, informative half-hour tours cover the wine-making process and BV's 100-year history. *1960 Hwy. 29, Rutherford, tel. 707/963–2411. Open daily 10–5, tours daily every half hr.*

S. Anderson. John Anderson, son of the late Stan (as in "S.") Anderson, does a wonderful job guiding you through his vineyards and candlelighted stone wine caves, modeled after those in the Champagne region of France. The caves hold more than 400,000 bottles of sparkling wine, awaiting their "turn" (champagne bottles are turned by hand in a labor-intensive process that removes the yeast). *1473 Yountville Crossroad, Yountville, tel. 800/428–2259. From Hwy. 29 in Yountville, take Madison exit and follow signs for Yountville Crossroad. Tasting fee $3. Open daily 10–5, tours at 10:30 and 2:30.*

RustRidge. While you're traipsing through Napa's backwoods, check out this winery, ranch, and B&B ($105–$170). You'll probably be the only visitor indulging in the free tasters, served in a converted barn, with the family dogs and horses roaming nearby. Someone might even have to run in from the fields to open the tasting room. You can picnic on the serene grounds of Catacula (Valley of the Oaks). *2910*

Lower Chiles Valley Rd., St. Helena, tel. 707/965–9353 or 800/788–0263. From Hwy. 29N, Hwy. 128 east; cross Silverado Trail, left at fork (look for Pope Valley sign), first right on Lower Chiles Valley Rd. Open daily 10–5 (winter until 4).

Nichelini. Napa's oldest family-owned winery (since 1890) lies 11 mi east of Rutherford and is worth every minute of the beautiful drive. Outside, under the shade of walnut trees and next to an old Roman grape press, you can sample several wines: Try one of their award-winning merlots. On summer weekends picnic to the strains of traditional Italian music on a hill overlooking the countryside. *Hwy. 128, St. Helena, tel. 707/963–0717 or 800/938–2783. Open May–Oct., weekends 10–6; Nov.–Apr., weekends 10–5.*

HOT SPRINGS

The majority of the Napa Valley's mud and mineral baths are in the curious little town of Calistoga, at the north end of the valley. The town's bubbling mineral spring became a spa in 1859, when entrepreneur Sam Brannan melded the word *California* with the name of New York's Saratoga Springs resort; Calistoga has been attracting health seekers ever since. Prices at the Calistoga spas are uniformly steep, but you can pick up discount coupons at the **Calistoga Chamber of Commerce** (1458 Lincoln Ave., tel. 707/942–6333), open weekdays 9–5, Saturday 10–4, Sunday 10–3.

A cheaper option is open-air bathing at rustic retreats like Harbin Hot Springs or White Sulphur Springs (*see below*). You won't get to play human mud pie at the outdoor spas, but you can bathe in natural springs and hike through rolling grounds far from the buzz of urbanity. Not only do these resorts offer many of the same amenities as the Calistoga spas, but you get an affordable room for the night to boot. If you opt for one of the indoor spas, call ahead for a reservation. Most accept walk-ins, but nothing is more stressful than being turned away from a longed-for massage.

They say, "Clothing optional," but you'll feel very out of place if you wear anything but a smile into the pools at Harbin Hot Springs.

Golden Haven Hot Springs. Golden Haven is the only Calistoga spa to offer private coed mud baths (sorry lovebirds, there's still an attendant). The full treatment (mud bath, mineral Jacuzzi, blanket wrap, and 30-minute massage) will run you $64 per person. If you're too relaxed to make it past the front door, you can crash in one of their rooms for $65 ($49 Sunday–Thursday, September–June), which includes use of the swimming pool and hot mineral pool. *1713 Lake St., Calistoga, tel. 707/942–6793. From Lincoln Ave. east, left on Stevenson St., right on Lake St. Open daily 9–9.*

Harbin Hot Springs. Forty minutes north of Calistoga, this 1,200-acre laid-back community is run by the Heart Consciousness Church, a group that advocates holistic health and spiritual renewal. The retreat, popular with gay men, has three natural mineral pools, varying in temperature from tepid to *very* hot, and a cold spring-fed "plunge" pool, all open 24 hours. To use the pools, you must pay $5 for a one-month membership or $15 for a year (only one member per group required), plus an additional day-use fee ($13 Monday–Thursday, $18 Friday–Sunday and holidays). There's also an acclaimed massage school, whose graduates are happy to show you their skills ($46 per hour, $60 for 90 minutes). Rustic dorm beds start at $23 ($35 on weekends and holidays); you bring your own sheets or sleeping bag. Private rooms with shared bath are $60 ($90 on weekends). Campsites along the creek and in nearby meadows cost $14 per person ($23 Friday–Saturday, $17 Sunday). Guests at the resort are invited to use the vegetarian-only communal kitchen and to share the community's vegetarian meals ($8–$12). *Tel. 707/987–2477 or 800/622–2477 (northern California only). Hwy. 29 north to Middletown, turn left at junction for Hwy. 175, right on Barnes St.; go 1½ mi to Harbin Springs Rd. and turn left. Rides can be arranged for those taking Greyhound.*

Lincoln Avenue Spa. With pleasant stone-and-wood massage rooms and a central location, this spa is posh for the price. Their body mud treatment ($40) is the ideal alternative for those squeamish about wallowing in mud someone else has already wallowed in: You get your choice of mud (herbal, sea, or mint) slathered over your body, a relaxing nap on the steam table, and a soothing facial mask. *1339 Lincoln Ave., Calistoga, tel. 707/942–5296. Open daily 9–9.*

Nance's Spa. Of the Calistoga spas, Nance's is one of the cheapest. For $62 you get the works: You begin by sliding into a tub of hot volcanic mud; then you shower and simmer in a bubbling mineral bath. Next you're swaddled in soft sheets and left to "set" like a human dumpling in preparation for a half-hour massage. Nance's facilities are sex-segregated and none too private: The amorous and the modest may opt to go elsewhere. *1614 Lincoln Ave., Calistoga, tel. 707/942–6211. Open weekdays 9–5, weekends 9–7.*

HUBCAPS AND MORE

Years ago, in Pope Valley, when Emanuelle "Litto" Damonte discovered that several hubcaps had been lost on a turn of the road near his property, he placed them on the fence for the owners to retrieve. Thirty years and more than 2,000 hubcaps later, the metallic splendor of his property is recognized as a registered California landmark and a tribute to American folk art. To reach the ranch from Highway 29, take Highway 128 east, cross Silverado Trail, and bear left on Chiles Pope Valley Road. When you reach Pope Valley, head onto Pope Valley Road—it's a couple miles farther on the right.

White Sulphur Springs. If you're planning to stay the night in Napa Valley, this longtime St. Helena resort is a bargain. Along with a decent room for the night—either in the rustic, dormitory-style carriage house ($85) or in the inn ($105), where each room has a half bath—you and a friend can enjoy access to 300 acres of land, plenty of hiking and biking trails, a Jacuzzi, a natural mineral bath, and even a stand of redwoods. For day-trippers, a sulfur soak, a sauna, a Jacuzzi, and hiking trails are a bargain at $30. Reserve two weeks ahead. *3100 White Sulphur Springs Rd., St. Helena, tel. 707/963–8588. From Hwy. 29N, turn left on Spring St. in St. Helena and go nearly 3 mi. Note: Do NOT take Sulphur Springs Rd. from Hwy. 29.*

OUTDOOR ACTIVITIES

If you're determined to beat the heat, it's a half-hour drive from Napa or Rutherford to **Lake Berryessa** (*see* Where to Sleep, *above*), where you can rent almost any kind of water vessel—from a Jet Ski to a ski boat—from one of the lake's many resorts. At **Skyline Wilderness Park** (2201 Imola Ave., Napa, tel. 707/252–0481), the 2½-mi Lake Marie Trail runs along a shady creek and past overgrown orchards and ruined stone dairies. Swimming in Lake Marie isn't allowed, but you can try your luck fishing for bluegill and bass. If you're spending the day in Calistoga, pay a visit to **Robert Louis Stevenson State Park,** off Highway 29, 9 mi northeast of Calistoga. Here you can hike to the bunkhouse of the Silverado Mine, where the impoverished author honeymooned with his wife, Fanny Osbourne, in the summer of 1880. That stay inspired Stevenson's *The Silverado Squatters*. The park is perched atop Mt. St. Helena, said to be the model for Spyglass Hill in *Treasure Island*. Its 3,000 acres are largely undeveloped; picnicking is permitted, but overnight camping is not.

LAKE TAHOE

Straddling the border of California and Nevada on the northern flank of the Sierra Nevada range, Lake Tahoe is one of the West Coast's best-loved outdoor playgrounds, drawing up to 100,000 tourists at peak periods. During spring and summer, when temperatures hover in the 70s, the lake (about a 3½-hour drive east of San Francisco on I-80) becomes a recreation arena for boating, fishing, waterskiing, and jet skiing; and the mountains surrounding Tahoe Basin satisfy even the most demanding rock climbers, hikers, bikers, equestrians, and anglers. During the winter season (usually December–April, sometimes extending into May), attention shifts to downhill and cross-country skiing and snowboarding. Tahoe has earned a worldwide reputation for its "extreme" conditions, thanks to the sheer cliffs and steep faces of the Sierra Nevada, while the Donner Summit is famed for its challenging rock-climbing faces.

The lake itself is 6,225 ft above sea level, for its size the highest altitude in the United States. The water is so clear you can see 75 ft below the surface, and plunging to a depth of 1,625 ft, it holds enough water to cover the state of California to a depth of 14 inches.

Although it's a somewhat subjective division, the lake's locales are usually designated as belonging to either the north shore or the south shore. Thanks largely to the popularity of 15 or so ski areas (compared with two in the south), the north shore is the domain of Tahoe's athletic set, while the south shore is largely overrun with family vacationers and casino-bound gamblers. The north shore's largest town is **Truckee,** about a 30-minute drive (12 mi) north of the lake, with a modern downtown area to the west and an old town (complete with board sidewalks, wood-frame storefronts, and an ancient railroad) to the east. Donner Pass Road connects the two sides of town and serves as the main commercial boulevard. On the west shore of the lake, **Tahoe City** has a small-town warmth largely lacking in Truckee. On the south shore, the city center of **South Lake Tahoe** is packed with restaurants, motels, and rental shops. The pace never flags in summer, and in winter popular ski areas such as Heavenly keep the town jumping. Butting up against the east side of South Lake Tahoe is the prosaically named town of **Stateline,** Nevada, with its four major (and two minor) hotel-casinos.

BASICS

The **North Lake Tahoe Resort Association Chamber of Commerce** (245 Hwy. 89, Tahoe City, tel. 530/581–6900) lies north of the Bank of America across from the Tahoe City Y (the intersection of Highways 89 and 28 that is impossible to miss). This site has free guides and maps, lots of community and historical facts, information on kids' activities, resources for travelers with disabilities, and details on camping. The **North Lake Tahoe Resort Association Visitors and Convention Bureau,** in Tahoe City (950 North Lake Blvd., near the Safeway, tel. 530/583–3494 or 800/824–6348) has deals on activity and accommodation packages year-round. The **Lake Tahoe Forest Service Visitor Center** (Hwy. 89 between Emerald Bay and South Lake Tahoe, tel. 530/573–2674) has beach access and nature trails, and the staff will tell you all

> *Going to the chapel? Then it might not surprise you that the wedding industry is second only to casinos for bringing the most business to the Tahoe area.*

you want to know about the lake's natural and human history. This is also the place to pick up campfire and wilderness permits for the Desolation and Mokelumne wilderness areas. Permits are free, but only a limited number are available. Depending on funding, the visitor center may be closed on certain days of the week—call ahead.

The **South Lake Tahoe Women's Center** (3140 Lake Tahoe Blvd., tel. 530/544–2118) has Spanish and English services and also operates a crisis line (tel. 530/544–4444). Gay-friendly information on recreational activities, support groups, businesses, and accommodations is found through the **Tahoe Gay Hotline** (tel. 530/541–4297). **Disabled Sports USA of Northern California** (6060 Sunrise Vista Dr., Suite 3030, Citrus Heights, CA 95610, tel. 530/722–6447) has information on skiing, waterskiing, rafting, and other outdoor activities.

COMING AND GOING

BY CAR

Both routes to Lake Tahoe take 3½–4 hours from the Bay Area when road and traffic conditions are at their best. To reach the north shore, follow I–80 east all the way to Truckee. For the south shore, take U.S. 50 east from Sacramento. You won't be allowed into the mountains without chains if it snows; bring your own, or you'll have to pay inflated prices for a set near the CalTrans checkpoint. Even if you bring your own, consider paying (about $10) to let someone else put them on for you. You will see swarms of jumpsuit-clad people with numbers on their backs at every checkpoint waiting to perform this service.

If snow doesn't slow you down, traffic might, especially on Friday and Sunday afternoon and during summer and holiday weekends. If you must drive to Tahoe on Friday, wait until 7 PM or 8 PM. Traffic is usually worst on I–80, so consider taking U.S. 50 even if you're headed for the north shore.

BY BUS

Greyhound Lines (tel. 800/231–2222) runs seven buses a day between San Francisco and Truckee, a 5–10 hour trip that's $34 one-way, and five one-hour trips between Truckee and Reno ($9 one-way). If you're headed to the south shore, Greyhound makes the three-hour trip between Sacramento and **Harrah's Hotel and Casino,** in Stateline, Nevada ($19 one-way), twice a day, with a $5 cash bonus on arrival. Both Amtrak and Greyhound use the **Transit Depot** (Donner Pass Rd., in Old Town Truckee, tel. 530/587–3822), a safe place to wait for connections. You can pick up information at the tourist office here; there are also a few coin-operated lockers.

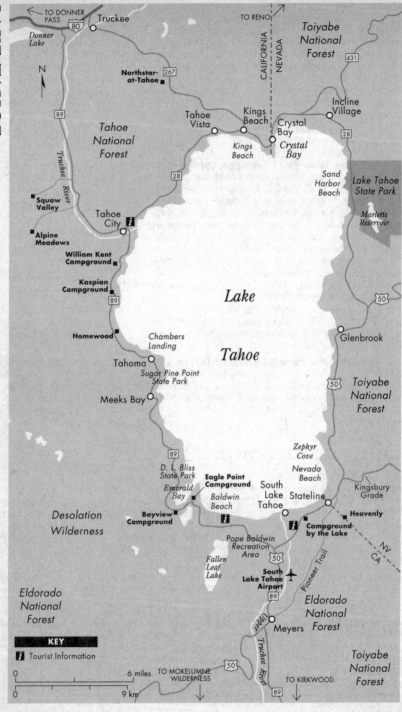

TO DONNER PASS

TO RENO

Truckee

80

Donner Lake

TO MOKELUMNE WILDERNESS

TO KIRKWOOD

N

Northstar-at-Tahoe
267

Tahoe National Forest

89

Truckee River

Squaw Valley

Alpine Meadows

Tahoe City

William Kent Campground

Kaspian Campground

89

Homewood

Tahoma

Chambers Landing

Sugar Pine Point State Park

Meeks Bay

89

D. L. Bliss State Park

Emerald Bay

Bayview Campground

Desolation Wilderness

Eldorado National Forest

Fallen Leaf Lake

Pope Baldwin Recreation Area

Eagle Point Campground

Baldwin Beach

South Lake Tahoe

50

South Lake Tahoe Airport

89

Upper Truckee River

Meyers

50

89

Tahoe Vista

Kings Beach

Kings Beach

28

Crystal Bay

Crystal Bay

CALIFORNIA

NEVADA

Lake Tahoe

Lake

Tahoe

Zephyr Cove

Nevada Beach

Stateline

Campground by the Lake

Pioneer Trail

NV
CA

Eldorado National Forest

Toiyabe National Forest

Toiyabe National Forest
431

Incline Village

28

Sand Harbor Beach

Lake Tahoe State Park

Marlette Reservoir

50

Glenbrook

50

Toiyabe National Forest

Kingsbury Grade

Heavenly

KEY

i Tourist Information

0   6 miles
0   9 km

BY TRAIN

Amtrak (tel. 800/872–7245) runs three train and bus routes a day between Emeryville and Truckee, with a transfer in Sacramento, a trip lasting five hours ($69 round-trip). If you're coming from San Francisco, take the free bus from the CalTrain Station at 4th and Townsend streets to the Emeryville Amtrak station (5885 Landregan St., at Powell St., tel. 510/450–1081). Amtrak also has four trains a week traveling the hour-long route between Truckee and Reno ($13 one-way). All trains arrive at the Truckee Transit Depot (*see* By Bus, *above*). Another train-and-bus combination serves South Lake Tahoe from Emeryville, again with a transfer in Sacramento, lasting five hours ($38 round-trip).

BY PLANE

At press time the only commercial airline with service to Tahoe was **Mountain Air Express** (tel. 800/788–4247). Its 19-seaters connect the airports at Long Beach and Oakland with tiny **South Lake Tahoe Airport** (off Hwy. 89, about 2 mi south of the Y in South Lake Tahoe, tel. 530/542–6180), from Thursday through Monday. Otherwise, your best bet is to get a flight to the **Reno-Tahoe International Airport** (2001 E. Plumb La., tel. 702/328–6499), then catch a **Tahoe Casino Express** bus (tel. 702/785–2424 or 800/446–6128) to South Lake Tahoe. Fare is $17 one-way, $30 round-trip; buses depart from the airport several times a day.

GETTING AROUND

For recorded information on road conditions, call CalTrans at 800/427–7623.

Three intersecting highways form a loop around the lake: **Highway 89** (a.k.a. Emerald Bay Road) skirts the west shore between Tahoe City and South Lake Tahoe; **U.S. 50** (a.k.a. Lake Tahoe Boulevard) intersects Highway 89 in South Lake Tahoe and follows the lake's east shore; and **Highway 28** (a.k.a. North Lake Boulevard or Lake Shore Boulevard) runs along the northern part of the shore back into Tahoe City. The intersections of Highways 28 and 89 in Tahoe City and Highway 89 and U.S. 50 in South Lake Tahoe are commonly referred to as the **Tahoe City Y** and the **South Lake Tahoe Y**, respectively.

The **Tahoe Area Regional Transit** (TART; tel. 530/581–6365 or 800/736–6365) has buses, most equipped with ski and bike racks, that serve the north and west shores of Lake Tahoe, traveling from Tahoma (Meeks Bay in summer) on the southwest shore to Incline Village in the north and up Highway 89 to Truckee. Fare is $1.25, and buses run from 6:30 to 6:30 year-round. Between **BUS PLUS** (tel. 530/542–6077) and the **South Tahoe Area Ground Express** (STAGE; tel. 530/573–2080), service runs 24 hours from the South Lake Tahoe Y to Stateline, Nevada; fare is $1.25 for STAGE. BUS PLUS ($3–$5) is for people who are too far from bus stops; if you call the number (*see above*), they will pick you up and drop you at the nearest STAGE stop. Schedules and maps are available from tourist information centers. Pending continued funding, the **Lake Lapper** (tel. 530/542–5900) is a great deal—$5 for an all-day pass on coaches that circle the lake, stopping at points of interest, connecting with STAGE and TART, and running 8 AM to 1:45 AM in summer and 6 AM to 4:30 PM in winter.

WHERE TO SLEEP

You'll face a mind-boggling number of options in choosing a place to stay in Tahoe. Hostels, motels, condominiums, cabins, and campgrounds abound. If you're just passing through for a night or two in summer, a motel or campground is the cheapest and most convenient alternative. But if you're coming for a week in winter to ski with a group of friends, consider a condominium or cabin on the north shore: It's more affordable than you might think (*see below*).

The quickest way to find a cheap (and perhaps fleabaggy) place to crash is to head to U.S. 50 between South Lake Tahoe and Stateline—cruise the strip and keep your eyes open for the neon. For a safer, quieter stay, opt for the area west of the South Tahoe Y, and travel up to either the north shore or Stateline from there. If you like to be in the middle of the action, look for cheap deals at the casinos on the Nevada side of both the south and north shores. No matter where you stay, reserve as far ahead as possible. On holidays and summer weekends everything is completely packed despite most places raising their prices indiscriminately at these times. All the hotels and motels listed below have private bathrooms.

SOUTH SHORE

El Nido Motel. The excellent amenities here include a hot tub and small, modern rooms with TV, VCR, and telephone. Flawlessly clean doubles start at $40 weekdays, $50 on summer weekends; in winter prices are about $10 lower. Call for details on discount lift-ticket deals. *2215 Lake Tahoe Blvd. (U.S. 50), South Lake Tahoe 96150, tel. and fax 530/541–2711. 21 rooms.*

Emerald Motel. This well-maintained building is 35 years old and the proprietors exceptionally friendly. Pope Beach and the woods are less than 2 mi away. Standard doubles start at $45 weekdays and $50 weekends, with rates $10 lower in winter. Groups get the best deal—two beds, sleeping four, for $45 on summer weekdays. Rates are negotiable for stays of four nights or more. *515 Emerald Bay Rd. (Hwy. 89), South Lake Tahoe 96150, tel. 530/544–5515, fax 530/544–2510. 9 rooms.*

Ridgewood Inn. Set on a 2-acre lot you can explore, these clean, well-kept rooms, some with kitchenettes, are a swell deal. Doubles in summer are $45, and a self-contained suite that sleeps five goes for $110. Some rooms have tubs, and there's also an outdoor Jacuzzi. *1341 Emerald Bay Rd., South Lake Tahoe 96150, tel. 530/541–8589 or 800/800–4640, fax 530/541–8712. 12 rooms.*

NORTH SHORE

It's hard to find a budget motel on the north shore, especially in Truckee. For better prices and a better location, check out the smaller communities around the lakeshore, like Tahoe Vista or Kings Beach. One of the cheapest motels on the North Shore is in Kings Beach: the **Big 7** (8171 North Lake Blvd., 96143, tel. 530/546–2541 or 800/354–6970), with weekday doubles $35–$45, weekends $45–$65.

North Shore Lodge. Across from Kings Beach, $60 gets you a double with a kitchen. The cabins are the best deal: One sleeps six ($115), and another sleeps eight for $125. Negotiate in winter: They've been known to take what they can get—sometimes as low as $25. In summer you have use of a heated pool. *8755 North Lake Blvd. (Hwy. 28) at Chipmunk St., Kings Beach 96143, tel. 530/546–4833, fax 530/546–0265. 11 rooms.*

River Ranch Lodge. The classy River Ranch Lodge is ideally situated beside the Truckee River between Truckee and Tahoe City. The rustic rooms (all no-smoking) come complete with tasteful wallpaper and antique furniture, and half have small decks overlooking the river. Doubles start at $40 on spring and fall weekdays ($50 weekends), $55 on winter and summer weekdays ($80 weekends). Several of the noisier rooms above the bar go for $10 less, and there's a cheaper double facing the parking lot. Continental breakfast is included. *Hwy. 89 and Alpine Meadows Rd., Tahoe City 96145, tel. 530/583–4264 or 800/535–9900. 21 rooms.*

Tamarack Lodge Motel. The North Shore's best budget lodging is a short walk from the beach. Knotty pine paneling and bike-trail access are big selling points, as is the TART bus stop across the street. Doubles start at $36 weekdays, kitchenettes are $10 more, and rates go up by $10 in high season. Stay more than four nonholiday days, and you'll get a 15% discount. *2311 North Lake Blvd. (Hwy. 28), Tahoe City 96145, tel. 530/583–3350 or 888/824–6323, fax 530/583–3531. 21 rooms.*

HOSTELS

Clair Tappaan Lodge. Managed by the Sierra Club, this coed hostel is about 45 minutes from Tahoe City. There are cross-country trails on-site, and they rent snowshoes and Nordic skis in winter. In summer they lead bird-watching, wildflower, and hiking workshops. Summer rates are $39 for nonmembers ($35 members) and include three meals per day. Rates in winter are about $4 higher. *19940 Donner Pass Rd., Norden 95724, tel. 530/426–3632, fax 530/426–0742. From Tahoe City, take Hwy. 89E, exit at Soda Springs/Norden. 140 beds. Check-in anytime.*

Doug's Mellow Mountain Retreat. At this laid-back private hostel about a mile from Heavenly and from the casinos, you can rent bikes for $5 per day and get your laundry done for $3. Doug invites guests to watch movies (he has more than 200), use his kitchen, and have barbecues on the deck. He'll even pick you up from the Greyhound station at Harrah's if you call ahead. Beds in coed rooms go for $13. Reserve ahead; if you're a party of three, ask for the studio ($35), which has its own kitchen, TV, and bath. *3787 Forest St., Box 2764, Stateline, NV 89449, tel. 530/544–8065. From South Lake Tahoe, U.S. 50 east, right on Wildwood Rd., left on Forest St. 15 beds. Check-in anytime.*

Squaw Valley Hostel. This privately run hostel, within walking distance of the Squaw Valley ski area, opens only during winter, usually from November 15 to April 15. During the week a dorm bed runs $22, $27 weekends. On weekends, when the hostel hosts groups, it's next to impossible to get a room unless you call well in advance. *1900 Squaw Valley Rd., Box 6655, Tahoe City 96145, tel. and fax 530/581–3246. From Truckee, Hwy. 89 south, right on Squaw Valley Rd. 100 beds. Check-in 4:30 PM–9 PM.*

WEEKEND AND WEEKLY RENTALS

As a rule of thumb, the more people in your group and the longer the stay, the more affordable rentals become. Contact the **Lake Tahoe Visitors' Authority** (1156 Ski Run Blvd., South Lake Tahoe 96150, tel. 530/544–5050 or 800/288–2463) or the **North Lake Tahoe Resort Association** (*see* Basics, *above*) to find out about weekend or weekly rentals. You should be able to find a basic two- or four-person condominium for about $100 a night or $500 a week in the off-season, with prices rising roughly 10% in summer. **R. RENT** (tel. 530/546–2549) specializes in north-shore budget rentals. If you have the time, you can save a few bucks by arranging a rental directly through a property owner. To find out what's available, check the classified ads in the *Tahoe Daily Tribune* for south-shore listings or the *Tahoe World*, a north-shore weekly that comes out each Thursday.

CAMPING

You can hardly drive 5 mi in Lake Tahoe without bumping into a public or private campground, and almost all lie in beautiful pine forests. All campgrounds close in winter until about Memorial Day. Temperatures can fluctuate widely in the region (from 60°F to below zero in a single 24-hour period), and many areas have snow until May. Call the Forest Service (*see* Basics, *above*) for advice and weather conditions before setting out. Free camping in the Tahoe area is restricted but still available at some lesser-known primitive campgrounds scattered around the lake. The Forest Service has maps, tips, and directions to free spots as well as a complete listing of campgrounds.

Besides being deep and blue, Lake Tahoe is also mighty cold (40°F–68°F throughout the year). You can swim in it, but most visitors just dip their feet in and scamper back to shore.

SOUTH SHORE • There are two inviting campgrounds just south of Emerald Bay on Highway 89. **Bayview** (tel. 530/544–5994 or 800/280–2267 for reservations), on the inland side of Highway 89, has 10 primitive sites amid the pines, with picnic tables and fire pits but no drinking water. A stopping-off point for journeys into Desolation Wilderness, it imposes a two-night limit on stays; but for those two nights you'll sleep for free. If all the sites in Bayview are full, head just up the road to beautiful **Eagle Point** (Hwy. 89, 1 mi south of Emerald Bay, tel. 530/525–7277 or 800/444–7275 for reservations). Here you'll find 100 well-spaced sites ($14)—all with fire pits, barbecues, drinking water, picnic tables, food lockers, and access to bathrooms and showers—on a hillside covered with brush and pines. Some sites have incredible views of Emerald Bay.

NORTH SHORE • On the north shore dispersed camping is available near the Homewood ski resort, in **Blackwood Canyon**. From Highway 89 south of Tahoe City, look for a sign BLACKWOOD CANYON on the right. After 2½ mi, veer to the right on an unmarked dirt road, and camp anywhere you please.

William Kent Campground (off Hwy. 89, tel. 530/544–5994 or 800/444–7275 for reservations) is a 95-site National Forest campground set well off the highway, 2 mi south of Tahoe City; its $12 sites are in a moderately dense pine forest within walking distance of the lake. Sites are $12. Just down the road to the south, **Kaspian Campground** (tel. 530/544–5994) is squeezed in between a highway and the lake in Homewood village, on National Forest land. Its 10 sites cost $12 each and have piped water and flush toilets.

FOOD

On the south shore food stops are concentrated along U.S. 50 between South Lake Tahoe and Stateline, Nevada. In Stateline itself look for bargain eats at casino snack shops and all-you-can-eat buffets. On the north shore there are plenty of restaurants in downtown Truckee (especially on Donner Pass Road) and on Highway 28 in Tahoe City. For fresh organic produce and bulk foods, head to **Grass Roots** (2040 Dunlap Dr., at South Lake Tahoe Y, tel. 530/541–7788) on the south shore.

SOUTH SHORE

Ernie's Coffee Shop. An unpretentious greasy spoon serving breakfast and lunch only, Ernie's has a host of regulars that keep their personalized coffee mugs hanging on the wall. Breakfast is served all day in retro green-vinyl booths. Meals range from the standard two-egg-and-toast breakfast to more adventurous creations like the tostada omelet. *1146 Emerald Bay Rd. (Hwy. 89), at C St., South Lake Tahoe, tel. 530/541–2161. ¼ mi south of South Lake Tahoe Y.*

Hunan Garden. The friendly, sometimes wisecracking staff at this flower-festooned joint serves up a lunch buffet (11:30–2:30) for $5.50, and another for dinner (5–9) at $7.95. *900 Emerald Bay Rd. (Hwy. 89), just northwest of South Lake Tahoe Y, tel. 530/544–5868 or 530/544–7268.*

Sprouts. At South Lake Tahoe's small, cheery vegetarian paradise, you can feast on great sandwiches and fruit smoothies on an outdoor patio. The produce is largely organic. *3123 Harrison Ave., at intersection of U.S. 50 and Alameda Ave., South Lake Tahoe, tel. 530/541–6969.*

Taquería Jalisco. With a blaring jukebox and great food, this spot attracts Tahoe's sizable Latino population. Hidden behind Rojo's eatery, Taquería Jalisco sells burritos, nachos, and tacos (some vegetarian) for under $2.50. *3097 Harrison Ave., at San Francisco Ave., South Lake Tahoe, tel. 530/541–6516.*

NORTH SHORE

Bridgetender Tavern and Grill. Housed in an old wooden cabin with high, beamed ceilings and tree trunks poking through the roof, the Bridgetender is a worthy burgers-and-beer stop. Huge beef patties and tasty veggie burgers are served with hefty french fries until 11 PM weekdays and midnight weekends. Sit on a patio overlooking the Truckee River or drink beer and shoot pool inside. *30 Emerald Bay Rd. (Hwy. 89), Tahoe City, next to bridge at Tahoe City Y, tel. 530/583–3342.*

China Garden. One of Truckee's best restaurants serves up veggie dishes, seafood, and other Mandarin standards. There are lunch and dinner specials for $5–$10 and a $7–$9 Mongolian barbecue buffet. *11361 Deerfield Dr., tel. 530/587–7625. In Crossroads Center, off Hwy. 89 just south of I–80.*

Truckee River Coffee Company. This homey café is furnished with couches, a few tables, and a piano. You can get a calzone for $3, but the real reasons to come are coffee and dessert. Try the old-fashioned hot chocolate, or the Coffee Nut, made of hazelnut espresso, hazelnut syrup, and vanilla yogurt. *11373 Deerfield Dr., Truckee, tel. 530/587–2583. In Crossroads Center, just south of I–80/Hwy. 89 junction.*

AFTER DARK

Events on the south shore are covered in *Lake Tahoe Action,* a free weekly entertainment magazine put out by the *Tahoe Daily Tribune.* The *Tahoe–Truckee Review* covers the north shore. Both are available at most motels.

SOUTH SHORE

The south shore is surprisingly quiet by night. On the Nevada side of the border in Stateline, you'll find a number of casinos and the usual array of Las Vegas–style shows and headliners. Just north of the state line, the gay club **Faces** (270 Kingsbury Grade, just west of Hwy. 50, tel. 702/588–2333) has a relaxed, friendly atmosphere, with dancing three nights a week until 4 AM (no cover). The **Brewery at Lake Tahoe** (3542 U.S. 50, tel. 530/544–2739), 1½ mi west of the California–Nevada border, is a microbrewery and restaurant popular with the après-ski crowd. **Ellis Island Café** (4093 Lake Tahoe Blvd., tel. 530/542–1142) is a gay- and lesbian-friendly spot with 10 microbrews on tap, live music every night, and fresh food.

NORTH SHORE

Tahoe City is without a doubt the center of the lake's nightlife. Loud, crowded, and filled with hard-drinking youth, **Humpty's** (877 North Lake Blvd., 1 mi northeast of Tahoe City Y, tel. 530/583–4867) features the best live indie music in the area most nights (cover $3–$20). When Humpty's is sold out, the overflow crowd heads to **Rosie's Cafe** (571 North Lake Blvd., Tahoe City, tel. 530/583–8504), a large restaurant and bar housed in an old cabin full of Tahoe City memorabilia. Across the street at the **Blue Water Brewery** (850 North Lake Blvd., behind Safeway in Tahoe City, tel. 530/581–2583), you can suck down microbrews, munch on fish-and-chips in beer batter, and shoot a game of pool.

Catering to a mellower clientele, the **Naughty Dawg** (255 North Lake Blvd., ¼ mi northeast of Tahoe City Y, tel. 530/581–3294) has a good selection of high-quality beers, as well as surprisingly good salads, burgers, and pizza. The **River Ranch Lodge** (*see* Where to Sleep, *above*) is an excellent place for a quiet drink, with a large deck next to the Truckee River and a stylish indoor bar. During the summer this place hosts an outdoor concert series with eclectic bookings ranging from jazz to hard rock (cover $5–$25).

OUTDOOR ACTIVITIES

In addition to its excellent skiing, Lake Tahoe is full of opportunities for just about every fair-weather sport imaginable. An abbreviated list would include hiking, biking, fishing, sailing, waterskiing, jet skiing, rock climbing, hot-air ballooning, parasailing, horseback riding, and river rafting. Many of the more exotic adventures are pricey, but Tahoe is a great place to splurge. Tourist offices and the Forest Service (*see* Basics, *above*) have detailed information about all these sports. For equipment rentals, **Don Cheepo's** (*see* Equipment Rental *in* Skiing, *below*) carries everything from water skis to backpacks and other camping supplies. Also try **Alpenglow Sports** (415 North Lake Blvd., tel. 530/583–6917), in Tahoe City, for information and equipment. **Gravity Works Rock Gym,** in Truckee (10095 W. River St., tel. 530/582–4510), is a good rock climbing resource.

HIKING

Almost every acre in the Lake Tahoe Basin is protected by some national, state, or local agency. **Tahoe National Forest** lies to the northwest, **Eldorado National Forest** to the southwest, and **Toiyabe National Forest** to the east. This means a whole lot of hiking trails for visitors, from easy scenic walks to strenuous climbs over mountain passes. The Lake Tahoe Forest Service Visitor Center (*see* Basics, *above*) has a complete list of day hikes.

One of the most interesting short walks is **Vikingsholm Trail,** a mile-long (one-way) paved path leading from the parking lot on the north side of Emerald Bay to the shoreline and the 38-room Vikingsholm Castle, a Scandinavian-style castle built in 1929. From the castle you can walk farther, to **Eagle Falls,** the only waterfall that empties into the lake. For something a little more woodsy, try the **Mt. Tallac Trail,** a half mile north of the Lake Tahoe Forest Service Visitor Center (follow the marked asphalt road opposite Baldwin Beach to the trailhead parking lot). A moderate hike takes you 2 mi through a beautiful pine forest to Cathedral Lake. For a serious day-long trek (with no potable water along the way), continue on the trail another 3 mi as it climbs past a series of boulder fields to the peak of Mt. Tallac, the highest point in the basin, at 9,735 ft. At the top you'll enjoy excellent views of the lake and Desolation Wilderness. The trip up and back should take seven or eight hours.

For extensive backcountry camping the choices are limitless. Off the southwest corner of the lake, 63,473-acre **Desolation Wilderness** is filled with granite peaks, glacial valleys, subalpine forests, and more than 80 lakes. South of the lake, **Mokelumne Wilderness,** straddling the border of Eldorado and Stanislaus national forests, has terrain similar to Desolation without the crowds. Before you enter any wilderness area, whether for a day or for an extended visit, it's crucial to pick up a wilderness permit from the Lake Tahoe Forest Service Visitor Center (*see* Basics, *above*)—if you don't, you may actually be kicked off the trails.

BIKING

Lake Tahoe has enough mellow lakeshore trails, steep fire roads, and tricky single tracks to satisfy any two-wheeled explorer. The Forest Service has detailed trail information, and the North Lake Tahoe Resort Association (*see* Basics, *above*) puts out an excellent brochure called "North Lake Tahoe Mountain Biking" that lists bike tours, trails, bike parks, and bike shops for rentals. Several paved, gently sloped paths skirt the lakeshore: Try the 3.4-mi **Pope Baldwin Bike Path,** in South Lake Tahoe at the Pope Baldwin Recreational Center, or the **West Shore Bike Path,** which extends about 10 mi south from Tahoe City to Sugar Pine Point State Park, near the town of Tahoma. Also worthwhile are the path along the **Truckee River** between Alpine Meadows and Tahoe City and the **U.S. Forest Service Bike Trail,** an 8.5-mi paved path (through pine forest and rare aspen grove) that starts at Emerald Bay Road just west of the South Lake Tahoe Y and ends at the lake.

Experienced riders may dare the famous **Flume Trail,** a 24-mi ride past several lakes and along a ridge with sweeping views of Lake Tahoe. The trail begins at the parking lot of Lake Tahoe–Nevada State Park, just north of Spooner Junction on the lake's east shore (take Highway 28 east from Tahoe City). The *High Sierra Biking Map* ($6) and its accompanying book ($9) provide a detailed description of the Flume Trail as well as several dozen other excellent rides in the area. If you like the idea of riding downhill all day, **Northstar-at-Tahoe, Donner Ranch, Kirkwood, Squaw Valley,** and **Sugar Bowl** (*see* Skiing, *below*) all open a number of ski runs for mountain biking June–September. All-day tickets run $10–$21 (bike rentals $30–$45).

BIKE RENTALS • Dozens of shops around Tahoe rent mountain bikes, generally for $4–$6 an hour or $15–$22 a day. On the south shore there's **Don Cheepo's** (*see* Equipment Rental *in* Skiing, *below*), near the east end of the Pope Baldwin Bike Path. On the north shore try **Porter's** (501 North Lake Blvd., tel. 530/583–2314), on Highway 28, east of the Tahoe City Y.

BEACHES

Of the many beaches scattered around the lake's shore, two of the best are **Chamber's Landing,** south of Tahoe City, a favorite of young north-shore locals; and **Baldwin Beach,** a gorgeous and usually uncrowded sand beach between South Lake Tahoe and Emerald Bay. **Nevada Beach,** a more populated spot just across the Nevada border in Stateline, has great mountain views. **Sand Harbor,** a crescent-shaped beach off Highway 28 south of Incline Village, is ideal for sunsets.

WATER SPORTS

Despite Lake Tahoe's often frigid waters, there's no lack of rental outfits specializing in sailing, waterskiing, jet skiing, windsurfing, kayaking, canoeing, and parasailing. Prices fluctuate a bit, but in general sailboats go for $30–$35 an hour, $85–$95 a day; Jet Skis run $50–$90 an hour; Windsurfers rent for $10–$15 an hour, $30–$40 a half day; and canoes go for $10–$15 an hour, $30–$40 a half day. Parasailing rides, which usually last about 15 minutes, range from $35 to $50.

On the south shore the **Ski Run Boat Company** (tel. 530/544–0200), with motorboats, canoes, kayaks, and other toys, is one of several shops operating out of **Ski Run Marina,** off U.S. 50 about a half mile west of the California–Nevada border. On the north shore you'll find rental outfits in the **Sunnyside Marina,** about 2 mi south of Tahoe City on Highway 89.

FISHING

The most convenient area is **Lake Tahoe,** stocked occasionally with rainbow trout by the folks at the Fish and Wildlife Service; to find the section of the lake most recently stocked, call 530/355–7040 or 530/351–0832. Also popular is the stretch of the **Truckee River** between Truckee and Tahoe City—just pick a spot and cast your line. Wherever you fish, licenses ($9 a day, $24 a year) are required by law and available from most sporting-goods shops. For sportfishing on the lake, contact **Tahoe Sportfishing** (tel. 530/541–5448 or 800/696–7797), in the Ski Run Marina, or **Don's Sport Fishing** (tel. 530/541–5566), in South Lake Tahoe. Half-day trips generally start at $60–$70, full-day trips at $75–$85.

SKIING

Whether you prefer downhill or cross-country, you've come to the right place. Unbelievably sheer faces, narrow chutes, and huge cliffs have attracted a new breed of downhill skier and snowboarder bent on pushing the sport to extremes. But novices shouldn't be intimidated: There are more than 24 ski resorts, and most have plenty of beginner-level slopes, both downhill and cross-country. In addition to the millions of discount rental and lift-ticket flyers you'll find all over the area, the tourist centers can give you the *Skier's Planning Guide,* the *Winter Travel Planner,* and the *Winter Visitors' Guide.* All have information on the various lift operators and advice about skiing in the area. Call the **North Lake Tahoe Resort Association** (*see* Basics, *above*) for tips on skiing specials—they change throughout the season.

EQUIPMENT RENTAL

Renting equipment from the shops run by the resorts will make it easier to get adjustments, repairs, or replacements midday. However, as a rule of thumb, the closer you get to the ski resorts, the higher the cost of renting equipment. For the cheapest rentals, try any one of the hundreds of stores crowding the lake's major roads. The best deal anywhere is the south shore's **Don Cheepo's** (3349 U.S. 50, about ¾ mi west of Heavenly, tel. 530/544–0356), where full downhill and cross-country rental packages (skis, boots, and poles) cost $9. Snowboards rent for $20, including boots.

Of the north-shore rental outfits, **Porter's** has low rates (full ski packages $11–$15, snowboards $15–$22) and three locations, including one in Tahoe City (501 North Lake Blvd., just east of Tahoe City Y, tel. 530/583–2314) and one in Truckee (in Crossroads Center on Hwy. 89, south of I–80, tel. 530/587–1500).

DOWNHILL SKIING

The "Big Five" ski resorts (*see below*) all charge about $45 a day, but if you're careful, you can avoid paying that price. Buying multiple-day or weekday tickets will save you $3–$7 per day; also scour local papers, motels, gas stations, and supermarkets (try Safeway) for discounts and deals. Beginners and intermediate skiers can save money and still get their money's worth at one of the smaller, less expensive resorts, some of which even offer midweek discounts. If you're coming from the Bay Area, you can save 30–45 minutes driving time by skiing at any of the Donner Pass ski resorts—Soda Springs, Sugar Bowl, Donner Ranch, Boreal, or Tahoe Donner. Of these five, **Sugar Bowl** (tel. 530/426–3847 for snow report), off the Soda Springs/Norden exit of I–80, is the largest and most beautiful. Sugar Bowl is especially attractive for experienced skiers, with 50% of its runs designated advanced, including some of the best tree skiing in Tahoe. A few miles farther down the road, **Donner Ranch** (Soda Springs/Norden exit off I–80, tel. 530/426–3635 for snow report) is Tahoe's cheapest ski resort, with lift tickets starting at just $10 on weekdays and $22 on weekends. If you have more than a day for skiing, consider **Ski**

Homewood (Hwy. 89, between Tahoe City and South Lake Tahoe, tel. 530/525–2900 for snow report): From its 1,260 acres of varied terrain you can catch magnificent views of the lake. Lift tickets go for $35 for a full day, $26 for a half. Better still, Wednesday is 2-for-1 day, when you and a friend can ski for $17.50 each.

THE BIG FIVE • Squaw Valley (on Hwy. 89, 8 mi south of Truckee, tel. 530/583–6955 for snow report) is a vast resort with more than 8,000 acres of open bowls, 2,850 vertical ft, and more than 25 chairlifts. Though it's unofficially known as the home of extreme skiing, Squaw Valley is actually an all-around ski area—70% of the mountain is suited to beginning and intermediate skiers. **Alpine Meadows** (off Hwy. 89, 6 mi northwest of Tahoe City, tel. 530/581–8374 for snow report) has a high base elevation of 7,000 ft (allowing for a longer season) and 12 lifts servicing more than 100 runs. Alpine has built its reputation on the abundant snow and sunshine that its two mountains enjoy—most locals agree it's the best place for spring skiing. Alpine Meadows is also home to the **Tahoe Handicapped Ski School** (tel. 530/581–4161), the first school in the area to offer ski programs for the mentally and physically challenged. **Northstar-at-Tahoe** (Hwy. 267, 7 mi south of Truckee, tel. 530/562–1330 for snow report) has a split of 25% beginner runs, 50% intermediate runs, and 25% advanced runs. It's worth coming here for a day, if only for the incredible views of the basin from the top of the 8,610-ft **Mt. Pluto. Heavenly** (west entrance off Lake Tahoe Blvd., in South Lake Tahoe, tel. 530/541–7544 for snow report) is officially the largest ski area in the United States, with more than 4,300 acres of skiable terrain, an incredible 3,500-ft vertical drop, and 25 lifts scattered over no fewer than nine peaks. **Kirkwood** (Hwy. 88E, off Hwy. 89 south from South Lake Tahoe, tel.

Alpine Meadows is one of the few resorts that does not allow snowboarders.

209/258–3000 for snow report) has the driest snow, which experienced skiers know means the best powder—all told, 85% of Kirkwood's runs are designated intermediate or advanced.

CROSS-COUNTRY SKIING

You'll have no problem finding a trail to suit your abilities at Tahoe's 13 cross-country ski areas, the most famous of which is the north shore's **Royal Gorge** (Soda Springs/Norden exit south from I–80, tel. 530/426–3871 or 800/500–3871), the largest cross-country ski resort in the United States. You can choose from 200 mi of trails running along a ridge above the north fork of the American River; fees are $18 midweek.

Eagle Mountain (tel. 530/389–2254), whose fee is $12, is strictly for skiers with at least some experience. With incredible vistas along 45 mi of trails, it's Tahoe's closest Nordic resort—about an hour west of Truckee. Exit I–80 at Yuba Gap and follow the signs. Two other cross-country resorts on the north shore, **Northstar-at-Tahoe** (tel. 530/562–1330), charging a $14 fee, and **Squaw Creek** (tel. 530/583–6300), which charges $10, are right next to downhill ski areas (*see above*), making them great choices for vacation groups with divided loyalties. Of the two, Northstar, with 40 mi of trails, is the more exciting destination.

On the south shore, only **Kirkwood** (*see above;* tel. 209/258–7248) has both alpine and Nordic ski trails, with more than 50 mi of cross-country for skiers of all levels ($12). **Hope Valley** (Hwy. 88E, off Hwy. 89, tel. 530/694–2266) occupies a beautiful valley of the Toiyabe (Toy-*ah*-bee) National Forest, on the grounds of Sorenson's Resort. Best of all, you can ski its 60 mi of trails for free (donation requested). The North Lake Tahoe Resort Association (*see* Basics, *above*) can also hook you up with packages, such as a $33 three-day ticket that can be used at any of seven resorts.

YOSEMITE NATIONAL PARK

REVISED BY JONATHAN LEFF

For over a decade tourists have been flocking to, awestruck by, and—all too often—abusive of Yosemite National Park. A hundred years ago this abuse came in the form of carved-up giant sequoias—making a hole big enough to drive a car through—and atrocities against the Native peoples; in today's era of eco-tourism, damage is the result of too much attention. Between 1986 and 1996 the number of visitors to the park increased from 3 million to more than 4 million—most came in the summer, and most went straight to the 7-mi stretch called **Yosemite Valley.** They came to gawk at **Half Dome** and **El Capitan**—two breath-taking but treacherous granite formations—as well as at the **Yosemite, Nevada,** and **Vernal falls.**

Though park officials have long known the undue traffic has been damaging the park (not to mention visitors' appreciation of it), little was done to alleviate the problem until 1996, when nature took matters into her own hands. First came the Ackerson Complex fires—the most devastating in park history. In August they burned 59,000 acres north of Tioga Road. A government shutdown closed the park for a record 21 days, and an 80,000-ton rock slide behind the Happy Isles Nature Center left a cloud of granite dust hovering over the valley for a week. Then came the floods of January 1997, the biggest flood recorded in park history. It was most destructive along the Merced River, the central waterway in Yosemite Valley: Two campgrounds were destroyed; several sections of Highway 140 were washed out; and drinking water, sewage systems, and power lines went down.

The cleansing effect of the fires and flood were naturally beneficial, as any ranger will tell you. The natural closure of the valley gave officials time to restructure the workings of the park, reducing the uncontrolled number of visitors by instituting a day-use reservations system. As a result, there will be fewer overall visitors to the valley; what this means for the other side of Yosemite—the undisturbed, forested backcountry with its massive granite formations and plunging waterfalls—is yet to be seen. Perhaps the less visited, nonvalley areas of Yosemite—**Tuolumne Meadows** (say it: *twa*-lo-mee), along Tioga Road; the giant sequoias of **Mariposa Grove,** off Highway 41 in the southwest corner of the park; **Glacier Point,** near Badger Pass; and the **Hetch Hetchy Reservoir** (north of Big Oak Flat)—will remain untrammeled and enjoyed by those who know their solitary wonder. Or perhaps the numerous turnouts and day-hike areas that make these areas fairly easy to reach from the highway will become crowded with overflow visitors from the valley.

Whatever the case, these natural disasters (or perhaps blessings) haven't for a moment dulled the natural, glorious sheen of this land, formed by glacial sculpturing and prehistoric activity at the earth's mantle. Slightly smaller than the state of Rhode Island, Yosemite is still packed with waterfalls, sheer granite cliffs, lush forests, and generous expanses of alpine meadows, and you can still find a quiet spot to call your own.

BASICS

VISITOR INFORMATION

For current events in Yosemite, check out the *Yosemite Guide,* available at all entrance stations. The visitor centers stock maps and brochures and distribute free wilderness permits (required for overnight camping in the backcountry; *see* Wilderness Permits, *below*). The **Yosemite Valley Visitor Center** (Shuttle Stops 6 and 9, tel. 209/372–0299) is 11 mi east of the Highway 140 entrance and open mid-June–early September, daily 8–7; off-season, daily 9–5. The **Tuolumne Meadows Visitor Center** (tel. 209/372–0263), open summer only, daily 8–7:30, is toward the east end of the park on Tioga Road. The **Wawona Ranger Station** (tel. 209/375–9501), at the south end of Yosemite on Highway 41, provides wilderness permits summer only, weekdays 8:30–5. The **Big Oak Flat Visitor Center** (tel. 209/372–0615), at the Highway 120 west entrance, is open from Memorial Day to Labor Day, daily 9–5. If you're not actually in the park, send a self-addressed, stamped envelope to the **Public Information Office** (Box 577, Yosemite National Park 95389, tel. 209/372–0265) for free brochures and maps or call weekdays between 9 and 5. For automated information call the **Yosemite National Park information line** (tel. 209/372–0200). At press time there was a possibility that restrictions limiting reservations would be required in 1998; call one of the visitor centers for an update.

WILDERNESS PERMITS • In 1972 Yosemite had to institute a permit system to limit the number of backpackers on the trails each day. Half the park's permits are reserved, while half are distributed on a first-come, first-served basis one day in advance. To make a reservation (available up to 24 weeks in advance), you'll need to pay a reservation fee of $3 per person and send your dates of arrival and departure, specific trailheads of entry and exit, your main destination in the park, the number in your party, and alternative dates in case your first choices aren't available to **Wilderness Reservations** (Wilderness Center, Box 545, Yosemite National Park 95389, tel. 209/372–0740). You may also call 209/372–0740 to reserve by phone.

For free first-come, first-served permits, head to the new **Wilderness Center** (tel. 209/372–0310), which is two buildings east of the Yosemite Valley Visitor Center (*see above*). When the Wilderness Center is closed (in winter), go to the wilderness permit station nearest your planned destination. Permits go

YOSEMITE NATIONAL PARK

Evergreen Rd.

Mather

TO HETCH
HETCHY
RESERVOIR

TO GROVELAND

**Stanislaus
National
Forest**

120

**Big Oak Flat
Visitor Center**

**Crane
Flat**

Merced

River

**Sierra
National
Forest**

140

South Fork Merced River

El Portal

41

**Wawona
Ranger
Station**

**Mariposa
Grove**

South Fork Merced River

**Badger
Pass**

Glacier

Point

Yosemite

Valley

**Bridalveil
Falls**

El Capitan

**Yosemite
Falls**

Bridalveil Creek

Rd.

**Sentinel
Dome**

**Yosemite
Valley
Visitor
Center**

**Curry
Village**

**Glacier
Point**

**Happy
Isles**

**Vernal
Fall**

**Nevada
Fall**

**Half
Dome**

**Yosemite
Wilderness
Center**

Big

Oak

Flat

Rd.

Cascade Creek

Tioga

Rd.

**White
Wolf**

**Yosemite
Creek**

120

Yosemite

Creek

**Porcupine
Flat**

May

Lake

Tenaya

Lake

John

Muir

Trail

Merced River

Merced

Lake

**Tuolumne
Meadows**

**Tuolumne
Meadows
Visitor
Center**

**Sierra
National
Forest**

**Inyo
National
Forest**

Waugh
Lake

Gem
Lake

Thousand
Island
Lake

Garnet
Lake

Grant
Lake

158

0

6 km

0

4 miles

N

quickly (some in just five minutes)—particularly for popular areas such as the valley and Tuolumne Meadows—so arrive early the day before your hike with a detailed itinerary, including trails and estimated overnight stops.

FEES

The park fee for one week is $20 per car or $10 per hiker or bicyclist. For $40 you can purchase an annual pass for unlimited access to the park.

WHEN TO GO

If possible, visit during spring or early fall, when crowds are less oppressive. Spring (late April–late May) is especially spectacular—the wildflowers are in bloom, and the waterfalls are at their peak of sound and fury as snow pack melts in the high country. Of the more than 4 million people who visit each year, 70% arrive during summer (June–August), when temperatures reach average highs of 90°F and lows of 40°F. In winter (November–March) temperatures drop to a chilly 45°F by day and a downright frigid 15°F by night—Tioga Pass and Glacier Point Road usually close by November due to inclement weather.

WHAT TO PACK

Rain gear is essential year-round since at any time you may have to battle one of Yosemite's sudden summertime tempests. Water-repellent shell pants and a warm jacket with polar-fleece lining are a smart idea, and don't forget wool or wick-dry socks—they'll keep you warm even when it's wet. If you plan to camp in winter, you'll need a subzero sleeping bag and a waterproof (or at least water-resistant) four-season tent. Hiking boots are a must for exploring the backcountry; bring snowshoes or crampons if you want to blaze your own trail.

GENERAL STORES

If you're coming into the park from Highway 120, stop first at Oakdale's **Newdeal Market** (888 Hwy. 120, tel. 209/847–5919), open daily 7 AM–10 PM. If you're headed in on Highway 41, stock up at one of the major grocery stores in Oakhurst. Otherwise you're stuck with the grocery and camping stores in pricey Yosemite Village (at Shuttle Stops 3, 5, and 10). The **Village Sport Shop** (tel. 209/372–1286), open from spring to fall, has fishing and camping gear. Both the **Village Store** (tel. 209/372–1253), open daily 8 AM–10 PM (8–8 in winter), and the **Wawona Store** (Hwy. 41, near south end of park, tel. 209/375–6574), open daily 8–8 (9–6 in winter), stock groceries and basic camping supplies.

Badger Pass Sport Shop (tel. 209/372–8430), open Thanksgiving through Easter (weather permitting), has ski clothing and equipment as well as limited picnic supplies. It's near Wawona and the Badger Pass ski slopes, off Highway 41 about 5 mi south of Yosemite Valley. Curry Village, at the far-east end of Yosemite Valley (Shuttle Stop 14), has a fair selection of stores, including the **Curry Village Mountain Shop** (tel. 209/372–8396), where you can purchase rock-climbing supplies and topographic maps at inflated prices, and the **Yosemite Mountaineering School** (tel. 209/372–8344), where you can rent camping equipment including internal- and external-frame backpacks, day packs, sleeping bags, bear canisters, and foam pads at reasonable prices. Only climbing students can rent climbing shoes.

MEDICAL AID

The **Yosemite Medical Clinic,** in Yosemite Village, offers full medical services and 24-hour emergency care. *Between visitor center and Ahwahnee Hotel, tel. 209/372–4637. Open daily 8–5.*

COMING AND GOING

BY CAR

You can reach Yosemite on three routes: **Highway 41** from the south, **Highway 140** from Merced in the west, and **Highway 120** from San Francisco (take I–580 east to I–205 and connect to Highway 120, a four-hour drive). Because of heavy damage from the 1997 floods, you can expect moderate to severe delays along Highway 140, especially in nonsummer months. Highways 41 and 140 terminate in Yosemite Valley, and Highway 120 becomes Tioga Road inside the park; Big Oak Flat Road connects the latter with the valley. In spring and winter the eastern portion of Highway 120 (from Crane Flat east to the Tioga Pass and into Inyo National Forest and Lee Vining) is closed until Memorial Day weekend, as is Glacier Point Road. Summer traffic is frequently bumper to bumper, especially around July 4 and Memorial Day.

From late fall to early spring you should carry snow chains. The highways can get treacherous, and the California Highway Patrol often closes the roads to all traffic without snow gear. If you get stuck, you'll have to buy an expensive set of chains ($60) from a gas station. For road and weather conditions call 209/372–0200, 916/445–1534, or 800/427–7623.

BY BUS AND TRAIN

There is no direct bus service to Yosemite from San Francisco; all lines stop either in Fresno or Merced, where you have to change coaches. Should the valley close to all car traffic, call 209/372–0265 to find out about the many bus services that will be shuttling visitors into the park from the surrounding towns. At press time a cheap option from either Merced or Fresno is **VIA Adventures** (tel. 209/384–1315 or 800/369–7275), which runs three buses a day ($20 one-way) from Merced's Greyhound station on 16th and N streets, a 2½-hour ride, and two buses a day ($20 one-way) from Fresno's airport and several downtown hotels (call in advance), a three-hour trip. In conjunction with VIA Adventures, **Amtrak** (tel. 800/872–7245) provides service from San Francisco to the park and back for $78. The train stops in Emeryville and in Merced, where you board the bus to Yosemite. All buses stop at Yosemite Lodge, Curry Village, and Yosemite Village in the valley. From San Francisco **Green Tortoise** (tel. 415/956–7500 or 800/867–8647) runs a three-day Yosemite and Eastern Sierras tour out of San Francisco that covers much of the park and surrounding forest. The tour costs $109, plus $31 for food (see Bus Travel in Chapter 1); they also have two-day winter trips for $75, including food. The friendly folks at **Incredible Adventures** (tel. 415/759–7071 or 800/777–8464) lead three-day camping and hiking trips to Yosemite from San Francisco for an all-inclusive price of $169.

GETTING AROUND

Curvy **Tioga Road** (Highway 120) runs the entire 60-mi east–west length of the park, climbing 4,000 ft in elevation. If you're on a bicycle (see Biking, below), you may want to limit yourself to the valley, since both Highway 41 and Tioga Road are often narrow, with extreme increases in elevation.

BY PARK SHUTTLE

Free shuttle buses operate throughout the year, though service hours vary according to season. The **Yosemite Valley Shuttle** travels every 20 minutes year-round, with stops at Curry Village, Yosemite Village, the Yosemite Lodge, and campgrounds and points of interest in between (see Where to Sleep, below). Starting in mid-April, the shuttle operates 7 AM–10 PM for most stops—excluding Happy Isles, the Mirror Lake Trail, and the North Pines campground, when service stops at 7:30 PM (campers in North Pines can easily walk from Shuttle Stop 19 at Lower Pines after 7 PM). In winter hours are reduced to 9 AM–10 PM, and some stops receive no service at all. Check the Yosemite Guide for a current schedule. During ski season a free shuttle leaves Yosemite Lodge for the **Badger Pass** ski area in the morning and returns in the afternoon. Another shuttle ($10 one-way, $19.50 round-trip) runs three times daily from mid-May to early October (weather permitting) between Yosemite Lodge and **Glacier Point** (see Scenic Drives and Views, below). Tickets can be purchased at a **Yosemite transportation** desk, which is in all hotels. Stops are well marked; just look for the SHUTTLE BUS signs along the main roads. From July until Labor Day an early morning backpackers' shuttle ($20 round-trip) runs once daily between Yosemite Lodge and Tuolumne Meadows. Call a visitor center for schedules.

WHERE TO SLEEP

Close to the ground—that's the way to experience Yosemite, and camping and backpacking are the best ways to do it. If you must stay in a hotel, keep in mind that the privilege of four thin walls and a bed doesn't come cheap. Beds and campsites go like hotcakes, and reservations are essential—especially in summer and fall.

One of the best-kept secrets of Yosemite accommodations is the **Yosemite Lakes Hostel** (31191 Hardin Flat, 17 mi east of Groveland, 95321, tel. 209/962–0121), 5 mi west of the park on Highway 120. It has all sorts of sleeping options: hostel rooms that sleep two ($19), cabins that sleep four ($28), fully equipped yurts (circular domed tents) that sleep four ($89), and wooded tent sites ($16). There are washing machines, a TV, and microwaves on the premises. And—best of all—they often have space for walk-ins. The hostel is open from mid-May to September.

SOME THINGS TO BEAR IN MIND

Yosemite is home to a good many healthy, curious, and hungry black bears. The good news is they have yet to devour a camper. The bad news is they have developed an appetite for your sunscreen, soap, toothpaste, hair spray, and any other scented articles you may have lugged along. Sustaining this diet requires a high level of curiosity, so be forewarned: Your tent, ice chest, backpack, and car are all fair game. Store all food and related supplies in the metal storage boxes provided at campsites or rent or buy bear-proof containers for backcountry trips.

HOTELS AND CABINS

Hotel reservations can be made up to 366 days in advance, and believe it or not, most places actually fill up that far ahead. All lodging reservations are handled through **Yosemite Concessions Services Corporation** (5410 E. Home Ave., Fresno 93727, tel. 209/252–4848). Because Yosemite is so mobbed, you probably won't have a choice when it comes to your hotel accommodations. If you can find a single vacancy, consider yourself lucky. Otherwise, try the hostel (*see above*) or check out the nearby towns of El Portal, Fishcamp, and Oakhurst, all of which have reasonably priced lodgings.

If you've got to get out of the moonlight, most people prefer the **Yosemite Lodge** (Yosemite Valley, tel. 209/372–1274), which has rooms for two starting at $87 (with private bath); although all shared-bath rooms ($70) were wiped out in the flood, they should be rebuilt by 1998. Accommodations in **Curry Village** (tel. 209/372–8333) include canvas tent cabins (starting at $41) and simple wooden cabins ($56, $73 with private bath). Or seek out the shantytown called **Housekeeping Camp** (tel. 209/372–8338). This site in the valley consists of more than 250 identical concrete-and-canvas "tent" units; they are huddled close together so they are ideal for people who want to camp but don't want to lug the equipment. They're not particularly comfy, but each structure can house four people in bunk cots for only $44 per night (extra cots are an additional $4 each). The camp is open from April to late October. A grocery store, laundry, bathroom, and showers are nearby.

CAMPING

Yosemite Valley's developed campgrounds share a number of characteristics: They're all large, flat, near a major road, and shaded by pine trees. Most have picnic tables, fire pits, flush toilets, piped water, and food lockers, but none has direct access to showers (for that you'll have to head to Housekeeping Camp or Curry Village). Unfortunately, they're all extremely crowded, especially the ones in the valley—reservations are a must. Campground reservations are available up to five months in advance through **Destinet** (tel. 800/436–7275 or 760/452–8787). If you're stuck, show up at one of the campground kiosks (at Curry Village, at Big Oak Flat, and at Tuolumne Meadows) and put your name on the waiting list in case there's a cancellation; remember that without reservations you'll need to get a day-use permit in advance. The campground kiosks usually call off names once a day (around 3 PM) for cancellations and no-shows.

If you can't get a reservation at any major campground, there are a few first-come, first-served sites you can try (but remember: if the day-use permits work out, these may also be put on a reservation system). In particular, check out the valley's only walk-in campground, **Sunnyside,** near Yosemite Lodge in Yosemite Valley. Its 35 sites ($3 per person), all with running water and toilets, are a favorite among hard-core rock climbers. For walk-ins outside the valley, try **Tuolumne Meadows** (*see* Outside Yosemite Valley, *below*), where 25 sites are reserved for backpackers with wilderness permits, and the rest are reserved for same-day reservations; check the visitor center (either in the valley or in Tuolumne) for availability. Other sites that have operated on a first-come, first-served basis include: **Wawona** (Tioga Rd., at south end of park), with 100 sites ($10); **White Wolf** (Tioga Rd., about 10 mi east of Crane Flat), with 87 sites ($10); **Porcupine Flat,** with 52 sites ($6); and **Yosemite Creek,** with 75 sites ($6). However, if the recently instituted day-use system becomes reservation only, any or all of these grounds could also become reservation only. The latter two are both off Tioga Road east of White Wolf. All the Tioga Road campgrounds close in winter, usually from mid-September or early October to early June. For information on backcountry camping, *see* Longer Hikes, *below*.

INSIDE YOSEMITE VALLEY • The 1997 floods knocked out a whopping 300-plus campsites—and two entire campgrounds (Upper and Lower River)—in the valley. Although the total number of campsites in the park should be back to around 1,800 by 1998, the additional sites will probably not be in Yosemite Valley. At press times **Upper Pines** was the biggest campground, with 238 tent and RV sites ($15 each), available from April through November. It's conveniently located at Shuttle Stop 15, near trailheads to Mirror Lake and Vernal Fall, and gets predictably crowded. Across the street at Shuttle Stop 19, **Lower Pines** is open year-round, with 80 tent and RV sites ($15) sandwiched between the Merced River and Storeman Meadow. Expect the same pack of RVs and families you see at Upper Pines. **North Pines Campground,** with 85 sites ($15) available April–October, is conveniently located at Shuttle Stop 18. Open to both tent campers and RV owners, this campground gives you spectacular views of Yosemite Falls and has many sites along the sandy (sometimes soggy) shores of the Merced River. It is also a great starting point for the short hike to Mirror Lake.

OUTSIDE YOSEMITE VALLEY • Look for **Tuolumne Meadows,** an enormous riverside campground perfect for exploring the east side of the park. Its 314 sites ($12) lie along Tioga Road (Highway 120) and are usually open mid-June–September, depending on the weather. This campground, in some of the park's most beautiful country, attracts its share of day hikers, but it's still one of the last to fill up. **Hodgdon Meadow,** just past Highway 120 at the Big Oak Flat entrance on the west side of the park, allows you to escape the chaos of the valley and still remain within striking distance (30–40 minutes). It draws nature-loving car campers year-round, except when snow closes the road (sometimes until late spring).

If you're coming in on Route 41, at the south end of the park, be sure to stop at the majestic Mariposa Grove, Yosemite's largest stand of giant sequoias and home of Grizzly Giant, one of the largest sequoias in the world.

FOOD

If you plan on camping, bring as much food as possible. Prices in Yosemite's stores (*see* General Stores, *above*) are predictably high. American eateries, from fast-food cafeterias to expensive sit-down restaurants, are the only other choice.

The **Yosemite Village** complex, 11 mi east of the Highway 140 entrance, has the largest selection of food in the park. The **Pasta Place** (Shuttle Stop 5, tel. 209/372–8381), which is closed in winter, is a cafeteria-style restaurant with basic pasta dishes and a $10 dinner special that includes a full pasta plate, Caesar salad, bread, and a large drink. Also in Yosemite Village, **Degnan's Deli** (tel. 209/372–8454), the valley's healthiest spot, has made-to-order sandwiches and salads.

In **Curry Village** (tel. 209/372–8333), on the west side of the valley near Happy Isles, there are a cafeteria, a burger stand, and a small pizzeria adjoining a bar. The cafeteria has burgers, sandwiches, and breakfasts for less than $6. Other options are the Terrace Bar, where you can get a pitcher of beer for $7, and a pizzeria. Both are open daily noon–9.

EXPLORING YOSEMITE

It can take anywhere from a few days to the rest of your life to familiarize yourself with Yosemite. To get a good overview in summer, drive along **Tioga Road** (Highway 120), stopping to take a walk or a hike wherever you're inclined. Scores of trails meander through the park, from relaxing strolls to highly demanding backcountry excursions. If you don't have a car, many trailheads are easily reached by shuttle bus (*see* Getting Around, *above*). In winter be sure to check trail conditions with the rangers before heading out. Not all trails and roads are open year-round; trails in Tuolumne Meadows and Glacier Point may be inaccessible. Those venturing off the beaten path will need serious snow gear in the winter months.

ORIENTATION AND TOURS

The **Yosemite Valley Visitor Center** (*see* Basics, *above*) runs a free 30-minute slide show throughout the day; check the *Yosemite Guide* for times. Also look for the center's documentaries about John Muir and

Ansel Adams, shown in the late afternoon and in the evenings (call for schedules). Ranger-led programs in the valley—nature walks, storytelling, and the like—last anywhere from 30 minutes to more than an hour and are a great way to learn more about the park; programs that are more in-depth, at Tuolumne, White Wolf, and Wawona, can last six hours.

All kinds of guided bus tours originate in the valley, from two-hour excursions ($16) along the valley floor (every half hour daily 9–4) to a day-long grand tour ($42) of Mariposa Grove and Glacier Point (late spring to late fall). For reservations contact the **Yosemite Lodge Tour Desk** (tel. 209/372–1240) or go to one of the tour booths at Curry Village, the Ahwahnee Hotel, or the Village Store in Yosemite Village.

SHORT HIKES

Yosemite Falls, also known simply as the Falls, is the highest waterfall in North America and the fifth highest in the world. It's divided into the upper falls (1,430 ft), the middle cascades (675 ft), and the lower falls (320 ft). From the parking lot, a quarter-mile trail leads to the base. To reach the top, head to Sunnyside Campground and take the strenuous 3.5-mi (one-way) **Yosemite Falls Trail,** which rises over 2,700 ft; you'll be rewarded by breathtaking views. If you're not up to the full trek, which is from two to four hours round-trip, stop at **Columbia Rock,** just past the 1-mi trail marker. You'll still get a good workout and dizzying vistas of Half Dome and the valley. Get off at Shuttle Stop 7 and follow the signs.

At the east end of the valley, the 3-mi trail around **Mirror Lake/Meadow** (Shuttle Stop 17) is the gentlest in the park, so nearly everyone takes it. From the Happy Isles Trailhead (Shuttle Stop 16), the difficult 6-mi round-trip trail to **Vernal Fall** (317 ft) and **Nevada Fall** (594 ft) takes two or three hours, but the view from the top is phenomenal. The first half of the trail (aptly named Mist Trail) is a great place to soak yourself on a hot day—kiss your hairdo good-bye. A fantastic overnight hike continues past Nevada Fall to Half Dome (see Longer Hikes, below). If you arrive in Yosemite along Highway 41, **Bridalveil Falls** will be your first view of the valley; it's a ragged 620-ft cascade that's often blown as much as 20 ft from side to side by the wind. The Ahwahneechee called it *Pohono* (Puffing Wind). An easy quarter-mile trail leading to its base starts from the parking lot. For fabulous views of some of Yosemite's finest, follow the **Pohono Trail.** The trek starts at Highway 41 at the Wawona Tunnel and terminates at Glacier Point. If you start on the west side of the tunnel, it's a mile to Inspiration Point, where looking eastward up the valley floor, you can bask in the shadow of El Capitan and Bridalveil Falls.

Numerous day hikes begin at **Tuolumne Meadows,** including an easy half-mile trail to **Soda Springs**—a potable naturally carbonated spring. In 1863 William Brewer of the California Geologic Survey called its water "pungent and delightful," though a more recent visitor said, "It tastes like flat seltzer." An arduous 1½-hour hike (5 mi round-trip) to emerald **Elizabeth Lake** wanders through mountain hemlock and lodgepole pine and across boisterous Unicorn Creek. These trails are less crowded than those originating in the valley.

LONGER HIKES

There are hundreds of possible day hikes in Yosemite, but to beat the crowds, you'll need to do some serious backpacking in the wilderness, miles away from civilization. All trails are limited to a certain number of backpackers to prevent overuse, and free wilderness permits are required for overnight stays (see Wilderness Permits in Basics, above). A permit gives you access to 800 mi of trails (ranging from 5 to 20 mi long) crisscrossing Yosemite's outback. These often involve strenuous climbs along jagged paths no more than a foot wide, and some trails take upwards of a week to complete. Fire rings are interspersed along the way, but you'll need to bring your own tent and provisions, including a water filter or iodine tablets to treat water. Park rangers highly recommend that you rent special 3-pound bear-proof canisters for $3 at Yosemite Valley Sports Shop, Curry Village Mountain Shop, Crane Flat Grocery, Wawona Store, or Tuolumne Meadows Sports Shop (see box Some Things to Bear in Mind, above). Order maps and a pamphlet of hiking suggestions from the **Yosemite Association Bookstore** (Box 230, El Portal 95318, tel. 209/379–2648). At any of Yosemite's bookstores, you can buy topographic United States Geological Survey maps ($4), but experienced backpackers swear by Trails Illustrated's waterproof topographic map ($8.95), available at the Wilderness Center in Yosemite Village (see Wilderness Permits in Basics, above).

If you're in top physical condition, take the hike out of Yosemite Valley, following either the John Muir or Mist Trail to **Half Dome.** Follow the trail to Nevada Fall (see Short Hikes, above) and continue past Little Yosemite Valley Campground to the Half Dome turnoff; then be prepared to climb an additional 2,700 ft until you've risen a total of 4,800 ft. This 17-mi round-trip hike takes from 10 to 12 hours and is not for those with vertigo; the last leg of the trip involves a steep area with guide-rail cables provided to help you keep your balance and to pull yourself up. At the top, if you can stomach it, lie belly down and hang your chin over the precipice. You can make the trek an overnighter by camping at **Little Yosemite Valley Campground,** but you'll need a wilderness permit (*see* Wilderness Permits *in* Basics, *above*). You can leave your pack at the campground or just before the cables section and climb the last 4 mi without extra weight.

Despite the massive dam and the record-setting fires of 1996, the **Hetch Hetchy** area still retains much of its beauty. Here you'll find the wonderfully isolated, moderately difficult **Rancheria Falls Trail** (13 mi round-trip), which leads to the eponymous lonely falls. You can do this trail in a day. If you have more time (five days) and excellent packing skills, go for the 52-mi **Rancheria Mountain and Bear Valley Loop,** a strenuous hike that rewards you with a terrific view of the grand canyon of the Tuolumne River and a secluded campsite near Bear Valley Lake. To reach the Rancheria Falls trailhead, exit the west side of the park on Tioga Road (Highway 120), turn right on Evergreen Road after 1 mi, and continue for 8 mi (you'll see signs).

The numerous trailheads near **Tuolumne Meadows** are great for backpackers who want to spend at least a few days in the wilderness. Serious hikers should consider the **Tuolumne Grand Canyon Trail,** accessed from either Tuolumne Meadows or White Wolf. Allow at least three full days for the strenuous 29-mi hike to White Wolf, beginning at Tuolumne Meadows. For the first 4 mi follow the river along the forest and then drop down along a series of waterfalls and cascades, where the trail gets steeper as it descends through the Muir Gorge into Pate Valley. From there it's a steep climb to White Wolf. Another popular trip out of Tuolumne Meadows from the John Muir Trailhead is the two- to three-day hike to **Vogelsang Lake,** about 30 mi round-trip: You'll hike up Lyell Canyon via the **John Muir Trail** to the **Rafferty Creek Trail,** which becomes steep and difficult. Get your permits early (*see* Wilderness Permits *in* Basics, *above*).

> *Yosemite is a mecca for world-class rock climbers; look around, and you'll understand why.*

SCENIC DRIVES AND VIEWS

During summer you can drive up to **Glacier Point** for a spectacular view of the valley and surrounding mountains. The 16-mi road starts at the Chinquapin junction on Highway 41. Better yet, take a shuttle (*see* Getting Around, *above*) to the top and take Four Mile Trail back down into the valley (three hours), coming out on South Side Drive. **Tuolumne Meadows,** the largest subalpine meadow in the High Sierra and the site of several backcountry trailheads, is on Tioga Road, 25 mi west of Lee Vining and U.S. 395. This is a gorgeous part of Yosemite, with delicate meadows surrounded by huge granite formations, and it's usually much less crowded than the valley. Tioga Road is closed during winter and usually opens by late May, but harsh winters can force the road to remain closed into July.

OUTDOOR ACTIVITIES

For those who want to take it easy, the National Park Service rents binoculars ($3) for **bird-watching.** Free 1½-hour **photography walks,** which lead you to prime spots for shooting Yosemite, leave several times a week around 8:30 AM from the Yosemite Lodge or the Ahwahnee Hotel; reservations are recommended. **Horseback rides** originate at the stables in Wawona and Tuolumne (in summer) and in Yosemite Valley; the valley stable didn't operate in 1997, and its future is still undecided. A four-hour trip is $45. In summer (June and July) you can take a leisurely 3-mi raft trip down the Merced for $13. Sign up at the **rafting** area in Curry Village, open daily 10–4. For more information on all these activities, consult the *Yosemite Guide* or check with the visitor center (tel. 209/372–0299).

BIKING

Bikes are not permitted on any hiking trails, but Yosemite Valley has 8 mi of paved bike paths. Try the spectacular trail to Happy Isles, off the road to Curry Village; the easy 3-mi loop takes well under an hour unless you stop for a half-mile walk to Mirror Lake. Rent bikes ($5 per hour, $20 a day) from **Curry Village** (tel. 209/372–8319) or **Yosemite Lodge** (tel. 209/372–8367). Serious cyclists should consider the 15-mi round-trip from Tuolumne Meadows to Olmstead Point along Tioga Road. The grades are difficult and the roads narrow, but the views are chilling.

ROCK CLIMBING

Basic and intermediate lessons ($150 for one person, $90 each for two) are available from mid-April to mid-October with the **Yosemite Mountaineering School** (tel. 209/372–8344). They organize trips from Yosemite Valley and Tuolumne Meadows. You can't rent climbing equipment in the park without enrolling in a class.

SO YOU WANT TO DO A LITTLE HIKING

You can hook up with the Pacific Crest Trail out of Tuolumne Meadows and continue hiking for a few days, months, or a year by following the trail for 212 mi south to Mexico or north to Canada. Routed in 1928 the Pacific Crest Trail starts on the California–Mexico border and winds through three nations, 24 national forests, seven national parks, and 33 wilderness areas for a grand total of 2,638 mi, making it the longest complete trail in America. For more information contact the Pacific Crest Trail Association, 5325 Elkhorn Blvd., Suite 256, Sacramento 95842; or call 800/817-2243.

SKIING

Yosemite's ski season usually lasts from early December to March. Call 209/372–0200 for weather conditions.

DOWNHILL • Yosemite has a small ski area, **Badger Pass** (tel. 209/372–8430 or 209/372–1000 for snow report), which won't pose much of a challenge to accomplished skiers. It's a good place to learn, however, and there are enough relatively uncrowded trails to keep intermediate skiers entertained. It's open daily 9–4:30 in winter. Lift tickets cost $22–$28, depending on the number of lifts open, which in turn depends on snowfall. They have five lifts, with three advanced runs and six intermediate runs. Ski rentals are $18 a day, snowboards $30 a day. Look for Badger Pass 6 mi east of Highway 41 on Glacier Point Road.

CROSS-COUNTRY • Yosemite has 90 mi of marked cross-country trails through the Badger Pass ski area to Glacier Point. A free shuttle from the valley runs to Badger Pass, departing twice in the morning and returning in the afternoon. **Glacier Point Road** is a good place to start: Beginners will enjoy the groomed track, and advanced skiers will get a workout if they take the whole 21-mi round-trip along the rim of the valley. The **Yosemite Cross-Country Ski School** (tel. 209/372–8444) offers two-hour lessons ($19) and four-hour lessons ($40, including rentals). A guided overnight trip—including meals and lodging—is $110 per person. Badger Pass (*see above*) has rentals ($12 half day, $15 full day). The **Tuolumne Grove of Giant Sequoias Trail** (3 mi round-trip), which starts at Crane Flat a few miles east of the Big Oak Flat entrance station, has a steep drop, but you get to ski among the largest living things on earth.

SNOWSHOEING

National Park Service naturalists conduct regular two-hour snowshoe walks from Badger Pass and sometimes at Crane Flat. These easy walks ramble around the ski areas and the Tuolumne Grove of Giant Sequoias; showshoes are available for $2. The **Yosemite Mountaineering School** (tel. 209/372–8444 in winter) rents snowshoes at Badger Pass for $11.50 per day.

SANTA CRUZ

Originally founded in the late 18th century as a mission town, Santa Cruz has long been considered a bastion of the California-bred cult of the individual. Old-time residents, many of Italian descent, still look askance at the liberal students and hippies who have been migrating to the town ever since the University of California opened its "alternative, no-stress" branch here in the 1960s. Back then Santa Cruz was a city-size incarnation of the hippie. Of course, that's no longer true, but people still call Santa Cruz a hippie town, and somehow that has made it so.

These days Santa Cruz is subject to the conflicts of any sizable California community, particularly anti-immigration hysteria. As migrant farmworkers, mostly Mexicans and Mexican-Americans, move to Santa Cruz County in record numbers to work on nearby farmlands, these newcomers often find themselves made unwelcome by the largely homogeneous community.

Nonetheless, Santa Cruz holds on to its idyllic beach-town atmosphere better than many. The carnival-like **Boardwalk** is Santa Cruz at its flashiest, drawing legions of hormone-crazed teenagers from Salinas and San Jose every weekend. Beyond the town lies the stunning coast. The rocks off the craggy shore are favored perches for seals, the beaches are thronged with surfers and their retinue, and the surrounding hills fade into redwood forests.

If possible, visit in early August, when the **Cabrillo Music Festival** brings symphonic music and other live entertainment to town. Tickets cost $6–$25, depending on the performance and seating; call the Santa Cruz Civic Auditorium box office (tel. 408/429–3444). From mid-July to August U.C. Santa Cruz hosts **Shakespeare Santa Cruz** (tel. 408/459–2121): six weeks of the Bard's works set against a backdrop of beautiful redwoods. Tickets ($15–$21) should be reserved a few days in advance.

BASICS

VISITOR INFORMATION

You'll find $1.50 maps at the **visitor information center** (701 Front St., tel. 408/425–1234). Gay and lesbian travelers can call the **Lesbian/Gay/Bisexual/Transgender Community Center Hotline** (tel. 408/425–5422) for listings of upcoming events and other resources.

COMING AND GOING

BY CAR

The most scenic route from either San Francisco, 1½ hours north, or Monterey, an hour south, is along **Highway 1.** San Jose is about 45 minutes away on curvy **Highway 17,** which meets up with I–280, I–880, and U.S. 101 and is the faster drive to San Francisco and the East Bay. Avoid Highway 17 weekend mornings, though, when the entire Silicon Valley seems to head for the beaches, and at night, when the sharp curves of the road are tricky.

Downtown has risen from the rubble of the 7.1-magnitude Loma Prieta earthquake of 1989, and many say the squeaky-clean new buildings symbolize a sea change toward conservatism. Still, Santa Cruz's sloppy individuality is still very much in place.

BY BUS

Green Tortoise (*see* Bus Travel *in* Chapter 1) lumbers from San Francisco to Los Angeles, stopping in Santa Cruz at the Safeway parking lot (2018 Mission St., at Younglove St.) once a week. Buses from San Francisco, a three-hour ride costing $10, arrive in Santa Cruz Friday at 11 PM. From Los Angeles buses arrive Monday morning, a 9- to 12-hour $30 trip. Reserve one week ahead in the summer. *Tel. 415/956–7500 in CA or 800/867–8647.*

Greyhound Lines (425 Front St., at Laurel St., tel. 408/423–1800) has direct half-hour service between Santa Cruz and San Francisco twice daily ($14 one-way, $15 weekends) and three-times daily service from Los Angeles, a 10-hour trip that costs $51 one-way. **Amtrak** buses (tel. 800/872–7245) link the San Jose CalTrain depot and the Santa Cruz Metro Center roughly every hour between 4 AM and 10 PM for $5 each way ($8 for two tickets).

GETTING AROUND

The layout of Santa Cruz is insanity on a map and even more confusing in practice. On the edge of Monterey Bay and bisected by the San Lorenzo River, the town is full of crooked and puzzling streets, so keep a sharp eye on a map. Highway 1 becomes **Mission Street** when it enters Santa Cruz and resumes its old identity on the way out of town. **Bay Street** and **High Street** both funnel into U.C. Santa Cruz, which stands on a hill 2 mi northeast of downtown, while the Boardwalk is on **Beach Street,** just west of the river. The Boardwalk and downtown (which centers around **Pacific Avenue** and **Front Street**) are within comfortable walking distance (1 mi) of each other.

SANTA CRUZ

Sights ●
Brookdale Lodge, **1**
Mission
Santa Cruz, **3**
Mystery Spot, **2**
Natural Bridges
State Beach, **4**
Santa Cruz City
Museum of Natural
History, **6**
Santa Cruz Surfing
Museum, **5**

Lodging ○
Babbling Brook
Inn, **7**
Harbor Inn, **9**
Santa Cruz
Carmelita Cottages
(HI), **8**

KEY

i Tourist Information

0   0.3 miles
0   0.5 km

PACIFIC   OCEAN

BY BUS

Bus service is efficient and fairly easy to use. The Santa Cruz Metropolitan District Transit (SCMDT), also known as Metro, operates from the **Metro Center** (920 Pacific Ave., at Laurel St.), adjoining the Greyhound station. Any bus in town will eventually take you to the Metro Center, where you can pick up a copy of "Headways," a free pamphlet that lists all bus routes. The fare is $1, but you can purchase a special all-day pass for $3 on any bus or at the Metro Center. Exact change, in coins or one-dollar bills, is required; change machines are available at the Metro Center. The center's phones are answered and the kiosk is staffed weekdays from 8 to 5, but you can pick up schedules and get exact change 24 hours a day. *Tel. 408/425–8600. Phones and information booth open weekdays 8–5.*

BY BIKE

Biking is the best way to get around Santa Cruz. Many streets have wide bike lanes, and the weather is moderate, especially in spring and summer. Bring wheels from home if you can, since renting can be expensive. **Pacific Avenue Cycles** (709 Pacific Ave., at Laurel St., tel. 408/423–1314), at the end of the Pacific Garden Mall, charges $23 per day.

WHERE TO SLEEP

In summer, especially on weekends, finding a budget room in Santa Cruz is next to impossible. During the rest of the year hotels slash prices to rope in boarders. Year-round, the best deal is at the youth hostel—if you can get a bed. Camping is popular in summer. If the campgrounds listed below are full, make sure you call the headquarters after 5 PM, when the Manresa and Sunset state beaches open overflow sites. Failing that, the Big Basin Redwoods State Park (*see* Near Santa Cruz, *below*) is 45 minutes away. The dorms at U.C. Santa Cruz (tel. 408/459–2611) accept guests from the end of June to the beginning of September, but the rooms are spartan, far away from everything, and pricey. A single runs $60, $67 with full board; a double is $30 per person, $37 with full board. The dorms and apartments are only available to those on official university business, so you may want to say you're considering enrolling, and then you should sign up for a campus tour.

HOTELS AND MOTELS

Facing the Boardwalk on 2nd and 3rd streets and Riverside Avenue are some seedy motels that lie in an area with sketchy boundaries known as the Flats. These places rarely fill up, but you'll find comparably priced places clustered on Mission and Ocean streets that are much more comfortable and equally convenient if you have a car. For a decadent treat, stay at one of several good B&Bs. At the downtown **Babbling Brook Inn** (1025 Laurel St., 95060, tel. 408/427–2437, fax 408/427–2457), rooms with country French decor are surrounded by manicured gardens and a beautiful brook. Twelve rooms come complete with private bath and a fireplace or Jacuzzi. Double rooms, which include a full breakfast, run $85–$165 per night.

UNDER $50 • Harbor Inn. In a residential area 10 minutes southeast of town, this inviting inn has doubles (starting at $45 in summer, $35 off-season) with a hodgepodge of old furniture and wooden beds. The inn often fills in summer, so call ahead for reservations. Most rooms have kitchenettes, and groups of four can get a suite ($65–$85, depending on the season). *645 7th Ave., 95062, tel. 408/479–9731. From downtown, cross river on Laurel St., right on San Lorenzo Blvd., left on Murray St., left on 7th Ave. Or Bus 67 or 6 to 7th Ave. 19 rooms, 14 with bath.*

HOSTEL

Santa Cruz Carmelita Cottages (Hostelling International). Two blocks from the Boardwalk on Beach Hill, these cottages are actually a cluster of houses made hosteler friendly ($13 for members, $16 for nonmembers). A curfew and a no-alcohol rule create a quiet atmosphere in the private and "family"

The forests around Santa Cruz are full of slimy little critters: Look for banana slugs (the UCSF mascot) and California newts, which have bright orange stomachs.

rooms (from three to five people), which cost $30–$40, depending on the number of beds. Cyclists can use the on-site repair and tune-up shop. Eager beavers show up around 3 PM for the 5 PM first-come, first-served check-in; arrive in a car, and you get last dibs. Write two weeks ahead (Box 1241, Santa Cruz 95061) or call for reservations. *321 Main St., at 2nd St., 95060, tel. 408/423–8304. From Metro Center, Bus 7 to Main St. 25 beds. Curfew 11 PM, lockout 10–5. Reception open daily 8 AM–10 AM and 5 PM–10 PM.*

CAMPING

Henry Cowell Redwoods State Park. Five miles north of Santa Cruz, this 113-site campground is buffered by a redwood forest and rests under madronas and mixed pine trees near several trailheads. In summer RVs and screaming teens tend to overrun the place, but otherwise it's great. Bike campers share one large, shady site for $3 each. Reserve through Destinet (tel. 800/444–7252). Both tent and RV sites are $17 weekdays, $18 weekends. *101 N. Big Trees Park Rd., Felton 95018, tel. 408/335–4598 or 408/438–2396. From Hwy. 1, Hwy. 9 north; from Metro Center, Bus 35. Drinking water, flush toilets, showers. Closed Dec.–Feb.*

New Brighton State Beach. High above the ocean on a large cliff, this popular tents-only campground is in Capitola, 5 mi southeast of Santa Cruz. What it lacks in privacy, it makes up for in beauty: A few of its 112 sites enjoy an incredible view of the coast. A steep path leads downhill to the soft beach below. Reservations, available through Destinet (tel. 800/444–7252), are a must between May and October. Sites go for $16 weekdays, $19 weekends. Follow signs from Highway 1. Otherwise, Bus 71 will take you to the corner of Soquel and Park avenues, leaving you with a long walk. *1500 Park Ave., 95010, tel. 408/464–6330.*

Sunset State Beach and **Manresa State Beach.** Slightly more spacious and private than New Brighton, these two campgrounds, both about 10 minutes south of Santa Cruz, are short walks from wide, sandy beaches. Sunset has 90 campsites, all with fire rings, picnic tables, and hot showers. Spaces, reserved through Destinet (tel. 800/444–7252), are $17 weekdays, $18 weekends. On the way to Sunset, you'll pass Manresa, which has 64 walk-in sites 100 yards from the parking lot, with the same facilities, prices, and reservation system as Sunset. Sites are on a plateau above the beach or set back in a sparse sprinkling of trees. Both campgrounds open overflow sites when they're fully booked; the Manresa overflow accommodates RVs only, and Sunset puts tent campers in the picnic area. *San Andreas Rd., tel. 408/763–7063 for Sunset and 408/761–1795 for Manresa. Hwy. 1 south to San Andreas Rd./Larkin Valley exit, right at bottom of ramp, right onto San Andreas Rd.*

FOOD

Santa Cruz's hippie days have left a legacy of organic, largely vegetarian cuisine. For fresh produce head to the **farmers' market** held every Wednesday from 2 to 6 on the corner of Pacific Avenue and Walnut Street; then trot over to Lorenzo Park (River St., between Water St. and Soquel Ave.) for a picnic. Also, look for the markets along Mission Street.

UNDER $5

For a tasty slice of late-night pizza, head to **Uppercrust Pizza** (2415 Mission St., tel. 408/423–9010), on the west side of town near the Highway 1 turnoff for Natural Bridges State Beach. For heaping portions of Mexican food, hit **Taquería Vallarta** (608 Soquel Ave., 1 block east of Ocean St., tel. 408/457–8226).

The Bagelry. This Santa Cruz institution specializes in hybrid bagel spreads like the Pink Flamingo (cream cheese with lox and dill) and the Luna spread (pesto, ricotta, and almonds). Spread your schmear on a hefty "three-seed slug"—a wide bagel without the hole. *320A Cedar St., at Laurel St., tel. 408/429–8049. Cash only.*

Zachary's. A basic breakfast—two eggs, tasty home fries, and your choice of homemade breads—sells for a reasonable $5, but you might want to splurge on a huge stack of pancakes or a family-size omelet. Expect a wait of up to an hour on weekends. *819 Pacific Ave., between Laurel and Maple Sts., tel. 408/ 427–0646. Closed Mon.*

UNDER $10

Dolphin Restaurant. Head to the end of Santa Cruz's municipal pier for crispy, freshly caught fish-and-chips. You can park yourself at the picnic tables adjacent to the Dolphin's serving window. *End of pier, tel. 408/426–5830. Cash only.*

Saturn Café. The Saturn is decked out with theme tables (*Charlie's Angels*, Richard Nixon, and Madonna, to name a few) and flying saucer–like lamps. Try their stellar tomato-garlic pesto sauce over the pasta of the day or a bowl of soul-warming chili. *1230 Mission St., near Laurel St., tel. 408/429– 8505. Cash only.*

CAFES

In a town with more than 15,000 college students, the absence of nighttime diversions for the under-21 set has fueled a serious café scene. In addition to being popular hangout spots for college students, cafés are also frequented by locals looking for a lively debate or a place to read a good book. **Caffè Pergolesi** (418A Cedar St., at Elm St., tel. 408/426–1775) is inside a big, rambling Victorian house with a huge outdoor deck. The **Herland Book-Café** (902 Center St., at Locust St., tel. 408/429–6636), conceived as a safe haven for women, has books grouped in categories like "Women of the Wild West" or "Women Respond to the Men's Movement"—all female-authored. You can get organically grown tea and coffee at the **Jahva House** (120 Union St., near Cedar St., tel. 408/459–9876), which occupies a large, airy, comfortable warehouse softened by Oriental rugs and ficus trees.

EXPLORING SANTA CRUZ

To explore the jagged coast, you'll need a car or a mountain bike. However, most of Santa Cruz's sights are within a walkable area downtown. The **Pacific Garden Mall** consists of specialty stores, antiques shops, restaurants, and cafés. **Logos** (1117 Pacific Ave., near Lincoln St., tel. 408/427–5100) is Santa Cruz's premier used-book and music store. The **Mission Santa Cruz** (126 High St.)—built in 1791, destroyed by an earthquake in 1857, and rebuilt as a half-size replica in 1931—has grounds overrun with colorful gardens and fountains.

SANTA CRUZ BEACH BOARDWALK

Thick with the smell of suntan oil and hair spray, the Boardwalk provides the stickiest, most commercialized sun-and-sand carnival west of Coney Island. At center stage is the **Giant Dipper,** created in 1924—one of the oldest wooden roller coasters in the world. The ride affords you a brief panorama of Monterey Bay before plunging you down toward the beach. Another Boardwalk favorite is the Ferris wheel, which provides one of the best ocean views in Santa Cruz. *400 Beach St., tel. 408/423–5590 or 408/426–7433 for recorded information. From Front St. follow signs to the ocean. Rides open Memorial Day–Labor Day, daily from 11 AM; Labor Day–Memorial Day, weekends and holidays only; call 408/426–7433 for details.*

U.C. SANTA CRUZ

The beauty of the UCSC campus makes you understand why so many people choose to attend college in California. The **campus bookstore** (tel. 408/459–4544), at the center of campus, is woody and natural, resembling a ski lodge more than a student union. Investigate the **limestone quarry** near the bookstore—it's a nice spot for a picnic—and take a self-guided or docent-led tour of the 29-acre organic growing system at the **Farm and Garden Project** (tel. 408/459–4140), near the base of campus. The **admissions office** (tel. 408/459–4008), at the campus entrance, is open weekdays 8–5 and has maps and tour schedules. Avoid the on-campus parking fee by parking along Meder Avenue at the far west end of campus and catching the free shuttle at Bay and High streets. Otherwise take Bus 1 from the Metro Center to the west entrance of campus.

SANTA CRUZ CITY MUSEUM OF NATURAL HISTORY

The museum is small but full of information about the Ohlone Indians—the area's original inhabitants—and the local seals and sea lions. A slippery touch pool allows you to finger sea slugs and anemones. In January the museum sponsors the **Fungus Fair,** celebrating the mushrooms that blanket the forest floor. *1305 E. Cliff Dr., tel. 408/429–3773. From downtown, walk or drive east on Laurel St., cross river, turn right on San Lorenzo St. (which becomes East Cliff Dr.). Or take Bus 67 from Metro Center. $2 donation requested. Open Tues.–Sun. 10–5.*

SANTA CRUZ SURFING MUSEUM

At Lighthouse Point on West Cliff Drive, there's a tiny exhibit on surfing—from its Hawaiian origins to the present. Included in the display is a board bitten by a great white shark in 1987, testimony to the genuine shark danger along the coast from Santa Cruz to Pigeon Point. Plop down outside the lighthouse and watch the surfers on Steamer's Lane, one of the best surf spots in California. A little farther out you'll see Seal Rock, the summertime home of thousands of shiny barking seals. *Mark Abbott Memorial Lighthouse, West Cliff Dr., tel. 408/429–3429. Bus 3A to Lighthouse Field. Admission free. Open Mon. and Wed.–Fri. noon–4, weekends noon–5.*

> *At sunset go to It's Beach, immediately west of the lighthouse. Almost every summer evening locals gather here to drum and dance as night falls. You can hang back or jump right into the middle of the fun.*

NATURAL BRIDGES STATE BEACH

The mudstone bridgelike formation that gives this beach its name is a nesting spot for pelicans and an unusual sight for visitors. There's also a **monarch butterfly colony** on the grounds: You'll find thousands of the brightly colored creatures clustered in the trees from mid-October to February. Call ahead for the latest information (and to make a reservation for guided walks). Tidal pools, picnic tables, barbecue pits, and plenty of soft, warm sand round out the list of attractions. Park on Delaware Avenue just east of the park entrance to avoid the $6 parking fee. *West Cliff Dr., tel. 408/423–4609. From boardwalk, follow West Cliff Dr. 2 mi until you see signs. Or Bus 3B from Metro Center. Open daily 8 AM–sunset.*

MYSTERY SPOT

This quirky little place lies in the redwoods 3 mi north of Santa Cruz and, in the minds of true believers, is at the center of a mysterious force that makes people taller and compels balls to roll uphill. It's kitschy, no doubt, but its gift shop is filled with everything you could ever want emblazoned with the Mystery Spot logo—from silver spoons to shot glasses to paperweights with scorpions stuck inside. Your $4 admission also buys you a Mystery Spot bumper sticker (that's why you see them everywhere). *465 Mystery Spot Rd., tel. 408/423–8897. From downtown, go south on Water St., left on Market St., go 2½ mi, then follow signs. Open summer, daily 9–8:30; winter, daily 9–5.*

AFTER DARK

Only a few bars in Santa Cruz feature live music; upcoming shows are listed in the weekly newspaper *Good Times.* Unless there's a big name playing, skip the **Catalyst** (1011 Pacific Ave., tel. 408/423–1336) and head straight to the **Kuumbwa Jazz Center** (320 Cedar St., at Laurel St., tel. 408/427–2227), which hosts jazz and blues shows throughout the year. Call for tickets ($2–$14) and scheduling information. Those with wheels might want to catch a double feature at the **Skyview Drive-In Theater** (2260 Soquel Ave., at Thurber La., tel. 408/475–3405) for $5 a head: Two first-run films and two not-quite-on-video-yet flicks play year-round starting around 7:30 in winter and 9 in summer.

THE CAPITOL OF THE COAST

The ocean-side town of Capitola, along the coast about 5 mi southeast of Santa Cruz, has a wide, quiet sandy beach and a rickety wooden pier—a welcome change from the sometimes frenetic pace of Santa Cruz. After you've soaked up enough sun, head straight to Mr. Toot's (221 Esplanade, tel. 408/475-3679), a café full of old wooden tables, comfortable couches, and a deck overlooking the beach. Catch Bus 59 from Santa Cruz's Metro Center or take Highway 1 south to the Capitola/Park Avenue exit and head toward the Pacific.

The **Blue Lagoon** (923 Pacific Ave., across from Metro Center, tel. 408/423-7117) is Santa Cruz's premier (read: only) gay and bisexual nighttime hangout (straights are welcome, too). There's a $2 cover on weekends and Tuesday—a small price to pay for some of the best DJ'ed dance music in town. The **Boulder Creek Brewing Company** (13040 Hwy. 9, tel. 408/338-7882), 25 minutes north of Santa Cruz, combines great beer and the best live music in the area. There's usually a cover ($3 and up) for their live bands, which might include anything from flamenco dancers to Middle Eastern musicians to blues artists. Despite its pastel-color stucco building and bland interior, the **Seabright Brewery** (519 Seabright Ave., at Murray St., 7 blocks east of the river, tel. 408/426-2739) is incredibly popular with locals, especially on Tuesday's Neighborhood Night, when homeowners mingle with renting students on the concrete patio. Friday brings live rock and blues from 6 to 10. The **Red Room** (1003 Cedar St., at Locust St., tel. 408/426-2994) is a snazzy dive bar and a true UCSC institution, especially among the über-hip. Occasionally you can catch rockabilly and alternarock in the rear Crown Room for a minimal cover. Don't look for a sign out front; there isn't one.

OUTDOOR ACTIVITIES

HIKING AND MOUNTAIN BIKING

Some of northern California's best hiking and mountain-biking opportunities are found in the redwood-filled hills surrounding Santa Cruz. Two or three times a week the local chapter of the Sierra Club sponsors group outings—hikes, camping, and canoe trips. Stop by their office (903 Pacific Ave., tel. 408/426-4453) for a listing of upcoming wilderness forays. If you're more hip to the solo experience, head directly to **Big Basin Redwoods State Park** (*see* Near Santa Cruz, *below*). Closer to town, the **Henry Cowell Redwoods State Park** (*see* Camping, *above*) has 20 mi of tamer trails, many of which meander through virgin redwood forests. Bikes are allowed on designated fire and service roads but not on hiking trails.

For a beautiful, albeit crowded, stroll among some of the park's tallest trees, take the **Redwood Grove Trail**; you'll find the trailhead off Highway 9. For a longer hike, walk up Pipeline Road from the nature center and turn left on Ridge Fire Road, which heads 2 mi uphill to an observation deck; here you'll get a beautiful view of the valley. From downtown follow Highway 9 toward Felton.

The less-crowded **Forest of Nisene Marks** (tel. 408/763-7063) is a favorite among hiking and biking locals. Here, among creeks, redwoods, and steep trails, you can view the ruins of a Chinese labor camp or walk 2 mi to the epicenter of the 1989 Loma Prieta earthquake; the trail is clearly marked from the end of the park's drivable road. There are also a few trails that mountain bikers are allowed to navigate—ask at the main gate. To get here, exit Highway 1 at Soquel and take Soquel Avenue a half mile east to Aptos Creek Road.

SURFING

Santa Cruz is the surf capital of northern California. **Steamer's Lane,** between the Boardwalk and the lighthouse, hosts several competitions in the summer; consult the free quarterly *Ocean Life* for dates. The city's **parks and recreation department** (tel. 408/429-3663) has the best surf lesson deals: Four hours of lessons over two days for $68; surfboards are included, and wet suits can be rented for $10 per class. **Cowell's Beach Shop** (corner of Beach and Front Sts., across from the wharf, tel. 408/427–2355) also rents surfboards ($15) and wet suits ($10) by the day.

NEAR SANTA CRUZ

BIG BASIN REDWOODS STATE PARK

The first forest deemed a California State Park, Big Basin overwhelms you with acres of gigantic old-growth redwoods, lofty Douglas firs, rushing streams, and flowing waterfalls. All sorts of wildlife call Big Basin home, including black-tailed deer, an occasional fox, bobcats, coyotes, and mountain lions. Just past the main entrance—where you'll pay a $5-per-car fee—you can pick up maps ($1) and trail information at the **park headquarters** (tel. 408/338–8860). If you have just an hour or so, head for the gorgeous **Silver Falls** and **Golden Falls,** about ¾ mi along the Skyline-to-the-Sea Trail. Here you can wade in the pools, shower in the falls, or skip across the creek on redwood logs. For a less crowded hike, try the **Howard King Trail** from the parking lot to Mt. McAbee. Along the way you'll pass through several different ecosystems before reaching the peak, which affords a supreme ocean view. You can return on Hammond Road for a round-trip of 5 mi in about two or three hours.

The truly fit should tackle the 12.5-mi **Skyline-to-Sea Trail**— arguably the most scenic hike in the park—which travels over hill and dale all the way to the coast. Leave a second car at the trail's endpoint at Waddell Beach, and either pay scrupulous attention to a map or accept the possibility of getting lost, since several trailheads converge a few miles into the hike. Mountain biking is allowed only on fire roads in the park, and unfortunately there are few good loops: Your best bet is to follow North Escape Road a short distance from park headquarters to **Gazos Creek Road,** a 12-mi fire trail that stretches to the coast, and then return on Johansen Road via Middleridge Road.

A river runs through the bizarre Brookdale Lodge (9 mi from Santa Cruz on Hwy. 9, tel. 408/338–6433), an oasis of drink during Prohibition. In those days a window behind the Mermaid Bar looked underwater into a swimming pool full of prostitutes.

COMING AND GOING • Big Basin is 23 mi northeast of Santa Cruz off Highway 9. Follow the highway north for 12 mi, then follow the signs for another 9 mi from Boulder Creek. If you're coming from the north on I-280, take Highway 85 south from Cupertino to Highway 9S, then pick up Highway 236 into the park. Bus 35 will take you 2½ mi short of the campgrounds; hike the rest of the way.

MONTEREY

Monterey—with the possible exception of Carmel—is California's tackiest and most unabashedly commercial seaside resort. John Steinbeck (1902–68) immortalized the busy fishing port in *Cannery Row* and *Sweet Thursday,* describing it as "a poem, a stink, a grating noise, a quality of light, a tone, a habit, a nostalgia, a dream." By the 1950s, however, the sardines were gone, along with much that was poetic. Visitors will still find the fascinating Monterey Bay Aquarium a worthwhile stop; unfortunately, much of the rest of the town has a Disneyland-by-the-sea feel—pricey gift shops sell plastic sardines, and lackluster restaurants feature "Steinbeck Specials." Still, Monterey's wealth has funded extensive public-space improvements—there's always a bench surrounded by a blooming garden just around the corner. And off Cannery Row and Fisherman's Wharf, historical conservation has preserved much of Monterey's past—it was the capital when Spain and Mexico ruled California, from 1775 to 1846.

BASICS

VISITOR INFORMATION

The **Monterey Peninsula Chamber of Commerce** (380 Alvarado St., at Franklin St., tel. 408/649–1770) provides free maps and information about the world-famous **Monterey Jazz Festival** (tel. 408/373–3366), held in late September, and the **Monterey Blues Festival** (tel. 408/394–2652), held in late June.

COMING AND GOING

Greyhound Lines buses have regular service to Monterey from San Francisco (a four-hour trip, $18 one-way) and from Los Angeles (12 hours, $49 one-way) via Salinas. The Monterey **Greyhound station** (42 Del Monte Ave., tel. 408/373–4735), in a gas station on the east end of town, is open daily 8 AM–10 PM.

The **Monterey-Salinas Transit** (tel. 408/899–2555) has regular connections to Carmel, Santa Cruz, and Salinas and a summertime-only connection to Big Sur ($1.50–$6). All buses depart from the downtown **Monterey Transit Plaza** (corner of Tyler and Pearl Sts.). For Big Sur, take Bus 22 (summer only); it will get you as far as the Nepenthe restaurant, on Highway 1.

GETTING AROUND

From Highway 1 the Pacific Grove/Del Monte Avenue exit will take you straight into downtown. The main drag is north–south **Alvarado Street,** with Fisherman's Wharf at the north end and Cannery Row (and the aquarium) 1½ mi farther northwest. Once in town, you can get around easily on foot or by bus. During summer and on holiday weekends, the shuttle bus **Wave** (tel. 408/899–2555) provides frequent service and stops throughout the downtown/Cannery Row area ($1, transfers free). Throughout the rest of the year, Bus 1 travels from the Transit Plaza to Fisherman's Wharf, Cannery Row, and the aquarium for $1.50. Because of summer tourism, both parking and crowds are a serious problem for drivers. The most reasonable parking garage downtown (between Alvarado, Franklin, Washington, and Del Monte Sts.) charges $1 an hour.

WHERE TO SLEEP

Monterey is almost devoid of cheap lodging—but if you're persistent (or if you have a tent), you may be able to scare up something reasonable. A slew of motels along North Fremont Street are close to downtown and accessible via Buses 9 and 10. Across from Del Monte Beach and one block east of the Greyhound station, **Del Monte Beach Inn** (1110 Del Monte Ave., 93940, tel. 408/649–4410, fax 408/375–3818) is a small bed-and-breakfast with 18 rooms ($50–$60) decorated by a Martha Stewart disciple. Make sure to check in before 9 PM. The 46 flawlessly clean, albeit dull, rooms at **Lone Oak Motel** (2221 N. Fremont St., 93940, tel. 408/372–4924) cost $42 weekdays and a whopping $80 weekends—but the price includes access to a Jacuzzi and sauna room. Eight miles north of Monterey in the town of Marina (take Highway 1 north from Monterey to Del Monte Avenue, or Bus 7 to Beach Road), the **Paramount Motel** (3298 Del Monte Blvd., at Beach St., 93933, tel. 408/384–8674) looks shabby on the outside, but the proprietor is friendly and the six rooms ($33 for a double) are secure, clean, and comfortable. Reservations are not accepted, so arrive early.

CAMPING

Just five minutes from downtown, **Veteran's Memorial Park Campground** (Via del Rey, tel. 408/646–3865) is a first-come, first-served campground on a grassy knoll in a quiet valley. Although it's not exactly the great outdoors, its 40 tightly packed sites ($15) are well maintained. Hikers and cyclists share one large site for $3 per person. Showers are available, but bring your own food. From downtown take Jefferson Street west; or take Bus 3 from Transit Plaza.

FOOD

On Tuesday afternoons Alvarado Street downtown is closed off for a **farmers' market**; at all other times you can find a plethora of seafood and health-food restaurants here, but unfortunately most are overpriced. At the **Lighthouse Bagel Bakery** (201 Lighthouse Blvd., at Reeside Ave., tel. 408/649–1714) you can load up on tasty bagels topped with cheese, avocado, or sandwich meat—all for less than $2. **Tillie Gort's Café** (111 Central Ave., Pacific Grove, tel. 408/373–0335) serves delicious Mexican and Mediterranean sandwiches with an emphasis on vegetarian dishes. **Fishwife** (1996½ Sunset Dr., Pacific Grove, tel. 408/375–7107) has fish dishes and pastas in the $10–$15 range.

EXPLORING MONTEREY

Monterey's main attraction is the justifiably world-famous **Monterey Bay Aquarium** (886 Cannery Row, tel. 408/648–4800), open daily 9:30–6 (10–6 in winter), where you'll find sharks and sea otters in convincingly natural habitats and a three-story kelp-forest aquarium. The new outer-bay exhibit, featuring the world's largest viewing tank, is engineered to make visitors feel as if they've taken a dive—odd jellyfish drift by, and mackerel schools circle endlessly. Admission is $14.75. Avoid hour-plus waits during the summer by purchasing your tickets in advance (tel. 800/756–3737 or 408/648–4937). AAA members can find $5-off coupons in *Motorland* magazine. From Highway 1 south follow signs from the Pacific Grove/Del Monte Avenue exit.

Cannery Row lies along the waterfront south of the aquarium, ending at **Fisherman's Wharf.** Both places have seen better days. The Laida Café—an "institution of commercialized love" in Steinbeck's time—is now a bright yellow ice cream parlor called **Kalisa's** (851 Cannery Row, no phone). To drown your sorrows over days gone by, head to **Bargetto Winery** (700 Cannery Row, tel. 408/373–4053), open daily 10:30–6, where tastings are free. Upstairs, **A Taste of Monterey** (700 Cannery Row, tel. 408/646–5446), open daily 1–6, charges $2 for a tasting—a bargain considering that you get the added bonus of superlative bay views.

History buffs can pick up "The Path of History Walking Tour" brochure from the chamber of commerce (*see* Basics, *above*) or pay $2 for a guided tour organized by **Monterey State Historic Park** (20 Custom House Plaza, tel. 408/649–7118). Monterey's old buildings are fascinating and well preserved, and most tourists ignore them for the artificial flash of Cannery Row. Don't miss Colton Hall, where the state constitution was written, and the Cooper Molera Adobe, or Custom House. Most buildings on the tour are free, but some charge $2. A $5 pass (good for two days) buys you admission to all the buildings.

Don't waste time at **Monterey State Beach,** where the wind will make you wish you'd worn thermals. It's nothing compared to **Asilomar State Beach** (tel. 408/372–4076), with its tide pools and enormous waves crashing on the rocky shore. Look for the beach 2 mi west of Monterey in the quiet town of **Pacific Grove** (Bus 1 will get you within walking distance). Here, between October and March, you can glimpse thousands of monarch butterflies who make their winter homes in **Washington Park,** at the corner of Pine Avenue and Alder Street. Pacific Grove is also home to the **Point Piños Light Station** (Ocean View Blvd., at Point Piños, tel. 408/648–3116), the oldest continuously operating lighthouse on the West Coast, since 1855. It's open Thursday–Sunday 1–4.

Jimi Hendrix made rock-and-roll history in 1969 when he burned his guitar in front of awestruck fans in Monterey. Later, horrified by the destruction of what he considered a sacred object, Indian sitarist Ravi Shankar almost refused to perform.

AFTER DARK

Skip the gimmicky clubs around Cannery Row and head instead to the **Three Spirits Gallery** (361 Orange Ave., tel. 408/393–2787), a tiny art space in the middle of a warehouse district in Sand City, 5 mi northeast of downtown Monterey. On some nights the gallery hosts go-go, surf, or indie rock bands for a $3–$5 cover; call ahead. From Del Monte Boulevard, go north, turn west on Contra Costa Street, and left again on Orange Avenue; or take Bus 20. For a more laid-back atmosphere, **Morgan's Coffee & Tea** (498 Washington St., at Pearl St., tel. 408/373–5601) is a café decked out like a medieval castle, with excellent coffee and occasional local folk and jazz performers. Word has it microbrews are on the way. Business is slower since the Fort Ord military base shut down a few years ago, but gay men still get down on the dance floor at **After Dark** (214 Lighthouse Ave., at Reeside Ave., tel. 408/373–7828). House music on Thursday night attracts straights who want to boogie as well.

OUTDOOR ACTIVITIES

BIKING AND MOPEDS

Moped Adventures (1250 Del Monte Ave., at Sloat St., tel. 408/373–2696) rents beach cruisers ($15 a day) and mopeds ($20 for the first hour, then $10 an hour; $50 a day). Call ahead to reserve; a driver's license and deposit are required. For $20 a day you can rent a mountain bike from **Bay Bikes** (640 Wave St., 1 block inland from Cannery Row, tel. 408/646–9090) and make tracks for the 4-mi paved path that stretches from the wharf past Cannery Row and Lovers' Point. Another great idea is to pedal down 17-Mile Drive (*see box, below*) for free, then on into Carmel or back to Monterey. Cyclists don't have to stop at the pay booth and can catch quite a few spectacular ocean views between the ritzy homes. Bay Bikes lets you return bikes to their Carmel location (near the south end of the drive) for an extra $8.

FISHING AND WHALE WATCHING

Contact **Chris's Fishing Trips** (tel. 408/375–5951), on Fisherman's Wharf, for half-day sportfishing trips ($28–$32); you'll pay another $15 for a license and equipment. Chris's also offers two-hour whale-watching trips ($15) between December and March, when Monterey Bay is filled with migrating gray whales.

KAYAKING

The kayaking off Cannery Row is superb, and you're sure to encounter a raft of otters, sea lions, or harbor seals. **Adventures by the Sea** (tel. 408/372–1807) can outfit you with a kayak, oars, wet suit, and a half-hour lesson for $25.

SNORKELING AND SCUBA DIVING

Monterey Bay attracts divers from around the world because of its vast kelp beds and magnificent underwater terrain. The bluffs and underwater caves off Ocean View Drive (between the aquarium and Asilomar Beach) are some of the best scuba and snorkeling spots in the area. Better yet are the pristine waters of Whaler's Cove, in Point Lobos. The **Aquarius Dive Shop** (32 Cannery Row, tel. 408/375–6605) has moderately priced equipment rentals for certified divers (about $70 the first day, $35 each additional day). A more feasible option for most people is snorkeling. Aquarius has gear for less than $34. Snorkeling lessons and a tour cost $50 more.

BIG SUR

Of all the scribes who've attempted to capture Big Sur with pen and paper, locals call Henry Miller their patron saint. Miller, who lived in a shack in Big Sur for many years, wrote of the land as "a region where extremes meet, a region where one is always conscious of weather, of space, of grandeur, of eloquent silence." Spanish settlers in the 1770s had called this forbidding wilderness *el pais grande del sur* (the big country of the south), which got shortened to Big Sur in the early 1900s. Come here to see precipitous cliffs, rocky beaches, and redwood forests and to revel in the solitude of open space. The local population is sparse, and the closest thing to a town is the group of stores surrounding the **Deetjen's River Inn** (Hwy. 1, tel. 408/667–2377), 22 mi south of Carmel. Locals head to the inn on Saturday night to hear live jazz or drum music; about a mile farther south, **Fernwood** (Hwy. 1, tel. 408/667–2422) hosts occasional live rock and roll on summer Saturday nights.

Much of Big Sur lies within the 167,000-acre **Ventana Wilderness,** in Los Padres National Forest, whose deep, wide valleys, waterfalls, hot springs, natural pools, and perennial streams foster abundant wildlife; you'll find plenty of deer and a few bears. **Big Sur Station** (Hwy. 1, just south of Pfeiffer Big Sur State

Park, tel. 408/667–2315), open daily 8–6, is loaded with information on camping and exploring the surrounding wilderness. For background information read *Hiking the Big Sur Country* ($16) or the latest issue of the free *El Sur Grande,* which contains a detailed map, hiking tips, and history; both are available at the station. Park at one of Highway 1's turnouts to avoid paying $6 on state lots.

WHERE TO SLEEP

Camping at one of Big Sur's 1,000-plus sites is the most economical sleeping option: If you don't have camping gear, consider renting one of the tent cabins available at private campgrounds for $30–$40. One of the nicest is **Big Sur Campground and Cabins** (tel. 408/667–2322), 3 mi south of Andrew Molera State Park (*see below*), where cabins sleeping two start at $45. **Riverside Campgrounds and Cabins** (Hwy. 1., tel. 408/667–2414), 25 mi south of Carmel, provides the cheapest indoor accommodations in all of Big Sur. Five rooms with gorgeous redwood interiors start at $50, and two larger double cabins go for $80. You will find rustic, romantic cabins at **Deetjen's River Inn** (Hwy. 1, tel. 408/667–2377), secluded behind redwoods 3 mi south of the Big Sur station. Each of the 21 rooms ($85 and up) comes with a down comforter—which you'll need. There's also a great on-site restaurant.

CAMPING

One of the few access points to the interior of Big Sur, Nacimiento Road, 4 mi south of Lucia, twists and turns to reach eight $5 sites at **Nacimiento Campground** (11 mi from Hwy. 1) and 23 $15 sites at **Ponderosa Campground** (13½ mi from Hwy. 1). Both peaceful campgrounds lie on the bank of a babbling brook, but neither accepts reservations, neither has showers, and only Ponderosa has flush toilets; make sure to bring your own water or a purifier. Better yet, remember you can camp off any wide spot in the road (there are several great spots between Nacimiento and Ponderosa) for free as long as you walk 100 ft from your car and obtain a fire permit from the Big Sur Station (*see above*).

West of Highway 1, 10 mi south of Palo Colorado Road, **Andrew Molera State Park** has more than 4,000 largely undeveloped acres with beach access and camping. The 50 tents-only sites ($3) are first-come, first-served, but they never turn anyone away, which means the park can become a beehive when overflow campers from other campgrounds stack up on weekends. Though payment is on the honor system, rangers make their rounds at 8 AM to hand out $25 tickets to weasels. If you want to soak up a view of a tremendous valley among the majestic madronas and oaks of the Ventana Wilderness, trek to the 11 first-come, first-served campsites ($12) at **Bottcher's Gap,** 5 mi south of Garrapata State Beach, and east 8 mi on Palo Colorado Road. Though there are no phones and no showers, there is running water and all the peace and solitude you could want. Hikers and tent campers vie for one of two secluded primitive sites ($17 weekdays, $18 on weekends) at **Julia Pfeiffer Burns State Park** (Hwy. 1, 38 mi south of Carmel), set in a cypress forest on bluffs overhanging the ocean. Even without potable water or flush toilets, these spots book early; reserve through Destinet (tel. 800/444–7252). For information on both environmental and developed camping, call or stop by the Big Sur Station (*see above*).

FOOD

Wise travelers stock up at the supermarket in Carmel or San Luis Obispo. If you forget to pack the cooler, the **Center Deli** (Hwy. 1, tel. 408/667–2225), 30 mi south of Rio Road next to the Big Sur post office, has groceries, pasta salads, and the cheapest sandwiches around, as well as fruit smoothies in summer. The **Big Sur Pub** (Hwy. 1, next to Deetjen's River Inn, tel. 408/667–2355) has burritos and sandwiches for less than $6.

EXPLORING BIG SUR

Eleven miles south of Carmel, Palo Colorado Road winds its way east from Highway 1 through the Ventana Wilderness for 8 serpentine mi before ending at **Bottcher's Gap.** From the parking lot, **Skinner's Ridge Trail** climbs 4 mi (roughly three hours) to Devil's Peak, which affords incredible views of Ventana's dramatic wooded peaks and valleys. South off Skinner's Ridge Trail is the eight-hour round-trip hike to **Pico Blanco**—a rugged mountain peak the Esselen Indians thought was the top of the world and the site of human creation. Winding partially through private property, the hike is not legal, but people do it anyway by trekking along the Boy Scout Service Road past the Boy Scout Camp and all the way up **Little Sur Trail.**

SYKES HOT SPRINGS

If you have two days and backpacking gear on your hands, make the 10-mi trek to Sykes Hot Springs. After a six- or seven-hour hike up steep ridges and along a river valley crowded with redwoods, you can soak in the thermal spring and sleep under the stars before heading back the next day or continuing on into the depths of the Ventana Wilderness Area. On summer weekends you may have to vie for space in the rock-dam tubs—aim for the winter months. The trail begins at the Big Sur station parking lot; register and get a fire permit from the rangers here before heading out.

Back on Highway 1, south of Palo Colorado Road, look for the **Bixby Creek Bridge,** a 550-ft concrete span built in 1932. Just before the bridge, the circular **Old Coast Road** curves inland for 10 mi and meets back up with Highway 1 opposite the entrance to Andrew Molera State Park. This is California at its rugged best—craggy cliffs, majestic redwoods, and views of the Little Sur River running its way toward the ocean. If you're the four-wheeling type, you'll like the road's gravel- and mud-plagued inclines; a regular car should be fine if the weather's been dry.

Double back a half mile north from Andrew Molera to check out the **Point Sur Light Station** (tel. 408/625–4419), which was built in 1889 on a huge rock outcropping to prevent shipwrecks along this foggy and rocky stretch of coast. Tours of the lighthouse are available on weekends and on Wednesday May–October ($5). Call first for times and make sure to show up a half hour early so the docents can let you through the gate. **Andrew Molera State Park,** once the site of a Monterey Jack cheese factory and a dairy farm, now has more than 10 mi of hiking and mountain-biking trails. The strenuous hike up the **Ridge Trail** takes you through 4 mi of stunning coastal scenery to the top of a ridge. Savor the spectacular view of the Pacific before you head down the **Panorama Trail** to the **Bluffs Trail,** which is especially striking in spring when the wildflowers bloom.

About 5 mi south of Andrew Molera State Park, **Pfeiffer Big Sur State Park** (east side of Hwy. 1, tel. 408/667–2315) is one of the most popular camping and hiking spots on the coast, especially during summer. Don't waste your time at **Pfeiffer Falls**—the hike is crowded and the falls are less than spectacular. Just south of Pfeiffer on the same side of the highway, Big Sur Station (*see above*) is the starting point for the **Pine Ridge Trail,** a local favorite that leads into the Ventana Wilderness and **Sykes Hot Springs** (*see box, above*).

Sycamore Canyon Road, a mile south of the Big Sur station, is unmarked save for a stop sign. If you can find it, brave the road for 2 mi, and you'll land at **Pfeiffer Beach,** a turbulent, windswept cove with huge rock formations and an angry ocean not suitable for swimming. About 2½ mi farther south lies **Nepenthe** (tel. 408/667–2345), an expensive restaurant with an extraordinary view (also the last stop of Bus 22, which runs from Monterey in summer only).

Head south from Nepenthe to the **Henry Miller Library** (Hwy. 1, ¼ mi south of Nepenthe, tel. 408/667–2574). More like a book collector's attic, the tiny one-room library displays the bohemian author's artifacts (sorry, no steamy letters to Anaïs Nin) and has rotating exhibits on artists and writers associated with Miller or Big Sur. The library is open daily 11–5 in summer; hours vary in the winter.

More spectacular than Pfeiffer Big Sur State Park, **Julia Pfeiffer Burns State Park** (12 mi south of Big Sur Station, tel. 408/667–2315) has excellent and often less crowded hiking trails. Few people blink at the $6 entrance fee that's required to see **MyWay Falls**—which was the most breathtaking sight in all of Big Sur before parking lots, postcards, and crowds demystified some of its natural wonder. From the parking lot, a half-mile path leads to a bluff with a phenomenal view of the creek at the head of the falls. If you're looking for solitude, take the rugged 6-mi **Ewoldsen Trail** loop through one of the best vegetation samplings of the Big Sur coast.

Three miles south of Julia Pfeiffer, a sign on the right side of the road reads: ESALEN INSTITUTE—RESERVATIONS ONLY. At the end of the road you'll find the world-famous **Esalen Institute** (tel. 408/667-3000), a one-time wacked-out hippie colony that specializes in the "exploration of human value and potentials." These days the grounds and natural hot springs are closed to the public during the day. However, between 1 AM and 3:30 AM you can relax in Esalen's natural hot springs, perched on a cliff overlooking the Pacific. At just $10, this is a pleasure that could run you 10 times that much during the day. Call the institute to make reservations.

The southern stretch of Big Sur—between the tiny towns of Lucia and San Simeon—is less populated and has a gentler geography than the sometimes violently beautiful north. There's not much to see besides the continually unfolding coastline, but you will come across some choice beaches every now and then. Ten miles south of Lucia, **Jade Cove** is a secluded, rocky beach with sweeping views up and down the coast. Just north of Gorda, quiet **Willow Creek** is another local favorite.

OUTDOOR ACTIVITIES

The main activity in Big Sur is hiking (*see* Exploring Big Sur, *above*), but to the dismay of many drivers, lots of people also bicycle along Highway 1. Cyclists should be experienced and familiar with the narrowness of the highway and the lack of road shoulder. Most state parks offer cheap campsites (usually $3) to those on two rather than four wheels.

Andrew Molera State Park is the only Big Sur park with single-track trails for mountain biking. Mountain bikers in tip-top shape can take on the steep, strenuous **Ridge Trail,** which is more than 2 mi long and has elevation gains of 1,200 ft. For a more relaxing ride, try the **River** and **Cottonwood trails** (2 mi), both of which wind through the park's meadows. Most trails start at the parking area or a half mile away at the beach. Elsewhere in Big Sur, you'll have to stick to the fire and service roads or risk a fine. One possibility is to head up **Nacimiento-Ferguson Road,** 4 mi south of Lucia off Highway 1 (*see* Camping, *above*). Bikes are not allowed to the left into the Ventana Wilderness, but off the right side of the road you'll see a few trails, most of which are quite steep in sections.

Locals scoff at the Esalen Institute's esoteric ideals, even though in the late '60s this was one of the first places to introduce Gestalt therapy. Today's classes have names like "Awakened Mind: Advanced Brainwave Training." Go figure.

INDEX

INDEX

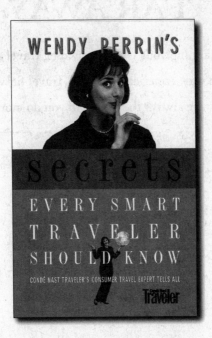

WHEREVER YOU TRAVEL, *H*ELP IS NEVER FAR AWAY.

From planning your trip to providing travel assistance along the way, American Express® Travel Service Offices are always there to help you do more.

San Francisco

American Express Travel Service
455 Market Street
415/536-2600

American Express Travel Service
560 California Street
415/536-2600

Ethan Allen Travel, Inc. (R)
1585 Sloat Boulevard
415/242-0277

do more AMERICAN EXPRESS
Travel

http://www.americanexpress.com/travel

American Express Travel Service Offices are located throughout California. For the office nearest you, call 1-800-AXP-3429.